Deadlier than the Male

Alix Kirsta was born in London to Russian and Austrian parents. Beginning her journalistic career simultaneously with a three-year stint as Dance Correspondent for LBC Radio and as a fashion, health and medical writer for *Vogue* and the *Daily Mail*, there followed a four-year period as Health Editor of *Woman's Journal* and *Options*. Moving into freelance writing as a contributor to publications including the *Guardian*, *The Times*, *Observer*, *Sunday Telegraph*, *Vogue* and *New Woman*, she began focusing increasingly on issues related to mental health, psychology, stress, crime, feminism and social change. Though living in London, much of her work is based on regular research trips to the United States and other countries. Alix Kirsta's previous books include *Skin Deep*, *Stress Survival* — so far published in ten languages — and *Victims*.

ALIX KIRSTA

DEADLIER
THAN THE MALE

Violence and Aggression in Women

HarperCollins*Publishers*

HarperCollins*Publishers*
77–85 Fulham Palace Road,
Hammersmith, London W6 8JB

A Paperback Original 1994
1 3 5 7 9 8 6 4 2

A catalogue record for this book is
available from the British Library

ISBN 0 00 637849 8

Set in Linotron Meridien by
Rowland Phototypesetting Ltd
Bury St Edmunds, Suffolk

Printed in Great Britain by
HarperCollinsManufacturing Glasgow

To JZ with love

Contents

Acknowledgments

Embarking on a book which covers such vast terrain, much of it new and relatively uncharted, would be impossible were it not for the guidance and help of great numbers of individuals, many of them professionals working in diverse disciplines and fields. Since the number of people I interviewed, both in person and over the phone, whose lectures and seminars I attended are far too numerous to mention, although each receives credit wherever necessary and possible in the bibliography, there are some for whose help I am particularly indebted, and whose comments and insight proved of such inestimable value and inspiration, that I want to express my sincere appreciation for their valuable contribution to this book. In America they include sociologists Kathleen Daly, Meda Chesney-Lind, Eloise Dunlap, Anne Campbell and Laura Fishman whose talks on women gangs at the ASC Conference in New Orleans proved so instructive, and in New York, Ira Sommers and Deborah Baskin who shared their latest findings with me, lawyers Adria Hillman and Holly Maguigan, Richard Curtis without whom I would never have had the guts to venture into 'the Well' district of Brooklyn, and Sharon Smrlish who got me into Bedford Hills Maximum Security prison. My special thanks too to Professors Ervin Staub and Pauline Bart, Dr Nancy Kaser-Boyd, Tom Mooney, Jeff Collins and Nancy Vogel for taking the time to hold long transatlantic telephone calls to answer endless questions. In Britain, I wish to express my gratitude to Professor Paul Brain for alerting me to the invaluable ISRA conference in Siena, and to Estela Welldon both for giving her personal time and for arranging for me to attend the Forensic Psychotherapy conference which she organized in London. Special thanks also to Philippa Weitz, who helped organize the first-ever conference I attended on female violence, which helped inspire this book, to forensic psychiatrists

ix

Dr Patrick Gallwey, Dr Brigid Dolan and Dr Jeremy Coid, John Harding and Peter Dalrymple of the Inner London Probation Service, criminologists Elizabeth Stanko and Susan Edwards, Pragna Patel of SBS, Chris Tchaikovsky of WIP, Fiona McLean of Clean Break, Susie Orbach, Mary McMurran at Rampton Hospital, Carol Sellars at Broadmoor, and especially Hazel Redsull, Wendy Chan, Anya Wilczynski, Michele Elliot, Cianne Longden and Willa Woolston who generously allowed me to quote their work and personal experiences. I am also grateful to staff at the American Embassy's USIS library, to Jill Phillipson for helping to put me in touch with Members of the Royal College of Psychiatrists and to Dr Raj Persaud, lecturer in Psychiatry at the Institute of Psychiatry, for taking the time and effort to help me in my research. My special warm appreciation to Alice Miller, for her kindness in granting me a number of lively, thought-provoking interviews on the patterns and origins of violence. Finally I want to thank my friends Claire Loew de Hausman for arranging my interviews with women bullfighters in Madrid and acting as interpreter, Franco di Giorgi for his translations of Italian transcripts, my editor Val Hudson and copy-editor Karen Whitlock for doing such an excellent job of tightening and shaping a very outsize manuscript and Gloria Ferris, my agent, for her ongoing support and invaluable feedback. Lastly, I wish to stress my immense gratitude to all those many women – and the men – who generously gave their time and energy to talk to me about their personal experiences of violence.

Introduction

As images of Utopia go, none is more warmly comforting or persuasive than that of a world which, because run exclusively by women, is free from war, conflict and cruelty. It is also, especially today, the most misleading and dangerous of images. Unlike other myths, what is so unsettling about this one is its widely proclaimed ring of truth, the crassest of fallacies masquerading as one of the great eternal verities. Of all myths inviting demolition, this one had it coming. As events have proved, never was there a more appropriate time for a writer to start hacking and chipping at that most sacrosanct of human beliefs – the non-existence of violence in women.

Looking back, 1991 was the year when what had seemed an entirely unremarkable phenomenon – the issue of female aggression and violence – first emerged as the hottest topic of controversy and debate. Its theme, the emergence of a 'new breed' of violent post-feminist woman, started to resonate with compelling urgency within my own environment. That year I found myself, for the first time ever, on the receiving end of a vicious barrage of obscenities and threats of assault, in daylight on a Soho street. The assailant was a young woman, her face contorted into an ugly, twisted mask of rage, spitting venom simply because I had glanced for several seconds at her haircut. A month later my purse was snatched by a little girl, aged no more than twelve, one of a gang of jabbering, jostling young gypsies who surrounded me in the Roman Forum.

At about the same time, a journalist colleague was rounded on by a woman at her health club who threatened her with violence simply for having asked if she could make less noise in the gym. An editor she knew had been subjected to similar foul-mouthed abuse by a group of drunken women having a night out in the West End. Another friend recounted to me in

horror how she had come home late one night and found herself
grappling with one of two burglars – the female half of the pair.
Subsequently an elderly relative of mine returned from a week's
holiday to find that a would-be intruder had smashed one of
her windows, as well as those of three other flats. Apparently
the girl who had tried unsuccessfully to burgle the flats had
been released from Holloway just before Easter. Penniless and
sleeping rough, she promptly gave herself up to the police in
abject despair. On hearing this story, a solicitor friend told me
about a woman client, a heavy drinker, who has repeatedly
been sent to prison for vandalism, yet soon re-offends after
being released because she has no friends, is homeless and has
become so alienated from the outside world that she only feels
secure within a prison environment. By now she has become
so well known in the small town and has been to court so often
that her chances of a fair trial are almost nil.

Later that year I heard two other horrific stories, one from a
friend, another on a radio counselling phone-in, both equally
mind-boggling because of their mixture of despair and rage.
My friend revealed that after recently having an abortion, she
learned from an acquaintance that her partner was having an
affair. The effect, she says, was as if someone had put 1,000
watts through her body. First she hurled herself around the
room, screaming and pulling her hair out. Later, with icy calm,
she took a razor-sharp seven-inch kitchen knife and set off in
her car with the express intention of killing him. With the knife
hidden up the sleeve of her coat she called at the flat where
she believed he would be. But he was out on a drinking spree.
Were it not for this she assured me she would have stabbed
him to death; she couldn't have cared less about the consequences, so overwhelming was her rage. Thwarted, she
returned home and smashed up their apartment.

The phone-in concerned a woman who had recently been
sexually assaulted – by a woman. Much of her trauma was a
by-product of having never reported the assault to the police,
because, as she pointed out, if some of her own friends were
loath to believe a woman could do this, how seriously would
the police treat her claim? Also, she knew that in law a rape

charge (and this *was* a rape in virtually every aspect) can only be made against a man, which made her even more bitter. And she feared that if she did press other charges the newspapers might get wind of it and make her life hell.

Some weeks after that call, a friend casually mentioned that her teenage daughter wanted to drop out of school. Long the victim of bullying and racist abuse, she was finally provoked into attacking her tormentor. It worked. The bullying stopped. But it proved a pyrrhic victory: because she had fought with her fists, her shocked classmates decided to exclude her from their group on the grounds that she was a 'weirdo'. By behaving like a boy she felt she was being punished for being 'abnormal' compared to other girls.

By now it was clear that there was a book demanding to be written. What clinched it for me was attending the first ever conference on female violence, also in 1991, a two-day event organized by the Forensic Psychiatry Department of St George's Hospital in London. Obviously this was not just a string of personal coincidences. A far larger issue was brewing, as testified by ever more sensational press coverage, much of it loaded with upfront or oblique moral judgements, of cases such as the Sara Thornton trial or that of Aileen Wuornos, America's putative first female serial killer. The subtext inevitably was, 'Give women more freedom and *see what you get*?' The backlash element was further underlined by the alternating tones of alarm and opprobrium elicited by the burgeoning trend in female gangster movies like *Thelma and Louise*. In what was clearly a radical new development in gender politics, numerous issues were springing up, most of them so thorny they could be counted on to touch not just the odd raw nerve but to prick away at a vast network of exposed nerve-fibre.

And so it turned out. Not only were violent women shouting to be heard but so too were their opponents, the oracles of doom and advocates of domestic fundamentalism. Numerous avenues of research which I might otherwise have missed were clearly signposted by the prejudices, sexist bias and ill-informed assumptions of others regarding the issue of aggression and violence in women. As a topic, this one guarantees kneejerk reactions of a wonderfully diverse variety. The most predictable response from friends and professionals – including doctors, psychologists, the police and judiciary – when I asked for their views on the subject was to assume I wanted to know about women as victims, not perpetrators of violence. I can't say I was surprised, having already come across this mind-set when writing previously about victims of violence; then, the implicit assumption was that I must only be interviewing women, rather than both sexes, and probably focusing on rape, when in fact my categories of violence included husband battering and violence between lesbian couples. All it proves is the melancholy fact that women's integration within today's insidious 'victim culture' is more total, their image as helpless, vulnerable – thus highly targetable – victims of crime projected with higher visibility than at any other period of this century. And an image that amplifies and advertises the message that helplessness is an inescapable dilemma of the female condition cannot but impede women's progress in all areas of life.

Whatever doubts I might have had about the advantages to be gained by women in becoming more assertive, aggressive, dominant, even violent when necessary, were rapidly dispelled by witnessing the growth of this victim culture and the climate of fear, much of it ill-founded and irrational, in which it flourishes. At once disabling and demeaning yet invested with hypnotic allure, the image of women as too powerless to avoid or surmount the dangers of urban crime and, above all, male terrorism, within the home or outside it, is one not only beloved by Hollywood and the media but, worse, is freely subscribed to by women themselves as evidence that all qualities associated with violence such as aggression, competitiveness and desire for power, by being inherently 'male' characteristics, cannot possess any potential for good and must therefore be abhorred and denied in their own sex. Abandon this notion and the central pivot around which much feminist ideology revolves, namely the inevitability of patriarchy, collapses. Likewise, the surest way to raise feminist hackles is to suggest that perhaps women haven't achieved the gains and successes they seek because they don't act aggressively *enough*.

Not because they can't, but because they won't – the image of female aggression being what it is. Those howls of feminist outrage that greet any suggestion that women may have an equal tendency to violence give the game away about just how much blinkered hypocrisy still skews the central premise behind much radical feminism. I hope one of the achievements of this book is to stand much of this dogma firmly on its head. Judging by many women's responses to the subject of female violence – that it doesn't exist, and when it does it arises only in response to male violence therefore women cannot be held fully responsible for their actions – a fatal flaw has been permitted to remain undetected deep inside the heart of feminism. That flaw undermines many of its aims and does a great disservice to women generally. The wilful refusal of the modern women's movement throughout its 25-year history to address, let alone attempt to understand, women's own acts of violence and desire for power over others, while succeeding in covering up the extent and nature of women's abuse and brutality towards other women, children, the elderly, male and lesbian partners and prison inmates, simultaneously devalues these victims and invalidates their suffering. Which amounts to just the sort of betrayal for which men have traditionally (though often justifiably) been blamed.

Asserting, as I have heard just as many women as men do, that women are by nature too nurturing, caring, gentle and empathetic to resort to acts of aggression, except perhaps when defending their children (talk of female aggression always leads to the well-worn cliché of angry lionesses protecting their cubs) is not only deeply patronizing but flies in the face of a considerable body of accumulated historical, anthropological, medical and social evidence to the contrary. Forthcoming chapters will reveal those tired old 'biological determinist' theories to be about as convincing as the newness of the Emperor's new clothes. The belief, as strong among women as men, that if women are antisocial or 'unnaturally' aggressive it must be because of hormonal chaos, or due to a frustrated need to fulfil maternal instincts (which, as one former probation officer told me, was usually both the standard explanation *and* cure

5

suggested by his colleagues, male and female, for the 'problem' of violent, antisocial or criminal women) sadly only reinforces the old man-made stereotypes of women as both servants and victims of their biology. That women should continue to cling to such reductionism beggars belief; surely to deny that they are capable of the full range of human experience, emotion and impulses, good and bad, is profoundly insulting, diminishing women as multidimensional and fully functional human beings?

The fact that research shows it is precisely *because* of the intolerable stresses of motherhood, single or otherwise, combined with socioeconomic deprivation, that many women turn to crime as a means of economic survival or to briefly escape, through alcohol, drugs or delinquency, from the pressures, boredom or hopeless isolation of a dead-end existence, defeats the proposition that crime and violence are uniquely 'natural' to men. And given that much of women's anger against men and towards a society that tacitly sanctions men's uses and abuses of women is entirely justified, why do so many women continue to deny the validity and power of that anger, whose origins often go far back to childhood abuse, both sexual and non-sexual, or are linked to spousal violence? There are no easy answers, but I have attempted wherever possible to address this complex question, especially within the context of very serious crime such as child murder and abuse.

Certainly, women's experiences of victimization cannot, and must not, be left out of the equation of criminal cause and effect. As more women enter the field of criminological research, examining female crime from a feminist perspective, women's subjective social experiences have formed a vital springboard for fresh analysis of the forces that lead women to crime and how as offenders they are often misperceived socially and unfairly treated by the justice system. As a result, the one important emerging concept, reflected throughout this book, is of 'blurred boundaries' separating victims and offenders. The frequent causal relationship between being a victim of violence and later using it intentionally or unintentionally against others, either because this seems the sole available outlet for the victim's anger or as a means of avoiding further injustices, is one of the most crucial areas of analysis in present-day research.

As I discovered from countless talks with American and British women prisoners or ex-prisoners, recognizing the existence and validity of their anger and finding a means to express it, even though this may have resulted in crimes as unconscionable as murder, arson or severe injury, often proved a turning point for a woman with a lifetime's experience of personal abuse. Perverse as it sounds, it is not uncommon to hear women say they hadn't consciously realized they were victims of violence until they ended up in jail and were forced to examine *why* they had acted as they did. Which is by no means to exonerate the offender or excuse the crime, merely to emphasize how crucial it is for us to attempt to understand more about the complex and disparate influences that may lead any person to commit crimes of violence. Whether women's subjective experiences of being female, in particular of their biological make-up, make them a 'special case' *vis-à-vis* the justice system is an emotive question particularly fraught with imponderables, to which – again – there are no straight answers. But with such 'conditions' as PMT and post-traumatic stress disorder increasingly being used by female defendants in mitigation in court, I have tried to present the special case argument as clearly as possible while avoiding any pat solutions.

That said, and heretical as some may find it, I agree with one of America's foremost sociologists and crime researchers, Kathleen Daly, that blurred boundaries are not unique to women, and it is surely as invidious to treat female criminals as a special case because we are more inclined to regard them as victims as it is to refuse to recognize that the roots of much male violence may similarly be traced back to an early history of abuse and neglect. And if hormonal flux can be used to explain a woman's crime, why shouldn't a man's fluctuating biochemistry be an equally valid contributory factor to his offence? Certainly, to differentiate between the psychological processes of men and women is to tread on dangerous territory. What Daly calls the 'harmed and harming' offender profile is not exclusively female, and why, as she and others have discovered, it is such a common one, and what exactly the dynamics behind it are, is a question with which researchers will long continue to grapple.

What is undeniable, however, is that ultimately the issue of agency, of assuming responsibility for one's actions, applies equally to either sex, which begs the question to what degree social attitudes, still blinkered and biased or outright ignorant, dictate the basis on which the courts, which after all usually include a jury composed of 'ordinary' individuals, judge an offender's level of responsibility. It has been suggested that after having been treated with excessive leniency over the years, because the idea of aggression and criminality among women seemed such an anomaly, today women offenders stand a greater chance of receiving unfairly harsh treatment, prompted by the belief that if they act like men they must be prepared to take their punishment like a man, if only to dissuade other women from getting 'out of line'.

But are women, as I am constantly being asked, really becoming more violent and aggressive? They are, but for reasons more demonstrably to do with changing circumstance than any sinister mutation, as often claimed. The problem is that the entire issue of female aggression and how it relates to appropriate or natural forms of self-expression has been for centuries so wholly shrouded in sexist myth and taboo that you first have to begin unpicking the weave and teasing apart each individual strand of thought that upholds society's construct of the 'unnaturalness' of female violence. My intention is to demonstrate clearly why female aggression and violence, and indeed assertiveness, bravery and valour, are almost certainly nothing new. Crucial to basic survival, qualities such as anger, dominance, competitiveness and the killer instinct were always present in women, but with the cult of motherhood and its attendant qualities of chastity, sexual modesty and passivity, such resources came to be regarded as incompatible with the virtues of ideal womanhood, especially in the developed countries of the world.

Today, with the break-up of 'traditional' family values and the nuclear family, together with the demystification of the mother as a superhuman deity, the onus is once again on women to fight in order to survive. Thus women are at last beginning to rediscover strengths and power that were always there from the beginning, but which centuries of male dominance seemed to have long conditioned out of them. The rediscovery of these qualities is in some areas rapidly helping to advance the empowerment of women – which is why, even when talking about crimes of violence, I cannot denounce female aggression as either unhealthy or wholly 'bad', whether for women or society as a whole. Even at its worst, crime may pay and violence is discovered increasingly by women and young girls to have survival value – a realization that has always been second nature to the great majority of men. The tragedy is that it is those with the least capacity for true self-assertion, let alone a way of safely yet effectively expressing anger and aggression or harnessing it productively, often because they are never given the chance, who are usually most likely to end up in prison. There they may have to learn violence in order to survive. To what degree this can be attributed to their own weakness, or to society's refusal to acknowledge such behaviour as appropriate because they are female, is what we shall now begin to unravel.

Alix Kirsta
London, January 1994

1

Angry Women:
The Rise of Machisma

The Notoriety of the Female Criminal

In Naples on the evening of 7 February 1993 the Special Crimes Unit of the city's Polizia Criminale held an impromptu celebration, knocking back the local grappa, hugging and backslapping one another with more than customary gusto. Well-earned plaudits from other police and criminal justice departments throughout Italy and the rest of Europe and America had been rolling in throughout the day. That morning they had scored a massive hit in the country's ongoing war against the Mafia. They had managed to track down and arrest one of Italy's most notorious and ruthless gangsters after thirteen years on the run, 56-year-old Rosetta Cutolo, a leading member of the Neapolitan Camorra. In her absence, the infamous 'godmother' had been sentenced to ten years' imprisonment for crimes including extortion and murder. She now awaits trial for another five similar charges, including filling an Alfa Romeo full of explosives and blowing up a wall of the psychiatric wing of the prison where her brother was being held to help him escape.

That same week in Sacramento, California, Mrs Dorothea Puente went on trial for the alleged murder of at least seven men and women, some of whose remains were dug up in her back garden, others being washed up on a local river bank. Over two hundred witnesses were lined up to testify over a six-month hearing after which, if found guilty, Mrs Puente would face either the death penalty or life imprisonment without parole. In Florida another serial killer, bisexual prostitute Aileen Wuornos, sentenced to death for killing seven men, awaited the outcome of her appeal to the Supreme Court to have her sentence

11

commuted, while in May, in Indiana, another death row contender, teenager Hope Rippey, went on trial for her part in the torture, sexual assault and murder of a 12-year-old girl, a crime so foul one could hear the West Coast wires buzz as scriptwriters' agents and film companies clinched deals and dramatized versions of the tragedy rolled into production. Which was exactly how three TV docu-dramas came to be shown within a single week early in 1993, presenting the story of New York teenager Amy Fisher's attempted murder of her alleged lover's wife, Mary Jo Buttafuoco, from three different perspectives, that of the victim, the criminal and the man in the middle.

Meanwhile in Britain, children's nurse Beverley Allitt, the country's most notorious serial killer since Myra Hindley, was charged with murdering four children, attempting to murder three and seriously assaulting six other babies in her care and would eventually be sentenced to serve thirteen terms of life imprisonment. Those who read the 'news in brief' columns in the papers may have also learned the following . . . That Scotland Yard has added the names and pictures of eleven more reported football hooligans to its files, who have fallen seriously enough foul of the law to warrant close surveillance at future matches. The latest eleven are young females . . . That Dewi Sukarno was recently released from two months' imprisonment for smashing a champagne glass in a woman's face, leavng a two-inch shard embedded in her cheek . . . That in Southern France, the local press is having a field day speculating how an all-woman gang of bank robbers has managed to cause so much mayhem in and around Avignon without getting caught. One of the theories is that this may be a copy-cat gang following in the footsteps of another women's group, the Amazons, who became similarly notorious in Nice, leading police a dance until their arrest in 1991.

So what? one might say. Female crime is nothing new. Everyone knows that women of every type can be violent, may kill calculatingly for money, for success, in fits of blind jealousy, sexual lust, unrequited or spurned love. Everyone, it seems, but the media, judging by the speculative and alarmist cant with which every such crime is trumpeted as evidence of a putative collapse of social and moral order. Why else should these crimes and those women have come to be regarded as any different or arrest our attention more than at other periods of time? Compared to Lizzie Borden or Bonnie Parker, why should we regard Aileen Wuornos or Rosetta Cutolo as particularly significant? What makes little Amy Fisher any more deviant and dangerous than Ruth Ellis was made out to be by a press which, after all, squeezed as much mileage from her alleged cold-blooded wickedness as from the poignancy of her end at the gallows.

The answer is twofold, and at first might seem oddly contradictory. There is no doubt that on the one hand, like famous female criminals of the past, many violent women hit the front page and gain disproportionate notoriety precisely because of their sex. This owes as much to tabloid prurience – aided and abetted equally by our obsessed fascination with all things supposedly 'wicked' or 'deviant' – as it does to society's need to reassure itself that these women are indeed, by definition, aberrant and inherently evil monsters like Myra Hindley or, like Nurse Allitt, dangerously deranged, so we can sleep secure in our beds, assured that they are as far removed from normal womanhood as Hannibal Lecter is from Essex Man, viewing them as egregious exceptions that prove the rule of nature as she truly is, and safe in the belief that while women continue to fulfil their traditional, instinctive, nurturing and care-giving functions, at home and in society, all is well with the world.

Until recently there existed a powerful and threatening subtext to all of this: beware the woman who veers too far from her designated role. The time was when a woman's notoriety as a calculating criminal or violent non-conformist rebel contained an implicit warning to the rest of womanhood, as a salutary example that society perceives criminals as interesting, complex and mysterious only if they are male, and as merely pathetic if they are female. While the male criminal was glamourized (consider the proliferation of books, films and TV documentaries that delve into the murky psychological recesses of male serial killers and mass murderers such as Jeffrey Dahmer, Dennis Nilsen and Andrei Chikatilo, the Russian Ripper), the female was pathologized (remember *Misery*?) since she represented an anomaly of gender.

But now another scenario has begun to unfold, in which the male criminal hero no longer holds centre stage. The new protagonists assembling under the spotlight share an altogether different set of characteristics: all are female, most are aggressive or violent, many, if not criminal, are delinquent or signally rebellious, antisocial and proud of it and all are of the era of feminism. Enter the anti-heroine, Hollywood's hottest property: 'macha woman'. And since it doesn't take long for life to imitate art, the media, predictably, have made it their business to publicize what is beginning to be regarded as the most significant sociocultural trend of the 1990s: the rise of the new female criminal.

It would be impossible to imagine a tougher, sweatier, more ruthless, un-prettied-up yet erotically charged androgynous breed of leading woman than the fearless personae of Nikita, Jamie Lee Curtis's gun-toting top cop in *Blue Steel*, Thelma and Louise, or hard-bodied Linda Hamilton of the iron-clad musculature in *Terminator 2*. Hamilton's role was so physically demanding that according to *Entertainment Weekly* she undertook six months of intensive weightlifting and circuit training, working with an Israeli commando on judo skills, learning to fight, shoot and move in every way like a human 'killing machine' and reputedly enjoying the power and freedom of attaining male standards of strength.

What has undoubtedly helped promote the ethos of independent, aggressive, post-feminist 'machisma' – some refer to it as female machismo, but if you're going to define a new species, why not properly adapt the gender – is that actresses portraying the new generation of hard, ballsy 'killer broads' are not far removed in spirit and attitude from their characters. Sharon Stone, who played the bisexual, manipulative seductress in *Basic Instinct* suspected of killing her male lovers with an ice pick at the point of orgasm, has stated proudly in interviews that she regards herself as a 'broad', adding, 'Nobody ever says I'm a lady.' She also declares that she took a sledgehammer and remodelled her home, smashing down walls unaided, and keeps two double-barrelled shotguns which she wouldn't hesitate to use. Nor is she a stranger to physical violence, admitting, 'I've hit a few people. I've knocked a couple of guys across the room.'

Undoubtedly aided and amplified by the industry's publicity machine, many actresses' screen personae now appear to be an extension of their true personalities, thus imparting substance and reality to the myth of the new gritty, cut-edged, aggressive modern female. Geena Davis (Thelma) has stated that: 'The exhilarating thing about *Thelma and Louise*, which could be inspiring to people, is you realize you can change your life and get your power.' Callie Khouri, who wrote the screenplay, has observed that the scene which had female audiences cheering, in which Louise shoots Thelma's would-be assailant in cold blood, not for attempting to rape her but because he retorts that he should have gone ahead and done it anyway, 'is a very cathartic scene for women. I've found myself in situations where saying "no" was not doing the trick, and I didn't have a gun. It's awful.'

Thelma and Louise was variously excoriated by (mostly male) critics as a 'hymn of hate to men' and 'a post-feminist howl of self-immolating fury'. Khouri stresses that the film's message is about the ultimate rejection of patriarchy (hence the male-dominated press vitriol) and the liberating influence of making personal choices, whether they turn out to be wise or foolish (the two heroines end up committing suicide by driving off a clifftop when surrounded by the police, making them winners or losers according to your outlook). 'I don't want anyone to be limited,' says Khouri. 'That's what feminism is to me, getting rid of the limits.'

Predictably enough, when Linda Goodmote and Bernadette Eadey were arrested after embarking on a so-called 'man-bashing spree' in Florida during the summer of 1991, luring men into their hotel room in order to rob them at gunpoint and shooting them if they resisted, they immediately became America's first 'Real-Life Thelma and Louise'. Yet these two could be dismissed as pussycats compared to Bella, the serial-killing anti-heroine of the film *Dirty Weekend*. The 1991 publication of Helen Zahavi's book on which the film is based elicited a violent kneejerk reaction of quite unmitigated venom, for in Bella we have a feminist avenging angel of death who embarks on a plan of revenge, systematically totalling a series of men who have variously abused, harassed, threatened or assaulted her.

Both the intensity and nature of the various responses were entirely predictable given the theme and content of the book. These ranged from self-righteous disgust – 'moral pollution' (*Guardian* columnist Melanie Phillips), 'more offensive than pornography' (Nicci Gerrard in the *Observer*), 'it sounds as if this woman hates men very much' (Dr Anthony Storr, psychiatrist), 'pernicious and shameful' (anti-feminist writer Neil Lyndon) – to praise both ecstatic and objectively balanced: 'brave, beautiful and brilliant' (Julie Burchill) and 'This is about the modern woman who has had enough of being humiliated, who says, "Go fuck yourself, I've had enough." I consider her an absolute heroine figure' (Michael Winner).

Disturbing to many must be Helen Zahavi's unequivocal vindication of the book's message. In interviews she has stated openly that the character is not a psychopath but a rational woman who is in control and simply goes one step further than the rest of us who can only fantasize about killing someone out of revenge and hatred. Bella's creator says: 'She is our suppressed side. We don't want to let her out. She is the darker side of nature, the side that goes on the rampage.' From Zahavi's comments it is clear that Bella is her own dark side made flesh. She began writing the book out of a sense of helplessness and rage after a series of violent attacks on women in Brighton and having suffered repeated threats by a man who lived nearby. 'First I wanted to run away. Then I wanted to lock myself in. One morning I woke up and realized I wanted to kill him . . . I wrote the book instead.' As she has accurately observed, judging by the excoriating attacks on her book by those who claim to be 'free thinkers' and 'the defenders of the liberal faith', 'those tender-hearted humanists, who write with such conviction of the freedom to dissent', it appears that a murderous, vengeful woman who gets even with those who have deliberately harmed her poses a threat so immense to the cherished order that her existence cannot be acknowledged, let alone her behaviour countenanced, even on the printed page.

In the music world, the new wave of 'psycho babes' whose aggressive tones and asexual appearance have put the boot into the soft-centred candy-floss image of the female singer seem to have so far escaped vilification, probably because they remain outside the mainstream of popular culture. But the strident iconoclasm of such androgynous rock performers as Katie-Jane Garside of Daisy Chainsaw, the loud grungy rock quartet L7, Kim Deal of the Pixies or the outrageous in-your-face misandry of Diamanda Galas is a further testament to the power of women's anger as an artistic force both for social comment and self-expression. It remains, however, the socially unacceptable face of womanhood with which many women, and great numbers of men, remain desperately uncomfortable. L7 had to sack their male drummer because, according to Donita Sparks, when he became drunk his resentment came to the fore, 'and he'd start calling us bitches. It got really ugly'. Sparks is well aware that in breaking new ground they may initially inspire fear and resentment: 'Some women are afraid to look ugly, but that goes with a lot of women, not just women in bands. You have to forget in order to be free, then you can really start to create.'

Performance artist Karen Finley, scourge of America's moral majority, believes that men fear women's anger as an emasculating force: 'When a woman is trying to express what she truly feels, a man will say, "That's hysterical, perverted, domineering."' Diamanda Galas, who dubs herself 'Tyson of the Voice', has bragged that she became a prostitute in her youth in order to be able to walk down the street 'in the worst fucking part of town and carrying a fucking knife and know that it was my street – our street, not their street . . . I learned to walk down the street without fear'. Today she owns a Smith and Wesson .38 special and advocates that all women should carry guns. In one of a series of profiles published collectively under the title *Angry Women*, the fury of Galas, as well as the obvious 'don't mess with me I'm dangerous' self-parody, is mesmerizing in its outrageousness. 'The only people you treat as equals are other

17

women. And when you want subordinates, you can fuck a man in the ass! That basically is probable in the future. I like violent men; I like the idea that I can terrorize them and they can take it. I don't want 'em to knock me across the room unless I hit them first – and can hit 'em back.'

Is Galas, and those like her, a startling product of the post-feminist age or simply the latest of a strong, assertive breed of women stretching back through history who have adapted and reacted to the climate of their times? This is the question we must attempt to resolve if we are to understand anything about the nature of aggressive women.

A Media Obsession?

We are now being challenged, even forced, to confront many new and to some people unacceptable aspects of womanhood – not only in literature and popular culture but every day in a multitude of different ways in all strata of society. It is surely no coincidence that at the same time as the present spate of tough girl and female killer movies began to hit the screen in Europe and America, a series of unrelated feature articles and news stories began slamming home the dangers of what many 'experts' interpreted as a sinister and predictable outcome of the feminist movement. Specifically these reports hinged on the apparently rapid growth in female delinquency and violent crime as attested by escalating crime convictions among young girls and women and an ever-soaring female prison population.

The media messages are mixed, sometimes warning against the dire consequences of women taking the law into their own hands, sometimes extolling the virtues of women who dare to fight back. Occasionally something about the circumstances leading to a particular crime serves to whip up a near hysterical public response towards the image of the offender. So it was on 2 April 1993 when 40-year-old mother of two Ellie Nesler walked calmly into a Californian courtroom, took careful aim with her .25-calibre semi-automatic pistol and pumped five bullets at close range into the head of Daniel Driver as he sat handcuffed awaiting a preliminary hearing on charges of sexually molesting four boys, including Nesler's 6-year-old son. The facts of the case were never in dispute. The real issue that divided public opinion throughout America was the morality of vigilantism: whether Nesler should not only be treated leniently for her crime but indeed praised for acting as she did, both in her child's interest as well as the interest of public safety. What transpired prior to and during Nesler's trial tells us as much about America's lingering and respected ethos of 'frontier justice' – now bolstered by burgeoning fears over violent crime – as it does about the growing fanatical moral outrage at child abuse. Within hours of the shooting more than a hundred people called the county sheriff's department protesting at her arrest. She was eventually released on $500,000 bail and supporters immediately launched a campaign to raise funds for her defence, eventually collecting donations from all over the USA and abroad totalling nearly $40,000. Thousands of letters of support flooded in from around the world. A singer even composed and recorded a laudatory ballad extolling Nesler's heroism, while a suggestion was seriously put forward for a statue to be erected in her honour.

With so much public sentiment in her favour from the outset the chances that a jury would find Nesler guilty of first degree murder, for which she stood trial, were reckoned to be slim. Defence claims that 'mad with pain' she was driven to kill as a result of years of accumulated mental anguish resulting from sharing her son's trauma after being sodomized by Driver only added to her victim-turned avenger status, while increasing her chances of reducing the charge to manslaughter on grounds of temporary mental insanity – even though all the evidence indicated that the murder was premeditated. A day after the killing she told her sister she had wanted to see justice done, stating that, 'I know I'm not God, I know I'm not the jury, but at that instant I didn't feel justice was going to get done.' The image of female avenging angel was irresistible to the press and public alike. That August the jury found Nesler innocent of murder but guilty of manslaughter, allowing her to remain a symbol of justice to all law-abiding, morally righteous folk who believe in their right to take an eye for an eye.

In contrast, extensive coverage of criminal trials and convictions of women charged with murdering their husbands, often violent men at whose hands they had suffered for many years, have yielded heated debates between lawyers, psychiatrists and women's groups about women's 'right' to defend themselves against extreme, apparently life-threatening male violence, including rape. There was, and still is, much agonizing over the dangers of letting female defendants off too lightly, with judges inveighing against women who 'take the law into their own hands' and warning that excessive leniency in sentencing would give battered wives a 'charter to kill'.

With the advent of the Gulf crisis there arose another violent controversy about whether women, especially mothers, should engage in active combat in the front line of war. Here was a custom-made platform to launch the mother of all feminist polemics. Female soldiers with children were denounced as 'wicked' mothers sacrificing their own well-being and that of their families for the sake of proving their equality, or if single were dismissed as token males, dangerous and irresponsible bimbos showing off in Rambo clothing, whose desire for kicks could only lead to disaster for them and for their fellow men whose activities would be hampered by having to support and protect their weaker female colleagues. 'IS THE BATTLE LOST IF FEMINISTS GO TOO FAR?' ventured *The Times*; 'SHOULD ANY WOMAN BE RAPED FOR HER COUNTRY?' thundered the *Evening Standard*, who at one point pulled off the trick of presenting equally emotive yet mutually conflicting messages on one page, asking 'WHY DID SO MANY ARMY WOMEN DIE?' in the top section and in the lower describing recently released Major Rhonda Cornum as 'FREED POW TOUGH AS NAILS'.

One thing that the media airing did achieve was to expose the extent to which sexism is still rife in the Pentagon, as in all other predominantly male establishments. Thus we were treated to the views of US Air Force chief Merrill McPeake, who told a congressional committee, 'I would rather put a less qualified man into combat than a better qualified female flier. I'm not anxious to shove women into combat, it's just a personal prejudice of mine.' And this was in the wake of Kelly Crank's nomination as helicopter pilot of the year for her bravery and skill in blowing up mines, rescuing pilots who had been shot down and saving her crew when their aircraft seemed certain to crash. Another US supremo, General Barrows, gave his opinion of women on the battlefield as follows: 'Women can't do it. Nor should they ever be thought of as doing it. And I may be old-fashioned but I think the very nature of women disqualifies them from doing it. Women give life. Sustain life. Nurture life. They don't take it.'

Schoolgirl bullies were targeted by the media as another scourge of civilized society, proof, they claimed, of an emerging generation of gymslip delinquents. Agony aunts, counsellors and helplines were suddenly besieged by TV and the tabloid press eager to whip up maximum public outrage over a girl who had committed suicide allegedly because of constant bullying, while another girl had made five suicide attempts and undergone psychiatric treatment for the same reason. In defiance, one teenager appealed to the High Court over her school's decision to expel her for being the ringleader of a gang which terrorized other pupils, indulging in offences that were alleged to be 'particularly nasty and sexual in content'. *ES* magazine ran a piece entitled 'SWING OUT, SISTER: WHATEVER HAPPENED TO THE GENTLER SEX?', featuring an already well-publicized incident in which 200 rival schoolgirl gangs went on the rampage, slugging it out in genteel, leafy Wimbledon, shrieking obscenities, coming to bloody blows, terrifying the locals and ending up in police custody confronted with a string of criminal charges. When asked by a *Times* reporter whether police were shocked, a Scotland Yard spokesman replied pointedly, 'Nothing much does that these days. This is London 1992,' a comment clearly intended to leave no room for doubt as to the slippery, downward slide of young British womanhood.

In one alarming example of the tendency to seek significant links between media imagery and real life tragedy, *The Sunday Times* devoted an entire page to an article that attempted to compare such screen characters as Thelma and Louise to battered wives like Sara Thornton, just jailed for life for killing her violent husband, a piece lavishly illustrated with stills of gun-toting film stars in their recent 'killer' roles. A year later the same newspaper ran another full-page feature positing that 'violence by women has increased dramatically', this time using as a springboard the tragic cases of Christine Dryland an army major's wife, and Susan Christie, a woman soldier, both of whom had brutally murdered their rivals in love. At the same time the article drew on a ludicrously over-hyped incident, so trivial it hardly merited the dignity of serious analysis, involving a jilted baronet's wife, Lady Sarah Moon, who had cut up thirty of her husband's Savile Row suits, covered his Mercedes in paint and given away all his vintage claret. The result was another superficial quest for significance, a vain attempt to identify and analyse a 'new social phenomenon' on the flimsiest of evidence by drawing parallels between these events and the latest crop of she-killer movies, this time, it being one year on, citing *Basic Instinct* and *Single White Female*. But since when was murdering the 'other woman' and lashing out at an errant husband either comparable or, indeed, anything new? The article and many others like it purport to say a lot – most of it speculative and, when quoting female crime statistics as allegedly being up by 350 per cent over the last decade, glaringly false – but in the end tell us little and explain virtually nothing.

The question is, does it really matter? Are such features any more than journalistic 'puffs', pre-fabricated media hype intended merely to arouse controversy, briefly titillate the reader and thereby hike up sales? The answer would be a simple no, were the subject not so reflective of two fundamental and highly emotive social issues, one being the public's growing fear of crime and concern about the apparent disintegration of our social fabric and the other, not entirely unrelated, concerning the changing roles of the sexes and the varying degrees of optimism, doubt, anxiety or condemnation with which society has reacted to women's growing independence, self-determination and attempts to gain equality in all spheres previously dominated by men.

It may be a well-worn adage that whatever trend or issue is born in America can be guaranteed to surface in Britain and the rest of Europe a decade later, but events have proved its unerring accuracy. Although Britain is only beginning to agonize over the apparent rise in female violence and growing delinquency among today's generation of girls, the spectre of the so-called 'new female criminal' is one which first began to haunt the minds of American criminologists, sociologists and, naturally enough, the media as far back as the early 1970s. In 1972 the *New York Times* ran a major feature about the threat posed by New York's teenage gangs such as the Bronx-based Ghetto Sisters and the 240-strong Savage Nomads, some mixed sex, some all-girls, who were taking to the streets in greater numbers and running amok due to the combined effects of poverty, boredom, lack of parental care and security and insufficient motivation at school. Interviews with some of the female gang members indicated a growing inclination to learn to fight and settle disputes for themselves, without help from the boys.

Ironically, however, when American criminologist Freda Adler first sent shockwaves through the women's movement by her assertion that feminism and crime were linked, claiming that the price to be paid for women's growing independence and visibility in the world was a concurrent rise in violent and criminal behaviour, it was to England that she pointed in partial illustration of her thesis. In her controversial work *Sisters In Crime*, published in 1975, Adler quoted a 1972 *Time* magazine article about Britain's menacing phenomenon of 'bovver birds', allegedly totalling thirty gangs in London alone, who regularly ran riot in Britain's city streets, terrorizing the elderly, viciously beating up other girls and women, mugging and robbing, often more for a lark than for great amounts of cash. An Old Bailey judge was quoted as saying: 'It was once assumed that if a man and a woman committed a crime, the woman was under the domination of the man. I think that's rubbish from what I've seen.'

In the first six months of 1972, Adler noted, muggings were reportedly up by 70 per cent in parts of London, with growing participation by females. One girl interviewed by a *Time* correspondent admitted she had formed her own all-girl clique who had no compunction about setting out for a spot of 'granny bashing' when the fancy took them. According to Trevor Gibbens, then a distinguished forensic psychiatrist and one of the few researchers into female crime, there was nothing surprising about all this. 'Girls who used to grow up in relatively sheltered homes now freely roam the streets just like the boys have always done. It is a natural result that, in becoming equal, they have become equal in all areas, including violence.' Although at the time the male crime rate was ten times higher for males (as it still is), between 1969 and 1977 violent offences among females in Britain were reportedly increasing faster than among men; they were apparently up by 200 per cent and about a third of the crimes were committed by girls under 17.

The fear expressed in the *Time* article – that because girls appear to be less threatening they can escape being spotted by the police and may eventually become more proficient than men in carrying out violent crimes – was partly echoed by Adler's thesis. Adler's theory that feminism was the wellspring of increased violence and criminality was, and remains, roundly condemned by many feminists, including social scientists and criminologists who have begun analysing crime from a feminist perspective. The main charge levelled against *Sisters In Crime* was its shaky methodology. Lacking solid, hard data, it was criticized for propounding a dangerously subversive antifeminist thesis on the basis of mere anecdotal evidence and random speculation. Another caveat was that Adler failed to address the predicament of women forced to endure domestic violence and increased risks of sexual assaults outside the home or the numerous socioeconomic pressures of single parenthood that may contribute to all forms of human behaviour, including crime.

Equally telling, however, was the outraged reaction of many women to the very concept of an emerging 'new female criminal' as a product of her age, revealing the ever-widening ideological divide of 'gender politics', a reflection of the chasm that still separates feminists of various persuasions. By highlighting women's strengths rather than their weaknesses, their ability to take positive, even extreme, violent action in order to survive

24

and fashion an identity for themselves as survivors, researchers like Adler are seen by many as traitors to the 'party line' that decrees *all* women to be helpless victims of patriarchal oppression. If Adler's early work did nothing more than challenge and refute the reductionist and insulting notion of an all-embracing and inescapable female 'victim culture' then its value is already considerable.

An equally bracing and more accurate picture of how – and why – patterns of female violence were beginning to develop in the 1970s and early 1980s emerged from British researcher Anne Campbell's extensive first-hand observations of girl gangs in Britain and America. Campbell's studies attest not only to women's noted resilience and infinite capacity to adapt to environmental change and adversity, including ever-increasing economic hardship, family violence and threats of male oppression and assault, but demonstrate to what degree this adaptive mechanism results in the development of group survival skills based in no small part on the use, when necessary, of force and aggression. What Campbell discovered was that wherever women's desire and need for male approval and protection declined, usually coinciding with a lack in certainty of being able to count on men's financial help and support, the stronger became their sense of solidarity and tendency to coalesce into semi-detached or completely autonomous groups. These existed either as auxiliary units to all-male gangs or, increasingly, broke away completely and went independent.

At the 1992 American Society of Criminology conference, Anne Campbell spoke of her continuing conviction that society's perception of female aggression as a weakness or flaw, representing a loss of self-control which can only be socially destructive and personally damaging, remains essentially a middle-class concept, one which no longer has meaning or value for girls growing up in environments riddled with poverty, drugs and crime, where intra-family violence is the norm. There, safety may only be possible for girls who stick together in numbers and work as hard on their reputation for toughness and craziness as the boys do.

*　　*　　*

At the 1992 ASC conference there was a general climate of agreement, especially among feminist researchers (of both sexes), that America as in the 1970s is again being afflicted by new theories of 'feminism-equals-violence', largely due to what Meda Chesney-Lind, Director of the Women's Studies Pro- gramme at the University of Hawaii, calls a 'media pile-on'. In a shamelessly tendentious slant on 'social trends', rising crime figures and women's new-found independence are deliberately and maliciously being causally linked and the alleged effects exaggerated by sensation-seeking reporters and reactionary social commentators as part of an attempt to whip up an ongoing feminist backlash.

The liberated female crook of today, according to the media, is more likely to be black, to carry a weapon and come from a poverty-stricken crime and drug-ridden neighbourhood charac- terized by its own insidious ecology of crime. Yet the differences between women living in inner-city areas and those who do not remain far more striking than differences between the sexes, as should become clear in the coming chapters, highlighting this as an issue of urban plight rather than an issue of female emancipation. And whatever circumstances and qualities mark out the aggressive or violent woman and set her apart from her more passive, law-abiding counterpart seem to be much the same now as a decade or two ago, so if there does appear to be a new wave of female crime then there is no doubt that it is largely a media fabrication. The female criminal not as a 'type' but as a cross-section of different types does exist – but she certainly isn't new, however disingenuously the press and com- mentators attempt to draw on rising rates of female arrests and imprisonment as evidence to the contrary.

It is true that between 1983 and 1986 there was a 53 per cent increase in the numbers of women who owned guns, bringing the total of female owners up to 12 million, and a poll conducted by Smith and Wesson found that the numbers of women think- ing of buying a gun increased from 8 million in 1983 to 15½ million in 1988. According to one instructor who holds two courses a month for women, each heavily attended, 'For years guns were seen as anti-feminine. Now women have realized that isn't anti-feminine to own a gun. It's a great equalizer.' But this increase in gun ownership has everything to do with women refusing to become victims, and much less to do with women becoming the aggressors.

If anything, the upward trend in crimes committed by women appears to have slowed recently. According to current FBI statistics, there was a greater rise in violent crimes by women in America during the late 1960s and 1970s than in the 1980s. Among women offenders, the increase between 1968 and 1977 ran at 61 per cent for homicide, 110 per cent for violent robbery and 159 per cent for assault. By comparison, between 1982 and 1991 homicides by women were reportedly up by only 12 per cent, robbery by 49 per cent and aggravated assault by 17 per cent, with the total increase for female crimes of violence over that decade standing at 62 per cent in comparison to the 400 per cent increase between 1930 and 1970. Quoting statistics, however, is notorious for its input of showmanship. And if there is one rabbit analysts delight in pulling out of the hat again and again it is the comparatively low rate of crime increase among males. By now a tired old trick, this is the one most easy to see through: violent assaults by women in America supposedly rose by 79.1 per cent over the past decade while among men they went up by only 43.3 per cent – but this comparison is almost entirely without meaning given that the vast percentage of all crimes of violence (with the sole exception of infanticide) are still, as always, committed by men.

In Britain, too, reporters have been tempted to dazzle us by juxtaposing crime figures and social trends with a triumphant flourish, suggesting that female violence, especially among young girls, is reflected in increased arrests and imprisonment of women. Although violent crimes committed by women went up by 67 per cent compared to a 10 per cent increase by men between 1981 and 1991, with a 12 per cent increase in the number of serious female offenders recorded by the Home Office in 1993, bringing the UK total to 101,000, acccording to the National Association for the Care and Resettlement of Offenders (NACRO) only one in every ten women prisoners is incarcerated for a violent crime while one third of women prisoners have no previous convictions – compared with 11 per cent of men. Figures for 1990 also show that 56 per cent of women remanded in custody were either acquitted or given community sentences, which already makes women's high profile in the crime statistics somehat skewed. Yet each time a murder or a violent incident involving a woman offender hits the headlines, especially where it involves drug or alcohol abuse, sexual promiscuity, lesbianism or some other behaviour seen to contravene the accepted female norms, these rising 'trends' are predictably trotted out accompanied by much anti-feminist rehetoric and general polemicizing about declining family values and women's abandonment of traditional roles.

According to Meda Chesney-Lind, today's female criminal is more feared and gives more cause for moral panic since she is usually young, non-white and may very well be armed. Apart from that, little has changed since women began – as much through necessity as by design – to challenge the *status quo* and find ways to become self-sufficient. 'We have rediscovered what was always there, which is that girls have *always* been more violent than our stereotype permits and that girls have always been involved in gangs.'

Theories of Criminality: Mad, Bad or Biologically Possessed?

Those outside the confines of academe might well be forgiven for failing to understand Meda Chesney-Lind's reference to the rediscovery of what already exists, indeed, has always existed. After all, the issue of female violence and criminality is explosive and controversial by mere virtue of its existence, which many take to be new. Women are perceived as the guardians and upholders of the law; the ones who can be depended on to control, calm and assuage anger and hostility in others and to suppress it in themselves. Anger in women is seen as unhealthy and aggression is worse – ugly, discordant and undignified, it is the antithesis of those quintessential elements of gentleness, selflessness and nurturing which have always been confidently looked for in womankind. Not surprisingly, crime, like all violent behaviour, has until recently been regarded as an inherently male activity with female misdemeanours by comparison so unusual and isolated in their occurrence, so anomalous among the 'normal' female population, as to make it virtually a non-starter as a topic for research.

It is for this reason and this reason alone that the study of aggression, still less that of crime and criminality, has until very recently signally failed to include women in its ambit. Hence the much touted phrase the 'invisibility of female crime', used as much to denote its non-validity as a topic for research as its insignificance in the world at large. Even those crimes to which women are believed to be drawn because of their temperament and physique, principally petty theft, shoplifting, killing their babies at or soon after birth and committing murder by such 'ladylike' methods as the use of poison, were traditionally dismissed as mere aberrations unworthy of in-depth analysis. And if it doesn't exist, how can anyone begin to investigate or analyse it?

Above all, the world of crime research, encompassing as it does psychiatric medicine, the police, probation service, penal institutions and the criminal justice system, is a world until very recently wholly constructed, run and dominated by men, whose views on female behaviour were entirely informed by centuries of traditional biological determinism, i.e. women's inherent physical and intellectual inferiority. Invisible in the world at large, women were destined to remain invisible in the world of criminological research. To read the bulk of textbooks on crime and delinquency written before the 1960s or even the 1970s is to step into a world devoid of female experience, a culture where male aggression dominates and is celebrated, even legitimized, as possessing survival value, and in which anger, assertiveness, hostility, competitiveness and the quest for dominance and power are accepted and praised as normal modes of male bonding, self-expression, success and survival. In such a world women cannot and do not figure on the agenda. And in as far as women were ever fleetingly and occasionally on this male agenda, it was only ever within the context of pathology.

It is significant, if not surprising, that of the tiny handful of early researchers who ever bothered to construe theories about female criminality, all were male and without exception all developed propositions heavily overlaid with value judgements, each one unashamedly sexist, racist, misogynistic and class-ridden in tone. A brief run-down of the four famous – or infamous – principal theorists of female deviance and criminality immediately reveals the almost unbelievable extent of bias and stereotypical imagery of 'mad' or 'bad' womanhood that persisted until very recently. Nor, by any means, has it entirely disappeared. Tragically, sexist assumptions still continue to inform current public and judicial attitudes towards women, dividing them to this day into either the 'madonna' or 'whore' category.

The first of the traditionalists was the Italian criminologist Cesare Lombroso, whose theories one could laugh off more readily were it not for the appalling fact that until recently they influenced the course and tenor of criminological analysis and attitudes more than those of virtually any other researcher. Known as the father of 'scientific criminology', Lombroso, writing with his son-in-law William Ferrero in 1895, stated that most criminal women were born abominably ferocious and could be identified by a large number of physical 'anomalies', including extra body hair, facial growths such as warts and hairy moles, extra dark skin and hair, facial asymmetry, deep-set eyes and fang-like teeth (accompanied by a forbidding hag-like expression) – in short, any physical type that did not conform to the ideal delicate refinement associated with white aristocratic or upper- and middle-class womanhood. In a nutshell, the female criminal was a monster, the she-devil incarnate. Even obesity was regarded by Lombroso as an indicator of criminality, particularly among prostitutes. Identifying these characteristics in male criminals also, he regarded all crime as an atavistic legacy, the survival of primitive traits once needed for the evolution of the fittest. Because like many men of his time he dismissed women (as well as all non-white races) as inherently inferior to the white male, when a woman differed from her biological ideal it was in his view a sure sign of moral corruption and sexual degeneracy, little different to the witches who were hunted down and burned at the stake by the million in Europe throughout the Middle Ages.

Lombroso also believed that women's capacity to sustain pain (which he interpreted as an inability to feel pain) made them impervious to the suffering of others and robbed them of moral refinement. In the end he reasoned that crime required passion and intelligence, qualities which women in general were too passive and apathetic to possess, therefore there were bound to be fewer female criminals since they must, by definition, be quasi males.

William Thomas, writing in the early to mid 1900s, was much influenced by Lombroso and also noted certain salient characteristics among non-European 'savage' women, including Red Indians and Africans. These women were without the desirable white female qualities of passivity and lack of sexuality which, in order for women to be ideal wives and mothers, had to be cultivated for the good of civilization. A more compassionate man, who did not share Lombroso's horror of deviant females as near witches possessed by evil, Thomas did, however, take the paternalistic view that delinquency was synonymous with sexual promiscuity, defining female crime principally in terms of prostitution, adultery and sexual freedom. In his book *The Unadjusted Girl*, written in 1923, there is much sanctimonious moralizing in which he advocates that women should be helped to readjust to traditional chaste, decorous modes of behaviour so that they can reconcile themselves to living a life of domestic virtue, sublimating their sexual desires in favour of preserving the sanctity of the family.

It wasn't that Thomas was unaware of the pressures and stresses experienced by women as a result of social change in which they felt their powerlessness and inequality more acutely. He was – but he believed their behavioural responses signified a maladjustment which should be held in check by cultivating the healthier 'natural' maternal instinct. As a contemporary of Sigmund Freud, who was by now a formidable influence on the study of human behaviour and whose position on women's roles was quite simply that 'anatomy is destiny', it is easy to see to what extent Thomas's views on women's need to reconcile themselves to the dictates of biology and learn to put up with men's domination as a necessary price to be paid for domestic cohesion were upheld as immutable and unassailable truths.

It is certainly hard to imagine anyone having a more powerful and enduring hand than Freud in delineating and reinforcing the traditional images of female duality – non-sexual, passive, self-abnegating mothers versus promiscuous, unhealthy, man-hating neurotics. Thanks to Freudian ideology, there are many who still not only believe that the well-balanced woman is the one who fulfils her inborn maternal instinct but that the unbalanced unhealthy one rejects that role in a futile attempt to emulate men, whose penis she envies and who seeks revenge for not having one. She may desire male power, but at the same time fears and hates it. Hence the assumption, elaborated and fortified by the cladding of Freudian doctrine, that stepping outside the female role can only result in deviancy and self-destruction. On the Freudian cast list we therefore find such stock neurotics as the rape victim driven by her masochistic sexual fantasies to lie about being assaulted, the 'prick-teaser' who accuses a man of rape through guilt at having led him on in the first place, or the woman who said 'no' when she meant 'yes' and whose fear and hatred of men makes her seek an independent sexually active life outside the home.

The last of the traditional 'biological' theorists on female crime was Otto Pollack whose 1950 publication *The Criminality of Women* (published in the UK in 1961 with a lurid cover depicting a witch beating a kneeling man) talked of the 'masked nature' of female crime. Although the first researcher to address the reality of women criminals who he believed were far greater in number than records suggested, their offences being vastly under-reported because they mostly went unnoticed, Pollack had merely hit on a new rationale to bolster the same age-old myths of women as victims of their reproductive cycles. Citing menstruation, pregnancy, menopause and sexual shame and repression as prime influences on women's behaviour, he believed that their expertise at secrecy, for example hiding menstruation and period pain, faking orgasm, attempting to prevent or succeed at conception or conceal pregnancy, reflected an essentially manipulative and deceitful nature.

Under the guise of respectable domesticity, Pollack believed women were free to avenge their anger and frustration against men and society by secret acts of treachery, including shoplifting, illegal abortions, prostitutes robbing their clients, petty thefts (especially by servants), poisoning and other 'refined' acts of violence against husbands, children and other dependants. The reason they got away with all this, he asserted, was because of men's blind chivalry, which could only conceive of the female nature as essentially gentle and beneficent hence first and foremost requiring protection. Women's crimes committed within the family might easily go undiscovered and those who were suspected or caught committing offences outside the home could count on the protective instincts of the police and criminal justice system to treat them leniently or let them off entirely. Ludicrous and offensive as this all sounds to us today, the fact that his work was published relatively recently and purported to offer the first serious analysis of female crime means that its impact has, like Freudian thinking, remained powerful and all-pervasive in determining how the justice system views women offenders.

Quite apart from the outrageously misogynistic flavour of, in particular, the popular theories propounded by Lombroso and Pollack – a putrid odour wafts nauseatingly off each page describing women's reproductive functions – the fact that historically and sociologically these are quite evidently a howling negation of women's acknowledged 'talents' (acquired or otherwise) for empathy, nurturing, compassion and skills at childcare and domesticity is something which few academics until now seem to have spotted. Pollack's notion of women's inherent vengefulness is impossible, for instance, to square with the concept of a 'universal' maternal instinct, showing up both theories as the ludicrous constructs they are.

It must be obvious by now to what extent even relatively modern criminological theory has colluded with ancient folklore to depict women as a species apart, their actions, mental stability and responses to environmental pressure determined by their hormonal make-up, especially in cases of deviancy or aberration. That economic hardship, family commitments, political upheaval or other factors such as racism, sexism, male oppression and violence against women and children may have a part to play in influencing a woman's decision or compulsion to behave antisocially and violently, perhaps turning to crime as a means of survival, seems only lately to have been considered relevant to the issue of female crime.

When you look at the past history and documented experiences of women it is staggering to see that what researchers appear to have wilfully overlooked, while piously genuflecting at the altar of biological determinism, is how often all such theories have been disproved by history. As far back as Queen Boadicea, who led her Celtic troops into battle against invading Roman armies having seen her husband Prasutagus killed and her daughters raped by Roman legionaries, we have persuasive evidence of women's readiness to take arms against brutal dictatorships, social oppression and injustice and economic privation. That the early Celtic women were often fierce, brave combatants, especially when it came to revolting against Roman invaders, is well documented by Plutarch and other writers of early or pre-Christian times.

Without the fury that gripped impoverished working-class Parisian women during the French Revolution, causing them to take to the streets in their thousands, it is debatable whether the arrest and execution of Louis XVI, Marie Antoinette and the entire Capet dynasty would have been such a precipitate or bloody event. The fury and mob-violence of the 8,000-strong almost exclusively all-female march to Versailles on the night of 5 October 1789 was a direct culmination of the earlier Bread Riots in which the women of Paris, enraged at the lack of food, rampaged in vain through the markets.

Much of the women's revolutionary bloodlust — they cut a swathe of terror on the road to Versailles, pillaging, looting, stoning shops and taverns and storming the National Assembly before finally murdering the Royal Guards and demolishing the Royal Quarters — was due to their central role and responsiblity in ensuring the welfare of their families. So female violence among the 'femmes sans culottes', which continued sporadically but vigorously throughout the war, was less about trying to 'prove' their bravery by fighting for the cause (although a few succeeded in serving at the front) and more about feeding hungry stomachs and obtaining employment. This did not deter the Parisian journalist Suleau from publishing a diatribe against the women of the revolution, accusing them all of being ugly or infirm crones who saw the uprising as an opportunity to recapture their lost youth! In response, a leading figure of the revolution, Theroigne de Mericourt – dressed as an Amazon she had led the storming of the Bastille and later joined in the invasion of the Tuileries – initiated the author's assassination. Ironically, she herself was later publicly flogged by a crowd of women hell-bent on a bloody reign of terror, as punishment for advocating a women's magistracy for peace.

Almost a decade later, in events leading up to and following the uprising of the Paris Commune of 1871, fighting French women took to the streets again with feverish passion, demanding equality with men in defending the city. Many thousands of women died as a result of erecting and defending barricades, fighting government troops or while acting as 'petroleurs' setting fire to public buildings. A study of those women who were arrested shows that the vast majority were 'respectable' working-class married women or widows aged between 30 and 50 who were employed in working-class occupations, mainly in the clothing trade.

Looking at female violence in this social and historical perspective highlights the nonsense of trying, as did some of the theorists, to attribute such 'deviant' behaviour to class and race. Although the French Revolution and the urban revolutions which erupted in 1848 in Paris, Vienna, Milan, Rome, Berlin and many other European cities and towns did involve large numbers of working-class women, many were also drawn from the ranks of the educated, middle-class intellectual 'élite'. Nowhere was this more marked than in the early anti-Tsarist demonstrations and terrorist activities in pre-revolutionary Russia of the mid to late 1800s. Here the women who spearheaded the radical socialist movement were exclusively drawn from the educated upper middle class and the aristocracy, since the remaining majority of the nation was still uneducated, many living as serfs under an ancient feudal regime.

The names of the early female revolutionaries have long been enshrined in the history of the fight against Tsarist tyranny and oppression. These women included teams of explosives makers and bomb throwers, of whom the most famous, Sophia Perovskaya, was hanged for her part in plotting and carrying out the assassination in 1881 of Tsar Alexander II. Perovskaya, a tiny graceful young girl, was said to possess 'a fearlessness that amazed the bravest of men'. But the price of such fearlessness, shared by many of her female compatriots, was often horrific. The leader of Perovskaya's group, Elizaveta Kovalskaya, once so severely beaten up by the police that it took her a year to recover, was sentenced to twenty-three years' imprisonment in Siberia for her role in this and other revolutionary activities. Many other female activists were routinely arrested and thrown into jail, put into solitary confinement and placed on trial, even exiled from their province, simply for looking like 'nihilists'. Guaranteed to put police on the alert was close-cropped hair and the standard 'feminist' uniform of a short dark skirt and Russian blouse cinched with a leather belt. In one region of Nizhny-Novgorod near St Petersburg, by order of the governor, women dressed thus were to be taken to prison, commanded to shed their clothes and put on crinolines. If they refused they were to be banished from the region.

The harsher their punishment the greater grew these women's determination to fight on for the freedom of the people. And fight they did, often with extreme brutality. Maria Bochkareva, a Bolshevik soldier who had previously fought with an all-male Tsarist regiment on the Western front, changed sides and formed the notorious Women's Battalion of Death in 1917, an all-female crack corps numbering 2,000 trained volunteers. So effective were they that similar units were formed and deployed throughout Russia. Indeed, there were more women involved in the revolutionary and pro-feminist movement in Russia than in any other country in Europe.

By taking an historical perspective such as this we again highlight the absurdity of the media's current obsession with the 'new' violent female.

Crime and Punishment

Despite the evidence that women's capacity for violence may equal men's and that criminal behaviour may be triggered by influences as diverse as political oppression, social injustice and the demand for socioeconomic change, or simply, as in most cases, the need to survive, the assumption remains that in women such behaviour denotes deviance – moreover deviance that so dramatically contravenes accepted norms of behaviour that it is usually suspected of being pathological in origin. While all crime and all acts of violence today are rightly an issue for growing social concern, men's violence is nevertheless understood because it fits into the accepted parameters of male behaviour. Even if the degree of male violence makes it menacing and problematic, it remains essentially non-deviant, except in a handful of isolated cases of serial and sadistic murderers and sexual offenders. Yet a woman's violence, by falling outside the parameters of acceptable behaviour, is considered by definition a problem of deviance. The fact that this apparent deviance is in many cases a normal manifestation of some women's conscious or unconscious rejection of the spheres of activity and behavioural norms designated to them over the centuries is something society as a whole is still unable – or unwilling – to accept. We need only remember how quickly women were again relegated to the domestic sphere after they had played their part and often given their lives in times of political unrest and economic hardship, as in Britain after the Second World War when women worked in the armed forces and were obliged to take over the reins in the hitherto male-dominated workforce, to see how shortlived has been any attempt to demolish male/female stereotypes for good.

Until now. Today's generation of women are certainly the first who are no longer prepared to walk backwards into the future. For one thing, in our rapidly changing economic environment such return routes have probably been cut off for good, like it or not. Having by now passed the point of no return in entering the 'real' world, the question is not whether liberated women are becoming more like men in exhibiting antisocial, violent behaviour, but how much like normal human beings they are, firing on all cylinders, in possession of the full range of human emotion and behaviour, including those once reserved exclusively for men. If taking up aggressive, male-dominated sports, entering once exclusively male professions like the army, police, construction industry or fire brigade, learning to fight like men, going out in groups or gangs, drinking alcohol, attending football matches or having to resort to tough, threatening, perhaps criminal behaviour to feed yourself, your child or your entire family is evidence of deviance then it is high time we began to redefine the term aggression and view it not as synonymous with pathology when applied to women but as an inherently normal manifestation of the coming of age of over half the human race.

Above all, the redefinition of deviancy is well overdue when it comes to women and crime. As long as society applies a radically different set of criteria in its evaluation and judgement of female delinquents, dropouts and offenders then the opportunity for women to obtain understanding from the community as well as their right to fair treatment by the law must remain severely limited. One of the most frequently stressed observations relating to women and crime is the leniency with which the criminal justice system habitually treats female offenders compared to their male counterparts. On the surface, this seems absolutely accurate. The 1988 British Crime Survey found that males were twice as likely as females to be stopped by the police because they thought an offence had been committed. According to a recent Home Office report, of the 509,000 offenders found guilty or cautioned for indictable offences in 1990 (remembering that a very great number of offences are not reported to or discovered by the authorities), 17 per cent were females and of these just under half received a caution, compared to a third of males (except in cases involving drug offences). As might be expected, the cautioning rate is highest for juveniles and steadily rising.

Of those young girls drawn into the criminal justice system in 1990, 96 per cent of 10–13-year-olds were cautioned for indictable offences compared with 85 per cent in 1980, and 86 per cent of 14–16-year-olds compared to 58 per cent a decade earlier. Although acknowledged to be incomplete, available prison and criminal statistics suggest that women remanded in custody remain less likely than men to receive a custodial sentence (30 per cent women compared to 40 per cent men) while women remanded on bail are also less likely to be sentenced to custody than men (5 per cent women compared to 10 per cent men).

This is where the 'chivalry' notion underlying women's lenient treatment by the courts acquires a distinct tinge of old-style paternalism, with women receiving 'treatment' rather than punishment on the basis, often entirely unsubstantiated, that their offences are due to illness or some mental disturbance which absolves them of responsibility. While men or boys get a rap on the knuckles, a short bout in prison, women go into 'care', often with the aim of helping them 'integrate' into roles they may have long ago rejected or found excessively burdensome due to external circumstances. Judicial leniency becomes chauvinistic benevolence. At the end of 1990, 17,200 females, many clearly seen as suitable cases for treatment, were either on probation or being supervised by the probation service under criminal court orders with psychiatric treatment a precondition, or were receiving 'aftercare'. Nearly a quarter of the women starting probation orders at that time had no previous convictions compared to just a tenth of the men. By now it seems that rather than being more lenient, the courts actually end up discriminating against women by being less ready to hold them accountable for their actions, opting for sentences which offer help and guidance – which, judging by the experiences of such women, may often take the form of psychiatric treatment, drug therapy and counselling or education designed to help women conform to more appropriate modes of female behaviour.

The fact that women who end up in prison are far more likely than men to have no previous convictions – in 1990, 33 per cent of female prisoners had no previous convictions compared to 11 per cent of men – also makes a mockery of the cherished notion of leniency. Many women imprisoned on remand for months, even years, will eventually be given a non-custodial sentence by the courts, but this can never fully compensate for the trauma and stigma of having been behind bars. The idea that if she isn't 'mad' the female offender must be 'bad' – and therefore imprisoned as an example to others who might think of following the route to deviancy – is hard to ignore. Yet the fact is that only one in every ten female prisoners has committed a violent crime; the remainder may be incarcerated for crimes as petty as non-payment of fines, poll-tax evasion, being drunk and disorderly (enough to constitute 'violence' in the context of feminine behaviour), for fraud or drug possession – both of which offences are rapidly on the increase among the female population worldwide.

Nor is it possible to ignore the disproportionately high number of black women in prison. Between 1985 and 1990 the percentage of non-white women prisoners rose from 17 per cent to 29 per cent. Equally disconcerting, considering the harshness of prison life and the well-documented levels of violence among prisoners and warders, is the high number of women remand prisoners awaiting trial or sentencing; 22 per cent of female prisoners, a lot of them youngsters, are there on remand, many of whom do not ultimately receive a prison sentence. If you take the view, as a great many male and female inmates do, that prison is the best training ground for a career in violence and crime, then these figures give ample grounds for alarm.

Even greater cause for concern is that while women make up only 4 per cent of Britain's prison population, they constitute *20* per cent of patients in special maximum-security hospitals ('specials') sent there for indefinite periods either directly from the courts or transferred from prison, again for often very petty offences. To be sent to an institution such as Rampton, Broadmoor or Ashworth – Britain's three largest specials – an offender has to be certified under the Mental Health Act (1983) as mentally ill, mentally impaired, severly mentally impaired or suffering from a psychopathic disorder. Yet as is clear from the suffering of women who have been incarcerated in these hospitals/prisons and as attested by growing numbers of mental health professionals working within such institutions, such labels often lack any precise meaning, making diagnosis an alarmingly flexible business, and may be abitrarily applied when women's actions fall short of appropriate norms. Excessive displays of anger or 'abnormal' levels of aggression and violence, extreme mood swings, self-injury and attempted suicide commonly come under the banner heading of so-called 'psychopathic disorder' or 'borderline personality disorder', under which many women in special hospitals are categorized.

Thus women may escape imprisonment only to face what many regard as the infinitely harsher option of being put 'in care' over an indefinite period. And care invariably means drugs – powerful, addictive, knock-out psychotropic drugs that often reduce women to glassy-eyed zombies, alternating between sleep and an artificial state of semi-alertness, each aggressive or violent outburst, whether against others or against themselves, liable to send nurses scurrying to fetch an extra heavyweight 'liquid cosh' – prison-speak for injections of powerful tranquillizing drugs. One former prisoner, Josie O'Dwyer, who spent eight years being shunted between various youth offender insitutions and prisons, has vivid memories of Holloway's infamous C1 psychiatric 'Muppet Wing' (a mini special hospital environment), a prime spot in which to observe what she wrily terms the 'Largactil twitch-and shuffle'.

'The women are so drugged-out they may be able to register pain, but they can't tell where it's coming from. They smoke a fag, burn their fingers, but don't know why. Their eyes are permanently dead. They gain weight from the drugs, lose their co-ordination, all their movements slow down. The nurses inject you straight through your jeans. There was an enormous eighteen-stone one used to come and sit on me, pushing all the air out of me till I thought I'd suffocate. They jab the syringe all the way in – whack – up to the hilt. The effects are instant and terrifying. You sweat, shake, get palpitations. It's scary, you think you're dying.'

The side effects may either turn the women into automatons

or make them more aggressive and bad tempered as their toler- ance rises. 'As you get more violent they give you higher doses, so everything just builds up in you, waiting to erupt. What they're really doing is drug 'em up to shut 'em up. Obviously some people do need to take drugs, but they may often give you the wrong ones – I was put on Haloperidol and couldn't lift my arm to clean my teeth or brush my hair. I'd forget to chew my food, just sit there with my mouth full, everything falling out. And on Largactil I put on masses of weight, I became unrecognizable. But the horror is, no one really cares, and you can't make anyone take notice or listen to you because you're too drugged out – and they know it.'

With violent attacks on staff in Rampton said to be five times more likely to be committed by a female than a male inmate, the thorniest question is not whether this proves that the women are fundamentally more dangerous, mentally disturbed or wicked, but whether such institutions, with their scarcity of specialized counselling, psychotherapy or rehabilitative pro- grammes aimed at increasing women's self-confidence and assertiveness, can in their present form be regarded as a suitable therapeutic environment for female offenders, for the most viol- ent and antisocial women are invariably the least confident and have the lowest self-image. Prison, because of its hierarchical structure from 'top dog' prisoners down and because of the power relationships based on aggression and dominance that develop between inmates and 'screws', often increases levels of violence and alienation in women. In the same way, special hospitals, with their reliance on drug treatment and emphasis on conventional standards of female behaviour, seem merely to reinforce many women's feeling of being isolated misfits. Their extreme youth is further cause for concern: one in six women held in 'specials' is under 20.

Terri Simpson, a founder member of the organization Women In Special Hospitals, was initially sent to Broadmoor at 21 for three and a half years for lighting a small fire in a shop doorway when sleeping rough and damaging a police cell while held in custody. Most of her childhood had been spent in children's homes, her teens marked by heavy drinking and drug use and the inability to find a job that interested her. Now a qualified plasterer, she maintains that had she been a man her drunkenness, swearing and rough appearance would not have led her to prison, let alone to Broadmoor. Once inside, there was nothing in the way of therapy. Even more appalling was the relentless continuing pressure for women to undertake such 'feminine' pusuits as needlework, knitting, hairdressing or soft-toy making, when their vehement rejection of such traditional roles is often what caused them to be locked up in a 'special' in the first place. Women at Rampton and other specials often complain of being encouraged to grow their hair long, wear make-up and feminine clothing and have their tattoos removed. This insistence on conforming to stereotype (it is surely no coincidence that women inmates at Rampton are referred to as 'our ladies') as well as the complete separation from outside life augurs ill for a woman hoping to resume a productive, independent life in the community.

Marian, who trained to become a classical musician and was sent to a special after suffering from mood swings and a nervous breakdown during which she committed various crimes of arson, resented the constant stress placed by staff on the need to 'conform', an attitude which merely intensifies society's condemnation of female anger. 'In my experience even simply to speak in a certain tone, or raise one's voice, use swear words, show anger, which would be normal in a man, is seen as very provocative. It's assumed you're going to act violently, which then means you're never allowed to express your feelings of frustration and anger openly. It's that which leads the emotions to stew and stew inside for so long until everything finally explodes, which happened with me. But then, when you get inside a place like that, the suppression continues and is enforced.'

She was charged with attempted murder while in Broadmoor and although the case was eventually dropped the charge remained on her medical record. She fears that the stigma of having been incarcerated under the Mental Health Act will affect her future chances of ever leading a healthy, fulfilled life.

With approximately 90,000 women currently behind bars in

American prisons and about 2,000 in England and Wales – including 3,000 or more on remand awaiting trial or sentence – another knotty problem is the amount of violence generated within the institutions themselves. Female prisons have long been a byword for violence and cruelty, more so even than men's. While some might attempt to use this as proof of Lombroso's theory, that criminal women are by nature more vicious and inherently 'masculine' in their behaviour, what it actually points to is the appalling power structure underlying such institutions, the 'institutionalizing' of brutality and the realization many girls and women arrive at – that it is only by resorting to violence that they can avoid ending up a victim of the system.

Most distressing is the evident absence of understanding within prisons of how often those who have been victims of violence may find themselves unable to control their own violent behaviour. Yet the virtual absence of therapy or programmes designed to tackle the root cause of women's destructive behaviour means that prison provides an ideal opportunity for women to cultivate, not resolve, their most destructive violent tendencies.

The general consensus among most prisoners is that the majority of prison warders thrive on the structure and discipline of institution life and depend on the sense of power derived through dominating or punishing inmates. According to one former inmate: 'They're prisoners themselves, who live, eat, sleep and drink prison life. They love torturing you and they know how to inflict the most pain. Like yanking your toes apart, which sends excruciating electric shocks up your legs. Ripping off your clothes when slinging you into a cell, all the tweaking and pinching of the nipples that goes with it.'

Sexual violence is another fact of life in a women's prison. Although many women do form intimate relationships, often for want of any other human closeness and warmth, the degree of brutality reportedly exhibited by some women, inmates and warders, defies the comprehension of those who have never experienced it. I have it on good authority, for instance, that the following experience, described by former closed ward inmate Sue Read in *Only A Fortnight*, is not so uncommon. Read describes in horrific and graphic detail how a co-inmate 'raped' her in the bathroom. 'If she had been a man it would have been called rape,' she says. Her attacker shoved her to the floor, biting her breasts, roughly pushing her fingers and mouth between her legs. When Read screamed for help a warder came into the bathroom and, seeing Read pinned to the floor, kicked the side of her head and threatened her, then stood by and watched the assault. As Read says, her experiences of enforced lesbian sex were of viciousness and brute force.

> Pauline would climb into my bed and roughly fuck me. She was strong and I was so scared . . . [She] would drag me into the loos. I learned not to say anything to dissuade her, because she would get me later. I'd sit or lie down, however she put me. I hated her with every fibre of my body. What she did to me was torture.

And if inmates don't fear sex, they certainly have to face punch-ups. Only by proving your fighting prowess, not just your ability to dominate and fight fellow prisoners but also to take on the screws, can you hope to become respected and feared enough not to be victimized by anyone else. To score points is to gain a reputation and a reputation ensures survival.

Little wonder, when Anne Campbell carried out a comparative study into the different attitudes towards fighting held by schoolgirls, former borstal girls and prisoners, the last two groups reported themselves far more likely to fight like men, punching, kicking, using weapons and continuing to kick an opponent who was on the ground, with the youngest (i.e. borstal) girls showing the most positive approach to fighting, seeing it as a good way of releasing anger and a legitimate means of settling conflicts or grievances.

One of the apparent ironies of prison life is that many come to depend on it as a lesser evil than the harsh hostility that passes for freedom on the outside. There is nothing so very mystifying about women who, when released, soon re-offend and willingly return to prison. Isolated for so long, having adapted perhaps all too successfully to the self-contained subculture of a penal institution without being adequately equipped with skills and resources to deal with the problems of unemployment, poverty, homelessness, the formalities of getting processed by the social security system or loneliness and estrangement from family and friends, who can blame offenders for consciously or unconsciously making a circuitous beeline back to the nick?

In defining the different 'pathways' that lead women into crime and the penal system, American sociologist Kathleen Daly has rightly pinpointed this lack of external community support as the key feature that keeps women, usually from deprived and abusive backgrounds, forever trapped in a vicious circle of law-breaking, imprisonment, alienation, deprivation and further law-breaking. As Daly points out, until we can begin to identify and tease out the myriad strands in a woman's life that lead her in the first place to become violent and commit crimes and that determine her status as a hardened 'crime offender' or a 'crime victim', whose crimes are in reality merely the end product of a long battle to survive, our understanding of *why* women abuse, harm and hurt others and end up being themselves brutalized by the law, must remain incomplete. And as long as society continues to see those women who fail to conform to feminine stereotypes as abnormal and continues to react with either excessive moral indignation or tabloid prurience to female crime, there is little hope for change.

Caution: Being Feminine Could Damage Your Health

The Aggression Machine

The year is 1963. The location: the Department of Psychology at Yale University in the United States. The objective: to assess how aggressively ordinary, non-criminal men and women are prepared to behave towards other individuals when under pressure to do so. The subjects, male and female, are young, well-educated, college graduates, volunteers who have agreed to participate in an experiment whose purpose they are told is to investigate the effects of punishment on learning. On arriving at the laboratory, each man or woman is assigned the role of 'teacher', and is told that another group of people, sitting at desks, have been given the part of 'learners'.

Each 'teacher' is asked to sit at a machine containing a control panel fitted with a series of buttons marked 1 to 10. They are told that each time the learner makes a mistake in the task they are trying to master, the teacher must punish him or her by pushing a button which delivers an electric shock to that person. The intensity of these shocks varies from very mild (button 1) to very severe and potentially lethal (10). What they are not told is that the readiness of each subject to use aggression will be monitored by researchers as they record both the intensity of the shock delivered by each subject as well as how long they keep their finger pressed on the button. (In reality the 'learners', who were part of the research team, felt no electrical impulse whatever but acted as if shocked, fearful and in pain.)

The appalling truth to emerge from these experiments is the degree to which normal, well-adjusted, perfectly *nice* human beings are prepared, under certain circumstances, to inflict pain and suffering – perhaps even death – without qualms, hesitation or apparent remorse. The second rather surprising discovery was that not only was there no significant difference between men's and women's readiness to aggress against their fellow humans by delivering these electric shocks but, if anything, women would press the high-voltage buttons sooner, more frequently and keep their finger depressed for longer than the men, despite pleadings and signs of distress enacted by their victims.

Such experiments have since been replicated numerous times in countries throughout the world, using random members of the public, adolescent delinquents, convicted murderers and other criminals, and the sorry truth is that when it comes to our readiness to inflict harm on others, most so-called non-violent, caring, peace-loving citizens act no differently, be they male or female, from the average cold-blooded psychopath. An amazing 65–90 per cent of subjects in the various studies have demonstrated their willingness to deliver the highest, very severe electric shocks! So much for the sweet celebrated virtues of womanhood.

Not surprisingly, many researchers have attempted to draw infinite numbers of conclusions from women's 'unexpected' propensity for aggression in these and similar studies, attributing diverse mitigating psychological explanations for their readiness to punish their poor unfortunate victims. One explanation centres on the argument that women are by nature law-abiding and thus more likely to defer to authority; therefore, if told by a white-coated official to carry out these punishments, they are more likely to comply promptly and efficiently than put up a fuss, which is one way of implying that women's capacity for autonomous free will, or for resisting what seems to be a harmful or senseless instruction, amounts to nil in the face of officialdom. Yet the point is that no one was forcing these participants to do what they did. They weren't locked in, no one held a gun to their head or threatened them with dire consequences if they refused to complete the study. (And, to be fair, some *did* refuse to carry on after a certain point.)

Even more sinister in its logic is the theory put forward by numbers of psychologists that women have an in-built tendency towards so-called 'pro-social aggression' (i.e. being cruel to be kind), whereby punishment, pain and injury are seen as justified provided they 'help' the victim attain a goal, master or learn a task or lesson more quickly. Drawing on the most socially sanctioned form of all human violence, mothers' physical punishment of their children, researchers believe that the women in the 'aggression machine' studies may merely have been delivering higher voltage shocks and pressing the high numbers for longer on the basis that this would 'help' the learner master the task faster and so escape further punishment. However, follow-up interviews with the subjects indicate that this was not the case. In fact, the overall majority of all participants, men and women, when asked why they had gone ahead with the experiments, admitted simply that it was because they were being told to do so.

Of course, what is really significant about the aggression machine studies is not so much what they tell us about women's inclination for violence as what they reveal about common attitudes towards it. If there is anything more alarming than researchers' attempts to prove that women are inherently the gentler, less hostile sex, it is their frenzied concoction of half-baked and addled theories indicating what devious psychological motivation is at work when women show themselves not to be as society wishes or imagines them but instead prove to be just as ruthless and inhumane as men are, by 'nature', believed to be.

One rational and honest voice in the fantasy world of academe, where misty-eyed reverence for the old male—female divide still persists, is that of American psychologist and aggression expert Robert Baron, who back in the 1970s pointed out that while there appeared to be significant differences in the degree of aggression shown by men and women in studies that involved exposing them to moderate provocation, the stronger the provocation used to try and whip up aggression the more negligible the differences between the sexes' responses. Although Baron theorizes that men may have a lower boiling point, and might be more easily aroused to anger through direct verbal insults than women, he believes it is more likely that the apparent disappearance of clear-cut sex differences in aggressive responses is due to general changes in sexual roles and stereotypes over the years, leading to less passivity and greater self-esteem and confidence in women, allowing them to be less inhibited about responding aggressively to direct provocation.

'If this is the case, then any remaining differences between males and females may continue to decrease and vanish entirely at some time,' he foresees. Yet what Baron has in mind is not so much a world terrorized by angry, violent women, as one in which men's aggressiveness is modified as they take on more of the 'female' attributes of caring and empathy. 'In short, the two sexes may gradually become equal in their propensity for violence, as well as their tendencies toward more desirable forms of behaviour.'

A prescient vision of closer harmony between New Man and Angry Young Woman – though as we approach the new millennium, there seems little evidence of it so far. The differences may be diminishing, but perhaps less for the reasons envisaged by Baron than because of social burdens and economic adversity which are simply impressing on women the need to catch up with the men if they want to survive.

Looking back on another fascinating variation of the hostility-measurement studies, there is yet more evidence (if evidence be needed) to what extent a threatening environment can sour and taint a person's normally empathetic, caring attitude and behaviour towards others. This particular study involved only female students from New York University and was conducted in 1969 by psychologist Philip Zimbardo, who wanted to determine to what extent subjecting individuals to hostile treatment would in turn increase their levels of hostility towards others.

The women were told they would be participating in a study on empathy. On arrival at the research centre, half were asked to put on hoods that covered their faces and large shapeless laboratory coats. Their names were never used and the women in this group were totally indistinguishable from one other. The other half, in complete contrast, were greeted by name in a friendly manner, given name badges to wear and generally treated as individuals throughout the study.

Then they were asked to sit in individual cubicles and deliver a series of 'electric shocks' to other women each time a green light flashed in the cubicle. Another light would then go on to indicate that the shock was being delivered and stay on for as long as the electric current was flowing. Just before the procedure began, the subjects listened to taped interviews with each of the 'victims' who were portrayed either as obnoxious, prejudiced and bitchy or as sweet, warm, loving and altruistic. As Zimbardo had predicted, the depersonalized group turned out to be nearly twice as aggressive as the others, showing no difference in hostility towards the 'nice' or 'nasty' victims. As he remarks: 'These sweet normally mild-mannered college girls shocked another girl almost every time they had an opportunity to do so, sometimes almost as long as they were allowed, and it did not matter whether or not that fellow student was a nice girl who didn't deserve to be hurt.'

At last, it is becoming ever more evident that the age-old idea of women as the weaker sex, inherently incapable of aggression and violence, except perhaps when defending their young, cannot stand up to close scrutiny. Not that the comforting nostrums of biological determinism, of women as 'natural' care-givers, the universal female 'instinct' for motherhood, etc., have been permanently laid to rest. Alas, far from it. It is self-evident why biological determinism – the idea that our nature and behaviour are pre-ordained by our biology – retains such an alluring, indestructible hold on public imagination. Compared to the infinite number of environmental, cultural, socioeconomic, political and other variables that influence human behaviour, the beauty of biological determinism lies in its extreme simplicity, its easy-to-follow formula of cause and effect. And it is that very crude simplicity that makes it not only so persuasive, but so dangerously pervasive, even today.

Just consider the underlying thesis: if man's hormonal make-up is responsible for his aggressive instincts, instincts which originally enabled him to fight, hunt, court and copulate with his mate, then woman – whose biological role in this unfolding drama of man's evolution was merely to submit to male courtship, give birth and care for her offspring – lacking testosterone, that all-important ingredient for aggression, should be now, as then, innately passive, since passivity in females like aggression in males, according to this scenario, has survival value. This shaky proposition, despite the absence of any concrete scientific evidence, is still perceived by vast sections of Western and Eastern society and by every major religion as an immutable hormonal imperative, dictating male dominance and perpetuating female subordination and inferiority.

The Tyranny of Biology

Many still passionately hold that to go against what is perceived as the 'natural' law is to invite inevitable global catastrophe. Thus, if we regard such feelings as anger, hostility, fury, rudeness, irritability, even extreme competitiveness and desire for power as predictable indicators of aggression or violence or precursors to criminality, then for a woman to display such characteristics – all that are deemed most detestable and ignoble, yet an inescapable *fait accompli* of nature, in men – it must follow that her behaviour, going against nature, is calculated to wreak damage unto herself and those around her, and ultimately untold damage to all of society.

This brings us slap up against another distinctly shaky premise: that it is impossible to effect any radical change in the sociosexual *status quo* without gravely jeopardizing the future of society. There lies in effect the cornerstone of today's passionate, even violent, debate on whether feminism has succeeded or failed in liberating women from the injustices and constraints of a hitherto male dominated society – and if it has succeeded, then at what price? An increasingly 'masculinized' aggressive new generation of women aping men's most destructive behaviour in a bid for equality? This polemic – progressive feminists versus reactionary guardians of the old order – more than any other issue, has led not only to bitter rancour between the sexes but, even more significantly, to deep schisms and ideological dissent within the women's movement itself.

Whether aggression is a force for good or bad lies at the heart of that debate, a debate that has the power to arouse such intense passions that, ironically, we have arrived at the stage where many anti-feminist men can now be heard arguing on the side of many an old-school feminist, those of the 'first wave' of the 1960s and 1970s who have tended to deify the nurturing, pacific, Mother Earth image of womanhood, accusing aggressive women of treacherously selling out to the enemy, gaining access to male liberties and privileges on the worst possible terms. The reasoning here is that women's 'natural' role as the custodians of peace and upholders of domestic harmony is too precious to be allowed to change, with the alleged inborn feminine virtues so densely interwoven into the social fabric that we unpick that weave or alter its pattern at our peril.

In essence, this amounts to nothing more or less than a form of inverted misogyny masquerading as chivalry, an insidious reversal of classic determinist arguments still used by some men to rationalize and justify the 'natural order' of patriarchy: that women's superior qualities of empathy, caring and selflessness must be celebrated and revered above all else because they ensure the harmonious organization of society and because they are *natural* to womankind. It is around this 'natural order', a mythic biological imperative which makes man the aggressive, warring hunter, woman the peaceful homemaker and mother, that all religious doctrine revolves, and never more so than in the observance of traditional 'family values' – which for women throughout the centuries has come to represent nothing more than biological tyranny by another name. As mutineers against any such further tyranny, women now find themselves at the cutting edge of more radical and permanent social change than at any time in history. What else, after all, lies behind today's mounting numbers of anguished Jeremiahs lamenting over the social evils caused by the collapse of this mythical 'lost' utopia than fear and fury over women's refusal to act any longer as the all-purpose social adhesive which could be counted on to bind and mask even the most cracked or rotting structure?

The depressing truth is that whenever women have sought to cast down the gauntlet, to broaden or step outside the boundaries of their traditional existence, and whenever female assertiveness or aggression have been instrumental in gaining greater freedom and equality, they have had to encounter the full wrath of the biological reductionists who, when not preaching on the need to uphold the sanctity of conventional family life, utter dire warnings about women's putative biological frailties which render them unfit for any form of equality with men. In the nineteenth century, medical experts even warned women not to study maths or science in case the exertion disturbed their reproductive capacities. Merely thinking too much, let alone becoming more physically active, was believed to place excessive strain on women's internal organs, and in 1886 Dr William Withers Moore went so far as to warn the BMA that educated women became 'more or less sexless' resulting in 'unborn sons'. Also writing in the nineteenth century, Alexander Walker took the view that healthy women were all too well aware of their inherent frailties: 'The consciousness of her physical weakness renders her timid and sedentary ... Woman ... fit only for sedentary occupations ... necessarily remains much in the interior of the house.'

In certain pagan societies women did enjoy brief spells of glorious freedom, although, alas, all too short-lived and usually followed by extreme oppression. Around 530 BC, in the Ancient Greek city state of Sparta, women had clout and status, owned two-thirds of the land and, as befitted a society famous for its cultivation of frugality, courage and extreme physical fortitude, those who were unmarried were expected to join in men's physical pursuits as their equals. Young women habitually practised gymnastics and exercises to strengthen their muscles, regularly running marathons and taking part in gruelling athletics and rough-and-tumble sports alongside the men, usually minimally clad, without risk of censure or harassment. In Crete at about the same time, young women were encouraged to train as bullfighters to cultivate and show off their bravery and skill.

It seems that along with physical freedoms women also enjoyed sexual liberation. An Attic Greek vase dated 4 BC, which depicts the goddess Atalanta stripped naked to the waist outwrestling the hero Peleus, offers just one of thousands of similar graphic illustrations of the lack of prudishness at that time and the freedom with which women partook in and excelled at mixed sports and athletics. Unlike the myth of the Amazonian warrior women, there are too many written and pictorial accounts of these women's unrestricted lives for them to be dismissed as mere legend. Plutarch describes Spartan girls throwing the javelin and discus, while running and wrestling along the banks of the Eurotas river. In a rather more reactionary vein, Euripides expressed his shock and disapprobation thus:

> The daughters of Sparta are never at home!
> They mingle with the young men in wrestling matches,
> their clothes cast off, their hips all naked,
> it's shameful!

Yet a mere century or so later in Ancient Athens, the cradle of modern civilization, women were universally regarded as inferior to men in every domain of existence and endeavour, their sole purpose being to bear as many sons as possible to ensure the continued glory of patriarchy. The Greek philosopher Aristotle summed it up simply: 'The male is by nature superior, and the female inferior; and the one rules and the other is ruled.' This basic law, the earliest example of female oppression justified on the basis of biological determinism, has been subsequently passed down through the centuries, embellished by religious beliefs, myth and legend, bolstered by ignorance and fear of 'sinful' woman's supposed powers of evil and witchcraft.

Can we really assert in all honesty that the fundamental spirit of this belief has been exorcised over the past century? We need not search far to discover that the same tired old determinism still provides a richly fertile breeding ground for much current anti-feminist rhetoric. In the view of Steven Goldberg, author of *The Inevitability of Patriarchy*, published in 1973,

> Women follow their own physiological imperatives . . . In this and every other society [men] look to women for gentleness, kindness and love, for refuge from a world of pain and force . . . In every society a basic male motivation

is the feeling that the women and children must be protected . . . the feminist cannot have it both ways; if she
wishes to sacrifice all this, all that she will get in return is
the right to meet men on male terms. She will lose.

Really. But lose what precisely? Judging by the experiences of
those women who have successfully joined men on increasingly
if not entirely equal terms, within such hitherto predominantly
male institutions as the armed services and the police force,
there has been precious little regret or dismay at having to
forego shelter and protection from danger and hardship, and far
greater genuine fulfilment and pride at being able successfully to
undertake 'men's work' on an equal footing. After all, what
evidence, if any, exists for man's inherent disposition towards
aggression and violence and women's innate passivity?

Given that there is little motivation to study what is believed
not to exist, it is hardly surprising that, as with female crime,
few researchers until now have deemed female aggression a
subject worthy of analysis. Such research is now steadily
increasing and, though still in its infancy, its emergence as a new
item on the agenda coincides, thankfully, with the beginning of
a greater closeness and collaboration in the field of aggression
research between those from radically different disciplines, from
neurophysiology and zoology to anthropology, feminist psychology and the social sciences. Another logical explanation for
the growing understanding and focus on female aggression and
violence, and the fact that antisocial behaviour is no longer
automatically classified as uniquely male, is the proliferation of
women in what used to be predominantly male, thus
undoubtedly biased, areas of research. It is only to be expected
that by examining women's supposedly 'deviant' or criminal
behaviour from, say, a cultural or socioeconomic perspective or
analysing anger within the framework of a feminist perspective,
that the full and wonderfully rich diversity of women's subjective
experiences of power, aggression and competitiveness – for so
long deemed inimical to 'true' womanhood – can begin to emerge.
By now, at last, the whole concept of aggression as nothing

more than an innate and instinctive evolutionary drive, comparable to that of other animal species, and over which we have little or no control, is beginning to be vigorously challenged and refuted.

One welcome upshot of the expanding multidisciplinary approach to the understanding of human aggression is that it has caused the tired and sterile 'nature versus nurture' debate finally to run its course. And not before time. Agonized nit-picking by ethologists, behaviourists and biologists about whether aggression represents an innate drive or a learned behaviour, whether it is the result of congenital or acquired brain injury with neurological dysfunction, an inheritance or a reflection of environmental influences and whether violence is the cause or effect of our adaptive capabilities, never yielded any clear-cut proof either way. How could it, since, as when trying to 'explain' such qualities as homosexuality, altruism and artistic creativity, so complex and interdependent are the diverse influences of both nature *and* nurture that measuring the precise role of either in determining a human personality and actions remains a virtual impossibility.

Undoubtedly the 'fight or flight' response common to humans and animals alike developed as an evolutionary mechanism by which all human and non-human species could adapt to their changing environment, flee their enemy and fight for their continued survival. Characterized by the automatic, sustained surge of a powerful cocktail of chemicals, notably adrenalin, whose principal effect is to switch mind and body to 'red alert', generating enough bodily strength and speed to confront extreme stress or emergency, this atavistic arousal mechanism is as capable of assisting flight through fear as it is of fuelling aggression and an angry determination to confront and fight. In adducing this response as proof of an associated violent 'drive', part and parcel of survival, which seeks regular outlet and, according to some theorists, arises also through frustration, aggression research has been bedevilled by the myth of the 'beast within', a primordial force ever dictating the baser actions of modern man (but not woman!), who remains as hard-wired for violence as were supposedly his prehistoric ancestors. Apart from making short work of the obvious influences of individual culture, changing society and environment that determine much self-expression, the reductionist nature of this theory is evident from its failure to differentiate between destructive, violent rage and rational controlled aggression – in short, from the lumping together of survival with violence. But whether man's putative 'killer ape' ancestry is in fact either as credible as has been suggested let alone serves to explain his modern day criminality and violent disposition is now hotly disputed, as the emergence of improved fossil records and rapidly developing fields such as molecular biology and primatology begin to point to an altogether less brutal and bloody past than earlier researchers would have us believe. Was 'man the hunter' really the savage and predatory brute the early post-Darwinian anthropologists made him out to be? According to Richard Leakey, for instance, the present fossil record suggests that the early hominids developed a peaceable, cooperative existence rather than a violent, antagonistic one, prompting him to comment that the concept of humans as just a step up from killer apes is 'one of the most dangerous persuasive myths of our time' – and one that contradicts Darwin's view of early man as coexisting peacefully with his neighbours rather than killing them for the sheer hell of it.

Female palaeoanthropologists have also argued that male bias within the profession itself has contributed largely to this distorted view of early hominid aggression and warfare, the persistent image of the 'beast within', and that since reason tells us that cooperation and non-aggression demonstrably confer greater benefits on groups as a whole, it is just as likely that our species learned this lesson early and therefore evolved as much, if not more, through cooperation between females and children as through the presumed savage instincts of men. Recent studies suggest that had women in the earliest hunter-gatherer communities left men to do all the work of providing food, the majority of groups would have regularly gone hungry or starved to death! Analysis of the oldest hominid teeth to be found so far shows that our earliest upright ancestors were either vegetarians or omnivores, suggesting that foraging had to be carried out by males and females, even children, to ensure survival.

Even once man became carnivorous, having started to manufacture crude weapons to hunt and kill large animals, anthropologists believe that since big game hunting was a chancy and unpredictable business prehistoric man almost certainly went on the kill for short intensive periods, perhaps one week out of four. This meant that at least 60–80 per cent of food came from plant sources – as is still the case among the 170 or so present-day nomadic hunter-gatherer communities that have been studied – with women responsible, then as now, for most of the collecting of plant foods and small animals.

Having studied the !Kung Bushmen of Botswana, whose hunting and gathering lifestyle has many parallels to that of earliest man, anthropologist Richard Lee worked out that collecting involves two or three days of work by women per week, during which they provide two to three times as much food by weight as the men. On that evidence, early hominid women were not the faint-hearted cave-bound slouches caricatured by cartoonists. On the contrary, almost certainly they would qualify as the earliest prototypical working mothers. Once they had succeeded in devising slings made from bark, leaves, reeds and animal skins to carry their babies on their backs, leaving their hands free to gather fruits, nuts, seeds, roots, etc., they could use similar containers to gather food 'in bulk' for storage and became more skilled in using simple devices made of sticks, stones and bones for more efficient gathering. All of which is a far cry from the mythic vision of man-the-hunter striding forth fiercely to stalk and slaughter his prey while the weak little woman cowered back in the cave, suckling her young, entirely dependent on her man's initiative and hunting prowess. According to this alternative evolutionary scenario with its more equal division of labour, anthropologists point out that there would have been no selection pressures for aggression and competitiveness in men, nor any advantage in female passivity, since survival demanded cooperation of the sexes, with as much resourcefulness, skill and adaptability as possible forthcoming on both sides. Thus there can be no basis for the argument that women have evolved with an innate lack of aggression.

* * *

It appears most likely that from humankind's earliest days we depended on our arousal instincts more for survival than to wantonly destroy and dominate our fellow humans. On the other hand – and this is the overwhelming and tragic mystery of *modern* humanity's aggression – our capacity to inflict consciously and purposely on one another infinite varieties and degrees of cruelty, degradation and torture, from the perpetration of wartime atrocities, genocide and racist violence to rape and often motiveless murder, even to derive pleasure from these acts, has no equal anywhere in the animal world. Could it be, as psychologists like Rollo May and Erich Fromm have suggested, that with the advancement of civilization and the fulfilment of our most basic needs for food, shelter and sex, it is when our higher 'existential' needs – for a sense of personal value and significance, for self-affirmation and self-determination – are denied that through a sense of demeaning powerlessness our aggressive and violent impulses may fulfil their deadliest, most destructive potential? Zimbardo's experiments with his hooded female students certainly seem to bear this out, as does the soaring crime rate among the poorest, most dispossessed communities of the Western world.

From his extensive study of ritualized animal behaviour, Konrad Lorenz proposed the existence of an instinctive aggressive drive which because it needed releasing resulted in the development of ritualistic activities that helped to strengthen and bind together social groups. Such in-fighting among groups of the same animal species rarely leads to serious injury or death because one individual member will always eventually submit or back off, whereas we humans have become killers through losing this inhibitory mechanism.

In Lorenz's view, mankind's only hope of containing and limiting the negative consequences of these aggressive impulses was to partake in forms of 'formalized competition', as in the Olympic Games. In view of the fact that all macho culture, from Roman chariot races and fights between Christian gladiators and the public spectacle of slaves being eaten alive by wild animals, to present-day football and boxing matches, represents socially legitimized forms of male violence and self-aggrandizement, in which women have always been forced to remain on the outside, we can only wonder what women would make of their long suppressed aggressive drives given half the opportunities enjoyed by men.

Is there a biological root for aggressive behaviour? Recent years have seen the emergence of increasing biochemical and genetic research aimed at trying to identify a possible 'marker' that could explain, in particular, the behaviour of very violent individuals who persistently re-offend, repeatedly engaging in anti-social and criminal behaviour. Some theories, like the notion that dangerous male criminals possess an extra Y chromosome, have remained by and large unsubstantiated; others, like the discovery of irregular EEG (brain wave) patterns, the existence of brain injuries, heightened insulin secretion, an imbalance in certain neurochemicals, principally serotonin, and various other types of brain dysfunction in violent offenders, while persuasive, leave too many questions unanswered. Why is it, for instance, that similar neural disturbances and chemical imbalances are also sometimes found in epileptics, depressives and migraine sufferers, or men and women exhibiting certain obsessive-compulsive disorders? And, more to the point, if brain injury or biochemical imbalances are responsible for violence, how can one account for the many violent criminals with no such disorders at all? Where all such biological theories fall flat is that they demonstrably fail to take into account the many other variables – poverty, discrimination, environment, social injustice, childhood experience, political upheaval – that almost certainly contribute to violence and antisocial behaviour.

Similarly, the theory that aggression and violence are unique to the male of the species and therefore attributable to the influence of testosterone, while containing a certain insinuating logic, is in fact riddled with inconsistencies. Despite continuous efforts to prove a causal connection between the male sex hormone and violence, and by inference women's lack of aggression and competitiveness, for every study demonstrating that violent men have higher levels of testosterone there is another to disprove the connection. This is one area of research where experts most regularly come unstuck. For one thing, most of the research into animal aggression has focused on the role of testosterone alone and ignored the role of other sex hormones and biochemicals such as adrenalin, yet some experiments indicate that where high testosterone levels were found to influence aggression, this effect only occurred once the male hormone had undergone conversion into one of the oestrogens, or female sex hormones.

Intriguingly, studies into human sexuality indicate also that women tend to become more sexually active or assertive – more inclined to masturbate or initiate sexual activity – during the mid-cycle phase of ovulation, when oestrogen levels are at their highest. And while it is true that some animal studies suggest a positive correlation between high testosterone levels and aggressive behaviour, this only applies to certain species. For instance, we know that male mice fight each other increasingly as testosterone production rises during puberty, while the tendency for them to attack strangers is increased by injecting them with androgens and greatly reduced by castration. On the other hand, similar research involving gerbils is far from conclusive: some studies indicate increased fighting linked to heightened testosterone, others indicate a decrease.

Despite numerous studies comparing hormone levels of violent criminals to non-violent men, there has been little consistent correlation between increased testosterone secretion and criminality, though what link there is seems more likely by far to occur during adolescence than later in adult life. This could also hold true for women: one study in 1980 found that among young women attending a clinic for behavioural disorders, those with histories of violence had comparatively high testosterone levels. In 1988, studies also found higher levels of testosterone in women convicted of unprovoked violence compared to those whose violence was an act of self-defence (i.e. abused wives attacking their husbands). It seems also that the amount of testosterone was related to the number of prior charges in a woman's record and parole board decisions about how long they should remain in prison. However, what no one so far seems to have addressed in any great detail is the fact that hormone levels may rise as a *direct result* of violent behaviour, and thus be a side effect rather than a cause of aggression.

Contrary to popular opinion, female aggression appears to be more prevalent in the animal kingdom than was previously believed. Aside from the cunning and murderous *femmes fatales* of the animal theatre of cruelty, notorious predators such as the praying mantis and black widow spider who decapitate, rip apart and with relish consume their mate in a fervour of post-coital relish, on a more prosaic level, aggression between female ger-bils and golden hamsters equals or exceeds that between males – a phenomenon apparently related not to testosterone but to the female hormone progesterone. Female mice will ferociously attack any intruder that might threaten their newborn and may deliberately kill and eat their young once they are weaned should they become injured. And lionesses have been found to incur severe injuries or death as a result of fighting off males attempting to kill their cubs.

When it comes to the study of primates, our closest animal relatives, aggressive behaviour seems to be quite equal between the sexes, with female members of different species such as macaques (including the rhesus monkey) and wild savannah baboons exhibiting a large variety of threatening, manipulative and competitive behaviours, including fierce sustained fighting against both their own and the opposite sex. Just who fights whom, and to what extent, depends on the nature of their social relationship, each member's status within the group's hierarchy and the context of the conflict. Far from being arbitrary or essentially destructive, much of what might appear to be random aggression among primates has been found to fulfil a beneficial purpose in organizing and maintaining the structure and cohesion of families and groups – something we might bear in mind when agonizing over the presumed social dangers inherent in female aggression.

Attempts to highlight the constructive pro-social goals and outcomes of aggressive behaviour have helped to prove how frequently animal and, to a lesser extent, human aggression, no matter how appallingly ruthless it appears to the outsider, may more often prove a force for good than for bad by achieving the desired outcome – from the perspective of the aggressor, at any rate.

Research in recent years by primatologists such as Sarah Blaffer Hrdy and Samuel K. Wasser has sought to demonstrate that if competitiveness is considered to be an asset in men, then presumably it also serves a useful purpose among women. When Samuel Wasser first arrived at Mikumi in the East African Savannah in the late 1970s to study the behaviour of female baboons, he was entirely unprepared for the viciousness and regularity with which groups of females would gang up to form 'coalitions', setting out expressly to beat up and kill other females and their young. He soon discovered that this had nothing to do with establishing rank but seemed to be the females' way of waging a form of 'reproductive terrorism', trying to keep down the numbers of new offspring within the various groups in order to ensure sufficient resources for survival of their own.

Given that among some species it is the female when on heat who selects her partner – a male who may not necessarily be a dominant member of the group – and the fact that the dominance hierarchy is often set by females, mothers conferring status on daughters from the eldest downward with the rank of the male entirely contingent upon his enduring membership of her troop, then it becomes blindingly obvious how much of the 'natural order' of male dominance and female submission is actually a man-made fabrication.

What applies to animals seems also to hold true for humans. Intriguingly, a system of 'reproductive terrorism' is also practised by women of the Kalahari Bushmen of south-central Africa, as described by Duncan Maxwell Hudson, echoing Wasser's reports of female primate aggression. This takes the form of what to us might seem ludicrous, even comical insults directed at women's genitalia in order to induce sufficient stress and trauma to prevent them ovulating and conceiving, so keeping down the birthrate and ensuring that mothers have enough food for the survival of their own children. Thus, when quarrels erupt between the tribeswomen, typical insults might be '*Du a*

!gum' – 'Death on your vagina'– or *'Gum twisi dinyazho'* – 'Long black labia'. Incredibly, so very seriously are such insults taken that the unfortunate victim usually ends up committing suicide, assaulting her attacker or creating a tribal split.

Undoubtedly, research into human behaviour has so far failed to prove conclusively that aggression is either an innate male characteristic or that it is tied to hormone levels, in spite of often extreme and sweeping assertions to the contrary. Attempts have been made to explain female aggression and the tendency of some girls to reject typically feminine interests and pursue 'tomboyish' activities at a very early age by the effects that extra levels of androgens might have on foetal brain development in females. In studying the behaviour of girls who, during foetal gestation, had been accidentally exposed to unusually high amounts of androgens in the womb, researchers John Money and Anke Ehrhardt found that not only were they born with partially male external genitalia (although with a normal inner reproductive system) but that they also conformed to a more tomboyish type, taking part in athletic activities and sports, playing in a vigorous, rough and tumble manner with boys rather than girls, expressing little or no interest in dolls or infant care, choosing to wear functional rather than pretty, feminine clothes, having few fantasies about marriage, pregnancy and motherhood and rather more interest in a career. On the other hand, the tomboys showed no greater aggressive tendencies or desire to fight than girls with normal hormonal profiles, and having undergone earlier corrective surgery they eventually got married and bore children.

Researchers have been tempted to conclude that the prenatal influence of testosterone was to 'masculinize' the girls' brains, pre-programming their future 'boyish' attitudes and activities, hindering so-called normal female maternal instincts and promoting dominance and assertiveness. What is equally plausible, as even Money and his colleagues now admit, is that the parents, recognizing that their daughters were born with a partially male physiology, tended to treat them differently than they would a child who was evidently 100 per cent female. Scoff we may, but the old 'pink for a girl, blue for a boy' mentality is as prevalent these days as in decades gone by. Study after study continues to prove that parents and adults generally display significantly different responses towards girl and boy babies from the moment of birth, attributing an infant's screams and cries to different emotions (fear in girls, anger in boys), talking to, handling and touching them with more or less robustness and vigour depending on their sex.

What such studies have proven, however, and vividly, is the very significant and crucial distinction between two concepts that are all too often confused or lumped together as a single, indistinguishable entity. One is the concept of 'sex', the biological category into which, by virtue of our chromosomal mix, we happen to be born. The other is our 'gender identity', which is the perceived image or sense of what being male or female means to a man or woman, as defined by behavioural criteria laid down within a given sociocultural environment. It is that latter subjective experience of what it means to be either male or female which in turn influences our interactions with others, leading us to take up – or perhaps challenge and even reject, as in the case of homosexuals or transsexuals of either sex – specific gender roles that are offered or thrust upon us as we begin exploring our environment.

So, although hormones obviously played a key role in fashioning the male-like genitalia with which the girls in Money and Ehrhardt's studies were born, their gender identity was almost certainly in part shaped by the degree to which their parents perceived their children as more 'male' than 'female', permitting or even encouraging their daughters to participate in boyish behaviour which might be discouraged in little girls with normal female sexual organs. Since the girls in these studies did not undergo therapy or surgical intervention until the ages of between 3½ and 7, one can only speculate on the overwhelming effect on a young girl, during the most crucial early development of gender 'identity', of possessing a boy's penis and of encountering not criticism or condemnation but positive approval for showing assertiveness and independence – in short the *opposite messages* most girls receive as part of their early social learning.

In spite of John Money's assertion that the job of prenatal sex hormones is to determine our physiological development as males or females, probably also laying down the blueprint for basic male and female codes of behaviour, what his critics have often chosen to overlook is his emphasis on the infinite freedom we still possess in being able to determine our own unique 'sexual signatures'. In other words, being born female, equipped to conceive and give birth, cannot and should not be regarded as an immutable formula which disbars a woman from choosing strenuous physical activity or dominance behaviour over maternal nurturing. By reminding women (as well as men) that they need not take up the option of their genital inheritance, Money acknowledges, as does the most ardent feminist, the degree to which culture dictates our destiny and determines appropriate behavioural norms relating to aggression and passivity – as much as, if not more than, biology. The mould, therefore, can be broken and often to extraordinarily good effect.

Reports from ethnographers who have travelled widely throughout Africa testify to the vastly differing sexual stereotypes, where warrior women – far from being an oddity – are much respected within the community. The African woman's strength often derives initially from her multi-faceted role as wife and mother as well as cultivator and market trader; control of the production and distribution of basic resources in turn confers political clout which, at times of unrest, gives her formidable powers as an activist. In 1929 10,000 Ibo women staged a massive and bloody two-day riot covering a 6,000 square mile area of South Nigeria. The uprising came in response to the imposition of punitive direct colonial taxation and was dubbed the 'women's war', so-called because the men remained passive throughout although fully backing their wives' actions.

Most legendary of all are the notorious Amazons of West Africa's ancient Dahomey tribe, whose sex-role orientation was founded specifically on the principle of androgyny. Worshippers of the cult of the god/ess Mawu-Lisa, which embodies the male–female duality of the sexes, the Dahomeans have long taken women's equality for granted in the public arena, including the army. As long ago as 1845 the King of Dahomey's 12,000 strong army included 5,000 women and in the late 1800s women warriors and reservists were expected to bear arms, including blunderbusses, muskets and eighteen-inch knives, which they reportedly used with equal efficiency and savagery as the men. A British writer at the time even observed that introducing a similar training and recruitment at home would eradicate the problem of 'old maids'! The boldest and toughest of all Amazon warriors were the Dahomean élite Fanti Corps, the famed elephant huntresses, who although forced to remain celibate and abstain from marriage until middle age, by all accounts led challenging and productive lives and were universally acclaimed for it.

Among the Vakinankaratra community of Madagascar the behavioural ideal is pacifism and the avoidance of all unnecessary confrontation. The male stereotype, as in most cultures, embodies this ideal. Conditioned from infancy to value and aspire to gentleness and pacifism, men may only buy fixed price commodities while the business of haggling over prices falls exclusively to women, as do the duties of scolding children and raising disputes with neighbours. When a man has a difference of opinion with another man, his female relatives are the ones who must do verbal battle on his behalf and when the imbroglio is over he steps forward magnanimously to assuage hurt feelings. What would a stranger to that community make of its womenfolk? Judge them as innately hard-nosed, quarrelsome, aggressive harridans, the very opposite of the sweet-tempered men, or – more accurately – as the prickly products of centuries of upbringing?

Among the Abipon of the Gran Chaco, one of the indigenous tribes of South America which lived in the centre of the continent before it was colonized by the Spanish in the eighteenth century, women's power, physical strength and daring as well as their freedom to hunt, work and fight alongside men, seems to have been exceptional. The Jesuit missionary Martin Dobrizhoffer, who lived among them from 1750–62, noted that the women operated as a collective to distribute and control food and other supplies and maintain order while the men were away hunting, working or at war. They would frequently become embroiled in bloody battles against enemy tribes, including the Spanish invaders, while internecine tribal disputes, often fierce and heated, could degenerate into a murderous free-for-all. The men would calmly stand back as observers, recognizing that this was 'women's way'. The women also had no reservations about physically attacking men. Ceremonial wrestling among the most powerfully built women was commonplace. After a chief's son was born, the strongest woman in the camp would lead a group of girls in whipping all the men. Women could, and often did, achieve the rank of chief, earning this distinction no doubt largely through respect for their considerable prowess and bravery as hunters and fighters.

What the aggressive actions of the women of the Dahomey, Ibo, Abipon and Vakinankaratra demonstrate clearly, is how effectively biology – in the sense of women's relative lack of physical power compared to men, and their reproductive processes – may be *overridden* by culture and the struggle to survive. To understand man's and woman's infinite capacity for adaptation as a means of serving their self-interest is to finally grasp why determinist theories are ultimately meaningless as a means of trying to explain differences in male and female behaviour. On any showing it seems we must regard the cult of 'true' non-aggressive womanhood as an outmoded sign of privilege, a luxury that an ever-declining number of women living either in great affluence or under constant protection from the real world, as in fundamentalist Muslim societies, can afford to indulge. To vast remaining sections of the female population it would be grossly insulting to suggest otherwise. We would also do well to remember that even in the developed world, women within farming communities and, as in the former Soviet bloc, those engaged side by side with men in grindingly arduous, dangerous manual labour (including coalmining in England until the middle of the last century), have always been forced to be physically tougher, more outspoken and assertive through the bitterly hard graft of everyday survival and the sheer force of necessity and circumstance, than women among the privileged upper classes.

Psychoanalysis: Myths and Misconceptions

Freud and his followers did not see the self-sufficient, assertive woman as any the healthier for her comparative freedoms. On the contrary. The psychoanalytic view of aggression, as the medical science view, is deeply and depressingly imbued with sexist bias. Freud, who saw all human aggression as borne of an inherent 'death instinct' – the impulse for self-destruction turned outwards against others – defined women (as discussed in chapter 1) as submissive, guilt-ridden and masochistic as a result of the ineluctable force of their penis envy! Given this in-built handicap, they had, he reasoned, little choice but to respond to provocation and hostility from others not with aggression but by developing an anxiety neurosis. Should a woman behave aggressively, this in itself was proof of a neurotic 'masculinity complex' – a delusion that her sexual equipment was *not* inferior to that of her father or brother and that she could masturbate without shame, enjoy sex without guilt and compete with men on equal terms. Freud's view of women who became assertive in male-dominated activities and professions was that they were driven by nothing more than displaced penis envy and in extreme cases were liable to end up as lesbians.

In a similar vein, Richard Von Krafft-Ebing described women's desire to go to war as a sign of homosexuality, even sadism, and diagnosed his girl patients who played with soldiers rather than dolls and preferred studying science to art as suffering from 'congenital antipathetic sexual instinct' or, put another way, the 'masculine soul' heaving within the 'female bosom'.

Such beliefs would be laughable were it not for their lingering and dangerously pervasive influence on psychoanalytic thinking and therefore on public attitudes to this very day. It is largely thanks to the original received Freudian wisdom on child abuse and rape – that such events were usually the result of women's or young girls' fantasies and desire for sexual domination – that society has so belatedly begun to acknowledge, albeit reluctantly, the full realities of incest and sexual abuse as described by children and adult women. Even a rational humanitarian writer like the eminent psychiatrist Anthony Storr, while identifying aggression logically as a necessary, potentially highly constructive life force through which we learn to understand and master our environment and develop our individual identity from early childhood, persists in seeing women, as did Freud, as prone to fantasize about being sexually dominated by men to the point of masochism.

In echoing the belief of the child expert and psychoanalyst Donald Winnicott that aggression only becomes potentially destructive when our attempts to assert our true selves and our basic needs are denied and frustrated, thence giving rise to hostility and violence, Storr rightly identifies certain amounts of aggression – perhaps more accurately described as assertiveness – as being an integral component of self-esteem. How is it, therefore, that he fails to challenge the traditional socialization of girls, which from early infancy often denies them a free outlet for the healthy, aggressive self-expression which he considers so necessary for balanced psychological development?

In view of the often tragically pervasive self-destructiveness that self-denial inculcates in many women, the failure of most psychologists even to acknowledge the existence of female aggression as a potentially creative energy force demonstrates to what extent orthodox psychoanalysis has until now effectively failed women, distorting and denying the subjective experiences of over 50 per cent of the human race. For it is only once we understand aggression as part of a mechanism through which we establish personal autonomy, build self-esteem and self-affirmation, that we can also begin to appreciate why so many women – even those who, paradoxically, are overtly aggressive or violent – admit to an insufficient supply of those qualities.

If, as analysts like Storr, Winnicott and Clara Thompson obviously fervently believe, our identity forms through opposition, from striving and struggling against opposing forces – the earliest and most formidable being our parents – then how can we justify our encouragement of boisterous fighting among boys as part of their healthy development while denying the importance of allowing girls to pursue similar aggressive forms of self-expression, should they feel the urge to do so? That the urge *does* exist is manifestly obvious. As recent studies show, many little girls when left to their own devices are far from being naturally 'sugar and spice and all things nice', with very young girls and boys showing little difference in the amount of competitiveness and aggression they display, although their style of expressing it may vary.

As long ago as 1977, researchers carrying out studies into the effects of watching violent television programmes on children noted that over the previous fifteen years the aggression 'measurement scores' of girls as young as 9 were equalling those of boys, a factor believed to be related to the increase in aggressive female characters on popular television programmes. Nor is there any evidence whatsoever that baby girls are born with less predisposition to aggression and violent emotion than boys. Quite the opposite. Very recent British studies aimed at determining whether differences exist between the way groups of boy and girl babies resolve conflicts, typically tugs of war over toys, revealed that the groups with the greater numbers of boys had fewer conflicts over toys, used less physical force and resolved conflicts in a friendlier manner.

A series of Finnish studies, which looked at the different types of aggressive behaviour in schoolchildren from primary to high school age, showed that although males tend to use more direct physical aggression than females at all ages, with girls' levels of physical aggression declining from adolescence on, the amount of verbal aggression, such as swearing, insults and other abuses, remains equal between the sexes. Girls from 11 on also begin to show a very marked tendency towards indirect aggression – trying to provoke a fellow pupil into losing their temper, attempting to make them look stupid, spreading vicious rumours and so-called 'backbiting'.

In the opinion of a leading researcher, Kaj Björkqvist from Turku University, such findings demonstrate not only how tenuous are the links between myth and reality concerning the absence of female aggression, but illustrate the need to identify and isolate the different patterns of aggressive self-expression in both sexes. In his view, girls' social conditioning teaches them from an early age to become adept at covert styles of aggression, including social manipulation, and the use of apparently rational arguments to cover up aggressive or hostile tendencies – findings that are further confirmed by studies of differences in aggression between adult men and women in the workplace. If one factor emerges from such studies, it must surely be a growing recognition of the positive value of much aggression – female aggression included – both as an efficient tool for resolving conflict and a means of self-assertion.

To suggest, therefore, that boys more than girls should be encouraged to have sufficient aggressive, even violent, outlets, whether through play or fantasy, in order to help them develop into autonomous, self-confident and independent adults, is bad enough. But to then make the very valid point that human destructiveness often results from feelings of powerlessness, humiliation and frustration, the unconscious legacy of our prolonged period of childhood dependency, and that the 'childish' adult feels especially disadvantaged in the dominance hierarchy, is at once to identify and yet simultaneously ignore, as does Anthony Storr, the crux of women's predicament of being socialized into non-aggression.

For what *are* many girls and women who were brought up to conform to traditional sexual stereotypes if not 'childish' in comparison to the qualities of confidence and assertiveness they perceive in men? I say perceived, because it is self-evident that male aggression, again due largely to the culture of machismo in which men are encouraged from infancy to pursue power, physical prowess and competitiveness at the cost of empathy, vulnerability or emotional openness, is rarely indicative of true inner strength and self-esteem. If paranoid projection (the tendency to attribute to others a generally non-existent hatred and hostility which drives us to attack and destroy them lest they should destroy us first) as well as the desire for power and dominance evolve, as Storr maintains, through our early experience of helplessness and dependency, then we cannot be too surprised at the women's movement's declared war against men, the ultimate enemy, or that the central thrust of militant feminist doctrine is to overthrow the detested politics of patriarchy. The fact that there are not *more* female psychopaths, serial killers and violent criminals might be less indicative of the calming influence of women's nurturing instinct than proof of how effectively the accumulation of centuries of cultural conditioning has become compounded and ingrained *as if inborn*, perfecting and reinforcing women's seemingly infinite facility for adaptation, self-control and self-effacement.

The implication for women in particular of Jung's warning that humankind ignores or denies at its peril the very real potential for destructiveness and evil that resides in each one of us seems particularly pertinent. He cautioned that it is only by acknowledging the existence of the dark side of the psyche, or what he termed the 'shadow', as an integral part of the whole, that we can develop a healthy, well-balanced personality, and so guard against the ability of the shadow to take on an independent life of its own. For women who were traditionally taught to suppress, reject or to fear any potentially destructive or unattractive aspects of their character, Jung's message takes on a particular and urgent resonance.

It should be a salutary reminder to all of us that Germany, the country which throughout the eighteenth, nineteenth and early twentieth centuries had the strictest, most repressive traditions of child rearing, resulting in clearly designated female virtues of decorousness, placidity and unquestioning obedience to male authority, also perfected and carried out the grossest of inhumanities in all history. With few exceptions, women were as inspired by Nazi ideology as men. Even more sinister and telling is the fact that quiet complicity and deference to authority, quintessential 'female' attributes, helped oil the motor that ran the entire murderous genocidal machinery of the Third Reich. Is it not likely, or at least possible, that a more aggressive, independent-minded attitude among Germany's women would have led to a greater sense of public outrage and furious dissent, a refusal to comply with orders, not only by women, but by whole families, husbands and children influenced by their wives' and mothers' anger and fury? Instead of the moral vacuum wherein evil found a space to fester and grow, taking on the aura of humdrum banality identified by Hannah Arendt during the Nuremberg Trials, might not the full and explosive weight of female disobedience and their courage to express ferocious indignation have held in check the rapid, all-encompassing spread of the Nazi virus?

Androgyny: The Best of Both Sexes

It is not difficult to understand social concern over the idea that women possess the same potential for aggression and violence as men. With crimes of violence, still largely committed by men, a growing problem throughout the world, and law and order uppermost on most public agendas, the fear that women may be catching up with the men in this area is understandable. But need female aggression always automatically be equated with male destructiveness? Indeed, could it be that for women to think and behave more like men, contrary to traditional, especially psychoanalytic, thinking, actually contributes positively to mental and physical health, thus indirectly influencing general social well-being?

The idea that women's conventional roles are weighed down with a multitude of stresses and strains, both physical and mental, is something which many feminists have rightly argued for quite some time. This claim is based on numerous findings on the positive health benefits enjoyed by married men, in contrast to the relatively high incidence of stress-related and emotional ailments suffered by married women and mothers, whether single parents or married, with the greatest problems occurring amongst lower socioeconomic groups. Career women in fulfilling professions, married or unmarried, especially those without children or those whose families have grown up, have been found to enjoy better health and higher self-esteem than their housebound counterparts.

However, part of the current backlash against feminism is founded on spurious claims that the stress of being a career woman – because it increases the incidence of aggressive and competitive i.e. typically male behaviour – is responsible for the rise of such diverse disorders as infertility, high blood pressure, baldness and facial hair, together with increased risk of heart disease, anorexia, depression, anxiety states and the ubiquitous 'burn-out' resulting from the strain of competing in a male-dominated world. Yet even the most perfunctory analysis of the facts reveals this to be so much dangerous anti-feminist cant. Not one of these claims is backed by any solid substantive evidence. Conversely, numerous surveys and self-reports into the causes and effects of modern stress suggest that if working women suffer debilitating burdens, it is usually because they are married or single working mothers who have no choice but to juggle domestic duties and job commitments with little or no help with household chores and childcare from their male partner, and extra stresses heaped upon them because of insufficient or non-existent childcare provisions within the community, poor pay – women are still generally paid less than men for doing identical jobs – and bad working conditions.

To claim that women's emergence into the workplace is hazarding their health by 'masculinizing' their behaviour is one of the most specious and subversive arguments ever to be used in the attempt to frighten women into relinquishing their hard won – and far from fully won – independence and banishing them back into the home. Additionally, in failing to identify such problems faced by women in the workplace as sexual harassment, sexual discrimination including lack of promotion and fear of redundancy following pregnancy, the extra-stress-is-bad-for-working-women argument is as dishonest as it is spurious.

When you examine the evidence more closely, there seems even less justification than ever for the belief that women who act more 'like men' are hell bent on the road to personal ruin. Far from proving that the espousal of what society generally acknowledges to be 'male' qualities and activities causes women to become frustrated, angry, violent and selfish, recent studies are beginning to indicate just how strongly a woman's well-being hinges not on her quintessential femininity but on the presence of a high quota of traditionally masculine personality traits and tendencies. Though calculated to upset and infuriate anti-feminist women, militant 'anti-men' feminists and traditionally chauvinistic men in equal proportions, there can be no doubt of the as yet unrecognized yet immense sexual and social implications of such findings.

Since the mid 1970s, much has been made of the theory that

androgyny – a personality composed of equally strong masculine and feminine elements – is in many ways preferable to being typically 'all male' or 'all female', conferring greater self-confidence, assertiveness and emotional balance, whatever one's sex. American psychologist Sandra Bem, who developed the Bem Sex Role Inventory (BSRI), increasingly used as a measurement of an individual's ratio of male/female personality traits, found that those people who display strong characteristics of both sexes in their psychological make-up are more versatile, possessing more appropriate traits in a wide variety of situations, as opposed to males or females who score high either in masculinity or femininity and who performed well only at tasks considered appropriate to their sex.

Essentially adaptable, the androgynous personality supposedly combines the best of both sexes. He or she is independent, self-confident and competent (socially desirable traits in men) and also warm, empathetic and sensitive (socially desirable traits in women), and therefore flexible enough to confidently perform tasks stereotypically associated with either sex. Although psychologists remain undecided whether androgyny measures a stable personality trait, or group of traits, or simply indicates an orientation towards certain social situations, many who have used this measurement to analyse men's and women's tendency to feel at home in their social, domestic and working environment, emphasize that individuals with a so-called High Androgyny (HA) rating are more able to express affection than male stereotyped individuals (men or women) and have more confidence in their opinions than female stereotyped people (again, men or women).

However, it wasn't until research began to probe further into the implications that HA scores might have for women's mental and physical health that the advantages of masculine over feminine traits came to light. For the first time we appear to have some quantifiable proof of something many women have long asserted, yet for which they continue to be derided or condemned: that their traditionally designated maternal and domestic roles and non-aggressive personality traits may be stressful and thus detrimental to their health. The effect of this discovery is of course to deal a mighty death-blow to the time-honoured belief that men and women are at their healthiest, most efficient and fulfilled when adhering to their specific sex roles.

Even more to the point is the discovery that while men's mental health does appear to be largely determined by their ability to successfully adopt appropriate 'male' behaviour, the exact opposite applies to women. Contrary to Freud's assertion that passivity, dependence and nurturance are healthy female attributes and assertiveness a sign of neuroticism, research conducted by psychologists such as Broverman and Abramovitz demonstrates that a high quota of feminine traits in women is positively associated with anxiety and negatively associated with the ability to adjust to change, high self-esteem, confidence and personal autonomy. Equally telling is the fact that this positive association between feminine traits and poor mental health holds even in cases where the individual displaying a preponderance of feminine traits is a man! So although having a fairly high ratio of both masculine and feminine traits seems to be the ideal in terms of positive self-image, the quality that ultimately tips the balance in favour of optimum mental health is not female docility but masculine assertiveness. Considering the findings, it seems surprising that psychologists have so far not made more of the apparent connection between sex-typing and mental health and the evident advantages to men and women of possessing a broader repertoire of behaviour.

So, to what degree does the fulfilment of conventional sex roles adversely affect women's health? In one comprehensive study of over a hundred women in the Bristol area carried out in the 1970s, researchers set out to correlate individual sex typing as determined by the BSRI with self-reported stress levels and health problems, which were also backed up by records obtained from the women's local health centre. Results confirmed that those women with HA scores reported the least amount of life stress, had the lowest incidence of self-reported psychological symptoms – not one single HA woman could be diagnosed as suffering from any form of psychiatric illness – and had visited the health centre least over the previous two years. The study also revealed to what degree high levels of self-esteem and personal autonomy, as in those with HA and HM (high masculinity) scores, determined women's assessment of whether the stress in their lives was controlled or uncontrolled. Not surprisingly, while HF (high femininity) women reported greater uncontrolled stress and less controlled stress than HM women, HA women were the least stressed overall, with most of the stress they reported being of the controlled variety. So, although a woman with more apparently male characteristics may actively seek out situations many of us would define as stressful, such as certain high-pressured, competitive or male-orientated professions and sports, her sense of confidence and belief in her ability to control the strains and pressures in such an environment seem either to neutralize much of that stress or render it more manageable than it would be for someone lacking sufficient assertiveness, adaptability and strength.

More recently, in 1986, a study conducted by Vonda Olson Long, a researcher at the University of New Mexico, further confirmed that competency-orientated masculine attributes are not only the most predictable indicators of women's self-esteem but also of self-acceptance – a crucial counterpart to self-esteem which entails the valuing of one's self despite one's short-comings. It is perfectly obvious, therefore, that any argument over the merits of women entering such overwhelmingly male-dominated activities as the armed forces, police, fire brigade, rugby, boxing, etc., where women's capacity to withstand extreme and prolonged physical and mental stress, utilize aggression, maintain emotional detachment and overcome intense fear seems always to be a central issue, must take into account not only such variables as sex-role typing but also the fact that this is probably as much a result of upbringing as an inherited disposition. On the strength of such findings, the notion that women's early conditioning and society's pressure on them to fulfil traditional sex roles can be an enormous potential source of stress and low self-worth has become more powerfully persuasive than ever.

There may be some reason to suppose that, in some cases, self-perception, assertiveness and biochemistry are in some way interdependent. Can our sex hormones, in particular testosterone, help to determine our mental outlook and behaviour – or does our body chemistry change *as a result* of that behaviour? Considering the enduring belief – so far unproven – that testosterone is responsible for male crime and pathological violence, it seems odd that little research so far exists into the association between testosterone levels and normal variations in dimensions of personality. As far as women are concerned, one of the very few studies into this area revealed that testosterone concentration is higher in women who express a need for personal achievement and autonomy, with female lawyers possessing significantly higher testosterone levels than female nurses, teachers and, for some inexplicable reason, athletes.

Another study, carried out by anthropologist Francis Purifoy and statistician Lambert Koopmans, to compare testosterone and androstenedione (a precursor of testosterone) levels in professional and managerial women and female students, clerical and service workers and housewives, found that students and professional or managerial women do have somewhat higher concentrations of both hormones. But as they pointed out, since stress can *lower* testosterone levels in both sexes, it is fair to assume that the amount of negative stress reported by those women in low paid, low status jobs or by housewives who did not work outside the home, could be just as responsible for depressing hormone levels as the sense of fulfilment, purpose and self-worth among professional women may be responsible for creating a reverse effect.

Whether a feel-good factor applies to women with higher testosterone levels is something researchers would also like to ascertain. So far the signs are promising. Far from being an indication of unhealthy stress, as some researchers claim, on the contrary it seems that higher testosterone in women is a healthy indication of positive self-image, fulfilled ambition, inner strength and resourcefulness. Another fascinating study, published in 1988, found that women with high masculinity and high androgyny personality scores had significantly more elevated measures of testosterone compared to those with high femininity ratings. Women with high testosterone levels were more likely to view themselves as 'robust', 'impulsive' and 'resourceful', independently determining the course of their own lives and more likely to be enterprising and action-orientated. In contrast, those with low testosterone concentrations described themselves as 'helpful' and 'caring', pursuing more conventional lives and with a disposition towards such negative moods as anxiety, depression and apathy.

Invidious as it is to make distinct comparisons between negative and positive personality types, or to suggest that one set of characteristics is healthier or more preferable to another, what does seem striking is how some women's sense of self-determination, the acknowledgment that they have the necessary freedom, assertiveness and strength to pursue the roles they see as most fitting for themselves, and the confidence that they will succeed at those roles, seems to have escaped the degree of socialization experienced by less independent and assertive women – a vivid confirmation of the truth of Jung's statement that we don't make images, but are made by them.

Traditional beliefs that upheld the old notion of male–female dualism are beginning to be shot down, thanks to scientific research. Which is the more 'masculine', which the more 'feminine', is becoming harder to define, given the continual reduction in polarity between masculine and feminine norms of behaviour. What precise role biochemistry plays in determining self-perception remains fiendishly difficult to assess: it could be that rather than causing women's assertiveness or aggression, testosterone levels, as well as other hormonal and neurochemical secretions, actually increase as a result of the positive or 'controllable' stress that accompanies a more active, risk-orientated lifestyle, a reversal of the testosterone-lowering effects of stress that has been found to affect certain men. Until researchers stop looking for evidence of biological factors as the underlying *cause* of aggressive and other pro-active modes of behaviour and instead examine more thoroughly the effect of behaviour and mood on body chemistry generally, the popular assumption that aggression is normal to males, hence unnatural to females, must not be allowed to go unchallenged.

3

The New Female Criminal

Down in the 'Well'

Buckled wallpaper is peeling away from the perished plaster. Beneath the window, mud-grey fungoid patches have begun to flourish, the unmistakable invasion of dry rot. Lit by one naked light bulb dangling overhead, the kitchen is bare apart from a row of largely empty cheap plastic shelves and cupboards and a rusty metal sink. We sit drinking Diet Coke at a cracked formica table, on rickety plywood chairs. My eyes are riveted by the 1950s-style cooker: the stained cream ceramic hob is alive with endlessly shifting dotted black trails, the crossroads for battalions of cockroaches busily *en route* from one hidden nook or cranny to another.

This is Marla's place. She keeps it as clean and tidy as possible for her four young children and the three elder ones who live there part time. Not easy, especially last winter when the temperature fell to -24 °F and there was no electricity or running water because the landlord failed to carry out overdue repairs. But this still beats her previous apartment in a condemned tenement block where not just cockroaches but rats would scurry after dark over the bodies of her sleeping children; where the only privacy available in a single bedroom shared by the children, Marla and sometimes her husband, was a blanket hung from the ceiling to divide the room. On one side, the sleeping children. On the other, when nights were good, Marla and Joey screwing; when they were bad, Joey beating her up or forcing her into degrading sex acts against her will, and shooting speed.

We sit in the damp, murky, roach-infested kitchen while in the adjoining room her three toddlers watch TV. On and off Marla starts to cry, quietly. Last night her brother was killed in a friend's home, stabbed in a brawl over drugs. She cradles her 14-month-old baby. The eldest three sometimes live with relatives and should be at school now, or so she hopes. More likely, she fears, they've played truant, got in with bad company on the streets. And in this Brooklyn neighbourhood, Bushwick, the infamous ten-block drug market which in the 1990s has become one of New York City's most dangerous, hopelessly crime-ridden, drug-infested ghettos, being on the streets means only one thing: crime. Committing it or being a victim of it or – quite commonly – both.

Marla should know. Now 28, since her teens she's been back and forth at random as frequently as anyone in the neighbourhood, seeing both sides – from the perspective of victim and that of offender. After years as a hardened 'dope fiend', shooting heroin, snorting coke, going on to become hopelessly crack-addicted, earning money to support her habit through prostitution, robbery and occasional drug peddling, she now lives on welfare, does part-time charring and, after undergoing a medical 'detox' programme, has been 'clean' for eighteen months. She knows she must stay that way and keep out of trouble if only for her children's sake. Her husband drops by sporadically without contributing financially – only two of the children are his. Anyway, she'd rather he stayed away for good; if not, she might end up killing him she says, pointing to the livid red weals around her neck.

'Yesterday Joey hit me so hard I was all set to finish him. I was so close to stabbin' him, I tried to, and I would have, but my little boy kept yellin' "Mom, Mom, don't kill him, you'll go to jail!" So I tell him, "You think I care about that right now?" And my brother dead an' all. I won't take all this from that little faggot. He may be my husband but I won't take no more shit like that. I left home as a kid because my dad beat me up, and my sister, since I was eight, burned our hands and legs on the stove, tied us to the kitchen table, locked us in the cellar naked. So I won't put up with this type of shit no more from nobody. The only reason I ain't killed him is because of my kids, I swear. I'd be put in jail and lose my kids. That would be like takin' my own life. Ain't nobody never gonna take my kids off me again.'

The last time Marla's children were taken into care was when she was too incapacitated by drugs to look after them adequately. Fear of losing them for good to foster homes or state care, as befalls large numbers of 'crack' mothers, is her prime incentive to avoid drugs. And fear that they too will take drugs and drift into crime has made her desperate to quit the neighbourhood for good. Some hope. As for the hundreds of other young girls and women here, and thousands more who were born into or have gravitated to similar urban hell-holes of poverty, alienation and lawlessness, with their all-pervasive drug culture, her chances are virtually nil. The name Bushwick – which police have nicknamed the 'Well' because of its unceasing supply of drugs, its ever-soaring crime rate and the relentless turnover of HIV-positive casualties of drug abuse – has become shorthand for urban despair and hopelessness, just one isolated subsection of the vast, festering underbelly of American inner-city deprivation. The scandal is that Bushwick is far from unique, either in the USA or any other part of the developed or undeveloped world. You will find its sordid counterpart almost anywhere, overflowing with human debris, junkies, ex-junkies and criminals like Marla, so many of them hardened and habituated to using violence to adapt to and survive their environment, whatever the cost.

Marla, who until her clean-up was one of New York's estimated 500,000 cocaine/crack addicts, has a relatively modest criminal career to date, her aggressive manner tempered by tears and anguished exhaustion at the evident lack of any possible escape route for anyone imprisoned in a ghetto community. Yet her manner belies a formidable reputation for violence. In her teens she is reputed to have knifed two men – she never knew whether they died of their wounds – but wasn't caught. Evidently ashamed, especially in front of her children, she refuses to elaborate on this, merely shrugging and explaining with tired resignation that 'Johns [pimps/menfriends] with too much attitude' should not be surprised if they got hurt. She also shot a heroin dealer in the leg when he refused to hand over money he owed her, threatening to kill her if she went to the police.

More recently her violence has been directed towards her husband, a 60-year-old crack smoker who beats her. She intimates that she is planning to hire a young black guy on her block as a hit man to get Joey 'taken out'. Unusually for someone in this community, she is now fighting to keep drugs out of her family's life. That takes guts: if there is anything more dangerous than possessing and selling drugs and being arrested for it, it is being seen or suspected by the local drug dealers and Dominican or Colombian 'bosses' as someone who might turn police informer. So afraid are local anti-drug residents of reprisals that a few brave ones, while unwilling to provide information directly to the authorities, recently agreed to facilitate police vigilance by secretly painting their addresses on their rooftops (houses are unnumbered in such neighbourhoods) to help night helicopter patrols distinguish which blocks to target as 'unclean'.

The last time Marla attacked anyone was when the wife of one of the drug dealers came to her home and threatened to smash her head in with a hammer for allegedly passing on their names to the police. 'Yeah, man, I cut her, I cut the bitch real good. I had to. I saw she was holdin' this hammer when she arrived, and started screamin' abuse at me. So I got a knife and hid it behind my back. Then she starts wavin' the hammer about preparin' to do me in, so I start wavin' around with the knife, and I got her in the face. '

Outside in the refuse-strewn streets with their abandoned warehouses, parking and storage lots – the few industries and businesses that once existed have disappeared since the expansion of the drugs bazaar – Marla takes me past the partly burnt-out or boarded-up shabby tenements, their graffiti-daubed walls and doors riddled with bullet holes attesting to the almost weekly homicides and police shoot-outs. On average, 5.3 murders take place every day in New York City, most of them in areas such as this, populated overwhelmingly by drug addicts and pushers. Between January 1991 and September 1992 there were 23 murders in one four-block radius that forms the nadir of the Well, nearly all drug-related. Between May and August 1992 in Bushwick there have been 626 arrests for drug selling and dealing, together with 303 arrests for possession and buying. The local police precinct has issued another 7,160 summonses for other minor criminal offences.

Marla points out both the casualties and the survivors of the Well. A black girl, glancing nervously over her shoulder every few minutes, sells syringes at one street corner. Teenage girls squat on the front steps of the houses and call out 'Bajando! Bajando', Spanish for 'coming down', when they see police approaching. Felicia, a longtime crack addict, tells me that because so many more women are out working the streets, touting drugs or selling syringes and equipment for cooking and packaging crack and other drugs, not only do the police now use far greater brute force when searching or arresting them, but women cops take particular pleasure in putting the boot into one of their own sex.

'You get beaten up bad. They're gonna stomp on you because they just wanna show you they can do it, be as horrible as the guys, you know? I won't deal no more 'cos it's too dangerous, too much violence, too many cops and I don't wanna end up in jail. These women cops arrested me a while back. They kicked me, they searched to see if I had drugs hidden in my breasts. One of 'em, she had these real long fingernails, she grabbed and squeezed my breast real hard, diggin' in till she left marks, just for the sake of being sadistic. And I wasn't even given' them a hard time, I wasn't fighting. You fight back, you get beat up worse, man. The other one had me on the ground and kicked my legs apart to see if I had something hidden. Yeah, the cops put you through all kindsa hell. They'll beat yous up just for still standing on the block two minutes after they told yous to go away . . .'

The major tragedy is that *not* to become involved in the subculture of drugs, whose tentacles search out and entwine themselves in a vice-like grip around every facet of daily ghetto life, is becoming less and less of a realistic option for women like Marla and Felicia. Like many of the inner-city poor, they often leave home as youngsters, especially if family life was violent or abusive, probably having dropped out of school early through lack of interest, drug use or criminal offences. Whether born locally or far away, as teenagers with limited education their chances of finding regular employment are remote and they frequently gravitate to areas such as Bushwick, lured by boyfriends with a pre-existing history of crime and drug abuse, bent on pursuit of 'good times' and financial gain. Inevitably, most end up selling their bodies on the streets or in 'freak houses' (where clients come to purchase and consume drugs and partake in bizarre sexual practices), sometimes sleeping rough, and peddling dope to support their addiction and keep themselves and their children alive. Since the crack epidemic exploded in the mid 1980s, communities such as these have not only had all hope sucked out of them, but are themselves increasingly sucked into an all-consuming vortex of despair: confronted on the one hand with an all-out war on drugs by the police, and on the other with dwindling social services, lack of community resources and an absence of economic alternatives to joblessness and crime. Those resilient and resourceful enough to resist destruction by this environment have turned their commercial energies to the creation of a new ruling enterprise culture based on flourishing supply and demand.

It is only within this context of social alienation and the anger, frustration and intolerable physical and psychological stresses that result from it, that it becomes possible to understand how being cast as a permanent member of the underclass in the world's wealthiest nation may turn an ordinary woman into a potentially lethal criminal. If there is such a breed as the 'new' female criminal, then ghettos such as these are the most fertile spawning ground, guaranteeing the evolution of the fittest of the species. In a world as palpably feral, where survival depends as much on the use of wits and verbal sharp-shooting as on physical force and ruthlessness, the name of the survival game is use the system or be used by it, even if that means adopting the same corrupt and immoral tactics of violence, extortion and terror that male hustlers have been encouraged to employ from birth. You live or you die, you rip off or you get ripped off — those are increasingly the sole choices, for either sex.

The first thing that street women like Felicia and Marla must learn is that drugs and prostitution are more synonymous with violence here than in almost any other environment, and that it may only be through resorting to violence that you can hope to avoid becoming a target of it. Gang rapes, brutal assaults and murders of prostitutes are commonplace. Diseases, including the HIV virus and AIDS, are rampant. If greater numbers of women reportedly carry knives and guns and act more ruthlessly in attacking or ripping off their 'tricks' or 'johns' (a pre-emptive aggression tactic known in crack parlance as 'viccing' – you victimize someone before they can victimize you), then can this really be interpreted as evidence of the effects of sexual equality or the 'masculinizing' influences of the feminist movement, as some social observers would have it, rather than as a tactic of sheer naked survival?

Actually, if there is anything to be learned from women's behaviour in a largely drug- and crime-ridden culture, it is how loath many still are to resort to violence, either because of their traditional upbringing or their fear of ending up in prison. Another explanation for these women's continuing comparative non-violence – one which serves again as a depressing reminder of the degree of disablement brought about by early conditioning – is the almost fatalistic acceptance of their lowly victim-status; street prostitutes in poor neighbourhoods, especially if selling themselves for crack and other drugs, know full well that their bodies have less value and that they are regarded by clients, whose resources may also be extremely limited, as a cheaper commodity than hookers working more salubrious districts, perhaps in midtown Manhattan. When market forces dictate the rise and fall in the price of sex, the easiest option may be to passively accept this devaluation of self, yet who can blame those who increasingly resort to extreme strategies to minimize the chance of exploitation? New York researchers Lisa Maher and Richard Curtis, who have conducted extensive studies of the hierarchy of the city's street-level prostitution, report one crack-smoking prostitute in Bushwick as complaining about the derisory offers men try to get away with. Her view is both logical and succinct: 'The price of pussy has gone down here tremendously. To $3 for head and $5 a fuck. Man, I got $600 rent to pay, you cannot give me $3 – I'm $597 short – move the fuck away from me.'

A prostitute and drug user for nearly thirty years, 42-year-old Candy has worked the Bushwick 'stroll' (streets designated for soliciting) since the late 1980s. She notes wryly that the cost of most commodities appears to go up over the years, except for 'the meat-rack business'. Consequently, not only do the men try to get it cheap, but one 'ho' (prostitute) will have less compunction about undercutting another. 'Everyone's out to cut everyone's throat,' she observes. Candy remembers one night when a local man she had known for some time offered her $2 for a blow job (the going rate had long been $5). Insulted, but broke at 5.00 in the morning, she had little option but to take the offer. Then, in the middle of being aroused, the man suddenly changed his mind, decided he wanted to have 'straight sex' and proceeded to take his trousers off. At that point, still enraged by his paltry offer, Candy noticed he had a large wad of notes in his pocket, so she snatched the trousers and left him standing in an empty lot in his underwear. 'Here comes this sucker offering me two bucks and he got a pocketful of money. Shit! That's a guy that's insulting you and, you know, I don't like that. Yeah, I mean, you going to get off on me? I'm going to get off on you!'

Another Brooklyn prostitute, known as Susie Q, 5-foot tall and weighing under seven stone, remembers cutting a man's face with a broken bottle, so enraged had she become at his attempts to change the terms of the prior agreement – $20 for a blow job and a supply of crack which she agreed to purchase for him. 'He took up most of my night . . . Later on, everything he wanted was different. He was talking about fucking me in the ass, and this and that . . . In the beginning I took care of him like he wanted. But all this time is going by and he is not giving me more money . . . He said that he had to go over to his house to get more money. In the middle of the highway he wanted to throw me out . . . I didn't know where the hell I was, how to get back, plus I didn't have any money at this point, and he is being a real scumbag . . . He wasted a whole night of mine. I could have been making money. So the bottle of soda that I had, I broke it and I cut him with it. I didn't stab him with it. For me to get mad it really takes a lot.'

Others admit to a more cold-blooded determination in using violence and threats to intimidate their clients. Although more women now carry weapons for their own safety, many see knives and guns as a means of controlling a potentially risky situation or making it easier to rob their clients. Contemptuous as many are of the men, very few deliberately set out to harm or injure their victim. As one girl puts it: 'I would rip off my tricks. I would get in the car with them and if I saw a lot of money I would just take it. I always carries a knife. Although I carried a gun when I had one. When you hold a gun people don't argue with you. But when you hold up a knife, a man might try to fight you back. I didn't want to hurt anybody but I wanted them to know I needed the money. It was just me trying to get straight. I didn't know them but I felt like this, if they were low enough to have me suck their dick for money then why not take what they had on them. I never had to use a weapon, they always gave it up.'

Another New York 'ho' talks about becoming increasingly incensed at men's blatant meanness and dishonesty: 'They want to buy you a drink and the next thing you know they're telling you to go with them to give them some head, they give you $3. I really desperately needed the money and they would do whatever they want with me and the next thing they tell me to wait here and they cut out on me. They don't give me nothing.' Eventually she started carrying a .22 automatic and would take all their money and jewellery at gunpoint. From there she went on to carry out armed robberies every couple of weeks, sometimes robbing strangers in the street but mostly robbing the men she had 'set up', planning everything in advance and carrying out the crime in their homes.

Researchers studying the phenomenon of the alleged 'new wave' of female violence point out that it is only by analysing the everyday context of such women's lives – in particular whether or not they are heavily addicted to drugs – that one can begin to assess how frequently the environment and daily pressures to survive lead them to commit both random as well as planned, opportunistic crimes, rather than their own inherent propensity for violent behaviour *per se*. Although many seem to gain considerable confidence and a feeling of control by carrying weapons and successfully ripping off their tricks, or even targeting strangers as victims, few seem to feel good about such behaviour or regard it as increasing their self-esteem or peer status. Violence for them is simply another means of survival, stumbled upon often accidentally and undertaken as a last resort.

Tragically, those women whose lives have come to be ruled by drugs will often use the greatest violence, out of a mixture of drug-induced aggression (most common and extreme in crack addicts) and crazed desperation over how to obtain their next supply. A Brooklyn university lecturer, living in a quiet, respectably middle-class neighbourhood, recalls how her neighbour was blasted in the face by an automatic rifle fired by one of two young women who rang the front door bell intending to rob her apartment.

One case involved an 18-year-old crack-addicted prostitute who had regularly worked the strolls in Harlem with her 35-year-old mother, who came bursting into her mother's apartment demanding money for more drugs. Her mother told her she had no cash, so the girl battered her over the head with a broom. When the mother's boyfriend tried to stop her, the girl pulled out a knife and stabbed him repeatedly. The mother died shortly afterwards.

Another tragic incident indicates just as vividly how not only the life of the drug addict but those of the people closest to them may become inexorably contaminated by duplicity, stress, vindictiveness and violence. In August 1992, 68-year-old Daisy Hutson finally shot her 48-year-old crack-addicted daughter to death after enduring almost a decade of lies, thefts and threatening demands for money. Distraught over the disintegration of her daughter's life, Daisy confronted her on the street intending to scare her with a .22-calibre pistol. She never intended to kill her, an explanation that was accepted by the judge at her murder trial who, sympathizing with 'the depth of Mrs Hutson's despair and the extent of her anguish', had her charge reduced to manslaughter with a possibility of plea-bargaining her way out of a prison sentence. In the context of daily life in the ghetto, Daisy Hutson and her daughter are just one more sad story.

Dealing to Survive

What seems increasingly clear is that although women may embark on a life of crime via a number of different entry points or pathways depending upon individual need and circumstance, what propels them there in the first place, especially in cases of robbery and assault, and then leads them to continue committing further, perhaps more violent offences, is principally drugs. According to one recent American study, female offending rates in New York City for robbery and aggravated assault increased 75.8 per cent and 47 per cent respectively from 1984 to 1989. From 1987 to 1990, black women, who are most likely to live in impoverished, crime-ridden neighbourhoods, accounted for 71 per cent of the female arrests for homicide, robbery and assault, Hispanic and white women accounted for 20 per cent and 8 per cent respectively. When it comes to assaults, America's latest National Crime Survey data indicates that arrest rates for white males and black juvenile girls appear to be almost equal, and are five times higher than for white women. In one New York study, researchers found the arrest rates for robbery and assault to be higher for black females than white males, and far in excess of similar crimes committed by Hispanic and white women.

Considering that of the estimated 2.4 million impoverished ghetto-dwellers throughout the United States, 65 per cent are black, 22 per cent Hispanic and 13 per cent non-Hispanic and other races, and that according to New York's Community Service Society, 70 per cent of the city's poor blacks live in neighbourhoods where well over 30 per cent of the residents subsist at below poverty levels (conversely, 70 per cent of the city's poor whites live in neighbourhoods where less than 30 per cent of the residents are impoverished), the apparent disproportionate involvement of black females (and males) in violent crimes begins to acquire meaning. So, too, does the fact that women's peak years for active offending, from assaults to homicides, begin later yet last longer than that of the average white male (women commit more robberies, burglaries and assaults in their early to mid twenties, unlike white men who are most active between the ages of fifteen and nineteen, and unlike black men whose burglary rate is highest between the ages of 25 and 29; women commit murder until well into their thirties, whereas men murder less in their thirties). Such findings could be interpreted as evidence of women's ongoing need to support themselves and their young children – very often their children end up being cared for by relatives or foster parents – and of their ability to 'space' their crimes and, when necessary, to adopt a more pragmatic and resourceful approach to offending, unlike men who carry out more unplanned, random crimes as much for sheer kicks as for self-preservation.

Having recently interviewed 65 violent female offenders and studied 176 records of women arrested for violence, together with another 93 of those imprisoned for crimes of violence, Deborah Baskin and Ira Sommers, sociologists at Manhattan's John Jay College of Criminal Justice, found that in 89 per cent of robberies women admitted that they needed to get money – and 81 per cent of these needed it for drugs. Only 19 per cent wanted cash to buy clothes, jewellery or electronic equipment, which rather explodes the current belief – a scenario much favoured by the tabloids – that schoolchildren and delinquents rob out of frustrated consumer greed and the desire to model themselves on the style of their favourite pop star, sports hero or movie icon. Certainly, a girl, or boy, from a poor background may mug or hold a gun to someone for the price of a new pair of Reeboks or simply yank someone's gold chain off their neck for themselves, but the vast majority are far more likely to do so to secure their next 'high'. The fact that many of the women in this study confessed a readiness to use violence and routinely carried weapons such as knives and guns indicates that commitment to violence had become very much a normal feature of their everyday lives, along with non-violent crimes such as fraud and forgery.

The most fascinating and telling aspect of Baskin's and Sommers's studies is how frequently drug-addicted women who commit violent crimes fail to regard themselves as criminals. On the one hand this could be seen as confirmation of the so-called 'subcultural theory' based on the premise that due to their unique historical experience of enslavement and white oppression, African Americans in particular have evolved a value system that legitimizes violence. According to this thesis, criminal offences such as assault and murder are interpreted as expressions of a subculture in which violence is condoned as the norm, not only essential to personal survival but of positive value in aggrandizing one's self-image. A less insulting and culturally reductionist explanation, however, and probably far nearer the truth in these cases, is the sad fact that as their lives become increasingly ruled by drug addiction, and their existence ever more devoid of close human involvement, reciprocal trust, friendship or any conventional commitments or responsibilities, these women simply saw their actions as dictated by economic necessity or borne of their 'drug compulsion'. Given that in refusing to acknowledge themselves as criminals they also abdicated any responsibility for the ill-effects of their actions, but readily referred to themselves in such disparaging and crude terms as 'junkies', 'cokebitches' or 'crackheads', the degree to which their lives had been devastated by their habit is all too tragically evident.

To find women who have not only learned the survival value of aggression and violence but, rather than drawing on those resources to feed their own addiction, use their toughness to improve their living standard and enhance their self-worth, we need to look at those women who are rapidly muscling in on what used to be exclusively male terrain – the world of drug dealing. Although some addicts do manage to boost their income considerably by selling or dealing on the side, only those who have overcome their dependence or can effectively control their own consumption can ever hope to make a go of it for any length of time. For those who stay 'clean' the financial gain may prove enormous, offering a toehold on the first rung of this shaky commercial ladder. It is here you are likely to encounter the more successful hustlers with recognizable street cred, the survivors of the scene rather than the casualties. Survival, it must be remembered, is entirely relative. To describe a drug dealer as a 'survivor' may amount to an obscene contradiction in terms, a seeming vindication of what is rightly acknowledged to be the most immoral and evil of all human activities; but to those forced to scavenge a living in the festering urban cess-pit in which, thanks to public and political indifference and institutionalized corruption, they have no option but to live, moral conscience is a luxury to which few can afford to aspire.

In a poverty-stricken slum where virtually all activities revolve around drugs, almost anything must be better for a mother with three children than to haggle over whether or not to accept $3 to drop her knickers for a man in a freezing car park at 4.00 a.m. And what allure can there possibly be in part-time cleaning jobs at $10 an hour when you can earn between $80–$100 in half an hour selling crack, and selling heroin may bring in up to $3,600 in one week? When your body has already been used as fodder for a system that exists and grows by voraciously cannibalizing itself, greedily sucking up and living off those that help to perpetuate it, where do you draw the line between human survival and human destruction? For the female dealer, as for her male counterpart, the system of drugs distribution, the need to remain four or five steps ahead of the law and the intense competitiveness not only mean that she must adhere to a strict code of rules, but also create a structure that is highly conducive to violence.

One young female dealer describes her earlier role as head of an eight-strong 'crew', seven females, one man, which proved more successful than an all-male group because females attract more punters and therefore sell more dope. 'Sometimes I used weapons, a gun, a knife, with me it didn't matter, anything in my hand was a weapon. Somebody would get in my territory, I'd shoot at them and tell them to get off the corner, you know, that's how it was generally.'

According to Eloise Dunlap, a New York-based researcher who has studied at first hand the New York crack market, becoming familiar with the female dealers and sellers, these women's emerging roles in the drugs industry not only make them a unique sector of the population but reveal a lot about how women's roles generally are changing in all aspects of American life. Although to the outside world women like these may be categorized, and pitied, as helpless victims of a corrupt, degenerate system, for the most part this is the exact opposite of how they regard themselves – or are regarded within their community. For many, whose lives from childhood were marked by violence, abuse, abandonment and rejection, whether by parents or institutions, leading to limited expectations for the future both in personal relationships and job prospects, proving to themselves and others that they are able to play an integral, active part in a business as dangerous, complex and male-dominated as drug dealing has proved a potent source of self-esteem, pride and empowerment. 'For many of these women, this is the first time ever that they have gained control over their lives through economic independence and that they perceive themselves as valued and respected in the community,' says Eloise Dunlap.

Respected *and* feared, since dealing is clearly only to be undertaken by the very tough, aggressive and fearless. Should these qualities be lacking, they need to be acquired fast for a woman to play any key role in the system. Generally a group of women will pool their resources, assuming allotted roles suited to their skills, temperament and lifestyle. Each woman or group of women therefore carves out a niche for herself on a particular level along the distribution chain. One, usually known as the 'holder', might have the best contacts for buying drugs at a competitive price, without too many hassles; some then buy and file down the glass phials to required size and pack up the crack ready for distribution; others are expert at cooking 'base' i.e. cocaine to make up top-grade batches of crack, guaranteed to give the 'best high', then bottling it for distribution. Others, sometimes called 'supervisor' or 'lieutenant', concentrate on the business of distributing and negotiating deals, keeping account of all the drugs and money coming in from the street that are eventually passed on to the boss, often directing the whole operation, delegating and issuing orders to her team, hiring and firing when necessary.

Street sellers are most likely to comment on the climate of violence that prevails, whether from police swoops or from other sellers trying to invade a particular individual's 'turf'. On some blocks there are a number of sellers trading often no more than ten, fifteen or twenty-five feet away from each other. The more congested the area, the greater the likelihood of rows, fights and flare-ups, especially late at night after many hours on the street. Says one seller: 'One time somebody didn't pay me money and I just hit them. You know, I really don't like to get into that . . . It was a girl . . . you standing out there and you hustling, that person can call the cops on you.'

The sanctioning of extreme violence may be an attitude that women develop through awareness of the need to adhere to consistent standards of professionalism. They may well behave more ruthlessly towards one of their own group who cheats or endangers the business than to an unscrupulous seller or buyer. As a woman, it pays to advertise your toughness, thereby ensuring faster promotion to higher perches in the pecking order, securing high-risk jobs normally carried out by men because of their bravado and strength. One of Dunlap's interviewees, Queen Bee, began selling marijuana while still at school and purposely chose to make a 'career' in the drug industry. She was hired to the position of door guard at a crack spot she had frequented previously as a smoker. Her duties were to search everyone wanting to come in, from head to toe, and to ensure no guns or weapons of any kind were brought in. What weapons were found had to be left at the door until the person left. This job was regarded as most important because the door guard had to watch out for stick-ups, police raids or any other trouble. Queen Bee brags that she did the job so well she even searched the boss when he came in, stressing that he had admired her nerve. From there she was promoted to the 'pipe and torch', which entails making sure customers buy their crack, smoke it without saving it, and when their time runs out either pay again or leave. If they didn't leave quietly, she would personally put them out. Eventually she was given the top position of 'chief' – managing the whole outfit.

As Eloise Dunlap discovered, women must be as tough as any man if they are to survive as dealers and sellers, because no special privileges are accorded a female who enters the arena. 'The position demands her to acquire certain attitudes and behaviour and she has to adjust.' Some, however, seem to gain extra satisfaction in erring too far on the side of aggression, even when unnecessary. One seller admits she gets a kick out of ripping people off, partly because of her contempt for them as hardened drug addicts. 'They'se be stupid enough to give me the money, to go get mother fuckin' drugs . . . I fuckin' go through one door and come out the next. That's it. No more details, just hope I don't get caught. Suckers, yeah, suckers; straight-up suckers, I see 'em comin.'

By the same token, a ruthlessly hard-nosed hustler such as this is also more likely to measure self-worth through her aggression and its effects on others, secure in the knowledge that she can use the system to her own ends, rather than be used by it. Selling drugs, she says, 'gave me a whole lot of self-esteem. I felt good about myself. Everything I had on was brand new. I could do whatever I want, eat whatever I want . . . it felt damn good. ' Especially in extreme circumstances of deprivation and limited options, the sense of independence and pride that comes from dealing drugs successfully and being in control of their economic lives must not be ignored or minimized. Such sentiments speak volumes, not only of the heady sense of empowerment fought for and accorded a member of a poverty-stricken, dispossessed community, but, equally important, of a woman's pride at attaining equality in a man's world where aggression has inestimable survival value.

Would the following words sound any less triumphant, the attitude any more understandable, coming from a woman, secure in her autonomy and the sense of being the ruler of her life, climbing the corporate ladder in the City or Wall Street? 'That's just how I am . . . I'm a hard motherfucker, OK? I like a lot of things. I like to travel. I like to get that fast money and I don't like the white man tellin' me what to do all the time, breathin' and holdin' over my neck. So this is the way I do it. I give a fuck about myself. That's what time it is.'

The Backlash Brigade

Of all the dangers lurking behind the current furore and media hype over 'escalating female crime', none is more potentially damaging to all women, whatever their status in society and *vis-à-vis* the law, than the lumping together of all female acts of violence as evidence of corruption and criminality. To many who attribute such moral turpitude to women's sexual and social liberation, this amounts to nothing less than a triumph of domestic anarchy over social cohesion. Yet the sweeping blanket condemnation of all women who commit violent acts as harbingers of a new 'species' of deviant, quasi-male thug, no more deserving of understanding or compassion than the original male prototype, carries an unmistakably sinister message, so far less stated than implied – if women don't want the cell doors to slam as hard on them as on men, they should get back into the home and stay there.

Given the tone of awed horror with which each new alleged increased statistic for female crime is trumpeted by law enforcement officials and media alike, quoted out of context and reported by sensation-seeking journalists with little understanding of the socioeconomic or psychological predeterminants of crime, it doesn't take a visionary to foresee a time, not that far off, when the violent female becomes society's newest 'antiheroine', in every way as threatening a symbol of urban danger as today's male psychopathic serial killer. Considering how little is known about why psychopaths commit sadistic and mass murders, what makes rapists rape, and how many pieces remain missing in the overall puzzle of male crimes of violence, the fact that society's paranoid fantasies are already beginning to embrace such new villains as the black girl gangster – a current favourite among the American popular press – and the glue-sniffing delinquent schoolgirl bully – a spectre much agonized over by the British tabloids – is surely cause for serious alarm.

It is futile to even begin to attempt to understand the varying patterns of women's violence without first distinguishing between the diverse geographical, ethnic, socioeconomic and cultural contexts of such behaviour. Which is why the violence exhibited by, say, a casual drug user or delinquent schoolgirl living in a working-class, multi-ethnic community such as Brixton in London, or that of a white middle-class wife who smashes up her husband's possessions because he has left her for another woman, is likely to differ widely in its nature, motivation and long-term outcome compared to the violence used by a drug-addicted single teenage mother living in an urban ghetto like Bushwick. With women so far removed from one another by environment, class, culture and circumstance they might come from separate planets, it would be ludicrous even to attempt to seek parallels.

If women are becoming more visible and active out on the mean streets, with the streets getting meaner by the minute, hustling to make money in an environment once dominated almost exclusively by men, it is certainly *not* as a result of female emancipation – or at least not in the standard middle-class definition of the term. On the contrary, the growing emergence of female violence, especially in very impoverished communities, actually reveals something highly significant yet paradoxical about women's perception of, and reaction to, their own vulnerability and fear of victimization. For in being forced, whether as single women, married or single parents, into a catch-as-catch-can front-line sometimes vigilante existence as sole or principal wage-earners, there can be no doubt that the physical dangers and financial hardship faced by women marginalized to such extremes is far greater today than at any time, affecting increasing numbers of the very young. That more women are turning to burglary, assault, mugging and opportunistic murder therefore serves as an indication of their increased burden of responsibility and heightened vulnerability rather than of any newly developed streak of savagery or venality.

Although statistical analysis of any number of women's arrest records, criminal charges and convictions admittedly reveals consistent and predictable patterns to women's crimes (as it does of men's), there is no such person as the 'typical female criminal'. Criminality frequently begins early – and according to present crime data is beginning at an ever earlier age, even pre-teens. Early antisocial behaviour such as school bullying and fighting, truancy, glue sniffing and under-age alcohol use, accompanied or superseded by teenage offences such as petty theft, shoplifting, vandalism and disorderly conduct, are often exacerbated by drug dependence, leading on eventually to more severe crimes including burglary, assaults, arson and murder.

Yet the temptation to draw on this data to construct an all-purpose offender 'profile' can in the end yield nothing significant or valuable in the way of insight into the psyche of violent women or offer any real understanding as to why they begin and, more importantly, continue offending.

Today's popular analysis of female criminality which categorizes violent women as misfits – either anarchic rebels without a cause or conscience, or butch bovver-booted lesbians whose aggressiveness represents a freak of nature – is as meaningless as it is misleading. The fact that women's aggression and violence is born of and nurtured by a diversity of complex environmental and psychological factors, usually originating in childhood, and that they may commit acts of violence for numerous reasons including poverty, boredom, isolation, fear, greed, kicks, desire for attention, power and dominance, in self-defence and for protection and day-to-day survival, is something which appears not yet to have penetrated the minds of most criminologists, law enforcement officials and psychologists. In the growing agonized outcry over soaring crime rates, what could be more convenient or expedient than to put the blame for women's increased participation in crime triumphantly at the door of feminism?

Never was an issue guaranteed to offer more mileage to the 'backlash' brigade than the spectre of growing violence among today's generation of young women. As a key weapon in the armoury amassed by anti-feminists, male and female alike, this is the sociopolitical equivalent of the H-bomb. Naturally enough, to point the finger of blame at feminism for rising crime waves was always bound to be an easy option for the lazy-minded or die-hard traditionalist defenders of the *status quo*. An easy option, but doomed to failure. Even a cursory examination of the lives, attitudes and experiences of many female criminals and violent women reveals the theory to be built on sand. Talk to any prisoner or woman with a previous criminal record or a history of persistent, repeated offending and it soon becomes glaringly obvious that – with the exception of political terrorists, revolutionaries and freedom fighters – they did not commit these acts out of ideological motives. Nor, for the most part, did

they find themselves on the margins of society, acting aggressively and violently in order to prove themselves equal to men,
but rather because their early environment failed to offer them
sufficient sustenance and security – be it emotional, physical or
economic – to make 'conventional' life a sufficiently beguiling
proposition in comparison to drifting and lawlessness.

The fallacy that feminism has given birth to a new breed of
criminal is most vividly illustrated in America, where dividing
lines between respective gender roles – and the whole issue of
gender-politics – among the inner-city poor, largely black and
other non-white communities, have become blurred by the
more pressing life and death issues of race. Pushed away and
isolated ever further on the outer margins of mainstream
society, men, women and children of the ghetto are increasingly
united in a joint struggle to survive in the face of the indifference, racism and white supremacy of the outside world rather
than divided by the battle of the sexes, in spite of the fact that
macho culture remains endemic amongst Hispanic, Latino and
black communities.

Women's violence in Britain, although also the upshot of social
deprivation, poverty, abusive and violent home environments
and easier availability of drugs, is far more readily identifiable
as a reflection of class. All crimes, especially those of violence,
are mainly a non-middle-class activity, and while offenders may
be far from proud of their crimes, they tend generally to be
fiercely proud of their working-class origins. If the popular
image of the young tearaway skinhead, crop-haired and scow-
ling, stomping and strutting around defiantly in Doc Martens,
black leather and chains, sporting tattoos on her arms and safety
pins or studs in her nose and ears, still has such a high visibility
long after the punk era of the 1970s, it is for one crucial reason.
It was only with the advent of punk culture – quintessentially
a working-class movement, reflecting the cynical hopelessness
of unemployed inner-city youth while glorifying violence, anarchy and lawlessness with frenzied energy – that women with no
desire or aptitude for traditional female roles finally discovered
a viable alternative means of self-expression, including the

venting of anger, hatred, hostility and aggression. It became 'in' to be ugly, to reject anything and everything that represented conventional 'fragrant' womanhood.

Brenda, who was in her late teens when punk fashion and studs and the leather look favoured by Hell's Angels motorcycle gangs exploded on the British scene, remembers the heady feeling of liberation that came through deliberately and defiantly rejecting everything that stood for accepted images of femininity. 'I had my shoulder-length hair cropped to about one-eighth of an inch all over and shaved around the sides and back in a sharply defined ring around my hairline. It was dyed black with bleached white spikes sticking up in the centre. The hairdresser also carved his initials into the hair at the back of my head! I then went home on the tube that evening and it was dynamite! People were looking at me with expressions of not just horror and disgust, but actual fear. They seemed obviously scared and kept moving away from me on the train. For the first time in my life I had this great sensation of power I'd never known before, but which I'd always sensed men had naturally.'

With the growing popularity of 'speed', drugs whose main effect is to increase energy and heighten aggression, punk followers could give full release to the heady nihilism born of a mixture of despair and rage. Punk gave girls permission for the first time to vent their aggression legitimately, as a kick in the guts to the white, middle- and upper-class establishment. At one Sex Pistols gig, Brenda was with a girlfriend who in a frenzy of excitement bit off her boyfriend's ear — and became the hero of her group.

In a recent interview with the psychiatrist Dr Anthony Clare, singer and actress Toyah Wilcox has confessed that violence became an important means through which she sought both to define her identity and to reject her conventional and emotionally repressive family background. As a teenager in the 1970s, she first learned the survival value of violence at school as a victim of bullying. After weeks of taunting and torture, she finally punched her attacker: 'And it never happened again, because from that time on I was feared.' The repercussions within her family of joining the punk movement turned out to be deeply destructive, especially in Wilcox's interaction with her mother, with whom she had had a tense, rebellious relationship at the best of times. 'I was always prevented from going out and mixing with "lower class" kids. Then I got involved with some gangs in Birmingham. We were all against middle-class conventionality. It was when I became a punk that my mother really became afraid of me. I became very violent as a teenager.' Under the surface veneer of middle-class respectability she remembers a lot of family violence, principally because of her father's alcoholism and the financial problems that beset the family. A major confrontation with her mother culminated in Toyah punching her repeatedly and going for her with a pair of scissors, something for which she confesses her mother has been unable to forgive her for to this day. Most of her youth appears to have been spent in a rage, terrorizing others. 'People were terrified of me. If a man made a pass – whack! I'd just hit him in the face.' Today, she has mellowed; she is more of a loner than a combatant and feels in control of her violence.

Young women's rejection of middle-class values, including notions of 'appropriate womanhood', may often be inextricably intertwined with hostility and violence towards men. Sian, now forty, recalls that during her twenties and early thirties, after being assaulted and almost raped by a college colleague, she was an unexploded bomb, smouldering with rage and waiting to go off at the slightest provocation. 'I'd been brought up believing that to express anger wasn't right or nice for a woman, that you should overcome it. But after that event something snapped, and I became entirely governed and motivated by hatred and a sense of pure outrage at that man, at all men, who seemed to be able always, repeatedly, to get away with such outrageous acts against women, while we women dare not and must not strike back or expect justice to be done.'

Although Sian's relationships with men seemed doomed to failure as a result of her aggression, she still believed she could use violence more to her advantage than disadvantage. 'Men sensed the anger and violence in me, like a sort of craziness, and consequently in relationships never tried to be violent towards me. I even chose to have affairs with seemingly aggressive men, to see if I could provoke them, but it never worked. And the tension that built up always made the relationship fail. That was the one adverse side I discovered. But as far as I was concerned, there was no negative element in attacking anyone who I saw as threatening my space or my safety.

'Once, in a train travelling back to London from Scotland, I was confronted by a group of youths who began verbally taunting me. I was finally so enraged I picked one of them up by the scruff of the neck – he was a big, burly, navvy type – bashed him up against the compartment door and shrieked at him repeatedly to stop. It worked. They were shocked, and they stopped. I felt marvellous. It was an entirely cathartic experience.

'Another time when working as a waitress a guy in a wine bar went to grab my boob and I just pushed him off his stool on to the floor. He left at once. When I was doing some street theatre in Covent Garden Piazza I saw a chap about to nick one of my props and I punched him with a karate blow. Another guy who came up to me in the street and blew in my face got punched on the nose and nearly knocked out. And I always felt better after I'd belted the person, never guilty or ashamed. I reckoned that they'd never do something like that to another guy and not expect to get as good as they gave, so I decided my sex was to be an irrelevance.

'What I resented was the feeling of powerlessness that had been conditioned into me by my background, by my parents, so that I had no choice but be forced into a position of vulnerability for the rest of my life. My brother had always tried, when I was little, to control and hurt me, and I was punished for hitting back, so this time, as a grown up, I swore I'd never allow myself get into that position again.'

Punk had, and has, no links or affiliation with feminist ideology. Quite the opposite. Punk males, like the teddy boys of the 1950s and 'rockers' of the 1960s, as a group espoused all the most primitive elements of macho-hooliganism. Blatantly sexist, to the point of parody, they effectively regarded girls as inferior sex objects, 'chicks' or 'birds' or 'slags' to be screwed, beaten up or relegated to domestic servitude. The point was that for the first time women could, and did, find a legitimate 'style', based on butchness and aggression, with which to carve their own individual alternative identities. This they continue to do to the present day. As former prisoner Chris Tchaikovsky, Director of the London-based organization Women In Prison puts it, 'These women have been far more influenced by the music and fashion revolution in punk than they have by feminism. Young women like this are concerned not with feminism but with being different from their mothers. Their denial of their femininity is not about being like men: it's about refusing to be "proper" women.'

Clearly, for the 'backlash' brigade to put the changing face of womanhood simply down to the feminist movement is desperately shortsighted and ignores the influence of many varied and complicated social and economic forces at work in the lives of women.

The Revolving Door

The price to be paid for rebellion may prove a hefty one for many women. Women like Toyah Wilcox, Sian and Brenda were fortunate in avoiding a run-in with the law. But many others, whose criminal record can be traced back often to childhood, may be destined, sometimes on the basis of no more than an initial petty misdemeanour – yet one deemed entirely inappropriate to their sex – to remain trapped within what American sociologist Kathleen Daly has defined as the 'revolving criminal justice door', moving between short but regular periods of imprisonment and short, regular periods of freedom spent often jobless and on the streets, living in temporary makeshift accommodation, involved in hustling, possible drug or alcohol abuse and crimes of violence – until their next arrest and conviction.

And once caught up in the revolving door, the longer the time spent propelled circuitously, with growing momentum, through phases of imprisonment and out again into a hostile external environment, the fewer the chances of ever stepping free for good. This catch-22 situation is particularly acute for women since, as outlined in chapter 1, they are more likely than men to be incarcerated when very young, for relatively minor first-time offences, often on remand for extended periods, awaiting trial, while also standing a greater chance of being diagnosed as having a psychiatric disorder and being sent to a secure hospital or detained in the psychiatric wing of a women's prison, undergoing often extensive, debilitating drug treatment. Although it appears that many girls and women consciously, even wilfully, opt for an ongoing 'career' in violence, and that others seem unable, through their own inability to control their destructive impulses, ever to resume a law-abiding, integrated existence in the community, how much responsibility for this should be laid at the door of the criminal justice system and how much may be put down to a failing in such women themselves remains the thorniest of all questions. It also fails to address another crucial part of the criminal equation – that of early home environment. As long ago as 1967, the late forensic psychiatrist Professor Trevor Gibbens, working with members of the Institute of Psychiatry, interviewed 638 women admitted to Holloway Prison, correlating the criminal records of a sample of 245 over the subsequent ten years, with their life experiences. His findings, which were that a disproportionate number of persistent and serious offenders reported unhappy, disruptive home circumstances, separation from parents, institutionalized care and ill-treatment in the family, serves as a timely reminder of where researchers today should concentrate their efforts when trying to establish patterns to rising female crime.

Josie O'Dwyer is something of a legend in the British prison world, famed – and feared by many – for her red-hot anger and violent outbursts against fellow prisoners, police and prison warders, her natural qualities as a rabble-rouser and phenomenal strength and skill as a fighter. Ex-prisoner Jimmy Boyle once told her she and her colleagues were too violent to join his violent male offenders' rehabilitation programme. Apart from having spent nearly ten years on and off from the age of 14 in a series of penal institutions including approved school, borstal, young custody centres and four closed prisons, Josie's notoriety is based largely on two major incidents in which she was the star protagonist.

In 1973 she initiated and led the Bullwood Hall riots, in which an entire wing was smashed to pieces by the inmates; it was four hours before the wardens could restrain Josie and her gang, by which time they had smashed up their cells, breaking their beds and chairs, and ripped out and torn apart all the kitchen and bathroom fittings including sinks, baths and stoves.

'We got hold of the piano and shoved it down a flight of concrete steps. We even got as far as the governor's office, and my friend Leanna shat in a drawer of one of her files and then shut it! It's like a fever when there are lots of youngsters together, all highly energized teenagers getting higher and higher on this big buzz. You need the violence for release — there's no other way to discharge all the aggro and energy. I never knew where the force and strength came from. All I know is that once something made me angry and made me snap, there would be this rush of energy, this very powerful hot sensation beginning at the feet, going right up my legs into my stomach, and from my stomach it just makes my head explode, so much so that I can't hold it any more. Then I just smash out — crack! I head-butted one of the screws so hard she had a broken nose, and I only hit her once.

'Another time something set me off when I was working in the kitchen. I got hold of the cooker, ripped it out the wall and hurled it across the room followed by a whole lot of cupboards. Then I somehow managed to lift up this giant tea urn which was bolted down and full of tea and shove that across the room. Don't ask me where the strength comes from. That's what really frightens me. Normally I don't have any strength really. It took me and another girl all our combined strength to slowly pull that cooker away from the wall, walking it on its base, when we were cleaning behind it, so how did I manage to rip it out, lift and throw it all by myself?'

Josie's other major claim to fame, one which really gave her the status of 'top dog' and made her a 'star' among women prisoners, is that she beat up Myra Hindley in Holloway. Aged 19 and having spent four years on and off in prison, Josie knew nothing about the Moors Murders. 'I was young, violent and bolshie, and had committed plenty of violent acts, mainly property offences, but I was very anti mugging old ladies and all that. I hated the nonces [inmates imprisoned for offences against children]. Then two prisoner officers gave me a copy of the *News of the World* in which there was an article about the whole case. That did it. What I read, all about the tortures and the tapes, made me shake with horror and fury so much they had to take me for a walk to calm me down. She'd just been put on to my wing. A few days later, when she passed me during a recess, I snapped and just went for her. I battered her and battered her, I punched and kicked and head-butted her, I cracked her head off the railings and wall. I broke her fingers stamping on her hands trying to make her let go of the floors so she'd fall off down to the bottom and be killed. I wanted to kill her. I saw bone show through her face when I bashed her. When I'd finished with her, her teeth were all loosened at the front, her nose crossed to the left side of her face, two black eyes, split lip, ear, knees. She had to eat through a straw for the next six weeks and needed cosmetic surgery.' Expecting severe punishment, Josie was treated like a hero by the staff. The incident, she then realized, had been set up – her reputation for fearlessness and violence ensured that she would react as she did. 'I heard one officer say to another: "I've been waiting twelve years for someone to do that."'

On the face of it, Josie is one of the survivors of the penal system, who found out as young kid how the 'system' worked, learning to outwit the screws or play them at their own sadistic games of manipulation and violence, undermining their attempts at 'setting up' and 'winding up' inmates for their own perverse thrills and amusement. She was strong and determined enough to use her aggression as a force for self-preservation, but has not escaped unscarred. Her long years – young, vulnerable years – of isolation and stigmatization as a delinquent, which included being diagnosed as psychotic and schizophrenic on the basis of mere 15-minute 'interviews' by psychiatrists to whom she would not utter more than one or two words, are a scandalous indictment of the penal system and its attitudes and treatment of girls and women whose belligerence and hostility would not be regarded as exceptional or unnatural in a young male.

When she talks about her childhood, it is easy enough to trace the pathway by which Josie stumbled on to the criminal circuit. She was brought up in a small town in Cornwall, the youngest of ten children. Her father, whom she loathed and feared, was a violent alcoholic who used to rape her mother and beat Josie at the slightest whim. 'He was a rotten, brute bastard and when he beat me I'd be in bed for a week. I hated him from a very young age and used to wish he'd choke on his food and die. I used to wet the bed, and got punished for that, so got even more nervous because of it.' Her elder brother tortured her mercilessly, once bundling her into a potato sack, shoving it into a box and sitting on the lid until her eyes were gritty with dried earth and she almost choked breathing it in. ''Course, I beat him up after. I was only ten and he was seventeen, but I walloped him just the same. Once I stuck a fork into his shoulder because he put some snot from his nose in my greens while Dad was saying Grace, and I knew I'd be forced to eat the stuff. Dad's reaction was to take me outside, stick my hand up against the outside wall and, lifting an axe, brought it right down on my fingers. From the pain I thought he'd chopped my fingers off, but I'd looked away when he did it. Turned out he'd used the butt end, not the blade, but the from the pain you wouldn't know. And in the background my brother was laughing. Then I got the axe and went to kill my brother with it – he was screaming by then in terror and running away. I'd previously thrown boiling water over him and stuck his shirt to his skin, so he knew I meant it.'

Josie ran away from home at 14, six months after her mother died. She was caught after having broken into a house in Bath and eaten some jelly out of the fridge. 'I'd gone in because it was the sort of grand house that looked like everyone's ideal home. I wanted to know how such people lived. I wasn't out to nick anything, and I hadn't. But the owners were trying to get some insurance compensation and they made out I'd stolen a grandfather clock, the TV and some hi-fi equipment. I was only a tiny skinny kid, under 5-foot – it was ridiculous for the police to think I'd be capable of carrying all that stuff off.' Convicted on two charges of burglary, she was sent to an approved school where she took her O levels. At sixteen she tried to find work in Cornwall but found her criminal record and her long isolation from the community an insurmountable handicap.

'I'd always had a terrible temper and now it came out in full force. Pure, undiluted anger. I felt I'd been punished enough for what I'd done, but now people were still punishing me, treating me as if I was bad or mad. They weren't giving me the same opportunities as my peers or the people I'd grown up with. I started doing a lot of burglary, being very violent, mainly against property. Chucking bricks through windows, shinning up drainpipes, that sort of thing. The Cornwall police just weren't prepared for a young girl to be doing the things that even men didn't do normally. Once they carried me into the police station with my teeth sunk into a copper's arse! I used to be terribly violent, fighting them off when they tried to catch me. It took a lot of force to restrain me. And that time three guys had got me into the back of an old Panda car and were sitting on me, and I bit into this one's arse and wouldn't let go. He was screaming in agony. The others were trying to prise my jaws open, but it only made me bite harder.

'I never worked with any chum or gang, always on my own, so I suppose I was more vulnerable. But I never knew any fear. I'd experienced so much fear and mental tortures through my childhood that anything anyone did to me I reckoned could never be as bad. I thought the best deal for me would be to get back in the nick as soon as possible.'

Control, as with many young violent women, is a crucial issue in her life. Five years ago she began having epileptic seizures and was put on medication for the rest of her life, which limited her social life and job prospects and prohibited her from drinking alcohol and driving her motorbike. 'I freaked at that. Now it seemed everything had been taken from me, and here was something over which I had no choice, no control.' In a frenzy of rage and despair she took a razor and slashed her arms and

111

wrists and carved deep gashes across her face from ear to ear, so deep that her teeth jutted out through the wounds. Prompt, expert cosmetic surgical expertise have left her with only very fine hair-line scars, but inside the emotional wounds are slow to heal. 'I tell you honestly, it's only Fury [her vociferous, lively Rottweiler] keeps me out of prison.'

Although now committed to helping young offenders avoid becoming casualties, like she was, of the penal system and advising girls – while liaising with the probation service – how to communicate their needs and problems to the authorities, Josie still prides herself on being able to use violence to defend herself when necessary. 'I seriously disabled a man sexually recently when he was trying it on with me. I don't regret that. My breasts are not for arseholes – especially male ones!'

One night a strange woman brandishing a crowbar and sledgehammer came to her home, threatening to kill Josie for supposedly sleeping with her husband and ordering her to come out into the street and fight it out with her. 'The police came and I was dragged in, kept in the cells overnight and charged with inciting her behaviour!' Yet another salutary warning: the one with the record gets the rap. A reputation for crime and violence dies hard – especially for women. And perhaps more particularly one who, though strikingly attractive and friendly, keeps a Rottweiler, works out at home lifting a collection of heavy weights, sports fatigues and cropped hair, has a sharp tongue with a good line in salty invective and a fast, powerful left hook. One wonders for how much longer O'Dwyer must pay the high cost of refusing to conform? As I leave she invites me to a party, six months hence, to celebrate her ten years of freedom. 'I hope you don't mind, you'll be probably the only non criminal there, the other five coming are all ex-prisoners!'

Talk to enough young violent women who are or were once on the wrong side of the law, and you find that to get to the real person you must first induce them to allow you a glimpse of who is actually hiding behind that formidably impregnable, almost professionally cultivated public image. This, in Britain, is usually modelled on standard punk or skinhead lines: regulation bovver boots or Doc Martens, torn jeans, boilersuit or overall, cropped or near-shaven head and ear studs. In its contemptuous rejection of all society upholds as desirably feminine, the look is studied 'bull-dyke' to the point of caricature. Depending on how far they think they can trust you as a sympathetic and understanding listener, the dialogue veers from monosyllabic sullenness or sneering bellicosity to cheeky, cheery, rather bracingly cocksure, tough-talking bravado, liberally peppered with expletives. Yet both the air and look of menace are often entirely sham. Once relaxed and trusting enough to stop trying to shock or impress, hopelessness, despair and cynicism, about themselves and about the system, become impossible to hide.

But just how alike is the inner fantasy world of male and female psychopaths has been revealed in recent studies carried out by Dr Jeremy Coid, a forensic psychiatrist at St Bartholomew's Hospital in London who has interviewed at length over ninety females, many of them dangerous psychopaths, in England's maximum security prisons, including Broadmoor and Rampton. It is by now common knowledge that the classic profile of the psychopath reflects an individual whose anger, inadequacy, desire for revenge and lack of concern for the suffering of others compels them to seek enjoyment from dominating, torturing, raping and killing without guilt or remorse.

Although only a small number of women, compared to similar men, fall into the various categories of violent psychopathic personalities, those that do display very definite sexual arousal from acts of torture and killing, whether real or imaginary. These include highly aggressive, promiscuous girls who casually pick up unassertive ones for rough, sado-masochistic lesbian sex; they are always the dominant sexual partner, enjoy beating up their lovers and frequently threaten them with 'rape' by some weapon kept to hand as a substitute penis. Desire for a penis, so as to be able to rape 'like a man', is often a part of the sexual excitement of violence. The most violent among these women have a repertoire of well-rehearsed masturbatory fantasies involving highly sadistic sex that leads to violent murder of their partner during orgasm. Others can only become sexually aroused by the thought of killing, usually a woman or child, occasionally a man, and may be compelled to do so. One woman described a fantasy in which she kidnapped a child and turned into a man before raping it, then turned back into a woman as she stabbed and decapitated it. Obsessions with knives and fantasies of strangling, suffocating and stabbing children, old people, animals – anyone weaker than themselves – may heighten arousal. Fantasies and violence usually begin in adolescence, or slightly afterwards, although many of the women interviewed by Jeremy Coid admitted having played killing 'games' as children, in which they put plastic bags over the head of a doll or a pet dog or cat to suffocate it.

The group who most resemble men are those whose coldly detached description of their homicidal urges belies the excitement derived from them. 'The idea of killing is extremely arousing and sexually fulfilling. Each time they masturbate they reinforce that feeling of satisfaction, and may go on to act out the fantasy, targeting and hunting down suitable victims, abducting and trying to murder them,' says Jeremy Coid. Sometimes they succeed, sometimes the woman is caught before she kills. In the course of his research Dr Coid found that one schoolgirl narrowly escaped having her head smashed in by a brick after being lured into an alley by a female assailant. Another woman, who had spent many months thinking about how satisfying it would be to kill someone, finally broke into a café at night and hid, knife poised, waiting to strike. She managed to stab a watchman who arrived in response to the alarm. Even when sexual arousal is not connected with killing, the accompanying adrenalin 'rush' is sufficient to ensure that an assailant experiences a sense of power and achievement, momentarily boosting their self-esteem and discharging the burden of accumulated anger and tension.

What seems very likely is that these women, like their male counterparts, are in some way addicted to violence and sadism. In a recent pioneering study published in the *British Journal of Psychiatry* Dr Coid has identified a violent mood swing disorder, unique to women but unrelated to PMT, which may occur every few days causing extreme anger, anxiety, tension and a particular form of irritable depression. This syndrome could provide the clue to the impulsive, bizarrely erratic behaviour of many violent women who periodically self-injure, starve or binge eat, abuse alcohol or drugs, and whose destructive urge is so overwhelming precisely because it holds the promise of instantaneous gratification and a brief return to 'normality'.

Arson, for which the great majority of women are sent to maximum-secure units, carries just such a cathartic charge, often representing displaced anger that they cannot express any other way. Arsonists typically describe an almost ecstatic sexual arousal, which involves not only the genitals but permeates almost the entire body, that accompanies firesetting. In addition there is invariably a sense of power and control that begins with striking the match and seeing the speed with which the blaze takes hold, as well as its hypnotic colours and flickering shapes. What is crucial about these findings is the light they shed on women's sexual fantasies – 'perverted' or no – and the broad range of female destructive behaviours. Psychiatrists like Coid are struck by the facility with which women with such so-called psychopathic personality disorders may substitute one fantasy for another, since attacking a person or property appears to work as well as a form of release from tension as self-injury. Some crimes being harder to commit and more easily detectable than others, a woman may end up in Rampton for arson simply because she happened to be caught while in a 'firesetting phase', as Jeremy Coid calls it, rather than a 'walking around the streets with a carving knife phase'.

Incarcerated at Rampton after being shifted around from various detention centres and prisons, including Holloway, Sharon Boast, now 30, is serving three life sentences for offences that include serious assault, attempted murder, arson and aggravated burglary. Sharon briefly hit the headlines in 1993 during Beverley Allitt's trial, having allegedly formed a lesbian relationship with the child killer in Rampton. Described enthusiastically by Allitt in letters home as having a skinhead crop, being very muscular and very macho, Sharon Boast's criminal career began at 7, her offences becoming increasingly violent throughout her teens. Revealed at her trial in 1990 as having an 'untreatable psychopathic disorder', she fits Dr Jeremy Coid's disordered female personality profile to chilling perfection, with mood swings ranging from deep depression to the ecstatic joys of fire-setting. During her most destructive phase she drove a high-powered motorbike from which she would siphon petrol to start blazes, torching mainly factories, shops and other properties in and around Leicester, which she recorded in detail in her diary. At one textiles plant the damage she caused totalled £150,000. Described as a 'danger to life and limb' by Judge Michael Astill at her trial at Leicester Crown Court, Sharon Boast's alternating phases of emotional stability, rationality and razor-sharp intelligence followed by profound depression followed by uncontrollable anger and violence are a disturbing reminder of the similarly unpredictable personalities of dangerously violent men and women and the futility of trying to ascribe their behaviour to any simple basic cause.

The sense of a girl at constant bloody war with the world and with herself was never more painfully evident than in the hard-nosed, up-yours swagger of Sharon Boast: 'I wasn't never influenced by nobody, not even at seven. I was the one who started nickin' things and made them join me, it was you fuckin' well do it or else! I'd be out on the streets 'cos my old man was violent and beat me. I hated 'im – but when I got bigger I beat 'im back. I got put in borstal the first time for doin' a whole loada burglaries, criminal damage and loadsa fightin'. Yeah. I was just bored. Of course you get a thrill outta doin' all 'em fings. It's excitin, innit? I couldn't ever be a conformist in society, like just go to work every day, come 'ome and sit watchin' telly, day in day out. And I never worried about gettin' nicked. You just do a few years 'ere, a few more there. But this time it's life – that's a bit of a pisser, innit?'

Like Josie, Sharon eventually enjoyed, or perhaps resolved to enjoy her borstal days, probably because she got a kick – literally – out of meeting the challenge to survive, or be a loser.

'I was all right there, 'cos there's riots all the time. Lotsa fightin'. You just go for it, you don't need no excuse. You gotta prove no one can mess with ya and 'ope to get away with it. Then I got out again and back to burglaries, beatin' people up. I always liked 'avin fights. I like fightin' men, 'cos I fight 'em better, they fight properly, not like women, who just scratch and pull your hair – that ain't fightin'! And I've fought a lotta men and won too, that makes you feel good about yourself. Specially when you've 'ad a few drinks. You feel you could take on the world. When I was burgling and robbing I used to get pissed nearly every night, 'cos of all the money I was makin' at it. And you gotta 'ave something to spend it on, don't ya? I took some drugs, like blow [marijuana] and a bit of speed, but I was never into 'eroin. I mean, that's a mug's game, innit? I used to 'ang around with lotsa guys, they respected me, they never thought of me as female. I was one of the boys. 'Course, I do feel sorry for some of the violence I've done in the past, causin' pain to some people. But listen, I'm a psychopath and I ain't supposed to feel no remorse, am I? They say I'm untreatable – uncooperative and hostile. And most of the time that's fairly accurate. I am pretty 'ostile.'

There is no way, according to the ward manager in charge of Sharon's wing, that she can hope to be released from Rampton in the immediate future. This, apparently, is because of her extreme violence, incitement to others to behave similarly, and her excessively aggressive anti-establishment stance. In the words of her ward manager, 'Sharon is so antisocial and so extreme in everything she does, always needing to be in a position of power and control. Don't believe what she tells you about liking prison, wanting to go back to Holloway or Styal because of the fighting. She'd like to think she's top dog, but because she isn't, because there are others there who are tougher, fight harder and have more power and reputation. She can't take it, she gets more violent and uncontrollable because of her frustration and resentment. Despite her intelligence and articulacy, she'll never be able to live without being completely self-destructive until she can reach an inner compromise to be more pro-social.'

But who is going to help Sharon reach a greater inner understanding and encourage her to develop the skills whereby she can turn her aggressive energies to a less destructive end, without any loss of self-esteem or sense of being out of control of her life? One-to-one counselling or group therapy for people with problems like hers are rare. Sessions with psychotherapists and doctors are limited and infrequent, often centred principally on discussing the inmate's drug regime. And the drugs, says Sharon, echoing Josie's memories of Holloway's CI psychiatric 'muppet wing' (see chapter 1), just space you out, numbing you and making you doubt your sanity. 'In prison they punch you in the 'ead, 'ere they just use violence inside your 'ead. They 'ave to use drugs, 'cos we're mental patients. I'm on Tegretol to stop my mood swings, but it doesn't work.'

Another woman on Sharon's ward, Marybeth, who is here for having set light to a friend's flat while drunk and completely destroying it, agrees that prison is a doddle compared to a closed hospital with its reliance on psychiatric drug treatment. 'Compared to prison screws, the nurses are a bunch of bitches. They just want to drug you up all the time. There's no sense of caring. Largactil, Paragol – you feel drowsy all the time, you sleep a lot. For a while I was on all of them. Then I came off them and got all agitated and tense [a commonly accepted symptom of withdrawal from psychotropic drugs]. Look, although I didn't regret what I did at the time, I know what I did was pretty dangerous and I'd never do it again, no way. I just want to get out and find a job and try and build my life up again. Therapy? That's a joke. I'm supposed to be seeing one next week and I've been here just over a year and haven't seen a single psychologist! There's so many people here and so few psychologists on the staff, that you get nothing in the way of counselling.'

Nor, as is commonly the complaint among women prisoners, is there anything in the way of hobbies, physical workouts and training or creative self-expression available to encourage women who don't fit the female stereotype to discover a positive, empowering route to understanding their internal conflicts and learning to modify their behaviour without the threat of losing self-esteem. Josie O'Dwyer provides an insight into the reasoning behind this: 'At one stage after I'd gone on the rampage and broken an officer's nose, the governor's instructions were that I was to be allowed an hour's gym and circuit training every day. After about two weeks the officers complained that I was getting too strong and fit and would therefore be harder

to manage, so my gym was curtailed.' Occupations such as car-
pentry and decorating, which Marybeth wants to learn, are only
available to more 'stable' inmates living a semi-unrestricted
existence in another section of the hospital. No wonder Sharon
would rather be in the nick – fighting is one way at least of
discharging pent-up aggressive energy. 'I need something to use
up my energies and give me something to concentrate on that
I might do one day when I'm let out. Like I'd love to do sports,
or work out in the gym, but it's the men, not the women, who
are encouraged to do that. I'd like to do a physical job like
gardening or cementing, but I wouldn't be trusted in the garden,
and they don't want no woman doin' the cementin'. It's takin
the piss, ain't it, expectin' a woman to sit all day in one room
sewin' and knittin'? Look, I know it'll be about twenty years
before I'm free again. Go back to society? I'd 'ave to calm down
before I get too old to be active! But I'm never goin' to become
a strict conformist. No way. And so I'll never get a chance out
there, will I? I think in the end I'll still be robbin' and that when
I'm about sixty. That's if I'm outta the nick!'

This sums up the most painful dilemma for any woman who
has got herself into trouble by kicking out too violently against
life's perceived inequities, reacting too viciously in a bid to buck
the system and refusing to compromise in asserting her own
identity: finally, having been processed by the penal system, do
you give in and conform, trying (like Josie O'Dwyer) to mend
the damage that comes from years of criminal stigmatization
and social isolation? And if so, how do you avoid the temptation
of falling back on familiar patterns? Many women who congre-
gate at CLEAN BREAK, the London-based organization set up
by and for former female prisoners and anyone formerly
involved in the penal system to provide advice and help with
housing, welfare and employment, as well as offering opportunities for creative projects like writing and producing plays,
emphasize that resuming a productive life is only possible
through some sort of 'safety net' like this. Given such a 'safe
haven', damaged individuals can begin to restructure their lives
and attempt to integrate into the community, reinforcing the
possibility of a future life free from crime.

Kim, who was once at Rampton and now writes poetry, is loath to underestimate the power trip that came from being recognized as a fighter – especially at school – and as a fighter who won, even against the boys. 'But I made enemies. And I discovered in the end I'd rather have friends. For a long time I was very wrapped up being this tough, naughty person that I actually deep down didn't really want to be. It became a matter of breaking away from my environment. My brothers were all violent, we were all violent with one another, and I sought out people like that in my teens. Once outside school, that behaviour stopped.

'I still shout a lot and get angry, but because I don't live near my family or my old friends, with whom I got up to no good, I've stopped getting into violent situations on purpose or setting them up. I got involved with violent men too, who would beat me – even though I beat them back. But I recognized that as part of a whole pattern of searching out violence, which I wanted to let go of in the end. A quieter life came from really wanting to change. I don't want to be around violent people any more, fighting to prove myself. I've done it. Now I'd like to know I can be somebody without having to do it by beating people up.'

Susan was in prison when a friend started having an affair with her boyfriend. After she was released, she picked a fight with the girl, who slashed Susan's face with a knife. 'We ended up both getting nicked, but she pressed charges for assault and I got six months on remand. We were both eighteen. A lot of my instinct to fight as a kid came from being bullied at school, often due to racism. So my violence was largely self-defence, teaching others not to bother trying it on or they'd end up hurt. But when she sliced me on the face, something just snapped in me and I started going around looking everywhere for fights. If someone gave me the hump, I'd just slap 'em! But I guess I've grown up. I'm twenty-three now and if I don't like someone I just tell 'em. I don't feel I have to prove anything any longer.'

Much of this 'quietening down' could be attributed to age – the transition from turbulent puberty and teenage rebellion to more confident maturity is generally marked, for males and females, by the acquisition of interpersonal skills and the building of secure relationships – as well as escaping a home environment made tense by constant violence and abuse, or alcoholism and drug taking, or a community atmosphere poisoned by racism and crime. Liz, who grew up in mixed ethnic communities in London's Ladbroke Grove and Wembley, was the constant target of racist attacks and bullying at school. 'All through my early teens I was quiet and retiring, because I'd constantly been stamped on, suffering racial abuse and bullying at the Catholic school I went to. I soon found out that if you fought back, you stopped being victimized – but as I got older I realized if I went on being violent it would get me into terribly serious trouble. But it still wasn't easy to stop. It's like a fever, or a drug. I'd fight men or women, I'd pick on anyone. I'd just lash out, and immediately I'd feel better, less aggrieved. Violence works. The problem is that I'm not scared of violence and aggression, and that's dangerous, because you lay yourself wide open to fighting.

'In the end, the only thing that changed me was having my first child. I knew if I got caught again I'd go to prison, so I stopped. But it was very difficult. The last time I attacked someone was a woman traveller who was racist and punched my 4-year-old daughter in the nose, making her bleed. So I beat her up and knocked all her teeth out. I still regret doing it, but years ago I wouldn't have. I'd have hounded her to give her more!

'I'm aware all the time of having to hold back my natural instinct to fight. All my family were violent and heavy drinkers. I constantly fought with my sister. And growing up mixed race doesn't help in certain communities. But I think what age and responsibility as a parent gives you is a sense of control and perspective. If I ever saw my son being violent to girls it would upset me terribly, but because of how I've tried to bring him up I don't think it'll happen. And my daughter now studies karate. That way I hope she'll really learn to defend herself properly.'

What seems clear is that for many girls who are naturally aggressive and violent and who pursue a very early life of crime, the discovery that there are *alternative* ways of cultivating self-worth and gaining control of one's life, though in no way simple and immediate solutions, can amount to the opening up of a new life, the birth of an alternative self for which they will gladly trade in their old fist-clenched persona. But such a metamorphosis is only ever possible provided sufficient support and guidance exists within their immediate environment or adequate opportunities are offered by the community to help a woman acquire the self-respect, interpersonal skills and feedback necessary to piece together her damaged psyche and heal her battered, fragmented ego. The alternative is to remain forever self-defensively 'on the kill', caught in the revolving door of crime.

Gang Girls – Survival of the Strongest

For some women, the adverse circumstances in which their early lives unfold may be such that they can only arrive at a point where it is possible to gain attention, let alone seek help and guidance, by first embarking on a criminal pathway, which evokes tragic echoes of the old theory of falling so low that there is nowhere else to go but up. Perverse as it sounds, there are some American researchers who have begun to define young female criminals and delinquents as the lucky ones, the survivors rather than the victims and losers of society. Robin Robinson of Rutgers University, who has interviewed a large number of female teenage offenders held on probation for crimes ranging from under-age prostitution to assault, car theft, attempted homicide and drug abuse, concludes that by their very actions, even if entirely by default, they have proven something of extreme value to themselves. Robinson interprets fighting and crime as an unconscious strategy, described by psychologist Albert Hershman as using 'voice' in order to speak up about one's suffering and thereby gain some power and control over one's life.

'Abused or neglected kids may simply withdraw into themselves, remaining silent about their experiences, unable to ask or demand alternatives to their present existence. They effectively exit from their environment and usually end up developing depressive illnesses, self-destructive behaviour and psychoses,' says Robinson. Having talked to girls in their teens who have spent years in and out of the courts and detention centres for delinquent behaviour, she was struck by how often they deliberately drew attention to themselves while committing offences such as theft, as if hoping to be noticed and caught. 'These girls are often trying very hard to get into the system, not escape it, because the alternative, being in a violent home with an abusive parent or boyfriend, or on the streets, has become too unbearable. They know, especially those who have been in and out of the child welfare system, that if you are just a kid out in the street you don't get much in the way of real lasting help, so they purposely escalate their delinquent activities in order to qualify for better services. The girls I see in the probation services are in fact the strongest, because they've done something to draw attention to themselves and their situation. The weak ones are those with personality disorders, who internalize the abuse and withdraw. We get the feisty ones who fight back.'

That most traditionally macho of all social groups, the delinquent teenage gang is, for increasing numbers of girls, proving to be a beguiling alternative to the misery of roaming the streets alone in frightened or desperate isolation or of remaining a prisoner in a violent or restrictive family home. Anne Campbell's research into the different modes of fighting tactics between schoolgirls, borstal girls and prisoners (as described in chapter 1) shows the extent to which girl gangs are proliferating in certain inner cities such as London, Glasgow and Liverpool. While all-male gangs were a hot topic of research in the 1950s, all the evidence at that time was that those girls who did 'tag on' to groups of boys fulfilled for the most part very stereotypical feminine roles, go-along groupies who incited the males to violent fights or crimes, or 'crumpet' valued only for their sexual favours. Only now, in the 1990s, have all-girl gangs, or male–female gangs whose members have near-equal status, become a new focus for attention, both in this country and in America.

Today's young girl gang member is far less likely than her mother to be a mere bit-player in an all-male drama, as was the case in the 1950s and 1960s. Not surprisingly, girl gangs are now almost certainly likely to be members of poor, mainly black or Hispanic communities, drawn together, like the women involved in drug dealing and distribution, by a common bond of poverty, a background of abusive early family life which they escaped while very young, or a culture of violence into which they were initiated by brothers, uncles and other relatives at an early age so that bonding with a gang, through the shared vocabulary of violence, has become a natural way of life while growing up.

Culture and race still tend to determine how much independence and autonomy a girl may have if she joins a principally male gang. In Los Angeles, where girls have been members of traditional Chicano gangs since the 1930s, Mexican–American females, especially from 'respectable' families, are expected to conform to traditionally subservient, domestic roles. It is usually because of addiction to heroin that *tecatas* – female heroin addicts – are drawn to a *chola* career in a gang, usually related to drug abuse and drug-related crime. Because of the stigma associated with gang membership, and their tendency to be exploited and dominated by male members of the group, until now the average Chicano girl gang member has lacked independence and autonomy. However, according to the Los Angeles Police Department, since the late 1980s there has been a threefold increase in the number of Hispanic girl gang members, a phenomenon attributed to the increasing accessibility of guns.

At present there are 1,000 gangs in the Los Angeles area, with 150,000 members, of which 10,000 are women. According to one senior woman police officer, Deputy Holly Perez, who has been extensively involved in combating gang-related crime, they are more vicious than the men, tending to commit more brutal assaults such as kidnapping, knifing or shooting their victims as much to obtain money for drugs as for the price of the latest hot fashion item. The most recent terror tactic is 'jacking': holding up someone driving a new and expensive car, shooting or stabbing them, dragging them out of the vehicle and taking the car and selling the parts. According to Deputy Perez, there are also more girls, or their children, getting shot, so they set out deliberately seeking retribution. In status-conscious California, schools such as LA's Lennox High now employ special security officials, usually themselves members of the local community, whose job is to crack down on 'gang-related' clothing in order to de-glamourize and de-mythologize gangstership generally. Girls or boys are immediately sent home to change if seen wearing over-large clothing or anything bearing a gang 'logo'.

In Chicago, another city whose history of gangs, mainly male-dominated, goes back to the 1920s, there are signs that women's membership is not only increasing but that they have become more independent, violent and more highly integrated into traditional crimes and warfare. Today, ever increasing numbers of young black girls have formed their own autonomous single-sex gangs, whose reputation for violence and concern with maintaining peer-group status is as formidable as that of their male counterparts. For example, the thirty-strong Vice Queens, of Chicago's lower-class West Side, may be an auxiliary to the Vice Kings, but this doesn't make their 'code' any laxer or their tactics any less ruthlessly aggressive or fearless. Perhaps this is because the nexus that links the Vice Queen members, aged mostly 13 to 19, is not only poverty but a sense of collective self-protection against the threat of undesirable male domination and violence.

Less rigidly hierarchical in structure than men's gangs, leaders of all-female gangs tend to be self-appointed, on the basis of one girl stepping into a particular confrontation or situation where she proves her leadership qualities by her authority, assertiveness or capacity to fight and dominate her opponents, so earning her status in the group as a result of her achievements. Unlike the gang 'molls' of previous decades, girls like the Vice Queens avoid sexual promiscuity and prostitution, sometimes forming lesbian relationships as a safe option. Like the boys, they become involved in relatively minor crimes such as robberies, purse-snatching, car thefts or ganging up in twos and threes and 'strong-arming' a victim into giving up their money or possessions. Ever resourceful, the women have devised flexible packages of hustling activities for maximum economic gain so as not to limit the scope of their activities and run the risk of getting caught.

Yet since a major dynamic behind any gang's *raison d'être* is simply aggro for aggro's sake – drinking, conflict and fighting – it isn't surprising that peer group status among the girls is now increasingly founded on how well they can fight. Laura Fishman, who has studied the activities of Chicago gangs from the 1960s to the present day, found that the reputation of a female gang member depends on her ability to fight like a man, using her fists. According to one observer, the girls may even fight tougher than the boys. 'They try to specialize in one punch knockouts. They get their balance just like a man would get his and they have nice left jabs. They can almost throw them better than the boys. The boys have a tendency to hook their jabs, which is very ineffective, while the girls throw their jabs right from the shoulder.'

Fighting other gangs is a dynamic used to maintain group loyalty and bolster a sense of solidarity between members. Fights rarely occur over personal grievances, but rather to enhance and confirm the group's reputation for toughness. Moreover, girls like the Vice Queens will fight anyone, male or female, and in any location – street, party, at the movies – when a dispute arises over an issue of loyalty or integrity concerning anyone in the gang. According to one local youth worker, the Queens 'have been known to jump on policemen . . . they weren't scared of nobody. They would jump on sober adults, they were that strong.' Not surprisingly, emboldened by the knowledge that they do fight as well as men and that they can defend themselves in the streets, whether against the police, potential sexual assailants or other thugs, their self-confidence boosted by their reputation for toughness, girls such as these – whose counterparts can be increasingly observed in inner-city ghettos throughout America – represent a new tough breed, determined to be survivors, not victims, whose capacity to adapt to apparently inescapable hardship has been very largely determined by their ability to adopt more aggressively uncompromising attitudes and violent forms of behaviour through sheer force of necessity.

On the plus side, it is impossible to overlook the empowerment, pride and confidence evidently gained by women who have taken control of their lives, as much by their wits as by their fists. That they are more likely, as men do, to gravitate from 'gangstership' to a life of serious violent crime is one of the more tragic, yet seemingly inevitable, by-products of this adaptation process. The one would not perhaps be possible without the other. It is often only through extreme violence and lawlessness that survival is possible for some. Without doubt that makes them criminals – but it doesn't diminish their status as survivors. If the new female criminal does exist, then she is a woman who is prepared to fight for herself.

4

In Cold Blood

A Woman's Touch

To *aficionados* of true-life tales of the grotesque and gruesome, the mere mention of certain dates, names and locations is sufficient to send shudders up the spine and flood the mind with images too nauseating ever to dwell upon. In the French town of Le Mans and its surrounding neighbourhood, the name 'Lancelin' still has the power to inspire just such a chilling *frisson* of horror in many an older resident. So gruesome was 'L'Affaire Lancelin' that it not only horrified all of pre-war France but was so widely reported as to grip the imagination of much of the world. When the police broke into the Lancelin home, at the request of a worried Monsieur Lancelin who had been unsuccessfully trying to contact his wife and daughter, the sight that greeted them could be counted on to haunt the rest of their waking and resting hours. Near the top of the hall staircase the first object they came across was a detached human eye. On the first-floor landing, lying at grotesquely twisted angles, were what appeared to be two life-size, mangled, crushed dolls, their heads by one account resembling 'blood puddings'. The face of what remained of Madame Lancelin no longer possessed any identifiable features; one of her eyes was found lying in the corner of the hall; there was nothing remaining that could pass for a mouth, all her teeth having been knocked out. One of the daughter's teeth had been pegged into her own scalp. Their fingernails were ripped out, their underwear pulled down and the flesh of their buttocks and thighs covered in a deep crosshatch of slashes. Their skulls had been virtually mashed to pulp. The walls and doors were splashed with blood almost up to the ceiling, the carpet reportedly so blood-soaked it resembled and felt like red moss. A battered pewter pitcher, a carving knife and a hammer were immediately identified as the murder weapons and the murderers – two servant girls, the Papin sisters, who had long held grudges against their employers – were led from their shared bed, which appeared to have been the scene of an incestuous relationship, and taken into custody.

Although the trial lasted a mere twenty-six hours, in which no adequate report of the girls' mental condition was presented, it emerged that the elder girl, outspoken, naturally violent and dominating, who exerted total power over her quiet, demure younger sister, had masterminded the massacre. The younger admitted freely that when told to she had torn out the women's eyes with her own bare fingers, adding with evident pride that it was she too who had 'done the slicing up'. It was the only case in criminal history where eyeballs had been removed from a living head without the use of an instrument.

Another more recent case, also in France, involved the frenzied, murderous assault on 45-year-old Colette Vail, a small, friendly, mentally retarded woman with numerous acquaintances who would visit and chat to her, amused by her penchant for wearing men's clothes. From the moment the Dieppe police surveyed the evident sexual and sadistic nature of the crime they were convinced they were dealing with a sexual psychopath of the most vicious and dangerous variety. The body was spreadeagled on the bloodsoaked bed, virtually naked, a gigantic Z-shaped knife wound slashed deep across her breasts, a crisscross of further deep cuts in the pattern of a chessboard covering the area between pubic bone and navel, and a Remy Martin cognac bottle rammed to almost its entire length into her vagina, rupturing the membrane walls and penetrating the intestinal cavity, probably while she was still alive according to the report. Her head had been smashed in.

What really mystified the investigators were the deep bruises on her arms where she had been pinned down while being assaulted. This made for a double mystery: no man, no matter how largely built or powerful, could possibly hold down a struggling victim with both hands and at the same time carry out sexual assaults of this type. Second was the fact that psychologists claim sexual psychopaths usually act alone. It was over eighteen months before the two defendants were finally caught and put on trial.

Delicate, pretty Patricia Nalais, half French, half North African and just 5-foot tall, had a history of violence going back to her early teens when she was thrown out of school for cutting up her fellow pupils with a knife. Having moved in with her first boyfriend, a gangster, at the age of fourteen, the first time he hit her she stuck the seven-inch switchblade that she always carried on her between his ribs. He survived but thought better of reporting the attack lest he should end up being charged for having sexual relations with a minor.

Several years later, Patricia met Gisèle Poulain, a 6-foot giantess with the muscles of a rugby centre-forward, who turned out to be an ideal playmate and confrère in petty crime and rabble-rousing. Gisèle was one of the most feared and respected bar-room brawlers in Dieppe. Blessed with powerful fists and feet and a readiness to fight dirty, which had also got her expelled from school, she had no need to carry a knife. Both girls had known Colette Vail, but neither could explain why they had tortured, sexually assaulted and beaten her to death. They made no attempt to defend themselves, saying only that they had come there originally with the intention of stealing a few francs.

That the vast majority of murders are committed by men goes without question. Save for child murders, which are carried out by an almost equal percentage of men and women, women are responsible for only about 12 per cent of all reported homicide. Also, it is a general conception that when women kill they tend to go about it in an altogether more civilized manner. Whilst men have a notorious tendency for brutal 'overkill', stabbing women in particular with an inexplicable savagery and force, sometimes going on to rip apart, torture, mutilate, dismember or disfigure their victims in an orgy of violence and for no apparent reason other than the sheer enjoyment of it, women – it is said – employ subtlety and restraint, killing with economy of force, perhaps because there is less frenetic anger spurring them on to more sadistic acts. Why shoot a man thirty times when one or maybe two well-aimed shots, straight through the heart or head, will do? Why all the mess of hacking, stabbing and gouging when a little judicious use of poison or a sleeping draught to put the victim out first will make the job all so much easier?

Best of all, why not keep your own hands clean and hire or cajole a hit man to do the dirty job for you? Like Maria Spence, who drove 236 miles with her former lover's mutilated body hidden in a wardrobe in the back of a van looking for a dumping site, after arranging for a male friend to beat, stab and crush him to death. Or Noeleen Hendley, whose ardent Catholicism prohibited her from seeking a divorce in order to marry her lover, but failed to deter her from paying out £5,000 for an amateur hit man to batter her spouse to death with a rolling pin and, for good measure, to punch her in the face to make the attack appear like an aggravated burglary. Had she known that even though hers was not the hand that slew her husband she would in the end still be sentenced to life imprisonment, she might have regarded this as a less than ideal way out of her marriage.

Any second thoughts, however, are more likely to revolve around their own fate rather than that of their cornered, unsuspecting victims. That much seems evident from the impassive attitude and breathtaking capacity for lying with conviction in court shown by Florence Samarasinha and Sandra Wignall, each convicted within weeks of the other in late 1993 at the Old Bailey for the murder of their husbands. In the case of Samarasinha, a senior local government officer, numbers of witnesses testified that she had asked them repeatedly and openly for help in hiring a contract killer. Weeks later, Nimal Samarasinha was found dead outside his home with one single stab wound through his heart – the mark of a professional hit man. Perhaps crueller and more treacherous, because of the nature of the trap, was Sandra Wignall's ruse of taking her recently wed husband into the woods ostensibly to feed foxes then disarming him with kisses, cuddles and oral sex while her lover and another accomplice overpowered and stabbed him to death. Wignall later sobbed to police that she and her husband had been attacked by muggers. Neither woman has admitted murder, yet in both cases any lack of courage to deal the actual death blow was amply compensated for by hatred, greed and absence of pity.

The image of the 'lady' killer, resourceful in devising the recipe for a perfect murder, ingenious and stealthy in its execution, owes more to Victorian melodrama and the gangster films of the 1940s than it does to the reality of modern women's existence, the increasing availability of weaponry (especially in America) once exclusively used by men and their skill in using this weaponry. And while restraint may be a characteristic of many domestic crimes committed by women, having heard of an American woman who eventually murdered her brutal boy-friend after embarking on a gruelling weight-training course in order to cultivate sufficient strength to strangle him and then hack up his body to facilitate its disposal, I'm not so sure how well this theory holds up.

Indeed, all the evidence today suggests that women who kill, whether in the heat of passion or in cold blood, may do so with as much sadistic savagery and overkill as any man. Two cases, again in France, demonstrate this. The first involved 45-year-old Jacqueline Carlot, who became so obsessed that her husband was about to commit incest with their daughter that she decided to drug his pineapple juice. Once he had passed out, she bludg-eoned his brain in with a lead pipe, stabbed him in the heart, dismembered his body in the bath with a butcher's saw, then boiled his head in a casserole to remove all identifiable features before placing it in the freezer prior to burial. The other woman whose crime kept all of France and half the world in horror-struck suspense during her trial was Simone Weber, the infa-mous 'she-devil' of Nancy, a tiny 60-year-old jilted mistress who expertly managed to operate a massive concrete chain saw, slicing her lover's body into segments which she then disposed of in the river and around the countryside.

Two other cases of equal brutality – all the more repellent given the extreme youth of the offenders – demonstrate the extremes of savagery to which women are able to go. Tammy Carr, a 15-year-old schoolgirl from Castle Bromwich, was found guilty of manslaughter on the grounds of provocation of 14-year-old Lisa Greenway in a 'gang' fight that went tragically out of control. Tammy, her 14-year-old sister and their father Daniel Carr, who reportedly goaded the girls into attacking their victim, grabbed Lisa Greenway and began punching and kicking her, then Tammy viciously plunged a steak knife into her eight times, ramming it into the girl's body so hard that the knife broke off when lodged in her back. As she lay dying from the knife wounds, one girl sat astride her while the other repeatedly kicked her in the face. Lisa died shortly afterwards in hospital.

A few months later two young Welsh girls, Maria Rossi and Christina Molloy, both 18, were declared by Mr Justice Scott Baker to be 'evil products of the modern age' and imprisoned indefinitely for the murder of 70-year-old spinster Edna Phillips. In this case the word murder fails to do full justice to the horrific carnage perpetrated by the girls on their victim, making this, in the words of Chief Inspector Reg Briggs of the South Wales Serious Crimes Squad, 'one of the most horrific crimes I have ever investigated'. Their long-standing record of delinquency – both came from broken homes and were sexually promiscuous, heavy alcohol and drug users and criminal offenders since the age of 11 – had made them notoriously feared in the community, not least by their long-suffering neighbour Edna Phillips, whose home they regularly vandalized, pelting eggs at her windows, smearing excrement over the panes and abusing her with foul language.

The bond between the two girls, whose parents had long given up any attempt to discipline them, strengthened as they became regularly turned on by drugs and violence. Each spurred the other on to new 'highs' of destructiveness, culminating in the fiendish torture and murder of the frail, near-blind pensioner. Having long singled her out as an easy target to bully and terrorize, in July 1992 they attacked her in her home after a drinking binge, strangling her with a dog chain, using a Stanley knife, broken glass and scissors to stab, gouge and mutilate her almost beyond recognition. Having criss-crossed her face with thirty-six slash wounds, stabbed her in the chest thirty times, broken her nose and five ribs, punctured her lung, battered her over the head and carved a crescent-shaped incision around her forehead, akin to scalping, they broke eggs over her mangled body and smeared the walls of her home with her blood and fragments of flesh before leaving triumphant, taking with them her vacuum cleaner, a radio and some money.

The next day, Maria Rossi's mother heard her singing gleefully 'We've killed Edna' to a tune from the *Wizard of Oz*, her demeanour calm, cool and unrepentant. Both girls were arrested that day, eventually pleading guilty. After they were sentenced, Chief Inspector Briggs commented: 'Over the years I have investigated numerous murders, but this has got to be the worst one. There were such horrific injuries and it is indeed sad to see a gentle old lady being murdered in such a manner. It is also sad to see that two young girls have committed this offence and yet show no remorse whatsoever.'

As with many brutal crimes committed by young boys, when girls embark on such killing 'sprees', it is almost always in groups of two or more, testifying to the contagious nature of violence, especially among youngsters. The conviction of two 11-year-old boys for the hideous, motiveless slaughter of 2-year-old Jamie Bulger in Liverpool finally rammed home this terrifying truth to a disbelieving and horrified world. Criminal experts believe that crimes such as the torture and killing of Edna Phillips are far less likely to be committed by a young person acting alone, whether male or female. A great part of the violent impetus is generated by peer pressure and 'winding up', in which the 'ringleader' becomes increasingly crazed and violent, determined to show off and prove their daring, as a result of being alternately incited to attack and praised for it. More hesitant, yet malleable members of the group, too unassertive to influence the course of action, are easily coerced, goaded or threatened into participating in the crime as much through fear as the desire for acceptance by their peers. The kick of violence, therefore, perhaps lies less in daring and doing as in being seen to dare and do. Which is undoubtedly why three Asian schoolgirls in Oldham ganged together to attack 81-year-old 5-foot tall Kathleen Kershaw in a subway, thumping her in the back, knocking her to the ground, breaking her hip and taking her pension book after rifling through her handbag, leaving her bleeding on the ground despite her pleas for mercy.

We delude ourselves if we really believe women's cruelty or ability to revel in gratuitous violence to be any less than men's. The extent to which women have proved their ability to add a sickening twist of inventiveness to their attacks on others, such as the Ohio teenager who, having robbed an octogenarian threw his artificial legs out of reach before making her getaway, or the 22-year-old London girl jailed for blackmailing a blind man by threatening to poison his guide dog, is surely the most chilling fact we are forced to confront.

Where a gang is made up of both sexes, the pressure on the girls to display bravado may be even greater, even if they themselves do not commit the worst atrocities. When two teenage boys and a girl set upon 41-year-old Shashikant Gondalika in August 1992, following him home from a pub and breaking into his flat, it was the boys who inflicted the foulest torture, the girl who watched and encouraged them as they coldbloodedly tied him up with electrical flex, cut him with a knife, whipped him as they demanded more money, burned his back, chest and face with a hot iron and then poured salt and bleach into the wounds. As Gondalike finally passed out in excruciating pain, he heard the girl ask calmly: 'Is he dead?' Later at their trial, the boys, aged 14 and 19, were sentenced respectively to three and nine years youth custody, while the girl, whose presence alone, according to the judge, merited a custodial sentence, was detained for nine months.

Evidence presented at the trial for murder of four men and two women who kidnapped 16-year-old Suzanne Capper in December 1992 and, over a period of a week, took turns to ritually and brutally torture her before burning her alive, reveals to what extent alcohol and drugs can stoke levels of violence to a fever pitch, even where a group consists of adults in their twenties. In transcripts of taped interviews read out in court, it emerged that 24-year-old mother of three Bernadette McNeilly, one of the gang, repeatedly laughed at the injuries she inflicted with the help of another mother, 26-year-old Jean Powell, when even the men held back. These included beatings, scrubbing Suzanne's lacerated body in the bath with neat disinfectant, ordering her teeth to be extracted and injecting her with speed. At the end it was a giggling McNeilly who assisted in the final act of horror when Suzanne was bundled into the boot of a car, driven into the countryside, pushed down a bank, doused in petrol and set alight. When finally discovered by the roadside with 70–85 per cent burns, Suzanne was identifiable only by her fingerprints, and died four days later in hospital.

Another devastating example of the ferocity with which girls operating in pairs or cliques can coldly plan, plot and finally strike in concert was shown recently in America by the grisly torture and killing of 12-year-old Shanda Renee Sharer in the small Bible-belt town of Madison, Indiana. This nightmarish case produces a heightened *frisson* of disbelief because of what remain shocking taboos, even in the sphere of female crime: lesbianism, sexual assault, sadism, lack of remorse and pity – and the sheer animal brutality and venomous hatred characterizing the behaviour of the criminals. Today, after a sensational murder trial, 16-year-old Melinda Loveless and 17-year-old Laurie Tackett, both self-confessed lesbians, along with their chum 16-year-old Hope Rippey, are behind bars beginning sixty-year sentences (of which they will probably serve thirty) while a fourth girl is serving twenty years for having been an inactive participant at the murder. Much as the defence tried to prove that the girls were traumatized by early sexual molestation and abuse, supposedly at the root of each girl's borderline personality disorder, in the end, given the elaborate and calculated planning that went into the abduction, torture and slaying of the victim by Loveless and Tackett, there could be no sentence other than life imprisonment. There are many in America, especially in this conservative, God-fearing part of the United States, who believe they should have received the death penalty.

Although only 12 at the time of her murder, Shanda Renee Sharer became Melinda Loveless's most hated enemy when she was rumoured to be 'dating' Loveless's girlfriend, Amanda Heverin. For this crime, Loveless swore Sharer would pay with her life. Together with Laurie Tackett – according to one crime reporter 'a girl who never showed any emotion and was pretty cool about the whole episode' – she planned to lure the hapless Sharer away from her father's home, nearly fifty miles away from Madison where she herself and her friends lived and went to school, and then drive back to their neighbourhood to carry out the assault. Having enticed her from the house, the four girls drove some way with the child then proceeded to subject her to a horrific ordeal of torture, lasting several hours. They forced Renee to strip off her clothes, then sexually assaulted her, slashed her legs and choked her with a cord until she passed out. She was then bundled into the car boot as the girls drove on, debating what next to do with her. From time to time as Renee regained consciousness she would bang on the boot lid in panic, attempting to get out. Each time this happened either Loveless or Tackett stopped the car and struck her over the head with a car jack, knocking her senseless again. Finally they saturated her body with petrol and set her alight, burning her alive.

Whether the massacre shows, as psychiatrists giving evidence for the defence have tried to maintain, what can happen when formerly traumatized children over-invest their emotions in someone they become attached to and then discover that the object of their affection does not fulfil their expectations, thus inspiring extreme hated in place of love, is highly debatable – and simplistic. Melinda Loveless's father, who allegedly molested her two sisters and, it is suggested, her too, is now in custody awaiting trial. But claims of abuse from the other defendants proved largely inconclusive. None of the girls, all of whom were white, was involved in drug-taking or alcohol abuse. Three came from 'respectable' working-class families, one from a more affluent middle-class background, so the usual theories of inner-city deprivation were entirely absent in this case, although Loveless was said to be academically 'backward'. Could it simply be that the two ringleaders in particular gained a horrendously perverse, unexpected enjoyment from the idea of masterminding and executing their plan of revenge, and having once embarked on their orgy of destruction were both unwilling and unable to stop? If, as American criminologist

James Fox maintains, the exhilaration and pleasure derived from killing stems from absolute control over others, and that each 'high' resulting from the act of killing increases the willingness to kill again, then it may be lucky for the Madison Four, and certainly for those with whom they would otherwise come into contact, that they are to remain behind bars for most of their lives.

Even a brief glance at the history of homicide shows that there has been no shortage of female protagonists, not least within the sphere of political intrigue and upheaval. From the murderous machinations of Lucrezia Borgia, the cunning duplicity of Charlotte Corday and the revolutionary zeal of Sophia Perovskaya, who helped plan the unsuccessful assassination attempt on Tsar Alexander II, right up to the unnamed member of the women's wing of Sri Lanka's Liberation Tigers of Tamil Eelam, the so-called 'Tamil Tigresses', who assassinated Rajiv Gandhi, blowing herself up in the act with true fanatical dedication to the cause, there is sufficient evidence to suggest that while women may not kill in anything near as many numbers as men, when they *do* their commitment and determination may equal, if not exceed, that of any man.

According to Professor David Canter, Britain's leading expert on criminal profiling, in any study of predatory crime and premeditated murder there is little to distinguish between killers of either sex when it comes to the underlying motives of revenge, anger, hatred and the deeply ingrained need to wield total power and control over others. In both men and women, cruelty and sadism are likely to reflect a deep lifelong inner sense of inadequacy, resulting in lack of power or control in their own lives, which can only be assuaged, momentarily, by attempts to dominate and destroy those who are fundamentally weaker and thus unable to defend themselves. A problem of our society, according to Professor Canter, is that while this 'male model' of violent crime and murder is accepted because it fits into the familiar culture of male violence, albeit as its most extreme and deplorable manifestation, women who act in a similarly brutal fashion cannot be placed into any such understandable or traditional context and hence will be defined as totally aberrant or deranged.

For instance, if a group of men, rather than women, from Charles Manson's 'family' had slaughtered Sharon Tate and her friends and, a day later, Leno and Rosemary La Bianca, would the world have been so prepared to buy the theory that they only did it because they were pathetically weak-willed, brainwashed drug addicts, entirely manipulated and dominated by Manson, whom they believed to be God? Almost certainly not. Nor, as it happened, did the jury buy the 'robot' theory, in which the defence argued that Susan Atkins, Patricia Kerenwinkel and Leslie Van Houten could not be convicted of first degree murder since they only carried out Manson's orders. In his summing up for the defence, Mr Maxwell Keith, acting on behalf of Leslie Van Houten, observed that: 'These girls can't be guilty . . . Those are thinking man's crimes. You have to sit down, talk about it and make up your mind. These defendants had no minds . . . I seriously doubt whether they could harbour malice aforethought.'

Nevertheless, all three women, who had already confessed to helping to plan, initiate and carry out the slayings, were convicted of murder and sentenced to life imprisonment without parole. Linda Kasabian, Manson's former girlfriend whose idea it originally was to commit the Tate murders and who was therefore also at first charged with murder and criminal conspiracy, escaped trial only because she agreed to testify against Manson and the other defendants and was in turn granted immunity by the prosecution. The fact that the women did indeed seem to be robotic and devoid of real emotion, with not one iota of remorse at having perpetrated such blood-curdling atrocities, obviously points to their disordered personalities – but that is still far removed from madness. More significantly, it also highlights their extreme dangerousness. The thrill they experienced from killing was frankly and disgustingly described by Susan Atkins to another prisoner when she was first imprisoned and awaiting trial. And as James Fox has noted, alluding directly to the Manson women, what passes for craziness may in fact be craftiness or deceit. Fox concludes that the

Manson family followed their 'messiah' not because they were hypnotized but by the promise of becoming important, special people who would make their mark on the world. Thus the killing, as for a terrorist, became part of a planned programme of action.

Much has been made of the phenomenon of so-called male 'instrumental' violence, seen typically as a coldly premeditated predatory act designed to serve a particular personal need, whether linked to sexual instinct, the bolstering of the male ego and the quest for power and dominance, or else, more prosaically, carried out expressly for material gain. In comparison, women's violence has tended to be classically defined as 'expressive', with aggressive crimes, including murder, usually seen as the outcome of an unthinking, spontaneous upsurge of heated passion, hence invariably followed by remorse, guilt, shame and contrition. So, whereas men's violence is held by experts to be merely a means to an end, women's – we are told – invariably lacks intent and thus should be regarded as an end in itself, an almost accidental, momentary lapse of self-control; further proof, so we are told, of female irrationality and emotional instability. In truth, both stereotypes are grossly misleading, often proving interchangeable between the sexes. Women criminals have tended to display a significant propensity for plotting and scheming acts which fit the archetypal 'instrumental' mode, while men have demonstrated how a sudden, blind passion may explode into uncontrollable 'expressive' violence. However, a woman who commits a premeditated act of violence and cannot be categorized as mad is still more readily branded uncontrolled, hysterical or simply evil, reflecting society's readiness to concede sexual equality in all spheres, save in the potential for a broad range of destructive, criminal behaviour.

Not surprisingly, as researchers have increasingly discovered, the real facts of women's violence consistently fail to fit this classic theoretical 'female model' of murder. Indeed, even if we take violence to its most abhorrent extremes – acts of vicious savagery and sadism like physical torture, the mass murder and maiming of innocent individuals including children, the elderly and infirm, and the terrorizing of hostages – then there are still striking similarities between the sexes.

It was not merely desire for power but a naked greed and avarice which lay behind the meticulously executed and grisly programme of action perfected by Sacramento landlady Dorothea Puente between 1985 and 1988. After one of America's longest running and most widely publicized murder trials of the 1990s, 64-year-old Puente was found guilty in August 1993 of the murder of three tenants who had lodged in her Victorian-style house on leafy F Street in Sacramento. Although charged with the deaths of another six victims there was insufficient evidence to support the charges. Puente was clearly was no fool: in targeting the elderly who were mentally unstable and in ill health, often from the effects of alcoholism and drug dependence, she could rest assured that they maintained only the frailest grasp on life while their lonely lifestyle was sadly prophetic of how little concern would be aroused by their disappearance.

Poor, indigent down-and-outs they might have been but there was one factor common to all which instantly clinched their fate: the social security payments sent unfailingly each month by post to their new address at F Street. Once installed in her house, her tenants had to agree to two things: to keep up their welfare and disability allowances, on which Puente helped 'advise' them, and not to touch the post before she had first sorted it.

A former diagnosed schizophrenic, Dorothea Puente had devised a surefire means of gaining the status, power and creature comforts she so craved. During her murderous career she managed to rip off the federal government to the tune of $80,000. As she began dispatching her ailing lodgers and their money rolled in, Puente started to dress smartly, claimed to be a medical doctor – her Christmas cards read 'Dr Dorothea Puente' – formed friendships with respectable members of the community, including former Attorney General George Deukmejian, and gained respect by purchasing tables at political and charitable events in Sacramento. The Boarding House on F Street became a well-established concern, developing a reputation among social services as a safe haven for Sacramento's dispossessed, drug-addicted and ailing drifters. As years passed neighbours commented on the lush profusion of roses, fruit trees and especially the succulent giant-sized tomatoes that flourished outside the house. Noticing how assiduously at all hours of night and day the grey-haired lady dug and tended her garden, and her comments about using special fertilizer to enrich her plants, they marvelled at her tireless devotion to horticulture. What visitors failed to recognize, however, was the source of the peculiarly acrid, cloying smell that began emanating from both house and garden. Complaints about the stench increased to the point where even the health authorities were alerted, but without success. It wasn't until a social worker contacted the police, suspicious about the disappearance of one of her cases, 51-year-old retarded immigrant Alavaro 'Bert' Montoya, that seven decomposed bodies, some brutally dismembered, were unearthed beneath Puente's lush vegetation.

All were thought to have been poisoned with sleeping pills and other potent medication or else suffocated. In addition a number of her very frailest, disease-ridden victims were prevented by Puente from returning to hospital for necessary medical care, thus hastening their demise. In all cases Dorothea Puente systematically looted their accounts, forging their signatures, assuming their identity in person, cashing their cheques and obtaining illegitimate documents allowing the transfer of funds to one of numerous bank accounts she had opened for that purpose.

The trial lasted eight months and involved 153 witnesses and more than 3,100 items of evidence. Puente claimed that all her lodgers had died of natural causes and pleaded guilty only to stealing their money and not reporting their deaths. Unfortunately there was no firm evidence as to the cause of death – not only had all the victims suffered from often multiple degenerative diseases usually exacerbated by drugs and alcohol, but all tissue recovered from the bodies was either decomposed, putrefied or mummified, making it virtually impossible to establish the presence or level of deadly toxic substances. Although found guilty of three murders, in some ways Puente still has the last lingering laugh: absence of complete, cast-iron proof for her deeds. That this was always the intention behind every calculating, murderous move made by this most ruthlessly cold-blooded of women cannot surely be in any doubt.

Although women's violent impulses are evidently not as frequently linked to sexual arousal as men's are (unlike men, women do not seem to use pornography as a stimulus or adjunct to violent acts) sexual sadism can at times play a part in some women's crimes of violence. And not merely in violence against other women. Anthropologist Bronislaw Malinowski once described hearing accounts of tribal women in the Trobriand Islands (now New Guinea), who reputedly partook in group sexual assaults on men, subjecting them to degrading and violent acts, sometimes to the point of murder. And while stories of women violently 'raping' grown men are rare indeed, they are not totally unknown. Sex therapists Philip M. Sarrel from Yale University and William Masters of the famed Masters and Johnson Institute in St Louis, have over the years recorded a number of such cases, identifying about twenty men apparently deeply traumatized by sexual assaults. These incidents include a 27-year-old truck driver who picked up a woman in a bar, took her to a motel and fell asleep. When he awoke, he found he had been tied hand and foot to a bedstead, gagged and blindfolded, and during the next twenty-four hours was forced to have intercourse with four women, one of whom held a knife to his scrotum and threatened to castrate him whenever his performance flagged. A 37-year-old man was kidnapped by two women with a gun, forced into an abandoned building, undressed and tied up. He was compelled to have intercourse and oral sex, then was genitally and rectally abused by them until he fainted.

Certain recent incidents suggest that the courts no longer react with incredulity on hearing of such assaults. In America a male employee won $1 million damages for what he claimed to be persistent verbal and physical sexual harassment by his female boss, adding weight to growing claims by men of having endured unwanted advances by both male and female employers. At the Old Bailey in June 1993, 25-year-old Lana

Hyman was jailed for three years for having threatened to rape Ahmed El Shafie, a 5-foot 4-inch tall restaurant manager, unless he handed over cash. According to Mr El Shafie, Hyman, who burst into his home with a male and a female accomplice, threatened they would kidnap him and take him back to her flat where they would smoke crack and she would rape him, warning they would cut off his head if he attempted to call the police.

The woman who raped university student Gennista Barrows after insisting on accompanying her home from a party where they had met briefly, managed to escape criminal charges only because Barrows was too frightened of the story being picked up by the tabloids if it went to court. 'If a man had done this to me he would have been charged with rape,' says Barrows. 'But because it was a woman, in spite of this being an experience so shocking that nothing in my life could have prepared me for it, there was no equivalent charge. It would only have been indecent assault. So my feeling was, why bother? What I feel bitter about is the fact that society's prejudiced attitudes when a woman is accused of being violent automatically ensures there is no justice for the victim.'

Although such cases cannot be singled out as representative of female violence, there is growing evidence that women are as wholly capable of carrying out certain despicable outrages as are men, with the same compulsion to dominate, humiliate and terrorize others. Their propensity to give full cathartic vent to years of pent-up hatred, fury and resentment, when they choose to unleash these, can equal, if not exceed, men's. Yet much of this fury will stay hidden behind closed doors, destined to remain unrecognized and unacknowledged, because those over whom women can most readily exert power and dominance are the weakest, least vocal or assertive individuals – namely the very young and very old, the sick or the retarded, as demonstrated in the Dorothy Puente case.

So, if we are to isolate any significant and major distinction between men's and women's 'style' of killing and the victims they choose, then we must begin by examining the demarcation line that exists between the 'public' and 'private' domain considered to be most 'appropriate' to each of the sexes. We must then question the origins of the differing value judgements which we, media and society alike, apply to crimes committed in these two arenas.

The First Female Serial Killer?

I can think of no more telling or pertinent example of the double standard which informs one image arising from society's stereotyping of male and female murderers (in this case the cold, calculating, sadistic female versus the irrational and irresponsible male) than that most notorious case of the 1990s: the bisexual prostitute Aileen Wuornos, universally hailed as the 'world's first female serial killer'.

The fact that Wuornos is a multiple murderer was never in dispute. When arrested she confessed readily to charges of the murder of seven men, claiming she had acted in self-defence when the men whom she had picked up as clients became violent or threatened to injure or kill her. Controversy has raged principally around whether she was or was not a professional prostitute, and thus more likely to be a victim of random attacks and threats by male clients. The prosecution portrayed her as a calculating, man-hating predator who carefully planned the killings, taking a 'murder kit' containing a change of clothes, a seven shot .22-calibre revolver and a bottle of household cleaner to clean up all trace of fingerprints on the road with her, targeting middle-aged men who would put up less resistance, slaying her victims after robbing them of money and other valuables and going out of her way to cover up all traces of her involvement in their deaths.

True, Wuornos's self-presentation hasn't helped to further her claim to be a victim of male violence, acting in terrified self-defence. She has stated repeatedly that the men deserved to die, one moment giving every impression of being an iron-clad psychopath devoid of emotion, the next dissolving into jolly, gleeful laughter or tearful fury at having been 'framed by law-enforcement'. Unfazed by TV interviews, she accepts her possible execution with an almost insouciant resignation, admitting she deserves to die. Yet when sentenced to a total of three death sentences in May 1992, she shouted at the judge: 'I won't see you in heaven because you'll be in hell,' raising her middle finger in a valedictory salute.

That the Aileen Wuornos case should offer limitless media fodder of unequalled proportions, not just now, but for years to come, could be easily foreseen. Understandable too, in an age unmatched for its insatiable appetite for 'real life' tragedy, violence and horror, its prurient fascination with living demons incarnate. The possibility that Wuornos may not be quite the monster the authorities and the media have dressed her up to be, and the fact that, whatever she is, she is far from the first of her kind, raise numerous deeply unsettling issues.

As usual, her media image tells us more about the society we live in, its perceptions of women and how they should behave, than about the woman herself. 'THE LESBIAN STREET-WALKER WITH DEATH ON HER MIND' screams an *Evening Standard* banner headline. 'THE HIGHWAY KILLER QUEEN' yells the *Sunday Times*. And, as might be anticipated, this angle from the *Miami Herald*: 'SLAYING CASE DEFIES THEORIES ON GENDER'. The first hastily published book (so precipitate it fails to include vital new evidence that may turn the Wuornos case around entirely) promises to tell the 'inside story of the world's first female serial killer'. So what is it about this woman that she should be celebrated as the new female icon of evil?

Her alleged status as a prostitute ensures immediate and automatic categorization as promiscuous or predatory, a 'bad' or 'sad' woman depending on your perspective. At any rate, an individual on the margins of society by virtue of her calling, and thus more likely to be a social menace, uncaring, amoral, turning to robbery and violence as an adjunct to her trade. She has a history of drug and alcohol abuse and was given to hanging out in rough, roadside bars frequented by truckers, adding yet more lurid colour to the picture.

As a lesbian she immediately qualifies for the label of deviant in society's eyes, especially since she played 'both sides' for profit. Under-age sex (she became pregnant at 13, possibly by her brother with whom she is said to have had a consensual sexual relationship, and had the baby adopted), a series of previous criminal convictions including cheque fraud, car theft and robbing a store at gunpoint, for which she served a three-year jail sentence, and holding up a policeman with a gun, further compound the image of a hardened, calculating criminal. Her early childhood history, which included sexual assault by a neighbour, an alcoholic grandfather who tried to attack her in outbursts of violent rage and a father who committed suicide in prison when convicted of raping a 7-year-old girl, have also been emphasized as further evidence as to why Wuornos grew up to become a murderous man-hating lesbian.

In every way, through each experience and episode of her unfortunate life, Wuornos is held up to us as the most undesirable, aberrant example of womanhood, a dangerous deviant who lived rough, used sex exploitively, robbed and eventually killed like a man. But, no matter how you define a serial killer, the truth is that Aileen Wuornos is most emphatically not the first of her sex to kill in such a way – nor indeed may she qualify as a serial killer at all, given most acknowledged patterns of the crime. The key characteristics of a serial killer include the existence of a large number of victims of a certain type but picked randomly at the time, who are usually sexually assaulted and tortured whilst or before being killed. Most recognizable seems to be an absence of motive and rationality on the part of the killer, sometimes explained by extreme psychopathology such as schizophrenic paranoia – the term psychiatrists used to diagnose Peter Sutcliffe, the Yorkshire Ripper.

Wuornos fails to fit that definition on a number of counts. Murder did not figure as an intrinsic element of her sexual encounters; she may have killed while on the job, but it did not feature as part of a 'trick'. Although psychologists' reports agree that she is highly immature and she appears riddled with neuroses, there is no indication that she displays any typical sociopathic or psychopathic tendencies such as being unable to relate fully to the outside world or lacking in conscience and emotion. On numerous occasions she has indeed expressed remorse and contrition, emphasizing that she was driven to kill out of terror for her life – which demolishes another central premise underlying the theory of serial killing, absence of motive.

In some ways she might fit the bill, but only on the more general basis that there was a pattern to her crimes: the men were all middle-aged, employed and had valuables worth stealing; and she used the same weapon and killed on numerous occasions, possibly with forethought, covering her tracks. At this point we get into really deep water. For what is there ultimately to distinguish the nature of her crimes from those of a great number of other women who have murdered numerous individuals with intent and motive, using identical methods over long periods? In the USA alone there are over fifty known cases of women convicted of such offences, and many more throughout the world. So what makes Wuornos so special? Why has she risen to celebrity status? Could it be that, unlike others of her sex who were recognized as 'care-givers' – mothers, wives, nurses, teachers, nannies, carers of the sick and elderly – she fulfilled no such role and, like a man, killed not while engaged in a woman's traditional private domain of domesticity, but in the public sphere of the big outside world, the sleazy world of bars, highways, trucks, motels and financial transactions.

Why else should a case like this be hysterically hyped as the world's 'first', and hers become a household name? Who today remembers Marsha Burton, a Boston nurse who in 1854 was found guilty of murdering thirty patients as well as numerous relatives and was suspected of killing up to a hundred victims? Or, to cite more recent cases, all in the 1980s and 1990s, what do the names Mary Beth Tinning (seven child victims) or Genene Jones (a suspected total of sixteen babies) mean today? Or that grim Austrian quartet, the so-called 'death angels': Maria Gruber, Irene Leidolf, Waltraud Wagner and Stefanie Mayer. All were nurses' aides in the geriatric ward of a Lainz hospital, convicted in 1990 of killing forty-nine elderly patients who, when deemed too bothersome or demanding, were subjected to lethal injections or had water painfully forced into their lungs.

Even today, with growing acknowledgment of women's capacity for violence, it is a brave researcher who can state confidently that motherhood or a 'caring' profession such as nursing may in some cases actually be a conduit for violence. Yet in a world where the existence of women's blackest dreams of revenge, hatred, greed and domination continue to be a closed book, and where most women's easiest and sole access to power still lies via the domestic route, can anyone honestly be surprised that some are driven to abuse that power, to pervert and make a mockery of their glorified role as 'care-giver'? How have we remained blind to the violent intensity with which some women hate men, whom they blame for their helplessness and suffering? Unbelievably, an all-woman murder ring responsible for poisoning over a hundred individuals, principally husbands and lovers but also some other vulnerable dependents, operated undetected for almost twenty years in the tiny Hungarian hamlets of Nagyrev and Tiszakurt. When the ring was broken in 1929 and arrests made, scores of women, their ages ranging between 44 and 71, stood trial. Eventually eighteen received prison sentences, eight were executed and some acquitted. Almost all had acted in collusion and under the leadership of former midwife and so-called 'widow-maker' Susanna Fazekas, to eliminate men they had come to dislike or whose death ensured economic gain. Significantly, virtually none of the defendants exhibited remorse, grief or a moral sense of wrong. On the contrary: they justified their acts on the grounds that the husbands had been unpleasant or cruel, or that by poisoning, rather than stabbing or drowning their victims, their deaths had been non-violent and 'pleasant'. Yet as Kerry Seagrave has pointed out in her study of women serial and mass murderers from the late 1500s to the present day, the idea that poisoners kill more compassionately or that a substance like arson is a particularly soft option for the victim is laughable, since dying takes longer, often involving lingering, drawn-out agony – searing stomach pains, violent convulsions, diarrhoea and paralysis.

By comparison to all of these, and many other women who are technically speaking 'mass murderers' or 'serial killers', Aileen Wuornos can claim one sole dubious distinction: she trespassed on traditional male/female boundaries and entered an arena where normally only the big boys roam and kill. In an age of increasing sexual equality, her achievements demonstrably equal those of any male murderer. She is therefore judged by society at large to be more ruthlessly calculating and lethal, less deserving of sympathy or understanding than most other women who kill. And perhaps it is also because her victims were clients and thus deemed to be her superiors, each one white, male and fully employed, that she is regarded as so formidable. Had her victims been people recognized as weaker or socially marginalized – children, babies, the old, retarded or infirm, ethnic minorities, homosexuals or lesbians – would the outcry have been as great?

Probably not. Nor might it have been if in her relationship towards her victims she had assumed a more traditional female role. As Su Epstein, a sociologist at the University of Connecticut who has studied female homicide, memorably remarked at a recent seminar on serial killers: 'If Aileen Wuornos had married each of her victims before killing them, the serial killer label would almost certainly not have been applied to her.'

As Epstein sees it, this case carries subtle implications for women's changing roles generally; its ripple effect adds up to more than a single, clear warning of what awaits those who might be tempted to a life of violent crime or murder. 'By continuing to create a dichotomy between public and private spheres, assigning women to the personal and men to the public sphere, those women who kill in the private care-giving role will continue to be treated differently from those who commit murder outside that role. That difference not only reflects continuing patriarchal distinctions of hierarchy but reinforces stereotypical sexist images.'

Thus the female killer is judged according to a double standard: if she kills men in the course of an 'outside' job, she becomes a public figure and may earn the starry title of serial killer; if she is a nurse or mother killing a helpless dependent she is seen as a weak person engaged in a menial if worthy occupation, labouring under burdensome emotional stresses, inevitably less glamorous and of lower status within society and therefore less likely to make it big in the celebrity stakes. In turn, the victims and their families are also downgraded and devalued, and therefore more readily consigned to oblivion by the press and public alike, for there is no denying that the prominence and publicity accorded to Wuornos's seven murdered clients far exceeds that given to the numerous 'anonymous' victims of previous female killers.

Most intriguing, however, is the fact that the tables could still be turned, and Wuornos may yet come out of this as more sinned against than sinning. For what investigators are now trying to establish is whether she had a fair trial.

What was always mystifying early on during the case was how quickly the trial and sentencing took place and the apparently hastily cobbled-together, threadbare nature of the defence. Although Wuornos admitted all the killings, she had pleaded self-defence, saying she murdered her first victim, Richard Mallory, a 51-year-old electronics repair shop owner, after he tied her to the steering wheel of his car, raped, sodomized and beat her, while threatening to kill her. She claims she managed to break free and shot him to prevent him carrying out his threat. Undoubtedly this would not have been the first time she was attacked during her years of prostitution – rape and other assaults being a common hazard faced by prostitutes, especially those who work a large area of different streets and highways – and Wuornos is claimed to have confessed frequently, even many years before the murders, that she had been raped numerous times by the men who picked her up as she hitch-hiked around the country.

The episode with Mallory, however, appears to have caused something in her to snap. In common with many rape and assault victims who suffer from post-traumatic stress disorder, her cumulative experiences led to increasingly extreme reactions of fear and terror which escalated to the point of paranoia, while her perception of reality became increasingly distorted. Viewed from this perspective of fear, her claim to have shot another six men in self-defence because, when they turned violent or threatened her, she genuinely believed her life was in danger, begins to sound less fanciful. The main problem she encountered at both her trials was that the defence had been unable to come up with any proof to back up her story about

Mallory's vicious attack which she claimed had had such a devastating effect on her. When she told the court that Mallory had beaten her up while threatening, 'You're gonna do everything I tell you to do, and if you don't I'm going to kill you and I'm going to fuck you after, just like all the other sluts I've done', and that after raping and sodomizing her he poured alcohol into all her orifices, the court didn't believe her. Nor did they believe it when she said he was going to use the alcohol in her eyes 'for the grand finale'.

In 1992, after a four-month investigation spearheaded by a team of American television researchers from NBC *Dateline* news programme, new evidence came to light that Richard Mallory was in every way the violent, brutal sadist Wuornos portrayed at her trial. Under state law, there will be an automatic appeal to the Florida supreme court, which is not expected to give a ruling until sometime in 1994. This evidence is almost certain to lead to a retrial, which, although it will not – and should not – lead to her release, may cause the death sentence to be commuted to life imprisonment. It might also erase the label 'serial killer' from her name in any forthcoming crime books.

The new findings could prove to be the stuff defence attorneys' dreams are made of. Mallory is now known to have had a horrific past record of violent sexual assaults on women going back as far as 1957 when, working as a delivery man, he entered the Maryland home of a wealthy socialite mother of three, Edith Little, and attempted to violate her. Although she has since died, her son has fully corroborated the story. Mallory was charged and convicted of assault and attempted rape, and, not surprisingly in light of a psychiatric report which declared him mentally unbalanced, he was sentenced to four years at a rehabilitation centre for violent offenders. There, officials found him to be so unstable and violent that they postponed the date of his release on the strength of a medical report stating that: 'He [Mallory] is still an extremely confused, impulsive and explosive individual who will get into difficulty most likely of a sexual nature.'

The report proved all too prophetic: Mallory attempted to sexually molest a nurse, causing him to be transferred from the centre to prison where he remained for ten years, frequently admitting that he knew he was insane and a danger to women, and that he deserved to go to the gas chamber. Other valuable evidence corroborating Wuornos's claim that Mallory was a deranged and potentially lethal assailant has come to light, including his collection of home-made pornographic videos and the testimony of a nurse who briefly dated him before she found out he had been in jail for attempted rape.

Many believe knowing Mallory is the key to understanding Wuornos and why she ended up murdering another six men, and on this basis the defence now appear to have sufficient information to present her crimes in an entirely different light. If she really is the cold-blooded man-hating killer the prosecution have made her out to be, then what are we to make of the testimony of another witness tracked down by the TV team, Tom Evans, a truck-driver and part-time musician who gave her a lift on a highway, five months after Mallory's murder. They spent a week together, forming a platonic friendship as he drove through the Southern states. Evans's impression is of a tense, suspicious, terrified woman whose long experience of beatings, abuse, rape, and of being drugged and stabbed on the road, had left her an emotionally dilapidated wreck. 'I am living proof that the girl is not a premeditated killer. And that's what I would have told the jury.'

Incredibly, Wuornos's defence team had been too incompetent to unearth any of this themselves. Or would it perhaps be more accurate to say that they simply could not be bothered, being under considerable pressure from the judge and state attorney to speed up proceedings to enable them to nail Wuornos as quickly as possible? No wonder it took the jury only ninety-five minutes to find her guilty of murdering Mallory at her first trial in January 1992. By now convicted of another four murders with two more outstanding, it is generally believed that the Florida state prosecution service wants to pin as many death sentences on her as possible to increase the likelihood of execution. Although there are three other women currently on Florida's death row and twelve in all have been sentenced to death, no woman has ever been executed in the state. Some legal experts believe Wuornos will be the first. They may have to change their minds once the true facts of the context within which she killed finally emerge.

Killing for the Cause

Whether in the end the full truth is ever known about Wuornos, and however she is represented in the annals of violent crime, we can be sure that just as she is not the first female multiple murderer, she is unlikely to be the last. Whether more women are likely to feature in the steady outpouring of ever popular 'true crime' books and films cannot be foreseen. My feeling is that they may. After all, the fact that women may and do consciously take up an existence dedicated to skilfully plotting and carrying out acts of extreme, deadly violence is indisputable. Also indisputable is the fact that, for many women, such activities become the means whereby they search, discover and continue to build their self-esteem and sense of personal identity and pride, thereby demonstrating the same ruthless drive for identity through power that has long been identified as a male trait.

This much is already clear from what we are beginning to discover about women's growing participation in organized terrorism and guerrilla warfare. In Germany, for instance, during the 1980s, 50 per cent of the membership of the outlawed terrorist Red Army Faction was made up of women, rising to two thirds in the early 1990s. In Northern Ireland, women's prominent involvement in the terror campaign conducted by the Provisional Irish Republican Army in the early 1970s during the internment of their male counterparts resulted in the PIRA suspending separate women's sections in favour of a unified command.

While terrorism may on the face of it appear to be the ultimate in male-type instrumental violence – no atrocity can be seen as too grotesquely horrific as long as it advances the doctrine or attempts to achieve the goals set out by the cause or movement to which the terrorist adheres – at the same time, the motivation that drives the world's most fanatically ruthless and committed 'freedom fighters', militant activists, call them what you will, is intense passion, searing emotion and a terrifying absence of conscience, logic or human compassion when it comes to the pursuit of their objectives. Were it possible to carefully dissect and analyse the complex psychological and cognitive structures of a terrorist, male or female, what would undoubtedly emerge would be a subtle meshing of ice-cold rationality, the quintessential predeterminant of 'instrumental' aggression with the blazing emotional heat that lies at the heart of 'expressive' violence. This, potentially, is the deadliest of all possible syntheses to make up the criminal psyche. And perhaps it is precisely this dangerous fusion of the two opposing modes of violence that accounts for the appeal of terrorism and guerrilla activities to so many young women, and explains also why a great number are highly efficient at it.

Women's active participation in covert organizations is by no means new or unusual. During World War II, hundreds of women in the French, Dutch and other European resistance movements resorted to acts of often extreme violence against the Nazis. During the 1941 German occupation of Yugoslavia, about 100,000 women fighters reportedly carried arms in a fierce, bloody and prolonged resistance. As members of diverse partisan, underground and guerrilla units battling in conditions of extreme danger, the casualty rate for women was immense: 25,000 deaths, 40,000 wounded and 3,000 disabled who became pensionable veterans. As in all wars and struggles against oppression, one individual's act of murder or terrorism becomes another's act of selfless bravery, heroism and quest for freedom and justice. And since these violent acts were committed within the context of what is regarded as the most 'just' of all wars against an enemy held to be the most evil, destructive force in modern history, few would suggest that such acts were not justified or deny that the perpetrators were saviours and heroes rather than criminals.

In Kenya during the 1950s, the Kikuyu women subverted their traditional roles and status, challenging the all-male power and decision-making base in the fight for liberation against colonialism so successfully that they eventually made up 5 per cent of the guerrilla movement. Many rose to prominent positions of leadership, ordering and carrying out the execution of enemies or traitors. In a bizarre ethnic reconstruction of the coronation of Queen Elizabeth in June 1953, a much respected female guerrilla, Wagiri Njoroge, was crowned on the same date, becoming acknowledged 'Queen of the Mau-Mau'. Wagiri 'ruled' for over half a year in the notorious Thompson's Falls District, a hotbed of Mau-Mau atrocities which included some horrific murders of the European population. When the husband of another high-ranking, respected forest guerrilla, Wambui, was killed, it was said she refused ever to remarry because, as one colleague explained, 'She could not be ruled. She knew everything. Her hands had become very light and she could easily kill a useless husband.' And around the same time in the Algerian uprising against French rule, women hitherto subservient and relegated to domestic roles took up arms and fought alongside their menfolk, even in the front line, risking their lives in acts of sabotage, murder and terrorism for the common cause.

If terrorism is the epitome of instrumental violence, then female terrorists are living proof that their skill, dedication and determination as agents of destruction rivals that of any man. Although legend has it that women only join terrorist organizations and take part in hijackings and other violent acts because they are lured or duped into doing so by their boyfriends, more recent analysis of the motivation and behaviour of female 'desperados' indicates that male coercion plays little if any part in their decision to espouse extreme political or ideological movements and to dedicate themselves to violence as a 'legitimate' means of achieving their goals.

Yet the popular 'Pattie Hearst' image of the female terrorist as a brainwashed moll whose passion to please her criminal lover is the prime motive for her own lawlessness is an enduring reminder of society's resistance to the notion of women as initiators and free agents of violence. If a woman joins an organization committed to violence in gaining its ends, then surely, the argument goes, it can only be because she is under the domination of some man? Criminologists have long advanced the theory of 'erotomania' as a prime cause of female terrorism, the obsessive sexual enslavement which causes an individual to abdicate all self-will and participate in any activity, no matter how perverse or wicked, as long as it satisfies their lover's demands.

David Ward, who has researched into female violence, believes that the key to understanding female terrorism is women's own image of themselves as weak and impotent. His view is that since all terrorist tactics, *per se*, represent the weapon wielded most typically by the weak struggling to attain power, then women, classically having been assigned the role of the weaker sex, are compelled to adopt the most repugnant aspects of male violence in a vain attempt to make up for their negative self-image. 'The strongest impression conveyed is that women are playing a male game using thinly disguised and poorly adapted male roles', states Ward. He also observes such women, especially those in the vanguard of terrorist movements, to be linked by a 'frightening bitterness and alienation and by a nihilism that is pathetic and saddening'.

All of which is fair comment. Granted, violence, especially if premeditated, is commonly the final refuge of the weak and insecure; and the alienation that a terrorist must experience both as a result of worldwide revulsion towards their attitudes and actions as well as the emotional and spiritual dissociation and the numbing of moral conscience that accompanies any long-term, considered commitment to violence, is indeed frightening and pathetic. However, such traits and deficits are by no means unique to women but demonstrably shared by all terrorists, male or female. The principal reason why women who live by a code of terror and violence evoke such extreme reactions is presumably because for the vast majority of people the image of woman as destroyer of life is so obscenely irreconcilable with that of woman as giver and protector of life that they can only explain her actions on the basis of diminished responsibility or male domination.

So, what *really* makes them do it? According to Eileen Mac-Donald, who in the late 1980s interviewed twenty female terrorists from varying cultures and organizations including ETA, the

IRA, the Intifada, the Red Brigades and the Baader-Meinhof group, there was little evidence of emotional immaturity and no sign of the need to compensate for a low self-image, let alone any suggestion that they had been manipulated or seduced into that life by their menfolk. Nor were they crazed fanatics forever engaged in bomb-making, target practice or gun maintenance, still less hobnail-booted, foul-mouthed 'bull-dykes' trying to prove a point. Far from it. The most significant finding to emerge from MacDonald's interviews is how utterly unremarkable the majority of these women appear to be, mostly friendly, unaggressive, sometimes shy, getting on with their everyday lives as wives, mothers or career women. In MacDonald's words they are 'disturbingly normal'. There is precious little evidence here to indicate the existence of deranged psychotic minds seeking the optimum outlet for sadistic and perverted fantasies.

The real clue seems to lie less within the minds and psyches of such women than in their subjective experiences of, and ultimate rejection of, their social environment and the political ferment prevailing in their country. It is no coincidence, for instance, that the great majority of female terrorists, women like Ulrike Meinhof and Astrid Proll or Leila Khaled, who were young during the early burgeoning of the women's liberation movement of the 1960s and 1970s, should be self-confessed militant feminists. They represent the first generation of women determined to become free agents and authors of their own, as well as their country's, future. And in those countries where centuries of extreme male domination and female subordination had passed unchallenged, as for example in the Middle East, the southern Catholic countries of the Mediterranean, or Germany with its prevailing ethic of stiflingly repressive religious puritanism, the advent of radical feminism awakened in such hitherto unliberated women ample anger and motivation to smash the established order and assert their independence.

Add to this newly awakened consciousness a nationalist 'cause' or ideology to which to harness their newfound energies and direct their fighting spirit – the Palestinian cause in Lebanon and Israel, the Basque separatist movement in Spain, the IRA's declared war against British rule in Northern Ireland – and the rationale for women's involvement in terrorism begins to take on a chilling logic. Not for nothing are they called the world's most dangerous women. There is certainly much more to this label than facile tabloid hype. Far from entering these outlawed groups casually or for a quick, temporary thrill, today's female guerrillas are noted in particular for their physical bravery and skill, their steely, unemotional mental edge and ruthless and undeviating commitment to their cause and the creed of violence that accompanies it.

Far from weakening or becoming deterred by an emotional backlash that would undoubtedly devastate the average person confronting the full horror of having been instrumental in blowing up a jumbo jet full of passengers or caused death, injury and unbearable pain and suffering to vast numbers of men, women and children, the unpalatable truth is that the thrill of pride and heady empowerment that comes with successfully carrying off such atrocities has proven to be an unprecedented, life-enhancing experience for many women. A frequent observation is the 'power of the gun' upon which they come to rely. Another is the intense relish and satisfaction they experience at knowing that explosives they planted went off as planned, causing the envisaged death and carnage they wished so fervently to inflict on the 'enemy'.

From their perspective, this is what true sexual equality is actually all about. This is empowerment of the highest order, which no 'ordinary' woman, especially one from a poor, deprived environment and a repressed, conventional upbringing, could imagine in her wildest dreams. It brings fame, peer adulation, glamour – and sexual power; the type of power women have traditionally admired and desired in dominant, successful and ruthless men, from political leaders to mafia gangsters.

So, when Leila Khaled talks of her feelings about going off on her first big mission, to hijack a TWA flight bound from Los Angeles to Tel Aviv in 1969 – which turned her overnight into a world 'star' terrorist – she emphasizes only her determination to carry out the mission successfully on behalf of the dispossessed Palestinian people, her thrill at the honour and glory of being chosen for a job of such magnitude, the amusement at having to fumble about for the hand grenade hidden inside her trousers and the enjoyment she derived from terrifying the crew and passengers by threatening to blow them up.

Although Susanna Ronconi of Italy's Red Brigades and the even more violent Prima Linea admits feeling nervousness prior to taking part in a strike – which typically included knee-capping fifteen students at a business school simply because they were 'guilty' of participating in a quintessentially capitalist endeavour – what comes across most vividly and compellingly in MacDonald's interview with her is her glowing description of the heroic dimension of her murderous activities and the sense of importance and pride at being able to 'influence the world about you, instead of experiencing it passively'. It is this ability to make an impact on the reality of everyday life, she stresses, that is important.

Which is not to say that women like Leila Khaled or Susanna Ronconi are natural-born assassins and saboteurs. For most, as is the case with male mercenaries, SAS paratrooper units or ordinary war combatants at lowest infantry level, some intensive training is necessary to acquire the skills, expertise and stamina required, as well as to cultivate the mental edge and control, the 'stress management' skills which prevent spontaneous human emotion from subverting the complex job at hand – namely planning and carrying out a hijack, controlling and terrorizing their hostages, negotiating with the authorities and, of course, killing. In the case of Sri Lanka's 3,000 or so Tamil Tigresses, the female faction, like their male counterparts, are forced to take vows to commit suicide rather than surrender – which is why there would have been no hesitation in the mind of Rajiv Gandhi's assassin about ending her own life along with his for the greater good of the Tamil cause. Recruits must undergo a rigorous six-month training in bomb-making, armed combat and self-defence, with tuition in how to effectively deploy the AK-47 rifle with which each woman is provided. The women are young, aged mainly between 15 and 30, and generally recruited from families with members of the terrorist organization, although the unit plans its own operations and members live in women-only camps. Many women are motivated to join the Tigresses only once they have lost close relatives or friends in battles with government forces or after hearing of alleged assaults and rapes committed by soldiers against Tamil women.

Just as fanatical in their readiness to kill and lay down their own lives for their political goals are the women terrorists of the ultra left-wing Shining Path or Sendero Luminosa, launched in Peru in 1980, whose campaign of violence against establishment security forces centres on their attempts to install a Maoist regime in Peru. An incredible 50 per cent of the Shining Path guerrillas are women, mainly young teenage girls, with two out of three members of the Sendero's ruling Permanent Committee and nine of the nineteen members of its Central Committee recently reported to be women. Since the capture and imprisonment in 1992 of the group's ideological leader, Abimael Guzman, according to a Peruvian TV station which claims to have contact with the Shining Path, the leadership allegedly has passed to 39-year-old 'Comarade Rita', aka Maria Jenny Rodriguez Neyra. As head of the new Central Committee, Comarade Rita, a former sociologist, is said to have ordered the assassination in December 1992 of Pedro Huillica, President of the Peruvian general workers' union and, in 1993, to have ordered the killing of one of Lima's leading community leaders. According to Rosa Malivias, a Peruvian sociologist, the women of the Shining Path, especially at committee level, are all from middle-class educated backgrounds, former teachers and university lecturers who embraced the Shining Path ideology because of its incorporation, superficially at any rate, of feminist doctrine. A survey conducted in 1990 of captured Senderistas showed that 10 per cent of the women had professional qualifications or postgraduate degrees, compared to only 3.9 per cent of the men.

Women have been responsible for much of the bloody violence that has claimed over 27,000 lives since Sendero's inception. Abimael Guzman is said to have promoted women in his organization precisely because he detected in them early on a quality of steadfastness and total commitment to the cause.

Grinding poverty and social frustration, according to General Antonio Ketin Vidal, responsible for Guzman's arrest, make women particularly keen to undertake the most savage atrocities. 'We found out that when a Senderista was given the job of administering the *coup de grâce* to the victim of a Sendero assassination, such as strapping explosives to the body and detonating it, it was usually a woman. The Sendero women are fearsome.'

In the wake of the disintegration and genocide taking place in what was formerly Yugoslavia, reports of women eagerly applying to join the ranks of Bosnian defence units – as well as female Serbian terrorists mercilessly shooting to death adults and small children, the sick and the old – grow steadily. For some, like Naima, an attractive 22-year-old textile designer from Sarajevo, the decision to fight in a specialist counter-sniper unit operating behind Serb lines was a simple choice: defend Sarajevo or die, along with her fellow citizens. 'I can't say I like it because it's a terrible job but at least I feel good because I'm fighting back. The first time I picked up a gun I felt empty. It's against all my principles and the way I was brought up. If you are a normal person, shooting at people cannot make you happy. It's an emotion mixed with madness and disappointment.' Having joined the unit after a 4-year-old girl was shot dead by a sniper in her neighbourhood, Naima admits that her motivation was partly revenge, but that she has managed to contain the emotion. 'I don't want all the enemy dead; I just want them to stop this. I do get frightened when I am preparing myself for an operation, when I pack my things, put on my uniform and get into the car. Then I am scared but when I'm in action there is no time to be frightened. I feel fury and anger but no fear.'

Among the 20,000 mainly Muslim soldiers, former civilians whose offensive to liberate Sarajevo from the tightening grip of the advancing Serbian forces has reportedly turned into an Islamic jihad (holy war), between 4 and 6 per cent are said to be women. They also qualify as the most radical members of the liberating army. Like the men, they talk with the hot-blooded bravado of those for whom nothing of value remains to be lost except life itself. One young former medical student, Sanja, aged 19, speaks with pride of having learned over the past months to fight and kill. 'When I liquidate an enemy soldier, my heart swells. I only feel courage and the desire to kill another.'

Most Bosnian fighting units are believed to have at least one or two women in their ranks. For many single young women this war has provided a welcome opportunity to join the men and prove that they have the skill and bravery to successfully carry out the same duty on behalf of their country – to kill with precision and conviction. One female recruit, Vezira Dugalija, a fighter on the front line who was once also a textile worker, denies any fear of infantry attacks. 'I don't know if I have killed anyone yet. But I can hardly wait to kill my first Serb.'

Bosnia's enemies, the Serbs, are also noted for their formidable, constantly expanding female faction. One female sniper, Radenka Odzakovic, became notorious in spring 1992 as the first woman operating in the front line to be arrested for shooting civilians in the Bosnian capital, and is charged with the massacre of seven people, including three children, some of whom had been courageous enough to queue for food during an apparent lull in the fighting. Although Odzakovic has become the most renowned woman fighter, the jail in which she is being held houses another fifty women inmates out of an approximate total of 180 prisoners.

According to Paul Slaughter, a former Metropolitan CID officer with extensive experience in dealing with terrorist crimes and hostage negotiation who now provides high-security services for individuals and business organizations, it is crucial to recognize that what makes female terrorists and guerrillas often *more* deadly than males is a combination of three interrelated factors.

First is their need to be seen to be more ruthless, more violent, in order to overcome sexism from male colleagues and so prove their worth and equality.

Second is such women's often fanatical, unwavering embrace of radical feminism. Since all men represent the 'enemy', a militant feminist guerrilla or kidnapper is less likely to show compassion towards a male hostage or any individual connected with an oppressive, patriarchal regime or institution. Says Slaughter: 'Men within the movements that spawn terrorism might be prepared to accept a settlement if sufficient progress were made towards addressing their grievances. This is less likely to be the case with women terrorists. Through their resort to arms, these women are seeking not simply a change in the immediate circumstances that sparked their aggression but a societal change overall: a furtherance of the cause of radical feminism.'

The third and last factor common to both sexes, but often a newer, more overwhelming experience for women brought up to observe traditional female roles, is the mind- and body-altering 'high' which inevitably accompanies or follows any dangerous strike or prolonged period of intense stress and life-or-death tension. Akin to the almost unreal euphoria and altered states of consciousness described by soldiers during and after combat, referred to variously as 'battle high' or, by Vietnam war veterans, as 'eye fucking' to emphasize the resulting height-ened sense of sexuality and comradeship, the phenomenon is an acknowledged aspect of post-traumatic stress disorder – and one of the hardest of aftereffects to fully overcome. On a physio-logical level it results from a massive outpouring of the body's natural stress chemicals, principally adrenalin, noradrenalin and dopamine, a cocktail so potent that for many the experience of feeling every sensation more keenly, of being in fundamental, immediate contact with life and death, has been described as on a par with taking heroin, cocaine or LSD. And, as with those drugs, the intensity of the experience and the desire to repeat it can lead to an addiction as total and potentially deadly as with any mind-altering drugs.

This seems to be especially true within Latin cultures where centuries of enforced passivity and subservience have left today's women angrily seeking empowerment, sometimes at any price. Being by nature often as passionately extrovert, sen-sation-seeking and ruthlessly aggressive as men, it was only a matter of time before Italian women born into Mafia families started demanding a piece of the action for themselves, perhaps not yet in the macho strongholds of repressive, backward Sicily but certainly in the more liberated climate of the Neapolitan Camorra. Here, all the signs are that having once tasted power, these new female gangsters are loath to abandon a life of violent crime, not least because of the improbability of tasting it to such a degree elsewhere. Although such noted women gang leaders as Rosetta Cutolo and Pupetta Maresca, who as a pregnant 19-year-old killed her husband's assassin and gave birth to her son in jail, might seem little more than loyal, loving wives or sisters turned henchwomen, carrying out orders on behalf of imprisoned or exiled male mobster bosses, their homely image belies a steely resolve and ruthless efficiency.

As reported recently by the Italian authorities, the notorious Anna Mazza, widow of Camorra capo Gennaro Moccia, returned from exile to take control of her clan, an exceptionally cruel dynasty dating back to the 1970s whose tentacles retain a murderous stranglehold over large areas of the Neapolitan hinterland. Anna Mazza, who gave her 13-year-old son a revolver, ordering him to assassinate the men responsible for murdering her husband, boasts a criminal career which includes armed robberies, blackmail, loansharking and murders-by-arrangement. Although Mazza's may not be the finger on the trigger, the Neapolitan police openly acknowledge that her charisma and qualities of leadership have made her a formidably dangerous leader of her clan, and the most powerful criminal woman in the region.

Another Camorra woman apparently quite without scruples about killing is 43-year-old Concetta Teccio, recently arrested for ordering, and possibly taking part in, the assassination of three men in 1991. Like Mazza, Teccio also took charge of her husband's clan, if only as a temporary caretaker while he served a prison sentence.

In comparison to their mothers' generation, the new post-feminist 'Camorristi', now in their early twenties, are proving more autonomous, self-motivated and deadlier by far, unrestricted by any need to dress up their actions in the respectable trappings of old-style matriarchy. The most notable to date are 24-year-old Cristina Pinto and 23-year-old Tatiana Imparato, now in prison on charges of extortion. Tatiana, a law student at Naples University and daughter of Camorra boss Mario Umberto, killed by police in 1993, was determined to avenge her father's death by taking his place, fearlessly and aggressively leading her clan in crimes of armed robbery and extortion. Cristina Pinto, although initially drawn into a world of organized crime through her boyfriend, a small-time clan boss, now plays a central, hands-on role, organizing robberies, providing murder weapons and outlining the plans of each strike. The speed, violence and accuracy of her reactions have made her one of Italy's most dangerous female criminals. While recently driving behind her boyfriend's car in her own vehicle, she noticed another car approaching, firearms protruding apparently in preparation to gun him down. Instantly she managed to cut across their path, forcing the would-be killers to halt. Armed, as always, with her .38-calibre revolver, Pinto got out and advanced shooting, forcing them to flee. The sense of power and triumph experienced by a young woman, living in a still overwhelmingly macho society, at having saved the life of her boyfriend entirely through her own skills and killer instinct in circumstances of extreme danger is scarcely imaginable, nor the undoubted desire to repeat the experience.

For many women, who have probably had fewer opportunities than men to channel their aggressive energies through rough contact sports, aggressive encounters or physically hazardous pursuits and adventures, the chance of becoming addicted to the excitement of terrorist activities may be greater than for a man, and the unfamiliarity of such sensations as power, pride, superiority and bravado, and of being the centre of attention, apart from inducing an icy mental calm and emotional detachment may also lead the female desperado to act more quickly and more lethally, ignoring or sweeping away all obstacles that might prevent her achieving her goal. In her interview with Eileen MacDonald, Susanna Ronconi describes her 'total suspension of all emotions' immediately following a violent act while maintaining that it is precisely because a woman is the giver of life that she also has a greater capacity than is generally acknowledged to take life. 'I do not believe that . . . putting aside emotions when you are being violent is exclusively male or female, or that it is something that women find more difficult than men. I have known quite a number of men who have told me that they could not have shot people', Ronconi says in MacDonald's book *Shoot The Women First*.

Yet the chilling truth is that although such women are not insane, sociopathic, perverted, wicked or cruel in any other area of their lives, certainly not with their friends and family, when it comes to their 'mission' they do appear to possess one principal characteristic of the psychopath: a complete inability to identify or empathize with the feelings, needs and suffering of others – except those who are part of the cause for which they are fighting.

Paul Slaughter and others have commented on how many female activists talk about the 'cause' or political movement, be it the IRA, Intifada or ETA, with a depth of passion and a specific phraseology that borders on the maternal. Is it possible that for many women adherence to an ideology amounts to a form of projection of the maternal or nurturing instinct? Slaughter and MacDonald have suggested that some vigilante or guerrilla women relate to their cause as to a surrogate child, and that this may account for their readiness to perpetrate horrific atrocities in its defence that men in similar positions might think twice before committing.

Yet since women's much-vaunted natural maternal 'instinct' is by no means the ubiquitous and universal dictate of nature it is generally perceived to be, such speculation – for speculation is all it amounts to – is only credible in the case of certain individuals. Far more telling is the fact that many mothers of young children, such as those of Peru's Shining Path, will willingly abandon their children and risk their lives because of the lure of these activities or, as in the case of the Palestinian Intifada, may actively encourage their children, boys or girls, some little more than toddlers, to train as terrorists and take part in stone-throwing and other street violence, sometimes against youngsters of their own age. Since such fanatical adherence to ideology and justification of violence as the principal means to an end indicates an unconscionable abandonment of parental responsibility coupled with a tragic absence of humanitarian instinct, it is hard to see how it could be identified as in any way a by-product or sublimation of maternal feeling. The truth is, women are every bit as capable as men of using aggression in the name of a cause, be it war, revolution or organized crime, if it is a cause they identify with strongly enough.

The Female Sadist: Fact or Fiction?

Considering the horrendously high, ever-soaring homicide rate principally among males in America, the single most persuasive reason why women who murder gain such inordinately massive media coverage, most of it salacious, prurient and inaccurate, is because so few do it. Yet a visitor from another planet might be forgiven for thinking otherwise, judging by the recent spawning of a particularly invidious new breed of 'slasher' or 'spatterpunk' movie in which women are portrayed as either hysterical, deranged or deeply evil creatures, wreaking unspeakable acts of vengeance on anyone, male or female, who thwarts their goals or fails to reciprocate their lustful passions. From the murderous girlfriend in *Fatal Attraction* and the bisexual sex killer in *Basic Instinct*, to even more absurd, loonier characters like the sadistic kidnapper in *Misery* or the control freak flatmate in *Single White Female*, the fear Hollywood is trying its lurid best to instil in us is that, when aroused, the modern liberated woman's sexual frustration, possessive jealousy and hidden lesbian or man-hating tendencies may turn them into murderous monsters whose capacity for cunning and sadism knows no bounds. And while it is easy to shrug off such images as commercial hokum, Grand Guignol in the latest modern genre, the implicit assumption that such women are all the more lethal nowadays because of their sexual and social liberation and equality leaves a deep, long-lasting imprint in the collective social unconscious.

Although for a few women sex and violence may indeed go together, there is little evidence – with the exception of a tiny minority of psychopaths – to suggest the existence of a female drive to kill in which sexuality is harnessed as a vehicle for anger and the urge to dominate, degrade and terrorize a victim, as occurs more commonly in men. If we look behind the glossy, soft-porn fictional images of say, the sexual seductress in *Basic Instinct* who stabs her partner with an ice-pick at the moment of climax, or a similar character in *Sea of Love* who dispatches her sexual partners at the same stage in the game with a gun, or even if we analyse the media's conjecture that Aileen Wuornos combined murder with sex, it is apparent that while women may murder for numerous motives, the drive for sexual power or heightened sexual gratification is not generally one of them.

Although it is indisputable that Myra Hindley participated with her boyfriend Ian Brady to a great degree, and with much excitement, relish and absence of conscience or compassion, in execrable acts of torture and murder, all the evidence suggests that she herself did not initiate the sexual perversions or become as driven by a sadistic urge for erotic arousal through torture as did Brady, who was diagnosed as a dangerous psychopath. As obscenely inhuman and irreducibly wicked and depraved as her part in the Moors Murders unquestionably was, it is more likely that in allowing herself to become manipulated and enthralled, body, mind and spirit, by the powerful, perverted will of her lover, she drifted willingly into a vast moral vacuum. It is this suspension of moral vigilance, the weakness and failure of certain numbers of us to live, as philosopher Mary Midgley puts it, as well as we are capable of, that we surely need to address and concern ourselves with, rather than attempting to pin often meaningless psychiatric labels on to offenders, or search for biological determinants where none exist.

As with terrorists devoted to an ideology or cause, or the vast numbers of apparently 'normal' men and women, even children, who helped plan and actively perpetrated the foulest atrocities of the Nazi regime, and did so with satisfaction, pride and a sense of total justification, it seems evident that the greatest danger facing all mankind is not of being possessed by evil and destructiveness as a positive driving force, but of allowing the development of a moral deficit, the opening up of a vacuum in which the precursors of evil – greed, vanity, jealousy, paranoid obsession, possessiveness, lack of forethought and above all, indifference – may take root and flourish unchecked like a poisonous fungus. And given that many women to this day are socialized to regard men and male dominated institutions as inherently more powerful, authoritative, wise and dependable, even when they are clearly not so, then perhaps the gravest, unrecognized hazard facing women now is the risk of adopting male 'models' of aggressive behaviour as a means of proving their equality and strength. As with many men who falsely equate brute violence with true inner strength, the tragedy is that such women may come to justify and glorify their brutality, slipping unwittingly into that moral vacuum within which much of the masculine culture of violence has been given licence to evolve.

When we examine the behaviour and personalities of very brutal, violently sadistic women, it is no simple matter to determine the degree of self-will that either precipitated their earliest actions or perpetuated them over time. Disturbing though it may be to contemplate, there is no escaping the fact that there are women who have become 'professional' torturers, and who took to it with gusto, notably such barbaric creatures as the World War II German concentration camp commanders – or 'Obergauleiters' – Irma Grese and Ilse Koch. The extent to which Grese's depraved mind was capable of thinking up ever new horrific forms of excruciating mental and physical tortures against women is virtually unparalleled in the history of wartime atrocities. Every one of her actions, her entire persona, was living testimony to Hitler's claim that: 'We are a race of savages and have no pity.'

Having joined the Nazi Youth movement as a young girl in defiance of her father's wishes, she soon became seduced by Nazi ideology, demonstrating a fanatical devotion to party politics in the conviction that therein lay moral salvation from the corrupt excesses of society under the Weimar Republic. On being finally placed in charge of over 30,000 female prisoners at Auschwitz, under license to unleash her full demonic powers, she managed to lend an incomprehensible new dimension of terror to the word sadism. Kitted out in a man's SS uniform, heavy hobnailed boots, a pistol and a whip in hand, she would toy with her prisoners, making them guess when they were due to be executed.

Grese would think nothing of personally slaughtering prisoners on any whim: a mother seen sobbing in conversation with her little girl through barbed wire was instantly beaten to death; and on seeing a woman staring at a truckload of newly arrived prisoners she walked up to her smiling, asking if she enjoyed the view, then pulled out her pistol and blew away her face. She was always accompanied by two savage Alsatian dogs, who were purposely kept semi-starved in order to better attack any hapless prisoner, woman or child, whom Grese wished to destroy; the dogs would disable the victim, pinning her to the ground, while Grese jumped on her stomach, then kicked or whipped her to death in an uncontrollable frenzy.

At the Nuremberg Trials she listened dispassionately, displaying not one iota of remorse or guilt while former prisoners told of these and other bestialities. Like numbers of other Nazi criminals, before being condemned to death and hanged, Grese justified her actions on the grounds that her prisoners were no more than a subhuman species of worthless 'dreck', proclaiming that she had no conscience and echoing Hermann Goering's statement, 'My conscience is Adolf Hitler.'

Ilse Koch – the notorious 'Bitch of Buchenwald' – was infamous for her rampant promiscuity and perverted acts of sexual sadism with both men and women. Her victims were predominantly the male prisoners of Buchenwald, whom she would order to be beaten, suffocated or shot to death, while she observed and helped carry out the slayings, transported on a tide of visible ecstasy.

Koch was first put on trial as a war criminal by an American court at Nuremberg, then was tried again in 1951 in Bavaria, accused of murdering 45 prisoners and being the willing accomplice to another 135 concentration camp killings. Unlike Grese she broke down in the dock, blaming her husband, the commander of Buchenwald, for everything, appealing for clemency on the usual well-worn grounds that she had had no knowledge of what was going on, pleading that, 'I was merely a housewife. I never saw anything which was against humanity.' Found guilty of all charges and sentenced to life imprisonment, she lived until 1971.

Today, as Serb forces in former Yugoslavia press on relentlessly with their own genocidal agenda, flushing out the Muslims of Bosnia, we can observe the nauseating ferocity with which the practice of 'ethnic cleansing' continues to be pursued – not only by the military, but by ordinary citizens. Long-suppressed nationalistic hatred and xenophobia can all too swiftly and rampantly stifle humanitarian compassion and free-will. The sentiments of callous indifference and hate expressed by Serbian snipers and Bosnian defence units – which include, as we have seen, large numbers of women – are an all too predictable part of the grim nightmare played out since the summer of 1992.

Can we therefore be surprised that the civil war in Yugoslavia should have spawned its own new generation of Irma Greses and Ilse Kochs? Events there illustrate the futility and foolishness of attempting to find simple reasons for women's violence without first examining the context of their past personal history and present socioeconomic and political environment. Before the incursion of Serb forces into Bosnia in 1992, Monika Simonovitch was little more than a social outcast, the uneducated 18-year-old daughter of a local prostitute, a nobody, a nothing, living in the Bosnian town of Brcko. The future held little likelihood of escape from her lot, of rising above her squalid and poverty-stricken surroundings, until the newly established Serbian detention camps beckoned.

For a girl who had only known abuse, insults and rejection, by her family and by the men she met, this was a perfect opportunity to wreak vengeance for life's injustices and wield the ultimate power – the power of life and death. Joining up as a guard in one of the local makeshift camps set up in 1992 by the Serbians principally for the incarceration of the Muslim enemy, she quickly showed a natural aptitude for the art of torture and gained a fearsome reputation. Reports were soon circulating of the enthusiasm with which she pursued her own favourite methods, including the breaking off of a bottle top to cut open the stomachs, gouge out the eyes or sever the ears and noses of the young men she interrogated. Her main aim was to force them to admit they were snipers who had fired at Serbian troops. The confessions started to come fast and willingly – by confessing, the victims at least could be sure of instant death, a welcome release from the agonies she inflicted upon them.

Certainly women such as these represent only a tiny minority of their sex. It is quite true that throughout history it has been the male of our species who has been overwhelmingly and indisputably guilty of crimes against their fellow humans. But would we not expect the majority of sadistic torturers and murderers to be men, given that it is almost only men who (at least until very recently) have made up the military service and the police force, who join vigilante, guerrilla and mercenary units, or are employed as guards, commanders and supervisors in state institutions? The question that now arises, and must be unflinchingly addressed, is this: if you put large numbers of women into such positions, would they too become as adept as men at exercising power and terror and as skilled at inflicting psychological and physical torture? Is the female psyche as susceptible to programming by unscrupulous ideologies and dictatorships founded on violence as a man's, and are women *en masse* likely to become as susceptible as men to contamination by the all-pervading virus of brutality and violence which runs rampant within male institutions of power at times of war, revolution and political oppression?

The growing number of accounts regarding the background and motivation of female terrorists certainly attests to that reality. So too do the experiences of many women prisoners at the ruthless hands of a great number of female warders. Judging by the countless hair-raising tales of prison life, some female prison warders appear to thrive on the intense hothouse atmosphere of high-security institutions, deriving intense satisfaction from exerting power over inmates and using violence often unnecessarily, sometimes to the point of sadism.

According to Dr Mika Haritos-Fatouros, Professor of Clinical Psychology at the University of Thessalonika, who has spent fifteen years researching the psychology of torturers, concentrating on those who from 1967 to 1974 worked under the Greek dictatorship, the last person you want to recruit as an efficient torturer is an emotionally unstable maniac – which confirms what we already know about the kind of women who make successful terrorists.

Having initially steeled herself to discovering a colony of heartless sadists, more monstrous than human, Dr Haritos-Fatouros found that, on the contrary, the successful 'professional' torturer must be absolutely normal and mentally balanced. In other words, what is so deeply disturbing about this is the notion that, given a certain combination of circumstances, *any of us* – male or female – could be driven to hurt another person, or even to torture them if ordered to do so. Like many other dictatorships, the Greek Military Police recognized that the only way to turn raw recruits into obedient instruments of torture was to train them – literally sending them to 'torture school' – to become emotionally detached, both in their relationship to their victims as well as with regards to their own self-perception of the acts they committed, in order to be able to follow orders obediently and efficiently and adhere strictly to the doctrine and goals of the system within which they operated. According to Dr Haritos-Fatouros, women could be trained in exactly the same way as men to become efficient torturers, a process that involved subjecting recruits to gruelling physical acts of exertion and other brutalizing psychological and bodily treatments, making them perform unpleasant or degrading tasks such as cleaning up a torture cell after a prisoner had been interrogated. The objective of such training is desensitization: the removal of all normal human feeling, inducing an automatic state of mind–body dissociation to the point where the trainee is transformed into an unfeeling automaton.

That human beings, male or female, can arrive at such a stage of de-humanization where acts of torture and killing become so commonplace as to be devoid of all meaning, or even capable of evoking satisfaction and joy, is a painful and obscene fact to contemplate. But Professor Haritos-Fatouros's findings tie in very largely with those of two other eminent researchers into the nature of evil and destructiveness, Robert Jay Lifton and

Ervin Staub, both of whom have also warned of the danger in assuming that only a select number of deviant or wicked, unfeeling individuals can be capable of such atrocities as mass murder and torture. Moreover, it is their belief that no special training is needed to cross the border from normal, compassionate behaviour to extreme destructiveness, and that in certain circumstances the process may happen automatically. In an attempt to explain the psychology of evil, especially in normally humane, caring people, American psychologist Robert Jay Lifton has defined an automatic, natural mechanism of adaptation to crisis, which he terms 'doubling' and which may just as easily help to preserve life, as in the case of individuals who are taken hostage, survive natural disasters, wars, rape or imprisonment, as to destroy it. It is usually preceded by a process of psychic numbing, a defence response which diminishes capacity for normal feeling and separates thought from emotion in individuals whose basic survival depends on their ability to commit atrocities. Inevitably they develop a fully functional 'second self', a double capable of perpetrating acts of the most obscene brutality without remorse or guilt, while at other times they can revert back to their ordinary, compassionate, humane selves.

We ignore at our peril, warns Professor Lifton, the fact that this facility is far from limited to extreme circumstances such as war. It may become the sole means of suspending doubt, revulsion or moral conscience for those routinely involved in an ideology or profession founded on a destructive or exploitative base, as for example the nuclear arms industry. As the technology of killing becomes more technologically sophisticated, human contact between aggressor and victim more fleeting or non-existent (as when a bomber plants a bomb in a pub or department store then detonates it miles away from the scene), the more pervasive the whole process of dissociation and the ability to justify violence becomes. The chilling fact that this mechanism is not unique to a handful of psychopaths and a few power-hungry despots and dictators but operates effectively in great numbers of ordinary men *and* women is inordinately hard for most of us to accept.

Just as depressing in its implied inevitability is Professor Ervin

Staub's notion of the 'continuum of destruction', which he believes causes us to learn and change by virtue of actively 'doing'. Its mirror image is the 'continuum of benevolence' by which altruists and philanthropically motivated individuals become increasingly more concerned for the welfare of others as a result of the personal development they experience from their involvement in the care of others. Neither altruism nor destructiveness are inborn qualities according to Staub – both are acquired and perfected through personal experience. Hence, destructive people in his view start off as mere ordinary folk like the rest of us, in possession of a set of motives, needs and goals, which, according to the prevailing cultural, economic and political climate, may only be attainable by embarking on a long progressive path of destruction. In so doing, and by experiencing, through the feedback of their own early, relatively minor antisocial or aggressive actions, that there are benefits to be gained from resorting to violence or ignoring the needs and suffering of others, the scale and intensity of these actions and the attraction of violent and inhumane political ideology may grow in direct proportion to their perceived advantages and survival value.

As Ervin Staub observes in his book *The Roots of Evil*, it is but a short series of steps from a person's very earliest indifference or hostility towards those whom they have targeted as the 'enemy' to full-scale murder and genocide, especially under extreme conditions of hardship and oppression.

Resistant though we may be to the proposition that neither the continuum of altruism nor that of destruction is the exclusive province of one sex, only by fully accepting this not as mere fantasy but hard fact can we begin to acknowledge that the infinite human capacity for confronting change, seeking self-expression and fighting for survival can, and does, include means that are vile, base and ignoble, born of motives ranging from the blackest malevolence and hate to the most abject fear and despair. To continue as we still do to revile men for being the principal inventors, architects and agents of destruction and regard women as a superior race apart is tantamount to denying men's capacity for altruism, selflessneess and caring. In recog-

nizing that the human potential for supreme good is shared
equally by women and men, it is foolish to suppose that the
potential for extreme destructiveness is not likewise shared by
both.

5

Deadly Intimacies

A Sentence to Fit the Crime
One set of clothing only; two visits from family members and friends per month, without recourse to privacy; no access to your children; rotten food, low in nutritional content; letters censored and checked for possible smuggling of drugs; windows so tiny and high up you see hardly any daylight, sky, birds, trees or signs of the seasons; locked into your dormitory or single room perhaps no bigger than 10 feet x 6 feet by 8.30 each evening. Is such punishment really all most criminals deserve?

Take the case of Devon housewife Pamela Sainsbury, who strangled her common-law husband Paul with a nylon cord then stuffed his body into a wardrobe for several days before sawing and chopping it up, putting the pieces into plastic rubbish bags and throwing them over a hedge into a deserted country field. The head she kept longest, in the woodshed; it was the last part of him she disposed of. Or June Scotland from Stevenage, who, with the help of her daughter, drugged her husband Thomas then clubbed him to death with a rolling pin and buried his body in the back garden.

Dangerous psychopaths who must not be let loose in the community at any costs? Not a bit of it. Much as it may strain the bounds of credulity, neither the fact that Asian housewife Kiranjit Ahluwalia threw a bucket of petrol over her husband and set fire to him, nor the fifteen shots, two in the head, thirteen in the back, with which Viola Williams of New Orleans finished off her live-in boyfriend, provides any real evidence that these offenders (and hundreds like them) are either too mentally unstable or callously wicked to be allowed outside a locked cell.

The history of female homicide is largely a history of domestic turbulence and violent family confrontation. Just as women are statistically more at risk of being assaulted, raped or murdered by their male partner or someone whom they know than by a stranger, so those whom they murder are overwhelmingly likely to be someone close to them, whom they probably know intimately, whom they perhaps still love or almost certainly once loved and shared a large proportion of their life with – spouses past and present, lovers, children, parents or other relatives. Crimes are usually enacted against a background of the banal and humdrum. Killings of one partner by another have occurred as a result of such trivial disputes as to why she put the mustard on the wrong side of the table, the overcooking of a fish supper, rows over which TV channel to watch, the mundane small print of everyday existence which may all too often act as a catalyst for the explosion of the most volatile human emotions, from fury and hatred to sexual jealousy, possessiveness and abject terror.

These domestic murders and crimes of passion may seem to the casual observer to be nauseatingly vicious and defying comprehension; the perpetrator, her sex notwithstanding, undeserving of either sympathy or clemency. Yet, as attested by increasing recognition of the plight of battered wives, the cumulative forces that may drive such women to desperate extremes as a last chance bid to save their own or their children's lives may be far from what they appear to be in the cold light of a criminal court.

The stark truth remains, however, that compared to men who murder their wives or girlfriends, women who kill their spouses, being fewer in number, are more likely to be deemed deranged or wickedly calculating and thus judged and sentenced with a degree of harshness that fails to take into account the extreme immediate circumstances, let alone the long-term history, marked often by collective experiences of violence in a woman's relationship with her victim, which may have driven her to kill.

In America, where 682 men were killed by their wives or girlfriends in 1991, many of whom are now serving life sentences or in some states face execution, about half are believed to have killed because of the violence they suffered at the hands of their spouses. A recent study carried out in New York suggests that a similar proportion of the 326 women serving time for homicide or attempted homicide during 1991 might have killed because of abusive relationships. Another irony is that many 'domestic' killers are unlikely to have had previous convictions for violent crimes and are therefore less likely to reoffend, which cannot be said for a large number of their male counterparts or for convicted violent criminals or petty offenders of either sex.

Separate and extensive studies carried out recently investigated the backgrounds of large numbers of convicted female murderers in comparison to those doing time for other serious crimes, and also examined the events and circumstances leading up to and finally precipitating each killing. In one study conducted in Florida involving 1,076 women it became clear that the murderers differed greatly from other convicted female offenders in that they were far more likely to have come from broken or violent homes and suffered violence from their partner – 62 per cent of those who murdered their partner had been abused by him regularly over long periods of their relationship right up until the killing – yet had less incidence of criminality in their family and committed fewer violent crimes themselves. Criminologist Carol Bullock of Florida State University, whose survey of female murderers was based on an analysis of daily homicide reports submitted to the Florida Department of Law Enforcement from 1976 to 1987, found that although more murders are committed by white and younger women, with a slightly higher number of women murdering strangers (mostly men), the vast majority of crimes remain domestic killings, most notably in cases where the husband or boyfriend was violent and abusive and a domestic argument had preceded the murder.

One veteran researcher, Professor Emeritus of sociology, anthropology and social work at Auburn University, Alabama, Alan Shields, a speaker at the 1992 American Society of Criminology's annual conference in New Orleans, tells of working as a volunteer counsellor at a women's prison in Alabama in 1956 where he forged firm, mutual friendships with numbers of 'remarkable women'. These included the chief librarian, the head of catering, the accountant and the gatekeeper. All were so-called 'heavies', the state's apparently most dangerous citizens, serving long or life sentences for murder – all, as he puts it, having been 'widowed by their own hand'. The majority had never had a single previous brush with the law, not even a parking ticket. 'These women ran the prison with great efficiency. They were not violent and they were probably the only real first-time offenders in prison, with the exception of youngsters on probation.' Shields's involvement with these women and the unexpectedly favourable impression they made on him prompted him to study not only the backgrounds of others like them committed to Julia Tutwiler Prison, but to evaluate the variations in sentencing for these offences over five decades, from the 1930s until the 1980s – analysis that was to embrace a total of 746 cases.

As foreseen, the data collected by Professor Shields, which was later analysed by his colleague Dr Penelope Hanke, showed that most murders were indeed a family affair, with violently heated disputes and confrontation a common catalyst in the murder of husbands and boyfriends, as well as other family members. Overall, the offenders were older, very poorly educated, mothers of one or two children and as likely to be from urban as rural communities. Knives and, in later decades, guns were the 'weapon of choice' (the rapid and immense increase in women's use of guns as opposed to knives in recent years offering an alarming reflection of America's violent 'trigger-happy' society). Yet as the other studies show, few of these women had prior criminal charges or convictions, and they were mostly non-violent by nature, those with prior convictions usually having been little more than drunk and disorderly. Echoing the Florida studies, it seems that white women are catching up with black in the domestic murder statistics; while 80 per cent of the women were black between 1929 and 1969, from 1969 until 1985 they made up only two-thirds of the female homicide inmate population.

On the basis of such findings alone, it would seem that the 'sling 'em into a cell and throw away the key' pro life-imprisonment lobby are skating on extremely thin ice. Arguments in favour of harsh, long-term prison sentences become shorter on logic by the minute the more apparent become the factors that lead certain women to kill, and also the more evident it becomes how inadequate prison resources really are in catering to such women's needs. Which in turn begs the question, how much of a threat to the community or to their own families or to themselves are most of these women?

The unequivocal answer, save for a few very notable and egregious exceptions, must be none at all. This much can be gleaned not only from the statistics, but from repeated observations of those who work closely with female murderers who have killed within a domestic context as to the degree of evidently genuine and extreme remorse and contrition they feel over their crime, hardly commonplace among persistent, hardened or dangerous offenders, male or female. Most women tend to report injuring or killing their victim immediately, usually calling an ambulance or the police or both, accompanying their dying spouse to hospital if he is not already dead, giving themselves up and freely admitting their guilt, usually without pressure to do so.

Cynthia Gillespie and Angela Browne, who have carried out extensive research into the experiences of battered women and appeared as expert witnesses for the defence in cases where these women murdered their abusive husbands, have both emphasized the recurring patterns of such murders, the predictability of every such scenario. Cynthia Gillespie, former director of the NorthWest Women's Law Center in Seattle, collected over two hundred stories from battered women who murdered and describes a typical domestic homicide as preceded by an explosive row in which the man threatens to gravely injure or kill his partner while lunging towards her, holding her down and beating, sexually assaulting or attempting to strangle her; the woman grabs a nearby knife or a gun – usually his – and points it at him, warning him to back off and leave her alone; he continues threatening or assaulting her and as they struggle either the knife punctures a vital organ or, as he tries to wrest the gun from her, she pulls the trigger. Panicking, she calls the police or ambulance; they find her sitting on the floor, cradling his head in her lap, begging him not to die.

In her book *Justifiable Homicide*, Gillespie comments that: 'This story was played out, with minor variations, so many times that I sometimes had the feeling that I was reading the same case over and over again.' There is rarely any dispute over who did the killing – the women virtually always give themselves up, confessing to what they did and why, and though invariably in an extreme state of numbness, hysterical shock and grief, do their best to cooperate with the police, answering detailed questions and making statements, sometimes under extreme police pressure, although clearly while in no fit psychological state to do so.

On the basis that the objectives of imprisonment are to protect society from the possible threat of danger posed by such individuals, to deter others from committing similar crimes and both to punish and, more significantly in recent years, to rehabilitate the offender, then it could be argued that there is little if anything to be gained from keeping these women under lock and key. Unlike men, who commit far greater numbers of random, opportunistic crimes of violence, including murder, and who also seem have a near monopoly on sadistic sexual assaults, women seem to kill in very specific and compelling circumstances – although one could well be led to believe otherwise listening to or reading some judges' views on the wickedness or the demented condition of many a hapless female murderer in the dock.

Does their imprisonment serve as a likely deterrent to others? In view of the fact that many such murders are far from premeditated, it is difficult to see the existence of any real deterrence factor. Those that appear to be so, as when a woman waits until her violent husband is asleep before murdering him, are now increasingly seen as the result of a battered woman's genuine terror that after repeated threats to kill her, this time he will carry out his threat. After all, if – as criminologists concur – capital punishment has demonstrably failed to deter individuals from committing murder and long prison terms have also proven notoriously ineffective in preventing convicted violent or petty criminals of both sexes from reoffending, then on what basis are we to believe that harsh sentencing could influence someone about to commit a crime in the so-called 'heat of the moment'?

How could it, when the main finding to emerge about women who stab, shoot, strangle or club to death their violent partners is that they often do so on 'automatic pilot', as Helena Kennedy QC, counsel for the defence, described Pamela Sainsbury's steady and relentless pull on the cord around her dying husband's neck: 'It was like eight years of anger coming out in an instant. She did not want to kill him but could not stop pulling.' In this case, Pamela Sainsbury's plight did appear to make sense to the court. Having denied murder but pleaded guilty to manslaughter on grounds of diminished responsibility, she was put on two years' probation.

What, then, of the much-vaunted rehabilitative powers of imprisonment? This, of course, is the most overrated, specious argument used to justify all prison sentences, whether served on men, women or youngsters, whatever their crimes. Again, because the majority of female 'domestic' murderers are increasingly recognized as having acted within the context of some form of sustained, often long-term physical and/or psychological abuse inflicted by the deceased, resulting in the woman's altered perceptions, heightened terror, helplessness and fear for her own safety, it seems nothing short of absurd that years of incarceration, with all the stigma and deprivation that this entails, can possibly help an offender who is herself very likely to be a victim, a long-standing casualty of abuse and injustice. In effect, the fate that awaits many battered wives who kill is nothing less than what post-traumatic stress expert Dr Martin Symons, former psychiatric adviser to the New York City police force, terms 'secondary' victimization – the first offender being their partner, the second one the state.

Thankfully, as the law in America and, increasingly, in Britain begins to address the complex dynamics underlying many such crimes, the time may be approaching when we can hope to see more just sentencing. In England, the overturning of the murder convictions of Amelia Rossiter and Kiranjit Ahluwalia who, previously sentenced to life imprisonment for murdering their violent husbands, finally walked free after their appeals had been heard and retrials granted, offers hope for women who have killed but do not by any stretch of the imagination conform to a criminal type. Still a matter of great concern is the very limited therapeutic potential of almost any prison environment. In view of the virtual absence of specialist counselling and adequate psychotherapy in prison for those with a past history of experiencing violence (for example, the first ever support group for former rape victims in any British prison was set up in Styal Prison in Yorkshire in 1993), it is baffling to suppose that any prisoner suffering from both the long-term consequences of domestic abuse, as well as the immediate trauma of having murdered someone close to them, could begin to pick up the pieces of their lives and rebuild their shattered self-image within a prison environment.

Much as lawyers are given to muttering about the risks of recidivism and the need to serve long prison sentences as an example to others not to take the law into their own hands and hope they can get away with it, there does appear, especially where women are concerned, to be a marked lack of consistency in sentencing policies, especially between America and England. For instance, it is hard to imagine what public interest could possibly have been served by denying parole to the aging, frail, Jean Harris who had served thirteen years of her fifteen-year prison sentence for the murder of her lover Hermann Tarnower, the Scarsdale Diet doctor. Harris, aged 68, who suffers from a serious cardiac disorder and who has always denied intentionally killing Dr Tarnower, was finally released in 1993 from Bedford Hills Correctional Facility, a maximum security penitentiary where from the outset she had proven to be a model prisoner, volunteering to work in the nursery and caring for babies born to inmates. She went on to extend and fund the nursery with proceeds from the sale of her books, *Marking Time* and *Stranger in Two Worlds*. New evidence that came to light after her trial in 1981, indicating that up to three days before the murder she had been heavily dependent on Desoxyn, a powerful antidepressant drug prescribed by her boyfriend that has since found to produce extreme withdrawal symptoms, has remained steadfastly ignored. It took three appeals for clemency before Mario Cuomo, Governor of New York State, agreed to Harris's release. Yet not by the wildest stretch of imagination could Jean Harris have been regarded as a potential public menace who, if released, might launch herself on a late career in crime.

By examining three very recent 'passion' murders committed by younger women who were clearly in control of their actions even if they were motivated by lust, jealousy and hatred, it becomes easier to spot those cases that obviously *do* merit long and severe punishment, and where, for the sake of the victims and their relatives, justice must not only be done, but be seen to be done.

Betty Broderick, convicted of murdering her former husband Daniel, a wealthy sharp-shooting lawyer, and his new, beautiful, young bride as they lay sleeping at home in bed, has been sentenced to life imprisonment. Broderick claims she went to the house in the fashionable San Diego suburb of La Jolla before dawn to discuss details pertaining to her divorce, and crept into the bedroom merely to confront them. The gun, she maintains, went off when she flinched, 'in one big explosion'. The pistol fired five times, hitting Daniel in the lung, his wife in the head and chest, and when, bleeding and dying, he tried to reach for the telephone, Betty Broderick smacked him on the wrist with the gun butt and threw the phone across the room.

Interviews with Broderick indicate a narcissistic, self-righteously indignant and emotionally detached woman, alternately glib and matter-of-fact, who repeatedly emphasizes the years of psychological abuse and cruelty meted out by her husband, displaying no genuine remorse, sorrow or guilt about the double killing, much as she attempts an unconvincing imitation of such sentiments. Ultimately she blames the victims for making her react in this way. 'I reacted very badly. But I still resent that they made me react, and that they made me defend myself that way. Because that's what they were doing. They were poking sticks in me. Watch her, watch her, watch her get mad, then we can say she's crazy.' What seems clear is that prison, hopefully in combination with long-term rehabilitation, can be the sole future for a woman like Broderick. She appears to take pride in her talent for duplicitous play-acting – during a recess at her first trial at which the jury failed to reach a verdict, one of her jailers quoted her as saying, 'I think my crying had a really good impact on the jury. They ate it up.' More chilling still is the extent of her moral bankruptcy, an inability to empathize with others' suffering or respect their views and a total obliviousness to the enormity of her crime, traits which would indeed make her a danger to the community.

Another, far younger, woman, 18-year-old Amy Fisher, who was sentenced in December 1992 to fifteen years' imprisonment for attempting to murder Mary Jo Buttafuoco, the wife of her alleged lover Joe Buttafuoco, seems also to be in dire need of help in attempting to overcome her emotional instability. This instability, combined with deadly intermeshing strands of evident cunning, cupidity and ruthlessness, makes her a potentially lethal individual, especially considering that she seriously disabled her rival but failed to kill her. In May 1992, Fisher rang Mrs Buttafuoco's doorbell and shot her point-blank in the head, leaving her for dead. Although Amy Fisher has publicly admitted sorrow and regret for what she did, she has consistently blamed her alleged lover for encouraging her to shoot his wife, claiming he began an affair with her while she was below the age of consent and still in high school, and tried to persuade her to work as a prostitute – charges of which Buttafuoco has been found guilty and sentenced to imprisonment. All the evidence suggests, however, that here we have no confused or frightened virgin taken against her will and coerced into violence, but a girl determined to satisfy her desires at any costs.

In sentencing Fisher at Nassau County Court in Long Island, Judge Marvin Goodman stated that: 'Her acts were not spontaneous or impulsive but like a wild animal that stalks its prey, motivated by lust and passion . . . You were a walking stick of dynamite with the fuse lit.' As usual, it is the less sensational, under-reported details that give the real clue to Fisher's character. A secretly made video during her detention shows her asking a boyfriend visiting her at the time to marry her so that they could have conjugal visits together while she is in prison. The video also records her saying she expected to make enough money from her notoriety to buy a Ferrari.

By comparison to such well-publicized American female killers and the appropiateness of their sentencing, it is difficult to understand by what logic the breathtakingly lenient five-year prison sentence was originally passed on former Ulster Defence Regiment soldier Susan Christie, who slashed the throat of Penny McAllister, the wife of her army captain lover.

Although pleading guilty to manslaughter on grounds of diminished responsibility – she was reportedly suffering from stress and depression – it became clear during the trial that this was a coldly pre-planned murder. The day before the killing, Christie had invited Mrs McAllister for a meal at a restaurant and they arranged to walk their dogs the next day in the countryside. During the walk she pulled out a sharpened boning knife and slashed Mrs McAllister's throat. She then ripped her own clothes, stabbed herself in the thigh and other parts of her body and fooled the police into believing that they had both been attacked in the woods. That this was a crime of passion and that Christie's mind had become unbalanced because of her obsession with her lover is all too likely; what is debatable is whether she was out of control of her senses when she murdered her victim.

Evidently the Appeal Court disagreed with the original suggestion that this was a sudden 'explosion of emotion' rather than a premeditated act, and by a majority of two to one the bench increased her original prison term from five to nine years, after ruling that she possessed 'considerable residual mental responsibility' for carrying out 'a wicked and evil deed'.

The very different motives and circumstances underlying these women's actions highlights the absurdity of current claims made by some radical feminist groups as to the unfairly harsh treatment by the courts of women who kill, as if their gender – implicitly linked to the status of the victim – were sufficient to abrogate personal responsibility while automatically deserving special leniency. Yet one has only to compare the cunning and cruelty of women like Christie and Fisher, or many of the groups of youngsters described in the previous chapter, to the distress of an evidently helpless prisoner of appalling circumstances, like Pamela Sainsbury, to recognize the need for punishment to fit each individual crime rather than the sex of the criminal.

Is Self-defence a Fair Defence?

It seems reasonable enough to assume that a woman being violently attacked by a man, whether he is her husband, boyfriend or a complete stranger attempting rape, is entitled to use whatever means she can to defend herself. But, alas, the legal doctrine of self-defence seems not to have been constructed with women in mind. In America and Britain, as in most other Western countries, the right to take an assailant's life to save one's own, or that of one's child or another close family member, is one of the oldest common law rights. Yet it is a right men may apparently avail themselves of infinitely more readily than women. Because the rules determining how much force may be used and the victim's perception of the imminence of danger are based on men's experiences of fighting one another as equals, women may find massive obstacles preventing them from getting away with such a defence – and end up being charged with and convicted for murder.

Proving that they used 'reasonable' and equal force to deter an attack – one of the prime criteria underlying the doctrine of self-defence – is no easy matter for most women, who are generally smaller and weaker than their aggressor and may need to use a weapon when he himself is unarmed, yet whose own bare body serves as an all too effective lethal weapon. Persuading a jury that they genuinely perceived the danger to be imminent is also less easy for a woman being attacked by someone she knows, especially a normally brutal, abusive partner, than for a woman who is savagely assaulted in the street by a complete stranger. Like the test of equal force, the so-called 'imminence requirement' fails to take into account battered women's cumulative experiences of violence such as terror of further possibly lethal attacks in the immediate future.

If a battered woman kills just after being attacked, when the man's back is turned or he has fallen asleep, the danger, it is generally argued, is no longer imminent, and there is theoretically nothing to prevent the woman from leaving home, escaping her attacker or calling the police. There again, the fact that many battered wives feel unable to leave either because they have nowhere to go or they are in terror of provoking their partner to further fury and brutality is a dilemma left wholly unaddressed by the doctrine of self-defence.

The final stumbling block a woman may come across — although much depends on the background, experiences and attitudes of the jury — is the legal concept of 'reasonableness', which also militates against women's experiences of male violence or of repeated domestic abuse. Since the law is based on what a 'reasonable man' would do if caught in identical circumstances it is obvious that a number of avenues of escape and options for alternative action — such as slugging it out with your opponent, knocking him out cold, breaking free and running away — simply do not apply to the average woman. It has been suggested that the fact that there is so far no female equivalent in legal textbooks to the hypothetical reasonable man reflects male assumptions that this would amount to a contradiction in terms, since female traits are perceived as the antithesis of reasonableness!

In some countries, such as Australia, Canada and the USA, the rules on self-defence have become sufficiently relaxed at times recently to allow more female defendants to justifiably and successfully run the defence in court. However, the route by which an apparent victim of assault suddenly finds herself on the other side of the tracks, being judged as an assailant, and then may find herself again back on the 'right side' of the law, is a narrow and slippery one, fraught with obstacles and laid with treacherously concealed traps.

An important test case in America involved Yvonne Wanrow, a Colville Native American woman who was originally convicted of second-degree murder, having shot and killed a known child-abuser who had broken into her home and threatened her child, but later had the conviction overturned. It was accepted that Wanrow, a 5-foot 4-inch woman, who had experienced much racial violence and discrimination, with a cast on her leg and using a crutch, confronting a 6-foot 2-inch drunk, white assailant, could only reasonably use a weapon to defend herself. At the retrial the Washington Supreme Court ruled: 'The defendant's actions are to be judged against her own subjective impressions and not those a detached jury might determine reasonable.'

In rape cases, the legal requirements of self-defence can reach supreme heights of absurdity. Should a woman who is under threat from a man act too soon, before he has initiated any specific sexual act such as pulling off her clothes and unzipping his trousers, then there may be doubt as to whether a rape really was about to occur. If she acts too late, after intercourse is completed, she may be suspected of having decided to kill him in vengeance. Presumably the only stage at which, in law, she may act in self-defence is the one when she is least capable of so doing – when pinned down in the act of penetration.

In America, two important precedents in particular stand out: one was the case of Inez Garcia, who was attacked by two men and raped by one of them. Twenty minutes after the ordeal, when the onlooker had telephoned her threatening he would return and do worse things to her, she went after them with a gun and shot the onlooker dead as he came towards her with a knife. Her initial conviction was overturned on appeal when the jury agreed she had acted not in revenge but in genuine self-defence against a perceived mortal attack, her terror made more acute as a result of the immediate effects of post-rape trauma. In another test case, Joanne Little, a young black woman imprisoned in a North Carolina jail, stabbed a white guard to death with his own knife as he was raping her. She was acquitted of murder and the case acclaimed as a victory not only by women's groups but by civil rights campaigners as an unprecedented triumph in a Southern area rampant with racism.

Judging by the number of cases where women have attacked or killed rapists and would-be rapists, trying to prove self-defence – like trying to prove rape itself – can turn out to be an ordeal of near unendurable proportions. In July 1981, 19-year-old Diana Lee was sentenced to a twelve-month suspended sentence for having stabbed a stranger who had confronted her, pretending to be a policeman, as she returned home from work along a country road after dark. He had dragged her into a field, thrown her to the ground and knelt on her, threatened to kill her and tried to rape her. She managed to pull out a small sheath knife she had used for cutting her pony's bales of hay and stuck it in his neck. What provoked outrage amongst many women at the time was the fact that the court showed more sympathy for him because of his injuries – things have come to a pretty pass when a rapist has to expect to get stabbed by his victim, for heaven's sake – than understanding of the terror she went through or acknowledgment of her right to protect herself.

Although the jury found 24-year-old Melvyn Maguire guilty of threatening to kill her, Judge Stanley Price, believing he had suffered enough, passed a twelve-month suspended prison sentence, remarking: 'This young lady inflicted a very considerable punishment on you.' *She* inflicted punishment on *him*? That a potentially lethal attacker should walk free because his victim took steps to guard her life and body must surely rank as one of the most iniquitous examples of sexist bias and a travesty of justice. Whether the outcome would have been the same had the potential rape victim, for argument's sake, been male, or the attacker a teenage burglar breaking into the home of an old lady who managed to biff him over the head or cut his face with a heavy object, is surely worth pondering.

Time and again, as such cases come to light, the single most distressing feature to emerge is the alternating attitudes of either bogus chivalry, patronizing sympathy or outright disapprobation adopted towards women who have had the temerity to act not in the accepted female mode of terrified submission, but managed to defend themselves or react in explosive fury against a violent attack in the way that any 'reasonable' man would be expected to under similar or less extreme circumstances. The belief that women maim, injure and kill men through vengeance, vindictiveness, hate or mental derangement and must be either severely punished or taken into care for rehabilitative therapy, while men assault women who have betrayed, taunted, nagged or refused to submit to their wishes and are to be shown sympathy, runs like an indelible stain through decades of law reporting and trial transcripts.

In 1988, when 28-year-old Yvonne Hey, an unsophisticated farm girl, shot her 55-year-old 'father figure' John France when he raped her, the judge made this statement on having her five-year prison sentence reduced to three: 'She had been raped by a man whom she had come to trust and consider almost as a father. We do think it would be proper to make some reduction.' Note the sententious use of the word 'proper'. Was a three-year prison sentence really just treatment for a girl who had suffered such extreme abuse and betrayal?

Although the trial of 38-year-old Janet Clugstone, a widowed mother charged with murdering her rapist, ended in her acquittal, the mere fact that she was forced to endure such further trauma – the trial took place in the full glare of publicity at London's Central Criminal Court – after suffering an appalling sexual assault, consisting of repeated rape and buggery, is an outrage in itself. When attacked by Stephen Cophen, who was high on alcohol, cannabis and glue-sniffing, she had recently undergone major surgery for throat cancer in which her larynx had been removed, so she could not cry out. Having met her *en route* to a discotheque, he had forced her into a friend's empty flat on a Paddington council estate and, during the attack, she found an open Swiss army knife on the floor with which she stabbed him, inflicting one lethal wound. She then staggered half a mile to Harrow Road police station with bloodstained clothes and ripped tights, carrying the knife, and explained what had happened. WPC Carol Rendelle, on duty at the time, reported this to be a very severe case of sexual abuse and degradation and quite evidently genuine: 'This was quite the most extreme case of distress I believe I have ever come across.'

Denying both murder and manslaughter, Clugstone was put on trial for murder in 1987, a year after the attack. Incredibly, the question of whether she had acted in self-defence or in revenge rested solely on whether or not Cophen had withdrawn his penis at the time of the attack, not on whether such repeated assaults constituted a terrifying, life-threatening experience. Yet all the research to date indicates that the abject fear and other post-traumatic stress symptoms suffered by sexual assault survivors may be equally extreme whether or not the attacker was armed or even whether or not the rape actually occurred, since the victim's perceived threat of death or mutilation remains the same.

Excerpts of the trial recorded by Sue Lees, director of Women's Studies at the University of North London, indicate that at times proceedings took a turn more reminiscent of high farce than courtroom sobriety. To quote Judge Hazan:

> The question is, did she kill him after he'd withdrawn – kill him in reasonable self-defence to stop him raping and assaulting her? In lawful self-defence, acquit. If she's not telling the truth – why isn't she? Is she a lady killing a young man in circumstances she's unwilling to reveal after he's withdrawn in revenge for the rape? *That is not lawful killing.* She should then be found guilty of murder – an unprovoked and unlawful killing with intent to cause death or serious injury.

Apart from this emphasis on penetration as the crucial determinant in assessing her motivation, what never seems to have been addressed is the fact that rape and murder often do go together, and just because he had withdrawn his penis was no guarantee that he would not go on to possibly strangle or beat her to death. In Janet Clugstone's words: 'I did not want to kill him. I just wanted to get away from him. He was like a madman.'

It is worth emphasizing that during her cross-examination about intimate details of the rape, Clugstone was also confronted with questions designed to establish whether she was a 'decent' or a promiscuous woman, and also whether she was a racist, at one point being asked whether she had previously had sex with other West Indians and whether she got on well with the West Indians on the housing estate. Yet as Sue Lees points out, in a rape trial questions concerning a woman's past sexual history are usually disallowed, except at the discretion of the judge. And although she walked free, Judge Hazan nevertheless trotted out the old familiar warning that rape victims should not regard this as a charter to kill their attackers.

Guilty by Gender?

Consider and compare the following cases. On the evening of 27 February 1991, Joseph McGrail came home from work to find his violent, alcohol and drug-addicted partner Marion Kennedy, as was customary during their ten-year relationship, in a drunken stupor. Unable to face her drunken abusiveness any longer, he kicked and punched her repeatedly in the stomach as she lay on the bed, causing her to die from a massive internal haemorrhage. At his trial, McGrail was found guilty of manslaughter and walked free from Birmingham Crown Court with a two-year suspended prison sentence. The judge, Mr Justice Popplewell, said Kennedy 'would have tried the patience of a saint'.

At the time, Pamela Megginson, who in 1983, aged 61, smashed a champagne bottle over the head of her violent 79-year-old millionaire lover in a fit of fury because he was throwing her out of the house and taking another mistress, was still in prison, serving a mandatory life sentence for murder. She maintained the only thing that excited him sexually was hitting her. She had agreed to have sex that night to try and persuade him not to throw her out, but when he hit her yet again, she lost control.

In 1987, Thomas Corlett, a civil servant, was sentenced to three years for the manslaughter of his wife, apparently a cold, wilful, unaffectionate woman, after she had put the mustard on the left instead of the usual right side of his plate. Judge Gerald Butler accepted Corlett's plea of provocation, describing him as a 'hardworking man who had snapped after skivvying after his wife for years', adding that she had 'ruined his perfectly ordered life'.

In 1988, 63-year-old Amelia Rossiter was tried at Maidstone for stabbing her husband through the heart with a steak-knife during a row in which he threatened to garrotte her. The judge, Mr Justice Boreham, said she had been found guilty of murder on 'the clearest possible evidence' and sentenced her to life imprisonment. Rossiter's history of prolonged sexual abuse by her husband, almost up to the time of his death, was not allowed to be presented as evidence at her trial.

Nicholas Boyce was sentenced to six years' imprisonment in 1985 for the manslaughter of his wife on grounds of provocation caused by her nagging. He had dismembered her body, cooked the parts to disguise them, then dumped them in plastic bags around London. After serving just over three years, he was released on parole and moved in with an occupational therapist who worked in the prison.

In 1983, Mabel Patterson was convicted for stabbing her brutal husband to death. In passing a life sentence, Lord Wheatley stated that: 'There are so many occasions when wives are subjected to the kind of rough treatment to which you were subjected. The difficulty is that I cannot establish a precedent to give licence to wives who take the law into their own hands.'

In 1992, Singh Bisla strangled his 'nagging' wife 'to shut her up' after two hours of alleged verbal abuse. Convicted of manslaughter, he received an eighteen-month suspended sentence, having been told by the judge: 'I do not see that sending you to prison is going to do any good and, more importantly, is going to do the children any good. You have suffered, through no fault of your own, a terrible existence for a very long time.'

The previous year in Birmingham, an Asian woman, Iqbal Begum, was convicted of murder, having fatally clubbed her husband with a metal bar as he threatened to kill their children. Due to the absence of an interpreter the court understood Begum to have made a plea of guilty when in fact she said 'mistake' – which in Urdu sounds like the word 'guilty'. Her defence of provocation was rejected and she was sentenced to life imprisonment.

When it comes to spousal killings, it has to be said that there is greatly conflicting evidence as to whether men and women stand equal before the law. There have been numerous instances to suggest that many men continue to get away with murder, frequently having their initial murder charge reduced to the lesser offence of manslaughter. According to Home Office figures, 25 per cent of all homicides are domestic. Of these, 37 per cent involve husbands or live-in boyfriends killing their spouses, while 6 per cent involve a woman killing her partner. In England and Wales every year between 12 and 21 women kill their spouses, while on average about 70 to 100 women are murdered by their husbands.

However, there appears to be an immense discrepancy in the figures quoted for reduction in charges, successful and unsuccessful defence pleas and sentencing statistics, depending on who does the quoting. The campaign group Rights of Women has consistently stressed that a far greater proportion of men get their murder charge reduced to manslaughter, usually on grounds of provocation, while only a small fraction of women succeed in doing so.

Other authorities hotly dispute that the scales of justice are weighed against women. Christopher Nuttall, Director of Research and Statistics at the Home Office, has repeatedly dismissed these statements each time they appear in the press, as 'extraordinarily erroneous' and serving only to perpetuate the unfortunate myth of women's harsh treatment in comparison to men. Having analysed the facts behind 1,071 domestic killings which took place in England between 1983 and 1991, Nuttall states that, if anything, it is men who are getting a raw deal. More than 90 per cent of those arrested were charged with murder. Yet at their trial, 22 per cent of women (one in five) and only 5 per cent of men (one in twenty) were acquitted of all charges, with self-defence believed to be the most successful defence mounted by women. Among the remaining defendants, 19 per cent of women were convicted of murder, as against 38 per cent of men, while 81 per cent of women were found guilty of the lesser conviction of manslaughter compared to only 62 per cent of men. In addition, Nuttall's findings seem to fly in the face of feminist assertions that women can only hope to escape a murder charge if they plead diminished responsibility. In his study, among those women convicted of manslaughter, 33 per cent used the defence of diminished responsibility, 34 per cent ran provocation and 33 per cent ran no intent to kill. The figures for men found guilty of manslaughter were respectively 47 per cent diminished responsibility, 32 per cent provocation and 21 per cent no intent to kill.

His research also reveals significant differences in sentencing, but again with men, not women, receiving harsher treatment. Between 1989 and 1991, 73 per cent of men convicted of man-slaughter received a prison sentence compared with only 29 per cent of women. The average sentence length for those men was fifty-six months and for women forty-seven months, while 59 per cent of women were either given probation or a suspended sentence compared with 12 per cent of men – which, depending on how you look at it, could also be seen as a reinforcement of the view that women who kill are sick, unstable and in need of care and protection. A smaller study involving 160 cases of domestic murder, conducted by Wendy Buck from Manchester University and Sandra Walklate of Salford University, seems to bear this last observation out. They found that women were more likely to obtain a conviction of manslaughter due to dimin-ished responsibility than men, and therefore more likely to be put on probation or go to hospital, with gender apparently hav-ing greater impact on the court's decision than the recommen-dations of the forensic psychiatrist. When confronted with the disparity in these figures, women's groups tend to argue that it is not the actual statistics which count but their interpretation – their view being that those who compile the figures and claim that women are less harshly treated fail to take into consideration women's 'special' circumstances and experi-ences. Although that contention undoubtedly holds true in a great many cases – as outlined earlier – like the assertion that women who kill are let off more readily in the courts than are men, so the notion that men manage to 'get away with it' more regularly than women is one of those blanket statements which cannot be so easily substantiated, given how little is ever dis-closed publicly about each individual case.

Persuasive though Nuttall's figures are, they seem to bear little resemblance to what we find when we examine actual case histories. So rigid and strict are the rules of defence under the 1957 Homicide Act and so great the odds stacked against a woman unable to produce convincing evidence that killing a partner was a true act of self-defence or response to provocation, according to its most precise definition, that there would seem to be little danger of women 'getting away with murder' under current law. Those who maintain that the requirements for both defences should be relaxed often overlook the fact that this might provide not only women but men too, with greater opportunity to walk free when facing a charge of murder. Some say they already do so far too frequently. The classic defence of the long-suffering husband increasingly put-upon by his nagging, shrewish or adulterous wife or unfaithful girlfriend who taunts him about his sexual inadequacy until he finally 'snaps' and kills her in a fit of sudden rage when goaded once too often may be a courtroom cliché, but as a plea for clemency it seems to work inordinately well to men's advantage. For women who similarly kill in the course of a vicious confrontation, though usually in response to far more extreme, apparently life-threatening violence and threats of death, the plea of provocation time after time cuts no ice in domestic murder trials, due largely to the apparent unacceptability of anger as a response to frustration on the part of a woman – or at least a 'reasonable' woman.

Social attitudes apart, the reason for this, while relatively straightforward in terms of the law, also highlights what some lawyers and a great many feminist groups see as a fundamental, long-standing inequity of the legal system, created originally by men, for men, reflecting – as in the rape defence attacks outlined above – predominantly men's experiences of being attacked by another man and acting in self-defence against someone of equal physical strength and size. According to the 1957 Homicide Act, for a provocation plea to be used successfully to reduce the charge of murder to one of manslaughter, the killing must be sudden and committed in the so-called heat of the moment – or as originally laid down by Lord Denning in his direction to the jury in the *Duffy* case (1949), demanding 'sudden and temporary loss of self-control'. Although nowhere does the Act specify that the killing must instantaneously follow on from the act of provocation, the words 'heat of the moment' and 'sudden and temporary loss of self-control' are crucial, denoting a sudden explosion of anger, fury and passion, which subsides almost immediately. As such, they have come to be interpreted in their very narrowest, most precise sense, irrespective of context or circumstance, allowing no leeway for manoeuvre or any accommodation of women's experiences.

With widespread publicity given to such offenders as Sara Thornton, who is serving life imprisonment for killing her violent husband after she went to get a kitchen knife, recent argument has centred primarily on whether the tendency to lash out blindly, in a sudden uncontrollable frenzy of anger, can be fairly and equally attributed to men and women. Women's experiences suggest it can't. While familiar enough with the sudden eruption of red hot fury, seemingly from nowhere, women's realization of their relative physical weakness compared to men often holds them back from instantaneously acting upon it – a delay arising more commonly from the instinct of self-preservation than cold premeditation. One might further contend that even the preceding unheralded 'explosion' of emotion, especially of instant 'blind' rage, is a stereotypic image, perceived as an inherently macho characteristic representing men's readiness to resort to violence, their shorter anger 'fuse' and higher boiling point when provoked, and their confidence at being able to resort to brute strength to attack and kill their partner.

By comparison, many women, lacking as they do men's physical strength and size, may automatically control and temper their rage, and act only once they can lay their hands on a suitable defensive weapon. Some, after years of habitually putting up with their partner's abuse, may be slower to arouse to anger, but once enraged the fire may smoulder and burn longer, proving just as all-consuming as men's much-vaunted 'momentary passion'. Indeed, the fiercest arousal of hatred and anger may occur just *after* a violent confrontation. Yet since the criterion of immediacy is central to the definition of provocation, any hesitation on the part of the accused, no matter how eminently reasonable and apparently justified at the time, more often than not causes the plea to fall flat in court. Yet the truth remains that the more we discover about the complexity of human behaviour and response, the more obvious is the existence of an intermediate emotional-rational stage, its boundaries admittedly so blurred as to defy precise definition, between icy detachment and going mindlessly berserk. For the most part, the law on provocation has failed dismally to take this into consideration.

Also militating against many women's pleas of provocation is society's, and thus the average jury's, attitude to 'normal' female behaviour. Who can seriously doubt that despite a decade or so of lip service paid to sexual equality, society as a whole still finds it hard to swallow that a wife and mother of many years, perhaps well into middle age, who has always appeared and acted calmly, rationally, even gently, and has no past criminal history, perhaps especially if she belongs to an ethnic community where women are still recognized as fulfilling traditional roles, would actually be capable of erupting into a blind fury and lethally attacking her partner in an uncontrollable frenzy. Harder still for many jurors to comprehend is the concept of a woman snapping after experiencing not just one act of provocation but as a result of 'accumulated provocation' carried out over a long period of time.

Here we are faced once again with the old familiar conundrum: if life with her partner was so unbearable, his actions so predictably cruel or violent, why didn't she leave him earlier? And if she stayed and put up with it for so long, how come she was suddenly driven to strike out and kill?

As defined in law, sudden and temporary loss of control reflects society's view of the classically male, visceral response, in which a man typically and, given many judges' comments, apparently understandably, uses his hands, feet or fists, to batter, punch, choke, strangle or kick his partner in an outburst of raw animal aggression. Such outbursts and responses are indeed all too terribly instantaneous – as attested by the suffering of thousands of battered women. For numerous other male offenders, however, the conscious act of looking for and picking out a suitable murder weapon such as a knife or hammer, though indicating intent, seems not to have disallowed a defence of provocation.

As, for instance, in the case of Peter Wood, who clubbed his girlfriend to death with a meat tenderizer, also smothering her with a pillow and strangling her for good measure because she had been trying to end their relationship. Running a defence of provocation, he was sentenced to six years for manslaughter and ended up serving only four. Or that involving Mumtaz Baig, who strangled his wife Rohila with a piece of rope, which he maintained she used for tying up a rubber plant (according to her sister, Rohila always tied it with wool), on grounds of her infidelity. Baig was found not guilty of murder and sentenced to six years for manslaughter. Yet for a woman, as illustrated by the cases of Iqbal Begum or Amelia Rossiter, the act of going to a kitchen drawer and pulling out a knife or fetching an iron bar from outside the back door then attacking their partner is usually sufficient to ensure the collapse of a defence based on provocation, indicating that the attacker had already regained control of their mind and actions. That intervening pause, perhaps no longer than a minute or two, or even a few seconds, can be enough to classify a hitherto ordinary, kind, caring and law-abiding senior citizen like Amelia Rossiter as a cold-blooded, dangerous murderer.

If Not Bad Then Mad

There is an alternative perception of women who murder their partners: if they are *not* calculating killers they must be either mentally ill or so irrational that they cannot be held fully accountable for their actions. In this case, a defence of diminished responsibility may also lead to a lesser conviction of manslaughter and avoidance of life imprisonment. But if ever a term has become overloaded with weighty, potentially explosive baggage, it is this one – especially where women are concerned. If provocation is by and large a classic man's defence, too rigid in its interpretation to allow for women's experiences of and reaction to danger, then diminished responsibility, with its implied irrationality, mental impairment and helpless lack of self-control, is seen traditionally as the 'safest', most appropriate defence for female offenders. According to barrister Helena Kennedy QC, women charged with murder – especially of a domestic nature – are more likely to plead guilty to manslaughter in the hope of a lenient sentence, especially if a report can be produced that she was suffering from a mental disorder at the time of the offence. Most find this preferable to the nightmare of a contested trial, hoping for an acquittal but knowing the very possible outcome could be a murder conviction and life imprisonment. Understandably, there is growing vociferous opposition to a defence that stresses mental instability and places the onus for a crime on a woman's mental state rather than, as in provocation and self-defence, on the actions of the deceased, but like it or not, all the signs are that in practice this defence remains women's best bet. Insulting and sexist as it may be in its implications, it may be the optimum chance she has to escape a murder conviction and life imprisonment.

There is no precise definition of diminished responsibility upon which legal and medical experts are agreed. According to some lawyers, the term was originally designed as a plea for psychopaths, to distinguish them from the classifiably insane, and to describe the gross mental abnormalities and distortions of their moral character that lead them to become violent killers. This definition would put a battered woman like Amelia Rossiter in the same league as Peter Sutcliffe, Jeremy Bamber or Moors Murderer Ian Brady.

Yet other lawyers, like Sir Ian Percival, a former Solicitor-General, tend to apply a broader, more liberal definition that encompasses far less severe temporary disturbances, such as anxiety neuroses resulting from extreme and prolonged stress. When asked whether a battered woman who kills in terror and desperation over her husband's constant violence can justifiably be said to be acting out of diminished responsibility, Sir Ian Percival, on a BBC *Newsnight* programme, warned of making 'too much of a meal of it' (i.e. diminished responsibility). As he put it: 'If somebody, and it can be a man, like a woman, is subjected to sufficient prolonged stress, then it is temporarily not their own mind as it normally would be, for very good reasons. Therefore their responsibility is slightly less than it would be if they were in full possession of their senses.'

Nevertheless, diminished responsibility still requires the back-up of a psychiatric report, heralding the attendant stigma of mental illness, the implied need for hospitalization, drug regimes or psychiatric treatment, which are often the conditions built into a suspended prison sentence or probation. In this light it is understandable that applying the label is regarded by many as heaping insult on to existing injury, and that to plead what amounts to, or is still seen by many, as a mental abnormality when in fact the woman has managed to live a productive, responsible life in the face of often intolerable odds, is an untenable proposition.

What American and Canadian psychologists and counsellors with long-term experience of working with battered women have emphatically argued is that women who live with violent, abusive partners do not suffer from a mental disorder or imbalance but rather develop an altered state of perception and a set of coping skills which constitute the so-called 'battered woman syndrome' (BWS), which in the end may cause them to murder in the absolute certainty that this is the sole option available to them should they wish to survive, since by not disabling or killing their partner, he will kill them. In America in particular, where increasingly in such murder trials an expert witness is permitted to give evidence that a woman is suffering from the syndrome, the act of killing is presented as a reasonable act of self-defence by a person who is not mentally abnormal or ill in any psychiatric sense, usually in response to an extreme act or threat of violence from the deceased, rather than a momentary explosion of passion or the result of an unbalanced mind.

One major breakthrough for the American battered women's campaigners was the unprecedented act of clemency granted in December 1990 by Governor Richard Celeste of Ohio to twenty-five women convicted for assault or murder, many who had long been languishing in prison. Celeste cited a ruling by the state's supreme court that allowed female defendants to present expert testimony of them being a battered woman, for the first time, as part of their defence. Since that testimony was unavailable to those women at the time of their trial, Celeste ruled that they should now be released. This gave the lead to Governor William Schaefer of Maryland who commuted the sentences of eight women convicted of killing or assaulting their batterers.

Although expert testimony on BWS has obviously had some success as evidence for the defence in Canada and the USA, the chief argument against its use, especially in Britain, is the fear that by depicting battered women who kill as justified in retaliating against their abuser, they may be seen as 'getting away with murder' and so setting a dangerous precedent for others to take for granted that they have a 'licence to kill'. However, all the evidence so far suggests that the 'licence to kill' argument amounts to nothing more than alarmist cant. In Australia, where the New South Wales Crimes (Homicide) Amendment Act of 1982 permits a time lapse between the provocative act and the killing, also taking into account the effects of cumulative previous acts of provocation, there is no sign that more women are taking advantage of these liberal laws to kill their spouses.

The difficulty now facing lawyers is how to measure the precise distinction between diminished responsibility in its broadest sense and BWS, which by virtue of the now ubiquitous overworked term 'syndrome', like PMT, denotes that a woman is not her normal true self but a victim of uncontrollable emotional turmoil. Indeed, in a number of recent British cases women have been acquitted of murder on grounds of diminished responsibility due to emotional and behavioural symptoms that sound virtually indistinguishable from those that come under the banner of BWS. Virtually akin to signs of post-traumatic stress disorder, these include the notion of 'learned helplessness', whereby a battered woman, like a hostage in a hijacking, no longer feels she has control or free will to direct the course of her life and regresses to an almost childlike state of dependence, intensified by abject terror of her partner's violence and continual anticipation of what worse injuries he might inflict on her, offset by brief intervening periods of positive hope, usually just following an attack, when she is truly convinced he will never attack her again. Central to the syndrome is an intrinsic belief that she can control and survive the situation by recognizing early warning signs in his behaviour and trying to prevent violent confrontations. This, coupled with his often very extreme contrition and expressions of love after an attack, are what cause her to stay on in the relationship, although mortal terror of what he will do to her if she leaves or presses criminal charges is another reason why she may be unable to take positive steps to leave. The longer she is subjected to violence, and the greater her fear, the more diminished are her perceptions of what realistic options are open to her to resolve the nightmare.

Borne of extreme stress, all these and other perceptions which to the woman appear quite rational and do indeed help her to cope and survive remarkably well, to all outside appearances can be represented as 'reasonable' behaviour within the context of family violence. It helps explode some common myths, such as the fact that battered wives are 'free to leave any time' or that they are masochists who enjoy being abused. US psychologist and lawyer Charles Patrick Ewing, advancing a new doctrine of 'psychological self-defence', essentially an attempt to escape not only physical injury but to reassert one's psychological integrity by refusing to endure emotional destruction, has drawn specific parallels between the experience of battered wives and hostages held captive for prolonged periods, where alternating psychological states of terror, denial, helplessness and attempts to rationalize one's situation are dictated by the closeness of the relationship between the victim and the victimizer. If clearly and succinctly put across, such analysis of the psychology of victimization can certainly help the outside world – and in particular the judge and jury – understand why a woman who seemingly puts up with her situation then goes on to attack and murder her partner seeing this as a rational and coherent response to her current situation.

The burning question that now needs pursuing is do we really want to create yet another victim stereotype, that of the 'bona fide' battered woman – to rank alongside such other notables as the PMT sufferer and the post-natal psychotic or depressive – kitted out with her own newly fashioned quasi-psychiatric disorder? The real feminist issue at stake here is whether by creating yet another 'syndrome' we aren't actually rendering the majority of women a thundering disservice, undermining their sense of responsibility and ignoring the really important key concepts that must prevail in any criminal trial, principally reasonableness, moral conscience, accountability and freedom of choice, or its absence, along with disclosure of the full facts to the background of the case. Surely it is not that women defendants need to offer yet more proof of the existence of forces beyond their control, but that the law on provocation and self-defence should be broadened to include the realities of women's and men's different experiences, and Britain's mandatory life sentencing for all murder convictions, irrespective of their context, thoroughly reviewed.

Although as defined by the experts BWS is indeed a normal adaptation mechanism and therefore no more an illness than post-traumatic stress disorder suffered by crime victims, hostages and war combatants, the real danger is that by being defined in sloppy, woolly or cliché-laden terms by non-experts, the average outsider (which includes your regular jury member) may regard it simply as confirmation of existing stereotypical images of women as irrational, emotionally frail and passive, in need of special protection and care. The result? A cast-iron reinforcement of the age-old image of woman as victim.

Already there are signs that those American lawyers who in the early 1980s helped formulate legal defence doctrine built around the 'special case' of battered women, presenting them as victims, not aggressors, are beginning to show a change of heart. For instance, Brooklyn lawyer Elizabeth Schneider, a chief architect of the more liberal legal defence incorporating expert testimony on BWS, admits that the defence may not work successfully for certain women. If, for example, a typically middle-class professional woman appears to be too capable, too assertive or emotionally cool and in control of her life, perhaps even having on occasions left her partner, pressed charges or – as may frequently be the case among West Indian or African women brought up to openly express aggression – fought back physically, her very lack of passivity and emotionality, by not fitting the 'ideal' victim image, may be construed as evidence that she murdered in cold blood.

Another problem is that the term 'syndrome' and the notion of reasonableness may appear mutually irreconcilable, thus undermining a woman's attempt to prove provocation or self-defence. So, calling upon an expert witness to testify on BWS can actually backfire in two ways: first, by perpetuating the stereotypes of passive, helpless womanhood and second, by failing to explain why and reveal how the syndrome operates in women who are by nature aggressive, assertive and apparently in control.

In a paper given at a British Psychological Society conference in 1992, Wendy Chan of the Institute of Criminology in Cambridge argued that there is the additional danger that the more BWS is used to justify or explain women's actions, including murder, the greater the chance that the prosecution will seize the opportunity to perpetuate further myths about battered women as a means of proving their unreasonableness. 'The result is that the woman is caught between two conflicting stereotypes, neither of which adequately describes the battered woman's experience as reasonable. The view is that if a woman does not leave or fight back, then the violence must not have been so bad and her fear is unreasonable. On the other hand, if she does leave or get help, she really is not a battered woman.'

Other feminist campaigners, like Jill Radford of Rights of Women, fear that once expert evidence is given in court by the defence, the prosecution will produce a counter expert in an attempt to refute a defendant's claim to be suffering BWS. With women's lives and experiences taking second place to a 'battle of the experts', just as many women as are included may end up being excluded from this defence simply by virtue of falling outside the precise, accepted diagnostic category. Rather than attempt to rely on yet another 'syndrome' defence, ROW recently submitted a proposal for an entirely new and partially separate defence to the charge of murder to the Royal Commission on Criminal Justice. The proposed defence of 'self-preservation', applicable to both women and men, would be based on evidence of domestic violence and abuse given by the defendant, their family, friends, neighbours, etc. Reasonable as this sounds, since the Government in June 1993 rejected demands by a Commons home affairs select committee to relax the law on provocation (which would have given more protection to battered wives), the defence of self-preservation seems unlikely to be adopted under British law.

At the core of the debate for and against the inclusion of testimony on BWS is the fact that the word 'syndrome' remains synonymous with sickness, introducing a medical slant to what are often essentially social or human tragedies. Understandably, many BWS 'experts' take issue with its definition as a mental 'abnormality' or 'impairment', a peculiarly British view of what Australian lecturer in law Stanley Yeo has described on the contrary as 'a mental state which "normal" people might possess'. As interpreted by the Australian courts, BWS may be manifested by women who are seen as wholly ordinary or normal, especially in their degree of self-control, and who differ from other women only in their involvement in severely violent relationships. Therefore, the syndrome, as applied in Australian law, allows the murder of a violent man by his wife after a provocative incident to be explained as a 'reasonable' action in the light of a history of provocation. Thus stripped of its clinical connotations, the word syndrome ceases to be defined as a mental impairment or disorder as it is in Britain and becomes instead a means of measuring to what extent such women's attacks on their husbands can be viewed as reasonable acts of self-defence. Seen in this light, the mind of many a long-suffering wife finally driven to kill her tormentor becomes, if not eminently reasonable, far from unhinged.

Perhaps the most decisive factor in the assessment of women's crimes, even the domestic variety, is still their overall stereotypical image as 'good' or 'bad', therefore deserving or undeserving of clemency. In Britain, the Taylor sisters, Michelle and Lisa, eventually had their convictions for the murder of Alison Shaughnessy overturned once it became clear not only that not a scrap of real evidence linked them to her murder but how much fictitious dirt had been dished up by the tabloids. From the moment a woman's reputation as fragrant Madonna or wayward whore grabs the public's attention, invariably through hysterical and tendentious press reports, her fate in court is largely sealed – as witnessed by the heroine status accorded 'avenging mother' Ellie Nesler, who escaped serving life for first degree murder. Yet the most egregious example of a woman deemed too wicked to warrant either understanding, compassion or forgiveness must be Omaima Nelson, sentenced to life imprisonment in March 1993 in California for the murder of her husband. In numerous ways hers is no different to the wretched history of pain, mental torture and subjugation suffered by hundreds and thousands of battered women who have finally killed their batterer, usually in self-defence. Yet rather than seriously examine the extent to which her suffering paralleled that of other victims turned victimizers, media and judiciary alike chose instead to focus on the grisly nature of Omaima's crime and her outlandishly bizarre previous existence.

Omaima Nelson went on trial in December 1992 for alternately bludgeoning and stabbing to death her husband of four weeks, 56-year-old former drug smuggler William Nelson, over Thanksgiving weekend in 1991. Her defence was that she had endured a month of sustained physical and sexual violence from her new husband and had finally acted in self-defence while he raped and attempted to kill her by slashing her body with a knife. Had this been all she did, both her lawyer and mental health experts working on the case are convinced she might have got away with manslaughter – especially given that she was diagnosed as psychotic. But death it seems was too simple, or perhaps too good an end for her torturer. Omaima admitted systematically hacking up Nelson's body over the next twelve hours, disposing of some parts down the garbage grinder and skinning others, including the hands and head, which she then cooked by various methods such as boiling, frying and barbecuing. She cut off his testicles and index finger and stuffed them into his mouth prior to cooking. Her motive for this butchery she said was partly revenge, partly fear and desire to remove all evidence of the body.

According to an interview she gave one psychiatrist, Dr David Scheffner, shortly after her arrest, she remembers putting on red lipstick, a red hat and red high-heeled shoes whilst butchering and preparing the body. She had become obsessed with the gleaming colour of his blood. Having cooked his ribs in barbecue sauce, she told Scheffer that she prepared the kitchen table and sat down, still naked and bloodsmeared, preparing to eat her husband's remains. Despite screaming headlines comparing Omaima to the likes of Jeffrey Dahmer and Hannibal Lecter, it was never fully established whether she actually ate part of him, or even attempted to, although the consensus is that she probably did not. Even so, according to Scheffner: 'She did his ribs like in a restaurant . . . then said out loud, "It's so sweet, it's so delicious . . . I like mine tender"'. Finally, as Omaima testified under cross-examination, she mixed up all remaining body parts with leftover Thanksgiving turkey to disguise their origins and threw the lot out with the garbage. Just over a week later the police, alerted by neighbours suspicious about William Nelson's disappearance, discovered his remains stuffed in garbage bags.

Were this Grand Guignol tale not sufficiently grisly to put a smile on the face of even the most hardened tabloid hack, there was also the matter of Omaima Nelson's own lurid background. An unemployed, unskilled, alcohol-dependent gregarious girl, who frequented the rough bars of Orange County picking up men, Omaima was described as a ruthless and dangerous opportunist who preyed on older men, accompanying them to their homes where she is said to have bound and gagged them ostensibly for kinky sex acts, but actually in order to rob them of their money, which she sometimes demanded at gunpoint.

This image provided crucial ammunition for the prosecution, who, claiming evidence that Nelson's ankles had been bound during a struggle moments before his death, argued that she had tied up and cold-bloodedly killed her husband in order to get her hands on the $10,000 cheque which he cashed just prior to their marriage. However, since only one uncorroborated charge of physical assault and robbery had ever been made against her by a former boyfriend, and the fact that given the state of Nelson's body the cause of any marks on his flesh would be hard to determine, the image of Omaima Nelson as a sadistic, violent predator, whose opportunist greed drove her to hunt down and mercilessly dispatch her weak and vulnerable male victims, seems fanciful in the extreme. Especially when you begin examining the facts behind Omaima's wretched, misgotten childhood, something barely touched on either by the media or the courts.

It is only by looking at that other violent side to her life – where she herself was the victim – that the possibility of a transgression of justice starts to seem more likely. When Omaima's defence attorney Tom Mooney and the psychiatrists involved in her case tell you that this is the most shocking, bizarre case they have experienced in their entire profession, they are only in part referring to the macabre slaying of Mr Nelson. Those who could be bothered to examine her chequered life history soon discovered a human tragedy of almost unbearably grotesque and painful proportions. Born into a poor Egyptian family, her earliest recollections, as she revealed to forensic psychologist Dr Nancy Kaser-Boyd during extensive therapy, was of her father beating the soles of her feet as she dangled helplessly from the branches of a tree or of him dangling her upside down into a well and threatening that the alligators which lived at the bottom would come and get her. It was an infancy of unmitigated anguish and abject terror which was to turn into an even more horrific nightmare when her mother, also a victim of her husband's regular, brutal beatings, became pregnant and finally fled, leaving 7-year-old Omaima behind.

It was then that she experienced the traumatic event that almost certainly, in Kaser-Boyd's opinion, was to trigger her psychosis, in particular the tendency to dissociate from reality as an emergency response to cope with extreme fear and pain. Omaima's father decided the time had come to call in a group of adult female relatives and villagers whose job it was, in time-honoured tribal tradition, to ritually circumcize the child. In Omaima's case, this involved not merely the removal of the clitoris but also the cutting away of half the labia majora, an excessively brutal mutilation still commonly performed on young pre-pubertal African girls, always by older women and in this instance without any form of anaesthetic. As two of the strongest women held down the struggling, screaming, terrified girl, others hacked and sliced at her genitals using crude, unsterilized instruments, finally firmly stitching shut the damaged tissue at the entrance to the vagina. So profuse was the bleeding and extent of the damage that the wounds began to fester and a severe infection set in, putting Omaima's life in jeopardy for several weeks. When her mother returned to rescue the child, she discovered plans for the funeral already under way. So very deep was the physical and psychological shock to the girl that, as happens commonly with casualties of major, near-death trauma, her only real chance of survival was to escape into a make-believe world and fantasize that someone else, not she personally, had experienced those horrors. And so began Omaima's identification with mythical Egyptian Goddesses, her morbid fascination with death and the construction of an elaborate fantasy life to escape the ongoing family violence in which her mother, now remarried, joined her new husband in further physical abuses towards the girl.

Early adulthood provided little escape from the fear and violence which made up the daily small print of family life. At 18 she was raped by an American, but couldn't tell anyone because to have lost her virginity meant almost certain retributive violence from her brothers for bringing dishonour on the family. Unable for that same reason to marry a Muslim, she married another American and left Cairo for the USA, where they divorced shortly after. The second man she lived with subjected her to two years of regular, often severe physical violence. Once divorced from him, she became alcohol dependent and frequented bars in search of someone who would provide her with a roof and kindness, naïvely believing that older men would be more protective.

The picture pieced together by Dr Kaser-Boyd of Omaima Nelson at the time she met and married her second husband William shows a gullible, sweet-natured child inhabiting the body of an exotically dark-skinned woman, an emotional cripple numbing the pain of her life with alcohol and Valium, drifting from the occasional casual unskilled job to a hand-to-mouth existence co-habiting with men she met in bars and who briefly gave her the adulation she craved. In the words of Dr Kaser-Boyd: 'The men would call her "Little Egypt" or "Princess". She liked to think of herself as Nefertiti.' Having worked occasionally as a model, Omaima's greatest ambition was to make the big time, to acquire the trappings of fame, glamour and success. Instead she accepted invitations from men, who were usually themselves pathetic ne'er-do-wells, to move into their homes. Her version of the alleged assaults and robberies is that it was usually the men who asked for 'kinky sex' and she who complied in order to keep them interested enough to supply her with food and shelter. In 56-year-old William Nelson, a pilot recently released from prison for drug-running, she truly believed she had found her knight on a white charger. Instead the man she married turned out to be foul-mouthed, cruel and sexually hyperactive, forcing her to have intercourse numerous times each day and to partake in degrading sex acts under threat of violence. To almost any woman this would have been insupportably traumatic; for Omaima, whose circumcision had denied her any sexual pleasure due to excision of the clitoris and extensive build-up of internal scar tissue, loss of elasticity, pain and bleeding during intercourse, the ordeal, compounding her previous emotional and physical injuries, was virtually unendurable – yet she believed she had no option but to endure it, observes Dr Kaser-Boyd. Even when he persisted in greeting her each night on arriving home, not with a hug or a kiss, but by roughly pushing his index finger into her vagina, saying: 'I married you, I support you, I own that pussy.'

Having previously raped and beaten her violently, threatened to kill her and hurled her new pet kitten out of the car on to the motorway, that Thanksgiving weekend as they went to bed after a bout of heavy drinking he demanded, as usual, that she perform oral sex. When she refused to obey he tied her by her hands to the bed, started cutting marks on her breasts and thighs with a penknife and sat on her face, raping her orally. She managed to break free, grab a heavy lampstand and knock him out, then killed him by stabbing him in the neck with a pair of

scissors and beating his head in with an iron. After intensive
sessions with Omaima totalling twenty-five hours, Dr Kaser-
Boyd, who has written extensively on post-traumatic stress disorder and 'battered woman syndrome', believes that there were
certain aspects about that final attack on Omaima which caused
her finally to be consumed by the utmost terror – in effect a
rerun of her circumcision when she nearly died – and finally
lose touch with reality. His act of stabbing and threatening to
kill her with a knife was significant in two ways. By reminding
her of the agonizing wounds inflicted on her in infancy, the
knife reawakened in her all the previously suppressed symptoms of uncontrollable panic and fear of dying. PTSD sufferers
commonly find themselves flooded by a surge of panic and anxiety symptoms when confronted by reminders of their original
trauma. Secondly, his attempts apparently to stab her to death
temporarily severed her already fragile contact with reality.
Becoming confused and agitated, Omaima believed that ancient
Egyptians were directing and helping her to cut up the body so
that Bill Nelson could not enter the 'nether world'.

In court Omaima testified that the moment she killed him
she instantly 'freaked out' and went into a trance-like state for
the remainder of the night. To Dr Kaser-Boyd she confided that
she heard voices and that there were other Egyptian women
helping her. These other women, says Dr Kaser-Boyd, represent
the split-off parts of her already extensively fragmented psychotic personality, a fragmentation not at all unusual among
survivors of childhood violence and abuse. But as Kaser-Boyd
also points out, not only did the horrific nature of Omaima's
actions blind the judge and jury to the psychodynamic and precise cultural symbolism of those acts, their failure to fully comprehend the nature of her psychosis and its early origins meant
she was destined to come across more as a sadistic assailant
than a helpless victim. Furthermore, as a dark-skinned Muslim
woman, yet one whose fondness for alcohol and apparent
aggression and promiscuity were antithetical to the traditional
chaste image of Arab womanhood, Omaima was perceived from
the beginning as one of the dregs of society, a sub-human
species from a far-off and primitive world.

The greater such public prejudice, the more remote were her chances of a fair trial. To understand why she mutilated the body so brutally is impossible without some acknowledgment of her identification with Ancient Egyptian culture and mythology, or a sense of empathy with her own repeated traumatization. Thus the act of cutting off William's testicles and his index finger, with which he had 'claimed' her on arrival home each night, and stuffing these into his mouth begins to take on a startlingly vivid symbolism. Likewise the act of cooking and preparing to eat the body: 'If you can devour something then that means you can control it,' says Dr Kaser-Boyd. 'Important in all this was Omaima's strong belief in life after death and her terror that if she left his body whole she might encounter William again in the "next world". She cut him up and attempted to dispose of him so thoroughly because by so doing she felt she would never have to meet him again.'

Dr Kaser-Boyd remains convinced that had Omaima not cut up the body, her plea of self-defence backed up by expert testimony on 'battered woman's syndrome' would have stood a chance. Even though the state of California has an unusually restrictive law on mental impairment, having abandoned the concept of diminished responsibility in 1982, an insanity defence may require a far higher degree of mental disturbance than that suffered by Omaima. Incredibly, there was no attempt to plead insanity, temporary or otherwise. Given the facts, how could Omaima's obvious psychotic state be so cavalierly dismissed by the court and her early background of abuse and assault deemed too irrelevant to be given as evidence, while her own supposedly predatory day-to-day behaviour instead became such a focus for attention? Had she not been sentenced to twenty-five years to life for murder, of which she will probably serve about sixteen years, Omaima might at least have been granted the opportunity to begin trying to heal some of her psychic injuries and rebuild her fractured personality with some serious, intensive psychiatric help. If on appeal she is granted a retrial and her conviction reduced to manslaughter on grounds of temporary insanity, she may still succeed in doing so. But the chances of someone so 'unworthy' being granted that opportunity seem negligible. 'Battered woman's syndrome', we are reminded, is not a condition women like Omaima Nelson can ever hope to use in defence.

Whether in the end 'battered woman syndrome' is adopted with as much vigour by women's groups and progressive lawyers in Europe as it is currently in America remains to be seen. In England it is only possible to measure the success or failure of such pleas as provocation or diminished responsibility according to the outcome of each individual case. Given that every person's subjective experiences of and behavioural responses to stress, trauma, disaster and grave life-or-death threats will differ significantly from that of another individual, depending on temperament, past history and variations in present circumstances, who can doubt that one woman's capacity for 'responsible' action, along with the balance of her mind, may be more diminished than that of another. Even from superficial reports, the salient points to emerge from certain cases speak volumes about the nature and extent of domestic stress – stress of such extravagant proportions that it is hard to imagine that it could *not* be a major factor in triggering mental imbalance.

Can one seriously doubt that when Sandra Fleming shot her common-law husband in April 1992, the scale of suffering she had experienced and the extreme steps she took to alleviate it had reached such a pitch that her mind would be likely to function less rationally and calmly than it would in a situation of harmony, safety and well-being? Sandra, 26, killed Christopher Porter, her childhood sweetheart and the father of her three children with whom she had lived since the age of 15. She had had her first child shortly after they moved in together and endured from then on a decade of torture and humiliation.

At her trial in January 1993, the court was told how Mr Porter, because of his own pathological fear of doctors, had forbidden Sandra to deliver her second baby in hospital, insisting on acting as midwife himself, breaking her waters, cutting her with a razor to remove the baby and then putting neat surgical spirit on her wounds. That night he forced her to submit to sex. On another occasion he stuck pins under her fingernails, having found out that she had undergone a routine smear test. Refusing to allow one of their own children to be seen by a doctor, he 'hired' a friend's baby to be sent instead. Increasingly overcome by terror, Sandra had a tattoo applied as a means of identifying her body if, as Porter often threatened, she were to be killed and dismembered. Enraged, he removed the tattoo with a knife heated on the kitchen stove. Given to frequent bouts of jealousy when he repeatedly punched, kicked, even stabbed her, he used also to push her head under the water so often when she took a bath that she eventually gave up bathing. Finally, after a particularly gruesome ordeal, she took a powerful mixture of drugs and alcohol to dull her pain then, as he slept, shot him dead with a gun he kept hidden under a floorboard in their children's bedroom.

A psychiatrist's report diagnosed post-traumatic stress disorder, by now overwhelmingly recognized as a perfectly normal reaction to extreme stress rather than a mental illness or abnormality. She was given three years' probation for manslaughter on grounds of diminished responsibility.

The fact that Pamela Sainsbury was not under the influence of a potent cocktail of drugs and alcohol, and, after strangling her husband Paul as he slept, hacked his body to pieces, storing them for days before dumping them in the countryside, keeping the head for months in the woodshed while telling friends he had walked out on her and not confessing the murder to the police until nine months later, may on the face of it sound like a foregone case of deliberate, pre-planned and cold-blooded murder. Given the facts, could she really hope to get away with pleading guilty to manslaughter on grounds of diminished responsibility?

Acting for the defence, Helena Kennedy QC stated that: 'There can be few cases as bad as this in documenting one human being's abuse to another.' Pleading guilty to manslaughter, Sainsbury was spared the ordeal of a contested trial. Her plea was accepted after the Plymouth Crown Court heard how Paul had forced her to eat her food from a bowl on the kitchen floor, put a collar and leash around her neck, whipped her with a cane, buggered her and made her perform other degrading sex acts, took pornographic photographs of her and kept her prisoner in their council home, and were told by a psychiatrist that Pamela was 'treated like a dog . . . was virtually a hostage and requires the same sort of help and treatment', her terrifying ordeal was evident enough to allow her to be put on probation for two years.

What, however, remains puzzling about a case such as this, where evidence of diminished responsibility is presented by the defence – and accepted – is that in his summing up, the judge, Mr Justice Auld, acknowledged that Pamela Sainsbury was so dominated mentally and physically by her partner that she 'lost even the nerve to run away from him'. Yet he also stated that, 'You killed him in a sudden and impulsive act, driven as much by fear and hopelessness as anger.' Something here doesn't quite gell. The fact is that Sainsbury's anger, like her terror, was real and extreme, and certainly justified not merely on past experience but due to the severe and prolonged beating she had received from him just before she killed him. Yet the fact that her actions seem more indicative of a visceral, explosive response to provocation rather than the result of diminished responsibility, and that, according to Helena Kennedy, recounting the case in her book on women and justice, *Eve was Framed*, there was no suggestion that she required psychiatric treatment after her trial, highlights two crucial factors to bear in mind when looking at how the law treats women who murder. The first embraces the immense inconsistencies inherent in all human behaviour and the minefield we traverse in attempting to judge an extreme act like murder without prior understanding and knowledge of the context and circumstances of the act. The second brings into sharp focus the fiendish difficulty, as the law stands at present, in assessing which defence is most likely to help a woman like Sainsbury walk free.

A Just Verdict? Miscarriages and Misconceptions

We cannot afford to ignore the fact that just as there are honest and corrupt policemen and women, some more sexist, racially prejudiced and bigoted in their attitudes than others, so there are competent and incompetent lawyers. The fact that from time to time cases *are* bungled cannot be ignored. That Iqbal Begum should be imprisoned for murder largely because nobody at Birmingham Crown Court, neither the prosecution nor the defence, deemed it necessary that she should be provided with an interpreter is nothing short of an abomination. Thankfully, with the help of campaigning women's groups, including the Birmingham Black Sisters, a counselling and advisory network for victims of domestic violence within the local Asian community, and the efforts of her solicitor, Bharati Pattni, Begum was freed after a successful appeal.

A more widely publicized case of backsliding incompetence on the part of the defence is that of Kiranjit Ahluwalia, another Asian battered wife and mother. In the words of Pragna Patel of the Black Sisters of Southall, who campaigned vociferously on her behalf between her conviction for murder in 1989 and her release in 1992, 'her trial was a disaster'. From the outset Ahluwalia's ten-year marriage, arranged by her family according to Asian custom, was a nightmare of physical brutality and psychological cruelty. Violence, often ferocious and sadistic, was an everyday event. She was humiliated, treated like a slave, subjected to rape, beaten with belts, shoes, pieces of furniture, threatened with lethal weapons and nearly strangled. There were strict curbs on her behaviour and she was forbidden to go out alone and visit her family. Even though Deepak Ahluwalia's own family were afraid of him, they sanctioned his violence. In spite of repeated attempts to break out – Kiranjit went to court twice and obtained injunctions restraining her husband from further acts of violence – nothing helped. Her own family urged her each time to return, to try harder to make the marriage work. At the heart of the tragedy lay the ancient, enduring Asian family tradition known as 'izzat', a powerful code of honour according to which the reputation of Kiranjit, her entire family and their community depended on her conduct as a 'good wife', as demonstrated by her readiness to live, or die, within the marriage.

Just preceding her husband's death, he had again beaten her viciously and pressed a hot iron against her cheek. Her intention, she stated at the trial, had never been to kill him, but to make him experience some of the suffering which he had inflicted on her for so long: 'Just enough for him to know what it was like to feel pain.' Waiting until he was asleep, she threw a bucket of petrol over him and set it alight. He suffered 40 per cent burns and died five days later in hospital. Kiranjit pleaded guilty to manslaughter on grounds of provocation, but might as well not have bothered. She didn't stand a chance since the defence failed to construct a case powerful enough to impress on an all-white, predominantly male jury the hideous extent of her suffering. Despite the family GP's report of physical marks she had sustained and the fact that her husband had visited a psychiatrist because of his violence, the treatment meted out to her was trivialized by the prosecution and reduced to simply 'being knocked about'. The judge stated that the violence she faced was not serious and when asking the jury to consider whether the acts or words of the defendant would be carried out by 'a reasonable person in her position' he omitted the battering as relevant to the case; 'The only characteristics of the defendant about which you know specifically that might be relevant are that she is an Asian woman, married incidentally to an Asian man, the deceased living in this country.'

Not surprisingly, her defence was rejected since the court did not find that she had been provoked. Because she had waited for him to fall asleep after the beating he had given her, it was argued that she had had time to 'cool off'. In December 1989 Kiranjit was sentenced to life imprisonment at Lewes Crown Court for murder, saying from Holloway that, 'Today I have come out of my husband's jail and entered the jail of the law. This is the essence of my culture, society, religion. Where a woman is a toy, a plaything, she can be broken at will. For ten years I have lived a life of beatings and degradation and no one noticed. Now the law has decreed that I should serve a sentence for life.'

It was not until September 1992 that she finally walked free, following a retrial in which her plea of guilty of manslaughter on grounds of diminished responsibility was accepted by the Crown on the strength of fresh evidence from five psychiatrists that she had been suffering severe depression at the time of the murder. The most pressing question is why medical evidence that must have been available at the time of her first trial was not presented by the defence. What also needs addressing is whether without such evidence, which was instrumental in helping to secure Kiranjit's retrial and her subsequent release, she would have been released. The irony is that women's groups hailed her release as a 'victory for women using the defence of provocation' and her lawyer Rohit Sanghvi stated that her case was 'the first nail in the coffin of the provocation law', yet what it actually demonstrated, yet again, is that battered women stand a better chance of being convicted of manslaughter and not murder if they plead diminished responsibility.

By comparison, the future augurs far from well for another acclaimed martyr of British justice, Sara Thornton. Feminist pressure groups, enraged at what they regard as failure by the courts to recognize the trauma caused by her alcoholic husband's repeated violence during their ten-month marriage, have blown this up into an ongoing *cause célèbre*. Because of her supposedly unjust imprisonment Thornton has been elevated as the totem of the British battered women's movement. Whether she should rightfully be accorded that status remains highly dubious. Anyone even superficially familiar with the case has heard how she was knocked unconscious, punched in the eye and on the back of the head and had an ashtray smashed down on her hands, and that at the time of his death Malcolm Thornton, an ex-policeman, was facing trial for an assault that landed his wife in hospital. Sara had gone to numerous agencies to seek support, including her GP, the Church, Alcoholics Anonymous and the police. Despite pleading guilty to manslaughter on grounds of diminished responsibility, she was sentenced to life imprisonment for murder and a subsequent appeal was rejected. She allegedly stabbed him with a carving knife which she fetched from the kitchen, first stopping to sharpen it, in the course of a violently abusive set-to in which he threatened to kill her once she was asleep.

But the claim that this represents a gross miscarriage of justice fails to stand up to close scrutiny. Closer analysis of the case, including facts disingenuously glossed over by women's rights campaigners, raises a number of uncomfortable questions. For one thing, was running a defence of diminished responsibility as much of an insult here as in many other similar cases, given that Sara was diagnosed as suffering from a personality disorder in her teens and asked to leave her public school at 16 and attempted to commit suicide on a number of occasions as a young woman? She had briefly been a patient in a hospital in 1981 under the Mental Health Act. There was a childhood history of emotional deprivation and sexual abuse. Even so, despite testimony from two defence psychiatrists that her responsibility was impaired, the prosecution psychiatrist refused to buy it, finding her of sound mind at the time she came to trial and during the period leading up to and including the murder.

After her sentence, the defence tried to pursue the route of provocation during her appeal, to see if it might pull more weight – but that too failed. Nor is it hard to see why. Weighed heavily against her are the following facts: four days before the murder Sara told a colleague at a business conference that 'I am going to kill him'; the following day she hand-fed him pieces of chicken containing ground-up tranquillizers, then phoned the doctor to say he had taken an overdose and was suicidal; two days after that episode, Malcolm Thornton told Sara he wanted a divorce.

Malcolm's 23-year-old son Martin, who was staying in the house at the time of the murder, testified in court that Sara was obsessed with obtaining possession of the house and had been terrified of losing it along with a share of some money due to come to Malcolm if he divorced her. The murder, according to Martin, did not take place in the heat of a violent confrontation but after she returned home from the pub and found him lying on the sofa in an alcoholic stupor. Earlier that day she had scrawled 'Bastard Thornton – I hate you' in lipstick on the bedroom mirror. According to Sara, she went into the kitchen to calm down after he called her a whore and threatened to kill her, looking for his truncheon in case she needed to defend herself. Unable to find it, she took a long carving knife, sharpened it and went back into the sitting room. They argued, he insulted and threatened her further and finally she brought the knife down slowly into his stomach. Sara claims she thought he would ward off the blow. Martin maintains that had his father been awake he would have done so. Martin's account of what happened when he came downstairs having heard no sound prior to his father's scream, was that Sara informed him she had killed his father. 'She said it to me like she was saying "Martin I've just put the rubbish out."'

When the police and ambulance arrived and efforts were made to resuscitate him, Sara was said to have told the team, 'I don't know why you are bothering, let him die.' She also said, 'I know exactly what I am saying, I sharpened the knife so I could kill him. Do you know what he has done to me in the past?'

In a newspaper interview Malcolm Thornton's first wife, Moyra Friend, with whom he had remained on close and friendly terms, claims that although Malcolm admitted to being violent and an alcoholic he had cited numerous instances of Sara's abusive, violent behaviour towards him, which included supergluing the volume knob on the television set so that he was unable to turn down the sound, holding a pillow over his head in bed and of being generally cruel and nagging. She also makes the point that no one, other than the recently formed feminist pressure group Justice for Women, has bothered to lobby on her behalf, not even her own family. 'Where are her friends? Why hasn't she got any support from people who know her, and why from only women's groups?' Why indeed. Even her own father did not attend the trial. More pertinent, why have her campaigners failed to get in touch with him to confirm the statements that have been made about her?

As for Sara herself, now in Bullwood Prison where she is serving her sentence, her view is that originally her trial received no media coverage as it was before the whole debate about battered women who kill really took off. She also believes that she presented the wrong image to the court, one that failed to conform to the popular image of the battered wife as helpless, terrified and totally under her husband's domination. 'It seems that women must have publicity and a spotless reputation to guarantee them justice. I'm now working to try and encourage women to relive their anger . . . it's very difficult for us because if you show your anger people say – well, what did we say, look at her.'

She cites other instances of women who killed their abusive husbands and got off on provocation, as, for example, Elizabeth Line, a former nun who had been subjected to beatings, rape and acts of gross sexual abuse over a two-year marriage. When her husband told her he was going to shut her up for ever and asked, 'Which knife shall I use to cut your throat?' she ran to the kitchen, grabbed a knife and stabbed him seventeen times. She pleaded provocation, was convicted of manslaughter and given a suspended eighteen-month jail sentence. 'Elizabeth Line was a former nun, which all the media focused on. The image of a young nun being violated by an older drunken man must have been a powerful factor in her defence. Women are expected to be "saintly" in order to qualify for a chance at the defence of provocation. And did you see the picture of her husband? He looked evil.'

Although Thornton may be right in saying that she was just unlucky her appeals in 1991 and 1993 did not succeed, the facts would seem to suggest otherwise.

Putting the Thornton case aside, there are some women who have managed to use provocation as a successful defence even where there appears to have been delay between the violent confrontation and her lethal attack. Barry Mitchell, a law lecturer at Coventry Polytechnic, writing in the *New Law Journal*, reports that in two out of twenty provocation manslaughters, defendants seemed to be in control when they carried out the killing. In one case the wife walked to a police station and complained that her husband had assaulted her, then went home, took a knife from the kitchen and went into the bedroom where she stabbed him twice in the neck. After he staggered around for a while she fetched a sharper knife and stabbed him once again. She was convicted of manslaughter due to provocation and received two years' probation.

Pauline Wyatt and Celia Ripley (both shot their sleeping husbands after threats and violence), Mary Bernard (poured paraffin over her husband while he slept and set it alight) and Rosina Ratcliffe (killed her husband six days after the last violent act when he tortured her with lighted cigarettes) are some of the British women whose provocation pleas were accepted in the 1980s. Having stabbed her violent boyfriend in the chest, neck and back during a brawl in which he repeatedly smashed her head against the kitchen wall, 52-year-old Janet Gardner was given a five-year prison sentence for manslaughter, then was released on appeal after serving one year. Having heard that Gardner was suffering classic signs of 'battered woman syndrome' – evidence not put forward at her first trial – Mr Justice Swinton-Thomas said she had been provoked 'in the fullest sense of the word' and placed her on two years' probation.

Evidently, there have been a huge range and variety of judicial responses to women who murder their violent partners. In Helena Kennedy's view, the outcome is still very much like a lottery, depending largely on the attitude of the judge and prosecutor – and the impression conveyed by the defendant. If women can hope eventually to be treated with more sensitivity and understanding in the courts, it will surely be because of the advent of a new generation of more liberal and progressive – and above all realistic – lawyers and a loosening of the strict, narrow guidelines on legal doctrine. This in turn can only come about through growing public awareness of the different, hitherto often unimaginable experiences of women caught in nightmarish domestic dilemmas frequently not of their own making. The signs of enlightenment are slight, but promising, as demonstrated by those cases where women have successfully pleaded provocation. In August 1991, Lord Denning, who originally fine-tuned the interpretation of the law on provocation, stated that: 'In the light of women's experiences, I would today direct the jury that, while it may not have been in the heat of the moment, prolonged violence over the years can result in provocation.'

Battered Husbands: The Invisible Men

Toeing the Official Line

Neighbours living close to the Hetheringtons' house remember their fights breaking out mostly at weekends. The street is in a peaceful, leafy, affluent London suburb where brawls, street crime and rowdy gatherings are virtually unknown, so the sound of two people locked in a bitter, violent dispute, seemingly on the point of killing one another, would not go unnoticed. Even above the blare of the television you could hear the sound of screamed obscenities, of crockery and glass being shattered, furniture crashing into the wall, the thud of bodies falling and, most distressing of all, a small child's plaintive whimpers of fear. Later, when silence fell, a hunched-up figure wrapped in a blanket could be seen sitting motionless, head bowed, outside on a bench in the back garden. Motionless except for the occasional bout of shivering, trembling – or was it sobbing? You could never quite tell.

'It was what I always did after being attacked. I'd go white as a sheet, ice cold and all trembly, and go and sit out there, wrapped up, in a state of utter despair and incomprehension. I confess too that there were times I also cried. The nightmare of it all would be going around and around in my head. Did she hit me because of something I'd done just then, or had I upset her unknowingly weeks before? Was it really my fault after all? I was always struck by how similar my reactions were to those I've read about being described by battered wives.'

Martin Hetherington is 5 foot 11, twelve stone, an Oxbridge educated lawyer; his wife Mariella is a university lecturer, daughter of a respected Dutch banking family – a couple the media would instantly categorize as members of the chattering classes. Meet the real people behind that stock comedy image, the cowering, wimpish husband and his sluttish, domineering wife, brandishing a rolling pin over his head as he slinks home sheepishly from the pub. Here, behind the classic caricature of the henpecked husband, staple stuff of mirth and ridicule among strip cartoonists and stand-up comics, lies the deadly reality of husband battering – the alternative face of domestic violence – where it is the women who attack, the men who live in fear.

It is over twenty years since shelters for battered wives were first established in Britain and America. Over the past five years, an increasingly get-tough public policy on domestic violence has led the police and courts to treat this as seriously as any other criminal assault. In 1992, rape within marriage finally became a criminal offence. Yet despite growing recognition by the authorities of the prevalence and severity of the problem, to this day the term domestic violence still means one thing: battered wives. With very few exceptions, the official line is that women are the victims, men the abusers.

More sinister still, there even exists a form of inverted sexism among 'experts' working with violent men – many of whom are men themselves. When researching an article on battered men in the late 1980s, the most hostile and summary dismissal I encountered was from Adam Dukes, Director of the Men's Centre in London, who accused me in no uncertain terms of being: 'socially irresponsible to even contemplate writing about this subject.' Did I not realize, he thundered, that my article would detract from the real problem, which is that there are two million battered wives in the UK, and the men who beat them merely use stories about attacks by women to justify and rationalize their own violence towards them? 'The fact that the odd man gets hit by a woman probably acting in self-defence, doesn't merit serious coverage,' was his parting shot.

Doesn't it? And is it really only the 'odd man', probably a batterer himself, whom we are talking about here? Not noted at the best of times for their sensitivity in recognizing or dealing adequately and promptly with the full horror of many domestic crimes, the police in some areas are now becoming increasingly aware of the phenomenon of husband battering. Helen Parnell, who runs the domestic violence unit at Kentish Town police station in North London, puts the figure at around 2 per cent, though she emphasizes that given the very low rate of reporting of such incidents by men this could well be a conservative estimate. Let's not forget that ten or twenty years ago the figures for wife battering were a mere fraction of the mind-boggling one in ten women estimated to have suffered domestic violence in 1993. Judging by the significantly higher rate of husband battering recorded by the West Midlands Police Force – an average of five or six men are included in each month's statistical breakdown on reported incidents of domestic violence by each of the eleven divisions within the force – it is not unreasonable to assume that the image of local police, how sympathetically, promptly and positively they respond to domestic and sexual crimes, must play an important part in encouraging men as well as women to report violent incidents. As Force Liaison Officer and policy adviser for rape/sex offences, domestic violence and child abuse, Detective Inspector Sylvia Aston is largely responsible for the 'caring' and user-friendly image of the West Midlands Police, recognized as being in the vanguard of UK policy-making on domestic violence. It is a tough policy which is non-gender based – or biased. This has resulted in rape examination suites being available to male as well as female sexual assault victims and a comprehensive approach to officers' training, focusing on all aspects of domestic violence, including assaults by wives and husbands, as well as attacks on and by siblings, grandparents, step-parents, co-habitees, former spouses, lesbian and homosexual partners.

'We've made absolutely sure through our training that no officer will ever dismiss a male domestic violence victim just because he's a man,' says Sylvia Aston. 'We don't take the attitude that a man can leave – many can't. And it's invariably the nice, sensitive ones who get battered. I think we risk going down a very dangerous path by discriminating between the sexes in these offences. Some of the most violent people I've dealt with as an officer are women, and if you don't judge a woman by her crime, but by her gender, then not only do you perpetuate the old, misleading stereotypes but you risk such offences recurring, perhaps in another relationship. Domestic violence as we see it is not a women's issue – it's a social issue.'

Police reports confirm what doctors have almost certainly suspected all along through witnessing the frequency of men's unexplained injuries. Leicester Royal Infirmary reports that 12 per cent of all accident and emergency admissions resulting from domestic violence involve women's injuries to men, findings reflected in US studies. In a study carried out in 1990 at Leicester University among 300 male and female undergraduates involved in long-term, co-habiting relationships, 29 per cent of women admitted that during arguments with their partners they had resorted to physical violence, including hitting, punching, slapping and attacking them with heavy or sharp-edged objects. In response to these attacks, men were just as likely to suffer emotionally as women victims, even to the point of tears, says medical psychologist Dr Kevin Brown, senior lecturer at Birmingham University Medical School, who carried out the study.

The study demonstrates only too vividly how misleading are current stereotypes of female victims and male abusers when it comes to everyday domestic incidents. Dr Brown's findings also confirm to what extent biology may be overridden by socialization. Both men and women who had experienced severe physical abuse and punishment in childhood were three times more likely to use violence to resolve conflict or stress in their own adult relationships.

More recently, in October 1992, Dr Malcolm George, a neurophysiologist at London University's Queen Mary and Westfield College, completed a survey of thirty-eight male victims of domestic abuse in an attempt to discover the backgrounds of both partners as well as the types of injuries and attacks most commonly sustained. In this instance, the majority of male and female partners had had little or no childhood experience of violence, although an interesting finding to emerge was that while most of the men grew up in the company of brothers and sisters, many of the women were only children and, if previously married, had a history of being violent with their former partner. There is ample support here for the old adage about the kitchen being the most dangerous room in the family home. Over 80 per cent of the men in Dr George's study told of violence involving the use of sharp-edged or heavy household objects like scissors, hammers, bottles, knives and other kitchen equipment, with such attacks occurring every few months at least, at most on a daily or near daily basis.

When asked whether they could identify reasons for their partners' violence, only 25 per cent mentioned premenstrual tension (PMT) and in only 2 per cent had a mental health problem been diagnosed. Yet apparently, and perhaps not surprisingly, this was at odds with the men's perception of their wives' behaviour. According to the study, the overwhelming majority of victims rationalized the women's violence in terms of some form of mental disorder, or put it down to a dominating, bullying, controlling personality, with a tendency constantly to blame others for any existing problems. Most described their wives as having little or no control over their impulses, especially anger, becoming violent and abusive in the manner of a spoilt child when their wishes remained unfulfilled. The saddest feature of all, observes Dr George, is that over 60 per cent – in spite of having suffered sometimes severe physical injuries – like many battered wives evidently thought it more prudent to suffer in silence than to seek police involvement.

As Common As Love

Such studies so far remain isolated one-offs in Britain. By comparison, numerous studies conducted in Israel, Puerto Rico, Finland, Denmark, Sweden – where men's refuges already exist – and especially in the USA, attest to the high incidence of violence by women against their male partners. Yet if ever there was a gender-sensitive taboo awaiting exposure, a politically correct myth ready to be exploded, this is the one. Perhaps we have to thank the growing vociferousness of Gay Rights activists, as well as the recognition of such hitherto unacknowledged crimes as male sexual assault (not, as is popularly supposed, a crime committed solely by and against gay men, but often involving heterosexuals), for the fact that battered men are beginning to come out of the closet about domestic abuse, although they undoubtedly face a tough road ahead if they are ever to gain serious acceptance of their plight.

To seasoned observers of the issues surrounding domestic violence, this is far from virgin territory. Nearly two decades of research into the multidimensional nature of intra-family aggression has led one eminent American researcher to state that: 'Violence between family members is probably as common as love.' Yet it seems quite incredible, given today's widespread and ever expanding recognition of wife battering in particular, that until the mid 1970s the term 'domestic' violence was used exclusively to define riots and terrorism taking place within one's own country! Paradoxically, even before the experiences of battered women had been formally identified and classified under the same label, and long prior to the establishment of women's refuges, the term 'battered husband syndrome' had been coined in the early 1970s by American sociologist Suzanne Steinmetz, author of *The Cycle of Violence*, one of the first books to disclose the frequency of women's attacks on their spouses.

In 1975 Steinmetz collaborated with researchers Richard Gelles and Murray Straus on the first US National Family Violence Survey, which found that an equivalent number of wives and husbands commit acts of violence against their partners (a statistic repeatedly confirmed by similar surveys up to 1991) and in 1978 she published an article outlining the phenomenon of husband battering. Extrapolating from their nationwide survey, Straus and Gelles estimated that throughout the USA in 1975 two million men were likely to have been victims of domestic violence, while Steinmetz, drawing on her own albeit small-scale study conducted in New Castle County Delaware, put the figure for American male spouses likely to be 'severely thrashed' by their wives at 250,000 per year.

Seizing on these figures with gusto, the American media had a field day. *Time* magazine, whose coverage to date of battered women had run to one or two column inches, ran a one-page article in 1978 featuring the 'newly recognized fraternity of victims: battered husbands', compensating for the paucity of real evidence by asserting – incorrectly – that Erin Pizzey, founder of London's first refuge for battered women, had set up a similar house for men. The American tabloid press and TV shows fell over themselves in an ignominious scrum to come up with sensationalistic hype, each trying to outdo the other in squeezing more mileage out of the limited data – data which many feminists had dismissed, with some justification, as a lot of baseless conjecture. According to some speculative press reports, because men's shame and pride prevented them from reporting their wives' violence, husband battering was almost certainly a more secret vice than wife beating, ergo, was this not likely to be the century's most unreported crime? It was a God-given opportunity for a touch of feminist-bashing.

Writing in the *New York Daily News* magazine, journalist Roger Langley pushed the original estimated national figure of two million battered men up to twelve million and, along with other commentators, disingenuously emphasized only the numbers of attacks supposedly perpetrated by wives, omitting the principal caveat contained in all the published findings: namely, that men's attacks on their wives resulted in many more serious and life-threatening injuries, making this by far the most grave form of domestic violence and the problem which must be of primary concern to social workers, health professionals and the law.

Can we wonder at the howls of fury that emanated from feminists and women's refuges in response to such hysterical and biased reporting of this newly discovered role-reversal? Recognizing the politically charged atmosphere that pervades the broad spectrum of gender-sensitive crimes such as rape, family violence and child abuse, and the inevitability of such a furore damaging their reputation as serious researchers into family violence, Gelles and Straus dropped the topic like a hot potato. 'We . . . have consistently refused every request for an interview or to appear on any talk show on this topic for fear yet again of being misquoted or misrepresented,' they wrote in a recent book, *Intimate Violence*, stressing that Steinmetz has also thought it better to steer a wide berth round the topic of women's attacks on men since the uproar.

In England, Erin Pizzey eventually parted company acrimoniously with others working in the women's refuge movement in the late 1970s largely because of her refusal to define domestic violence as a feminist issue or allow herself to become embroiled in the politics of the women's movement. The view for which Pizzey most came under fire from other women's refuge workers was that women possess an almost equal potential for violence towards their partners as do men. Writing in 1979, she put the proportion of violent women who came to the Chiswick refuge at a third, observing that they were frequently as violent as the men they had left and that beating their children was often a reflection of the same violent tendencies.

With hindsight it is obvious that the 1970s, when the increasingly militant and vociferous feminist lobby was gaining ground, was hardly an auspicious time for men's 'rights' to get a serious airing. The so-called 'men's movement' still lay a long way ahead and battered husbands then were a mere overnight media sensation. So, fifteen years on, have we really come any closer to acknowledging the true scale of women's violence towards their male partners? Alas, far from it. Though still calculated to raise feminist hackles, new evidence suggests that while statistics for wife battering remain shockingly high – in London an estimated one woman in four is believed to be battered by her spouse – the incidence of husband battering is undoubtedly more prevalent than is commonly supposed. Further American studies by Gelles and Straus (whose 1985 survey involving 6,000 couples found, as in 1975, that the frequency of women's attacks on men equalled that of men against women) and other researchers up to the present day continue to reveal the same findings.

In 1985, a US team of researchers into family violence examined one month's computerized police reports in a Texas town, filed in the officers' own words, on almost 400 cases of domestic violence, and in 11 per cent of cases it turned out that the women had initiated the violence or were as violent as the men they lived with. Around the same time, sociologist Richard Breen studied 884 Texas university students, married and unmarried, and found that 18 per cent of men, compared to 14 per cent of women, reported having experienced a violent assault by their partner. Among the married men who took part in the study, 23 per cent were punched, slapped or kicked by their partners, 30 per cent were pushed or shoved either in private or in public, while 9 per cent had partners who hit them with objects and another 9 per cent had sustained visible welts, cuts, bruises, etc. In 1992, a support group for domestic violence victims based in Santa Ana, California, reported seeing approximately a hundred men each week, of whom on average 38 per cent had visible signs of injury.

In Britain, ironically, we have women to thank for much of the information. When former battered wife Jenni Manners opened Swindon's women's refuge in the late 1970s, she was initially surprised to receive the occasional phone call from men living with violent partners. Rare though they were, she took them as seriously as any woman's cry for help. From the early 1980s, when she set up a special telephone crisis line for men (the first and so far only service of its kind in England) until today, the numbers of distraught men seeking advice have escalated from several every few months to over fifty per year. 'One in every five calls we receive now is from a man undergoing some form of abuse or violence from his partner. The number who have contacted us now runs into the hundreds,' she says. Reported physical injuries include skull and rib fractures, crushed fingers and toes, cuts, scratches, burns and extensive bruises.

In 1984, when Janine Turner first launched Lifeline, a support and counselling network for all domestic violence victims, in only 10 out of 350 families did the man admit to being on the receiving end. By 1989, with 4,500 families registered, that figure had doubled. Often it is only when the woman's anguished recognition of her actions and the suffering she is causing drives her finally to seek help that the man's predicament will come to light in the first place.

At one time it was believed that the low profile of battered men was due to their unwillingness to regard themselves as victims, or inability to admit that being 'battered' amounted to a problem. Even today, Suzanne Steinmetz, who has very recently resumed her early studies into male victimization and is still the chief US researcher in this area, suggests that unlike their female counterparts these men retained their self-esteem and saw only their wives as having a problem.

From what we now know, almost certainly the reverse is true. Men do feel humiliated and ashamed about coming forward and admitting they are victims. And therein lies the clue to men's invisibility as victims in the domestic arena, especially within the officially reported figures: quite simply, due to pride, shame, fear of ridicule or disbelief, men on the whole do not talk about such incidents to friends or family, let alone to doctors, police or lawyers. How could they, after all? In a society that by and large still buys the notion that 'real men don't cry', so-called real men, especially those who are solidly respectable, ordinary citizens, and to all appearances contentedly married or living harmoniously with their girlfriends, will certainly be unable to admit to being attacked, dominated or terrorized by their partner, let alone control or defend themselves against her attacks.

For a man like Joe Edwards, a TV technician who is 6 foot 2, fourteen stone and a former rugby player, the prospect of confessing to colleagues that his petite 5-foot 4-inch wife's typical repertoire of attacks includes trying to jab a broken bottle or a knife into his arms and cheek, or knocking him out cold with a plank of wood, then kicking and pummelling him as he lies on the floor, hardly comes easy. 'I put up with such attacks for twenty years, with usually just two- or three-week periods of peace and happiness in between the violence. The hardest part was explaining away my injuries by inventing accidents. I told no one the truth. Who would believe someone my size, with an apparently strong character, holding down a responsible job, would let himself be beaten up repeatedly? It's not part of the macho image. You'd be laughed off as pathetic or ridiculous. So you shut up about it.'

Joe's silence and acute awareness of the perceived ignominy of his position is typical of the vast majority of men who have contacted Lifeline and the Swindon helpline. Moreover, contrary to the popular Andy Capp caricature of battered men as weedy and invariably working class (the latter image still erroneously extends to all areas of domestic violence, including battered women), husband battering cuts across social class, age and type. Both Jenni Manners and Lifeline counsellors and, more recently, Dr Malcolm George in compiling his survey, have encountered such men in all walks of life, from solicitors, doctors, airline pilots and company directors to firemen, policemen and unskilled labourers. For the majority, the shame, isolation and humiliation that battered wives experience can be equally if not sometimes more damaging to men's confidence and emotional stability, especially if they are schooled in the classic ideal of macho invincibility.

If you are a beefy, 6-foot martial arts student, recognized by your mates for your no-nonsense swagger, then how do you go about explaining your domestic nightmare? The answer is you don't. 'None of my mates at work would believe what I put up with. Anyway, in front of others she behaves so correctly, is so quietly feminine and charming, we look to all the world like Mr and Mrs Average, everyone's image of the ideal couple. If they knew how she knocks me about, and the fact that every time it happens she manages to take me by surprise, catching me off guard, can you imagine how they'd take the piss?' says Roger, who holds a senior position in the Edinburgh fire brigade. Although few men would go to such tragic extremes as the US army sergeant who put a gun in his mouth and blew his brains out because he could no longer reconcile his public authoritarian image on the parade grounds with the shame of allowing himself to be abused and attacked at home by his wife, the pain of alienation, of believing you are the *only* person to suffer such humiliation, seems unique to men.

This points to another dismal corollary to the old inverted sexist notion that only women and children get battered and abused in the home and that men always do the abusing, namely that men cannot ever suffer seriously as victims since they possess all the necessary physical wherewithal and financial resources to escape or defend themselves. In one widely quoted text that attempts to refute the existence of husband battering through the most simplistic of arguments, researcher

Mildred Pagelow asserts that men can always beat a hasty retreat if their wives become violent since, unlike women, they are more likely to carry everything they need – money, credit and identification cards, car keys, etc. – on their person, and have no need to hunt for purses or handbags, find transport or money. The idea that men do indeed go around at home at all times wearing suits, weighed down with such possessions, or that there is nothing else to prevent them from leaving home, would be absurdly comical were it not so insultingly presumptuous, especially in cases where men have responsibilities as caring, protective fathers.

The most disconcerting aspect of this particular 'iron man' mythology is that it is men themselves who continue to perpetuate the aura of invincibility by their reluctance to speak about their experiences. As long as there is silence we can never fully comprehend why it is that when the going gets tough the tough don't get going – neither striking back nor getting the hell out. Apart from ensuring their continued invisibility in statistics on domestic violence, men's silence serves to feed these myths, myths which compound their isolation and shame over their own 'unmanly' behaviour. As counsellors and those few men who can be persuaded to talk about their situation constantly stress, it is precisely men's awareness of their superior strength and potential to inflict serious physical damage which acts as a brake on the urge to strike back and which in turn leads to the conflict and inner frustration that distinguishes men's and women's experiences of victimization.

'I know without doubt that if I had really clobbered her the first time she ever went for me it would never have happened again,' reflects Andrew Bellton, an accountant, whose immediate reaction was to soil his trousers the first time his wife hurled a glass ashtray across the room, ripping his cheek open. 'It was the shock of someone you love and think you know intimately undergoing such a complete personality change, determined to say and do anything to harm you, like some crazed animal. But in spite of this, the idea of belting her, the idea of hitting any woman, especially someone dear to me, entirely revolts me, and I knew I could have injured her seriously with my size.

From that day on she always knew she could get the upper hand, count on my pacifism. In a sense by not reacting violently, and yet keeping my pride and standing my ground, I believe I provoked even greater fury. It's a classic male no-win situation: you don't or can't hit back but you can't back off either and you suffer more because of it.'

Why Do Men Stay?

When compared to women's experiences of victimization the term 'battered husband' is something of a misnomer. That in general men suffer fewer physical injuries and are less subjected to the types of sustained, repeated, brutal — at times lethal — assaults that men often inflict on their spouses is undeniable, by the mere virtue of men's greater physical size and brute force and women's relative weakness and smaller build. But we should not underestimate the degree of harm and potentially life-threatening injuries some women, even those of small and delicate build, can cause by throwing heavy or sharp-edged objects, hurling scalding liquids, wielding knives, scissors and other dangerous weapons, scratching, biting, kicking or kneeing in the crotch, and often attacking unexpectedly from behind while their partner relaxes unawares or is asleep.

A member of one men's group talks about waking just in time to see his wife coming at his throat with a fully operational electric carving knife. In another episode which went to court in 1990, 54-year-old Lady Frances Izard was sent for trial accused of wounding her 62-year-old husband by trying to saw off his head as he slept. Some men are less fortunate than these last two. In a notorious case that made the headlines in 1991, 40-year-old Dorreth Currithers managed to rip off one of her husband's testicles with her fingernails.

Even more bizarre is the attack on 26-year-old American nightclub bouncer John Wayne Bobbitt, whose wife Lorena chopped off his penis in a fit of fury while he slept, after allegedly having sexually assaulted her. The incident, which took place outside Washington in June 1992, made worldwide headlines, mainly because of the farcical turn of events immediately following the hapless Mr Bobbitt's dismemberment. Having severed the offending organ, Lorena Bobbitt left the family home with it in her hand, drove off in her car and hurled it from the window on to a motorway verge, then called the police to report having been raped by her husband. Under pressure she also revealed where she had disposed of the penis; police hurried to the spot, located it and packed it in ice, whereupon Mr Bobbitt was rushed to hospital where it was stitched back, apparently successfully.

As is now increasingly the case when a woman seeks violent revenge for sexual assault, public response to the incident provides an intriguing illustration of the underlying climate of feminist debate, especially concerning sexual relations. According to the *Guardian*'s American correspondent, Martin Walker, this case has become folk legend, a parable for a time of confusion about sexual roles and rights. Lorena, pleading temporary insanity due to years of sexual violence, was found innocent of malicious wounding at her trial and ordered to undergo 45 days' psychiatric hospital treatment. John was found not guilty of charges of sexual assault which would also have carried twenty years. Yet vast numbers of the public have unreservedly rooted for one or the other. Both have received thousands of letters and calls of support, including many cheques for legal fees. Women's groups have actively campaigned to raise funds for her 'cause', believing that she acted reasonably and justifiably, since like the majority of men, her husband assuredly 'had it coming'.

Extreme and unusual as it is, the Bobbitt case naturally enough stands principally as a cipher for female fury, albeit a terrifyingly salutary one. But to suppose women as a whole possess limited power to injure men physically is merely to endorse the classic stereotype of female helplessness, as well as the traditional concept of women choosing as partners men who are bigger and stronger, which with women's increased participation in sport and fitness training is no longer as common as it might once have been. Men's main advantage is that those who encounter violence from their spouses are usually able, by dint of size, brute strength and speed of reaction, to avoid very serious injury or control the attack through physical restraint – something most women cannot, on the whole, do as effectively.

'Being agile kept me alive on numbers of occasions. You learn to duck and dive, and develop a finely tuned instinct for danger. It's the assault from behind, perhaps when you're drowsy, sitting in front of the TV or asleep, that's the most potentially dangerous,' says Andrew, whose wife once tried to stab him in the shoulder with a pair of scissors while he dozed in an armchair. 'Most of the time I'd know when it was about to happen though. We'd be having some trivial argument, or I'd contradict her over some small thing and suddenly there was this Jekyll and Hyde transformation. She'd explode and hurl herself at me like a banshee, punching, kicking, clawing, screaming obscenities like a crazed lunatic. The only way to control her was to grab her arms with full force and with all my weight bring her down on the floor, pinning her arms and legs, sitting on top of her until all her energy was spent. Then she seemed to pass out, or get all tearful and confused, becoming distraught and terribly apologetic. It was over as fast as it began. The closest thing I can liken it to is someone having an epileptic fit.'

Afterwards, Andrew would invariably start to shiver with cold and become nauseous to the point of vomiting. Later still, as she kissed and caressed him with tears of contrition, promising she would never allow herself to do this to him again, Andrew persuaded himself yet again that this really was the last time, that he wouldn't allow himself to do anything untoward to risk provoking her rage, that he would ensure their life was so harmonious there could be no trigger for her violence. 'Another reason I stayed so long is that the way I was brought up, you learned marriage is for life, that when things go wrong you hang in and work it out. I know it sounds incredibly naïve but I took my marriage vows very seriously. Also I loved her and truly believed she'd change.'

It all sounds too depressingly familiar. The echoes of self-blame, the belief that through love as well as his own skill and prescience he can surely succeed in controlling his partner's violence, or at least contrive to maintain an atmosphere in which negotiation of disputes and peaceful resolution of conflicts prevail over enraged confrontation and conflict, are no different to the comments made by many battered women. The false, tortured logic of it all, the illusion of believing oneself capable of controlling the violence, are classic indicators of the battered wife syndrome. Ask a male victim of domestic violence why he doesn't just walk out and end the relationship and you will receive answers which more often than not accord remarkably with women's replies to the same question: love for their partner, in spite of the violence; love for the children and a strong need to protect their well-being, especially if there is any evidence the woman will, or already does, act violently towards them; and practical considerations such as having a hefty financial stake in the family home and insufficient resources to live elsewhere, often an insoluble problem of considerable magnitude, particularly for a man who is unemployed, faces the possibility of redundancy or bankruptcy or is struggling to hold his head above water while grappling with financial debts.

Another double bind that confronts many men is the risk that if they leave home, the wife may file for divorce on grounds of desertion and use this as an argument to limit his access to the children. According to the men's support and campaign group Families Need Fathers, who estimate that about one third of their members – numbering 500 in London alone – have suffered domestic violence, a very great number of married men begin to experience violence from their wives only when the relationship begins to break up or just prior to divorce proceedings. It is at this point that a battered husband has potentially everything to lose, which is why he may delay the break-up or divorce, putting up with the violence and abuse through fear of enraging his wife further, to the point where she may make formal counter-allegations about his instability, cruelty or abuse so that he loses contact with his children, especially if he leaves home precipitately during or after a violent confrontation. It is at such strategic turning points in a marriage that a man's response to his wife's violence may dictate the entire outcome of his future *vis-à-vis* divorce settlements and his role as a father.

*   *   *

In the case of filmmaker Tony Roell, physical fights between him and his wife Sandy were nothing new. Her attacks on him were usually a culmination of some bitter dispute over alleged infidelities on his part or how their daughters should be brought up. Sandy herself used to admit to friends that when she could no longer find words to express her anger and distress her frustration mounted until she felt compelled to use blows instead. Tony understood this mechanism and, while he restrained himself from hitting her back, as he is powerfully built he was easily able to restrain her, even if it meant using a certain degree of force.

'The last occasion this happened we had decided to separate and eventually divorce. I had come to begin packing my things to move to a new flat. Some minor disagreement came up and suddenly she flew at me like a wild cat and ripped my T-shirt right off me in shreds, drawing blood. I managed to hold her down, pinning her arms to her sides, which left red marks and bruises started forming. On seeing this she immediately called the police, told them I'd beaten her up. They came round and locked me up overnight in the cells. The next day she filed assault charges. Thankfully we managed to talk it through and friends persuaded her not to go to court. But you see how a perfectly reasonable act of self-defence by a man against a violent partner can be interpreted as an assault – and how readily, in this climate of awareness over battered wives, but ignorance over battered men, the police will believe the woman's version.'

According to some men, police attitudes and actions vary from area to area. Tony Roell lived in a part of London where one of the more militantly feminist women's refuges and the local police domestic violence unit work in close collaboration. In some cases, physical injuries must be fairly extensive before the police will believe a man's claims of being attacked by his wife, or that she initiated the violence.

Martin, who finally hit his wife across the face after she gashed his forehead with a broken bottle, actually had little trouble persuading the police who was the victim, who the offender. 'She got herself registered as a battered wife at our local hospital and wanted to press charges. But when the police saw my wounds they persuaded her not to bother and warned her that the next time this sort of thing happened they would take her into custody for assault. That is exactly what happened a few weeks later, and that time I called the police after she'd lashed at me with a hot poker, burning my hands and cutting my lip. They had no compunction about locking her in the slammer for the night.' As a result of that final event, Martin took out an injunction against his wife, mainly to prevent her harming their small daughter. They are now legally separated and the authorities are taking her violence seriously enough to consider allowing him to have permanent custody of the children.

However, in many similar cases, or more specifically, where mutual violence is a feature of the relationship, culpability – especially who struck whom first – may be impossible to prove. Given such variables as one or other of the partners being drunk or on drugs and the tendency for a man or woman to retaliate with greater ferocity and strength to a relatively minor initial act of provocation – she shouts obscenities at him, he slaps her, she hurls a heavy ashtray at his head or stabs him with a knife – any attempt to differentiate between victim and offender, or to define who initiated the violence and whether each person's action was retaliatory or in self-defence or committed purely through spite and anger, may be doomed from the outset. As one American researcher sums it up: 'Who gets defined as the victim and who is finally charged as the assailant may only be a matter of who called the police first and filed assault charges.'

The Balance of Power

Why men stay seems easier to explain than why women act violently towards their partners in the first place. As usual with cases of so-called 'uncharacteristic' female behaviour, many experts have been quick to pin various neat pathological labels on to the causes, thereby implying yet again that there must be external factors to blame for a woman's violence which are ultimately outside her control. Those working with alcoholics, drug addicts and the mentally disturbed all stress the greater likelihood of women with such problems behaving violently towards their partners and their children. And so they do, but this only accounts for a minuscule part of the overall picture.

Female biochemistry is another factor often seized upon. As ever, endocrinologists and support groups for PMT and post-natal depression sufferers emphasize women's reproductive biology as the villain of the piece, with raging hormones as the fount of irrationality and violent mood swings leading to aggression and violence. All of which are perfectly plausible explanations, bolstered by considerable amounts of evidence. But they still only reveal a relatively small part of the picture, probably no more than a quarter.

That the influence of alcohol and other drugs may decrease inhibition and thus increase women's aggression, as it intensifies men's violence, is undeniable. According to Al Anon, a support group for the families of alcoholics, a large number of those attending meetings are the husbands and relatives of women whose violence is directly related to alcohol dependence. Similarly, such organizations as the Women's Nutritional Advisory Service and the National Association for Premenstrual Syndrome have no shortage of women on file whose premenstrual symptoms include violence, and who have responded successfully to either dietary or hormonal intervention. Yet in the vast majority of cases, according to those men who do respond to polls and questionnaires and who are beginning to speak openly about being victims of their partners' violence, such explanations by and large rarely square with their own personal experiences. Out of a hundred men who contacted TV producer Pamela Smith during her research for a documentary on battered husbands, only a handful mentioned alcohol, drugs or PMT as causative factors behind their wives' attacks. 'From what I've learnt from these men, the booze excuse really is a red herring,' she asserts, a finding so far confirmed by the existing, if limited, studies into the subject. So far all the evidence suggests that women's, like many men's, propensity towards marital violence is rooted largely in early childhood experiences of abuse, abandonment or violence, whether as a victim or as an observer of aggressive interchanges between parents or other care-givers.

In Dr Kevin Brown's study, both men and women who had been either physically abused or severely physically punished in childhood were three times more likely to behave violently themselves in an adult relationship. Interestingly, those who were emotionally and verbally abused were more prone to end up as victims, male or female, presumably due to consistently low levels of self-esteem and confidence, factors which are commonly mentioned by women to explain why they continue to put up with their husband's violence and domination over very long periods. Brown's study failed to come up with any significant or dramatic difference in tactics used by men and women during an argument that eventually turned into a violent confrontation. Both sexes admitted resorting to verbal abuse and threatening or actually using physical violence, including hitting, slapping, punching, throwing and hitting with objects. The only difference appears to lie in the intensity and duration of the violence and the subsequent injuries, men's violence proving, as would be expected, more brutal, intensive and sustained and thus more damaging and potentially life-threatening than women's, and with women tending to curtail or contain aggressive confrontations by drawing on negotiating skills as opposed to men's tendency to escalate the violence.

By now such parallels and distinctions are continuing to emerge too frequently and predictably in every survey of family violence in America for there to be any real room for major dispute. Increasing emphasis on the distinction between what are assumed to be essentially female '*expressive*' forms of aggression, the spontaneous outpouring of red-hot, raw emotion, often a combination of anger and frustration, and inherently masculine '*instrumental*' violence, reflecting men's need to punish, dominate, coerce and generally terrify women into submitting to their desires and demands is useful in so far as it illustrates the dynamics underlying the two different modes of violent behaviour in both sexes. But to define women's aggression as 'typically' expressive and men's as 'inherently' instrumental seems a dangerously divisive exercise in that it merely perpetuates popular stereotypes of women as irrational beings, helplessly swept away by seething, uncontrollable passions and men as coldly calculating, cruel misogynists.

By dwelling too much on the theories for presumed biological differences in men's and women's expressions of anger and frustration it is all too easy to ignore the all-important context that gives rise to such violent interchanges in the first place – the most obvious being the context of power. One has only to listen to the experiences of women who have suffered often extreme physical violence, emotional abuse, cruelty and degradation by their lesbian partners, moreover lesbians who are self-confessed feminists, to realize to what extent a woman's determination to exercise power and control over her partner in a supposedly 'equal' relationship may resemble a man's. It would indeed be ironic if by speaking out more frankly – as is now slowly beginning to happen – battered lesbian women rather than abused heterosexual men were to be the ones to present us with a fuller picture of women's potential for control and violence within the sphere of domestic partnerships.

Those working with battered women continue to take issue with the methods used by researchers to obtain information on marital violence, stressing that the much used Conflict Tactics Scale (CTS) used to measure violence in the home oversimplifies the complex issues surrounding marital violence. This is because it only covers violent episodes that may have occurred in the single preceding year and fails to take into account previous contexts and past circumstances when other attacks occurred or the nature and scale of injuries sustained, indiscriminately lumping together different violent acts while omitting violent attacks such as rape and other sexual assaults. Were such surveys to interpret men's and women's violent acts according to the overall long-term climate of the relationship, taking into account the subtle dynamics underlying the couple's past history, their habitual mode of resolving conflicts, each partner's skill, or lack of skill, in communicating their wishes and feelings and above all by analysing the exact nature of the confrontation which precedes a violent act, critics argue that a far more accurate, if complex, picture of domestic violence would emerge.

In the case of husband battering, many women maintain that women who strike their partner probably do so in self-defence, or after years of suffering when they can no longer endure being controlled, emotionally abused, manipulated, criticized, verbally or physically assaulted by him. A frequent criticism of such surveys is that they will usually classify a man who has battered his wife over a ten-year period and is finally punched in the stomach by her with a broom handle, perhaps when he is coming at her yet again with fists raised, as a battered husband. Absurd, but true – and dangerously misleading. Without sufficient background information and the full facts of such couples' past life together it would be pointless to waste time speculating about who is the victim, who the initiator of violence, and who qualifies as the true battered spouse.

The problem, of course, as with all surveys involving large numbers of individuals, randomly chosen (i.e. 'quantitative' research), is that in order to conduct fairly extensive research into one particular area of human behaviour, especially concerning sex or violence, rigid categories and simplistic generalizations become inevitable as a result of the necessary omission by researchers of any theoretical interpretations of the findings (i.e. 'qualitative' research). It is a valid criticism that the CTS-based surveys fail to take into account women's vulnerability and men's greater potential for inflicting grave physical injury – criticism which even the inventors of the CTS, Professor Murray Straus and Richard Gelles, by now largely acknowledge. But it is equally true that men's own violence, like their victimization, may similarly come across out of context, without allowing for such elements as wives' provocation, verbal taunting, humiliation and abuse.

As many men have testified, their physical wounds are often nothing compared to the emotional damage inflicted on them, more hurtful and lasting than the blows struck by any weapon. 'My wife not only used to scrawl disgusting insults on my study wall, but because I'm Jewish, came out with anti-Semitic abuse against my dead parents, saying things like it's a pity Hitler didn't do his job properly and do away with all of us. It's the most painful attack anyone could ever live with,' says one divorcee now living with his children.

References to sexual inadequacy, accusations of infidelity, homosexuality and fierce possessiveness are other forms of emotional devastation described by abused men. Aaron, who lives in fear that his Lebanese wife may leave the country with their small son, finds the steady stream of humiliation, ridicule and abuse about his lack of masculinity far harder to endure than being knocked about. That, and the sexual harassment. 'She subjects me sometimes for nights on end to hours of verbal abuse. She goes through my pockets, my wallet, my diary, accusing me of unfaithfulness. But worst is the threat of what damage she will do to me or our son if I don't satisfy her sexually. She's punched me in the face more than once for refusing to have sex. If you've ever heard that fear makes it impossible for a man to perform – forget it. For one thing, there's much more a woman may want than just penetration. And fear can make you go on doing it just to save your skin. She'll demand it over and over again, knowing I'll be too knackered from lack of sleep to work efficiently the next day. By angering me with her accusations of being a lousy lay she also gets me at it. And by her so-called proof that I'm unfaithful to her, that I've just slept with someone else by analysing my volume of semen when we have sex. Then she demands that I "pay" for my infidelity by doing it again with her.'

Before we can ever hope to gain any real and helpful insight into domestic violence, and how to reduce it, we must take into account the fact that women's potential for abuse, domination, aggression and even extreme violence towards their partner can be as great as a man's, even though most lack the force to wreak anything approaching the scale of physical damage that characterizes the more savage elements of wife battering. It is in trying to ascertain not *whether* women are violent in the home, but *why*, that the real complexities of inter-family violence become most apparent – the blurring of roles of 'victim' and 'perpetrator' that arise out of the constantly shifting dynamics of power between partners, and each one's need to control the other.

In their experience of working with groups of family members, including former spouses and partners, grandparents and step-parents, as well as currently warring partners, counsellors such as those affiliated to Relate and Lifeline recognize only too well how, in the absence of adequate emotional insight into past experience, present stresses and anxieties can trigger unconscious 'flashpoints', in effect unconscious traumatic memories from the past which serve as a wellspring for a woman's violent outburst. A typical example quoted by Janine Turner might be the case of a woman's father having deserted the family which as a little girl she experienced as a deeply painful rejection and which she has never fully confronted or forgiven. Now, as a wife, she unconsciously relives all the fear and despair of that early rejection each time her husband leaves home unexpectedly, returns home late or unintentionally ignores her. The only way in which some women can suppress the tide of frightening emotions that threaten to engulf them, and whose origins they cannot identify, is by allowing more familiar and expressible feelings of fury and aggression to erupt and to project these against her partner who has come to symbolize her parent.

In Jenni Manners' experience, however, the background of many women who use violence against their partner does not always conform to the victim-turned-abuser stereotype, and may actually turn out to be quite the opposite. 'We have found that it is often women who were only children, or the eldest, and had a very close relationship with their fathers, often ganging up with him against the mother – who may have been a weak, placid type – who end up demanding power and dominance in their relationship with a man.'

The role that a woman's early history plays in contributing to her violent moods may be gradually revealed in certain forms of intervention therapy where women are required to keep a detailed 'danger diary', in which they record the date and time of each violent episode, the type of situation during which violence occurred, identification of the thought processes prior to the event, appraisal of the severity and duration of different emotions that preceded, accompanied and formed the aftermath of the violence, and the eventual outcome of the confrontation. Learning to recognize potentially dangerous trigger situations allows women, with the help of counselling, to defuse and avert violent outbursts, sometimes with the help of special audiotapes, de-stressing techniques and imagery designed to resolve the original childhood experience and disconnect its hold on the present.

More sad and complex still are those cases of female incest or sexual abuse survivors who, according to Janine Turner, are sometimes driven to form relationships with quiet, placid men whom they know they can dominate or abuse, using anger as a means of 'getting even' with their early abuser. Invariably when men talk about the immense problems of living with former incest survivors the overwhelming obstacle to peaceful co-existence is always the woman's store of pent-up hatred and anger. It may be a cliché now to say that abused children, be they boys or girls, become abusers in later life in an attempt to 'master' or 'make sense' of their early trauma as well as through an unconscious determination to avoid further victimization, but like all popular generalizations it contains, deep down, a hard, bitter kernel of truth.

Sometimes in the wake of that anger comes shame or regret, sometimes not. Judith, an interpreter, says she often came close to walking out on her family after realizing the full and terrible impact of her behaviour. 'The only detail I remember is this immense, intolerable build-up of red-hot fury, and an overwhelming desire to hurt those I love most. I'd purposely pick a row, about anything, nothing, with my husband, then this phenomenal inner energy seemed to boil up, driving me to smash out at him. At that moment I hated him more than anything else. Then things went blank. Later, seeing his poor face, the weals and blood, his state of shock, was utterly horrifying. I was so scared eventually at not perhaps being able to stop myself killing him, or that I'd harm the children, that I asked my sister to move in as protection and I finally rang a crisis line for battered wives, asking them if they knew of help for abusers.'

Guilt and reluctance to let themselves off the hook for losing their temper or becoming violent even where there might have been some justification for their actions, seems, as one might imagine, to be more common among women than men. As her two-year relationship with her live-in boyfriend became increasingly soured by rows, sulks and sexual difficulties, Meg, an advertising copywriter, genuinely believed that if only she could make Graham talk openly and honestly to her about the problems he was having at work and with his finances, she could be more supportive and understanding and help him through his difficulties. But the more she tried to probe, the more withdrawn and resentful he became, until, 'the barrier between us prevented him from trusting me or truly committing himself to the relationship. My frustration and sense of impotence became unbearable in the end. I started resenting him deeply. Finally I began hitting at him in desperation once I saw that nothing I said, no way I explained anything, would get him to consider my feelings at being pushed away. So one day I began shoving, kicking, hitting him – I even pushed him downstairs once. It was partly blind instinct, partly premeditated – I wanted to hurt him. I'm nearly six foot and very physically fit and he's quite slight. So I knew I had an advantage and I used it, purposely, knowing I'd get no come-back, I'd be safe. But even though I was violent a few times, afterwards the sense of shame and disgust at myself for sinking to such a low level, for using brute force when I'm a person whose job relies on using words and strategy to communicate, was horrendous. We soon split up. I wouldn't have been able to live with myself any more in a relationship based on my capacity for violence.'

Remorse, or lack of it, may depend very much on what fault or failing a woman perceives in her partner that causes her to attack him in the first place. For a usually unassertive woman lacking adequate verbal or other communication skills to negotiate conflicts and disputes, violence – murder, even – may come only as a final long-delayed act of revenge against a husband who has abused and dominated her throughout the relationship, not necessarily in the physical sense but by more insidious means. This was the experience of Audrey, whose memories of her marriage are principally of being derided for looking frumpish, admonished for not keeping a tidy home and rejected for being unsexy in bed. 'In the end I felt totally useless in every area of my life. He ignored me in bed, having made me feel worthless throughout the day. I began to feel this unbearable tension building up inside me and eventually I exploded, began biting and scratching him, pulling his hair, like a wild animal, or someone in a lunatic asylum. It terrified and ashamed me when I saw what I was capable of. This was a new part of me, coming out of an alien world I never knew existed. I felt absolutely cheap and nasty – especially the screaming, like a fishwife, so different to what I'm normally like.'

In contrast, one 65-year-old American grandmother who took part in a US national survey on domestic violence admits to having no compunction about punching her husband in the gut every time he calls her 'a dumb Polak'. Another, who admits that both she and her husband have always fought, often resorting to immense physical violence throughout their fifteen-year marriage, states candidly that it is, 'because we both want to be the boss'. Evidently, if two such essentially assertive and uncompromising partners remain together, it must surely be because, rather than in spite of, the fact that their bloody battles for equal power are part of the domestic deal.

What really lies behind women's aggression in the home, in particular towards her partner, is a conundrum in itself, especially as so little is yet known of the mechanisms that generate female violence and motivate women's need for power. Unlike much male violence, women's is rarely used as an adjunct to sexual domination or as a means of bolstering their gender image or self-importance. In some cases, for instance, women use anger against their spouses not as a weapon of attack but as a perfectly understandable, if not always legitimate, response to a man who fails to meet their needs. To an outsider, those needs may seem particularly complex, even perverse, as in the case of a formerly abused woman who may want the man she lives with to demonstrate his strength and authority over her in order to give her a licence to continue playing the role of the defenceless victim, becoming violent and hostile when her partner lacks the necessary characteristics of dominance.

Grotesque, even kinky, as this might appear – and of course the mere idea that any woman would genuinely wish her partner to dominate and control her must seem like the grossest of heresies to many women – such cases are by no means unknown or unusual in the field of family therapy and domestic violence research. Given that many women without any previous history of abuse, physical punishment or cruelty are still brought up to expect men to assume positions of authority or dominance in society and the family, such tactics may well help to explain the paradoxical nature of some of what passes for wife battering, but to which there may be much more than meets the eye.

Researchers Straus and Gelles provide two particularly illuminating cases. One was a woman who had frequent physical and verbal fights with her husband, each of them retaliating, defending and putting equal amounts of energy and violence into their punch-ups, yet who acknowledged that, 'I only feel fully alive when we're fighting.' The other concerns a woman who frequently provoked her husband into violent outbursts, taunting, teasing, even hitting him until he hit back or beat her up. The reason she gave for persisting in 'winding him up', even when she knew it would almost certainly end with him beating her, was that he was essentially a passive man who avoided making decisions, leaving these primarily to her. Having been brought up to believe that the man 'should wear the pants', his passivity so angered her that she taunted him, knowing that in the end he would at least react by, 'doing something that a man is supposed to do,' as she puts it. Unbelievable? Perhaps. But surely no more so than the finding that one in four women approve of husbands slapping wives under certain conditions, showing to what extent women themselves continue to buy into the old 'real man' macho myth.

Both these examples also provide a glimpse of the danger area Erin Pizzey pinpointed in those battered women whom she came to regard as being 'addicted' to violent relationships. Pizzey's remarks were misinterpreted and she was ostracized by the women's movement for accusing women of 'inviting' men's violence or 'enjoying' being beaten by their partners. Yet she never actually said this. On the contrary, she has stated openly that: 'I have never met a woman who enjoyed the actual beating.' But when you carefully analyse the experiences which certain women described to her, and Pizzey's own insight into those women's emotional make-up (almost all, as she acknowledges, grew up in violent homes and came, tragically, to equate violence with love), it is clear that what made them feel 'fully alive' was not being violently beaten and injured by their husbands but the build-up of tension and sense of danger preceding the violent episode and the excitement of the 'adrenalin rush' immediately before an assault, which some women described as akin to a sexual orgasm in its intensity and pervasive power.

Whether this need for excitement through a violent confrontation arises from a woman's childhood history, her own inability to express anger or communicate emotion in other ways, or from the fact that her partner is emotionally unresponsive and she is compelled to 'kick-start' him into some sort of semblance of life, is difficult to say, though very likely it may be a combination of all three. Feminist therapist Susie Orbach has also found that some women can only deal with their own inner anger by living with a violent man who becomes in effect a 'container' for her inexpressible feelings, acting out the aggression on her behalf of which she herself is incapable.

Also, one cannot help but suspect that as with other aspects of personality and behaviour, so too with aggression, and that opposites may perhaps attract. Placid or slow-to-arouse men and volatile, aggressive women may be drawn to each other out of some deep unconscious need or dependency. Is it mere coincidence that so many of the men who have contacted crisis lines and begun to talk openly about their experiences appear to be fundamentally peace-loving, non-confrontational 'new men', the very antithesis of brutish or dominant machismo? If so, then this may help explain women's violence by placing it within a specific framework – the power vacuum resulting from men's abdication as traditional 'leaders' of the family. It would appear, at least on the surface, that such men are fated to lose out on several counts in a partnership with an aggressive woman. Like Andrew Bellton or Joe Edwards, they will be unlikely to strike back at a woman who attacks them, and they are both too loving, forgiving or optimistic – some might say gullible or self-deluding – to back out of the relationship.

More significantly, do some women, like so many men, in fact have a desperate need for a human punchbag against whom they can let out their pent-up aggression? If so, then it is these very qualities of forbearance and patience, qualities that some women may interpret as weakness or passivity, or even just emotional inaccessibility, that are most likely to provoke women whose aggression is intended to evoke positive, even aggressive responses from their partner. Compared to a wife who derives satisfaction from dominating her partner and who relies on his remaining submissive and malleable, using his weakness as an excuse to justify her actions, for another woman, abusive language, physical blows, humiliation and ridicule may turn out simply to be randomly chosen weapons of last resort when he refuses to engage in any emotional dialogue at all.

The Symmetry of Violence

According to Christopher Clulow, director of the Institute of Marital Studies at London's Tavistock Institute, violent wives are too easily dismissed as hysterical, man-hating viragos when in reality their attacks on their husbands can be more accurately interpreted as a desperate cry for help, a last ditch attempt after years of patience and denial of their own emotional needs to get through to a placid, undemonstrative man who is 'emotionally unavailable'. Clulow's explanation highlights the basic premise that has given form to the recently developed 'systems' theory of family violence: that the complex underlying dynamics of violence and aggression between relatives and family units as a whole need to be examined, an altogether more painstaking exercise than simply placing 'victim' and 'offender' in neatly separate categories, one meriting care and protection, the other odium and punishment. The 'systems' approach rightly jettisons the paranoid notion that domestic violence, in essence, boils down to no more than men's hostility towards women and that by eradicating misogyny, battering and abuse would cease to exist. Some hope.

Instead, this undiscriminating, infinitely more broadly humanitarian approach recognizes the often symmetrical nature of intra-family violence, believed to be a characteristic feature or handicap of the so-called 'dysfunctional' family. Again, whether couples and families today are any more violence-prone or dysfunctional than they were decades or centuries ago, especially among the very poor and dispossessed, is a moot point. The fact that it was ever thus, and that child abuse, husband battering and wife beating are evils as old as time, until recently accepted as commonplace injustices within domestic life which are only beginning to be acknowledged as a widescale social problem today, is almost certainly closer to the truth.

One can understand why some researchers see family violence as a microcosm of increasing social and world hostility, evidence that the 'culture' of violence now so densely woven into the basic fabric of our society has become a linking pattern within the family system itself. Psychoanalysts, however, are more likely to emphasize the role of the unconscious in creating powerful bonds between individuals whose interlocking neuroses may breed a dynamic relationship (as much among gay men and lesbian women as heterosexual couples) which itself feeds on violence, yet whose impetus may originally have been set in motion and is perpetuated by pre-existing violence between other family members. This explains why, increasingly, therapists try to work not only with 'victim' or 'offender' but with entire families and co-habitants, and also indicates that their claim to be able to trace family violence back four generations (as when therapy involves participation with a child, its parents and its grandparents) may amount to rather more than idle speculation.

Is this type of therapy the fastest, most dependable route to achieving greater domestic harmony? It must be interpreted as a positive sign that many women, unlike most men, seem to be driven by their guilty conscience, shame or fear over their destructive behaviour to seek help in controlling it. Also encouraging is the broadening, multidimensional approach adopted increasingly by agencies in trying to understand and solve the problems underlying domestic violence.

But, at the same time, we must never lose sight of the fact that understanding women's (or men's) violence towards their partners is a long way from excusing, let alone condoning, it. To propose that a woman may have no other outlet for her aggression and is justified in resorting to violence when trying to communicate with a non-communicative or violent man, is entirely untenable, for it gives women the very same licence to abdicate responsibility for which we rightly revile men who behave violently in similar situations – the man, for instance, whose sentence for murdering his wife was commuted when the judge stated that, 'her nagging would have tried the patience of a saint'.

Is it any more reasonable for a woman to be encouraged to take refuge in such arguments and defences? Except in those very few isolated and extreme exceptions where domesticity has turned into a life-threatening nightmare to be survived by any means, most emphatically not. If there is anything more dangerous than our refusal to recognize women's capacity for domestic violence, it is the temptation to manufacture excuses, whether it be female 'hormonally induced' irrationality or, as men have traditionally done, citing their partner's 'unreasonable behaviour' to legitimize their violence (the bottom line being that the victim was somehow responsible for provoking their own assault). For women to similarly shrug off their accountability and deny their capacity for free choice and responsible action would be to slow the progress of sexual equality – if not halt it for ever.

Killer Carers

Murder Most Foul

Outrageous as it may sound to us, Queen Victoria's notorious refusal to believe in the existence of lesbianism is unlikely to be entirely apocryphal. Nor can we be too confident that such myopia doesn't exist today. Although the present climate of moral and sexual liberalism is hardly conducive to social or sexual naïvety, a vestigial trace of 'Queen Victorianism', particularly the unshatterable trust of many women in the inherent incorruptibility and moral superiority of their sex lingers, even today.

Though it may be fashionable to denounce it, somewhere – deeply embedded within society's collective unconscious – unrealistic ideals of female virtue still beckon alluringly, obscuring the crude reality of certain female crimes in myth and taboo. Continued disavowal, especially by many feminist groups, of women's assaults on husbands, boyfriends, even lesbian partners, is a prime case in point. And as for the ultimate 'unmentionable', we need look no further than the explosive issue of women's violence towards children. Having seen most forms of human perversion and violence, the average forensic psychiatrist doesn't shock easily. However, there can be exceptions. At a recent conference on adolescent and female offenders held by the International Association for Forensic Psychotherapy, one speaker decided to run a videotape made by a local health authority using a hidden camera. Doctors had become suspicious about a baby frequently admitted to hospital with inexplicable symptoms of severe physical trauma. The film showed the screaming baby struggling to breathe as a woman, a close family relative, while changing a nappy repeatedly forced her hand over its nose and mouth in an apparent attempt to asphyxiate it. Murmurs of distress and disbelief echoed through the audience. Something about the sight of this tiny human creature, writhing helplessly while what seemed in contrast a disproportionately giant hand threatened to snuff out its frail existence, sent a collective chill around the room. Was it because the hand was a woman's? Or rather because, as it later emerged, she escaped criminal charges and was sent only for psychiatric treatment for symptoms of depression, soon after being deemed harmless enough to be allowed to remain in the community, where she continued to be entrusted with childcare?

It is a brave psychiatrist who publicly stirs up such a hornets' nest, not only by presenting evidence guaranteed to repel, but by openly challenging society's continuing tendency to let such women off the hook. Whatever its outcome, the enquiry ordered after the conviction of that most egregious of all 'killer-carers', Beverley Allitt, will almost certainly leave vital questions unanswered. Such as what in the end turns an apparently normal, fully functioning woman into a child murderer? And, more crucial still, how many women with severe emotional problems may be teetering on the brink of fully blown homicidal psychopathology? Yet could the real reason for our ignorance about what makes the female serial killer tick be the fact that because they raise a host of deeply repugnant, taboo-ridden issues, we still shrink from asking such questions in the first place?

If media hype is to be believed we are currently facing a growing and particularly abhorrent new crime wave – the abuse, torture and murder by women of babies and young children. From reports of children being assaulted by molesters and paedophiles masquerading as social workers to alleged ritual and satanic abuses, as in the recent Orkneys investigation, women have begun increasingly to feature in such tales of depravity and perversion.

In the 1990s, the new spectre haunting our dreams and stalking our waking hours is the 'killer carer', one hand rocking the cradle, the other poised to assassinate. Never slow to spot a trend or to make a fast buck out of exploiting human fear, Hollywood has played no small part in contributing to parental paranoia by portraying a new breed of monster women, like the murderous nanny in *The Hand That Rocks the Cradle* or the vengeful matriarch in *Mother Love*, women who appear to be the epitome of middle-class respectability. Not that the portrayal of filicide (the murder of a child by its parent) is anything new; it has always been an original and horrific source of inspiration to dramatists, most notably in Ancient Greece. Indeed, the murder by Medea, that most celebrated and tragic of female killers, of her female rival and her own two sons in revenge for her husband's adultery and abandonment is more bloody, more coldly premeditated and her actions more deeply shocking because the slaughter is accompanied by stark recognition of and total responsibility for the tragic scale of suffering she has chosen to inflict, not least upon herself.

Today's real life tragedies are no less gruesome in their magnitude and impact but, unlike the horrors served up to us by the Ancient Greeks, they lack the moral contextual frame which might help us to identify with such terminal despair and comprehend how the intolerable burden of life's injustices could drive a woman to kill her children. Nowadays, doctors would label Medea a psychopath, as they did the American 16-year-old girl who smashed in the face and head of her little brother with a bronze statuette, in order to get back at her detested, abusive father who had worshipped his little son. Believing, like Medea, that instant death was too good for a man who had caused her so much grief, she opted instead to make his life an everlasting hell by killing the thing he adored most. A further explanation for the massacre is Medea's own anguished and furious recognition of women's comparative lack of power in dictating the outcome of their lives, an impotence with which countless women continue to identify. Psychotic or no, many an abused child or adult survivor will undoubtedly recognize the motivation and empathize with the desperation leading to such acts, even if they are unable to condone the act itself.

Yet for the most part it is the frequent wanton arbitrariness, the apparent absence of motive or of any sign of mental illness in the criminal herself, whose image is usually nearer that of Mary Poppins than Lucrezia Borgia, which in the end is so deeply disturbing. A case in point is that of 28-year-old nanny

Carol Withers, an archetypal Sloane Ranger, blonde, elegantly dressed, her voice reflecting the influence of her expensive English education and Swiss finishing school, who in January 1992 fractured the skulls of two 3-week-old babies in her care. The infants survived, and Withers was jailed for fifteen months. Yet two psychiatrists' reports failed to diagnose any mental abnormality or emotional disturbance. To this day, there has been no explanation of why Carol Withers, the daughter of a wealthy agricultural magnate, should have assaulted her charges. Nor can we begin to fathom how an apparently ordinary young mother could dip her small son's penis in hot tea and whirl him around inside a spin-dryer, as in a case heard by a Nottingham court in March 1988. Or how another young mother, in Ealing a year later, could calmly plunge the feet of her yelling 18-month-old baby into boiling water.

In November 1991, Beverley Allitt, a 23-year-old nurse, was arrested and charged with murdering three babies and a 10-year-old boy, and attempting to murder another nine infants at Grantham and Kesteven hospital in Lincolnshire. The assaults, which caused some of these children to suffer heart attacks, respiratory failure and irreparable brain damage, ranged from the injection of massive and lethal doses of drugs such as insulin and potassium chloride to suffocation, interference with their oxygen supply and the crushing of their ribcages. Not surprisingly, bail was withheld after the initial charges, to which she pleaded not guilty, and throughout the very long period of criminal investigations she was remanded in custody for her own protection. When finally committed for trial in February 1993, Allitt faced a total of twenty-six charges – four of murder, eleven of attempted murder and eleven of causing grievous bodily harm with intent. When sentenced to thirteen terms of life imprisonment on 28 May 1993, Allitt had been convicted of all four murders, three attempted murders and six other serious attacks causing grievous bodily harm on babies in her care. When sentencing her, Mr Justice Latham stated that he would have sentenced her to life on each count of grievous bodily harm had she faced those charges alone.

*   *   *

Motiveless attacks by ordinary women who have suddenly broken down? Mentally deranged women, part of whose condition is the deceptive façade of normality? Women who have gradually ceased to retain control over powerful destructive impulses? Women who derive personal pleasure from cunningly planning the destruction of human life? Which is it? Surely such horrific actions as those described above must be classifiable under one of these categories? Or so the newspapers would have us believe, until one begins to analyse the small print beneath the lurid banner headlines. An important if tiny fragment of a clue lies embedded in part of Mr Justice Latham's sentencing of Beverley Allitt: 'I accept that you are severely disturbed [Allitt, diagnosed as suffering from the personality disorder Münchausen Syndrome by Proxy had subsequently developed severe anorexia while in custody, becoming too ill to attend her trial] but you are cunning and manipulative and show no remorse for the trail of destruction you have left behind.' Here we are presented, in a nutshell, with a frightening paradox: a disordered psychopathic personality by no means indicates that the offender is either helplessly devoid of intelligence and responsibility for their actions, bereft of mental acuity or short of any capacity to calculate their every fiendish move with ice-cold precision. Their overwhelming deficit is in the realm of care and compassion, a tragic failing that is the quintessential mark of the psychopath. Often fully aware of the difference between right and wrong, a killer like Allitt may repeatedly do wrong but with complete indifference to the pain and anguish resulting from their deeds, since only the gratification of their own needs is important to them.

To call such women simply 'mad' is for the most part dangerously misleading, since the genuinely mad, including those suffering from psychotic illnesses such as schizophrenia, rarely have any real capacity to function normally, lacking control for greater or lesser stretches of time over many, sometimes most of their actions. To judge them bad, unless you subscribe to the notion of original sin, provides no insight into their behaviour while missing the point about the infinite complexity and as yet unrecognized factors, environmental and biochemical, that conspire to shape – and to fragment and corrupt – the human personality.

Take the case of Margaret Kelly Michaels, a 23-year-old American nursery school teacher who was convicted in April 1988 on 115 counts of sexually abusing nineteen children aged between 3 and 5 who were in her care at a New Jersey nursery school. The court heard that Michaels allegedly performed sexual acts on them and forced them to participate in activities that the judge called 'sordid' and 'bizarre'. When sentenced to forty-seven years' imprisonment, her lawyers argued that she should be released on bail pending an appeal, on the grounds that a psychiatrist's report concluded Michaels was not psychotic and therefore could not be regarded as a danger to society. During the interview with the psychiatrist, she had commented that her family life was normal and that she had always been treated with respect. Yet while in prison awaiting the result of the appeal, a visit by Margaret's parents soon revealed the opposite. Prison warders observed that Margaret and her father engaged in passionate embraces, intimate fondling and French kissing, while her mother looked on unperturbed. The incestuous relationship had clearly been established long ago. Not surprisingly, the court ultimately declined Michaels's appeal. What is highly unlikely is that Michaels had intentionally set out to deceive the authorities by describing her 'normal' childhood. The disconcerting truth is that like the majority of child abuse survivors, as most therapists can testify, in order to survive her experiences she *genuinely* came to believe in the normality of her past.

More unsettling still are the number of as yet unanswered – perhaps unanswerable – questions surrounding a recent British case, in which an 11-year-old babysitter murdered an 18-month-old baby, battering, punching and suffocating him when she lost patience with his crying. The trial attracted sensational media coverage and raised understandable public feelings of revulsion. Not only did it seem incomprehensible that a girl so young could act with such brutality towards a tiny child, but just as sinister was the cool assurance and expertise with which she managed, minutes after the murder, to assure the child's mother that the evening had gone 'fine'. Later, when testifying in court, her self-possession showed no sign of weakening: confidently denying committing the murder, she gave a series of elaborate yet plausible explanations for the bloodstains found on her clothes. According to the judge at Newcastle Crown Court the girl's composure was such that for twenty minutes after the mother returned 'she presented an entirely normal attitude'.

Found guilty of murder, she was sentenced to five years' detention at a centre for young people. The giveaway here is less her mendacity than the enduring, all-pervasive conviction accompanying it. According to Dr Peter Woods, a forensic psychiatrist, this is a perfectly natural defence reaction that many offenders display in response to their own violence. In his words: 'She is not mentally ill. She is intelligent and has the intellectual facilities to know what she has done. But because of the enormity of the offence and its horrendous nature, it is very probable she has unconsciously blocked it out of her mind using the defence mechanisms we all have.'

The real clue lies in the extent and duration of the denial – a mechanism which in some measure also affects many victims of violence such as rape, survivors of war, torture or natural disaster. Exactly why certain victims exhibit a far greater tendency than others to suppress all memory of their ordeal to the point of denying the event ever happened, or believing it happened to someone else – a recognized feature of severe post-traumatic stress disorder – is unknown. Yet one explanation given by psychologists treating rape victims with severe PTSD symptoms is that any pre-existing trauma resulting from early abuse, shock or violence is more likely to intensify the effects of future trauma. This reveals a second vital clue to the puzzling behaviour of offenders such as this girl (whose name has never been publicly disclosed). So far we can only speculate as to her early experiences. The odds are, however, that they are likely to have been hair-raising.

Everything points to her inability to live in the real world or to react with any spontaneous emotion to the magnitude of her dreadful deed. Nearly a year and a half after the murder of little Sean Graham, reports indicated that his killer, now 12, steadfastly continued to deny her actions, remaining unconcerned, unrepentant and unable to understand why she has been locked up when she insists that someone else did the killing. In the experience of Professor Masud Hoghughi, former director of the Aycliffe Centre for children whose fifty-three inmates include an adolescent girl who mutilated and drowned her brother, another who tortured an elderly man and then burnt him alive and a girl who is there for seriously sexually assaulting another girl, these children are far from being 'the hairy black underbelly of this nation . . . children labelled as beasts by the public', but youngsters, often from violent, unloving backgrounds, needing and deserving the best of care and treatment.

The Good Woman Giveth – And Taketh Away

No other issue is quite so guaranteed as child assault and murder to snap open in each one of us a Pandora's box of emotion, that might occasionally encompass unusual insight, empathy and understanding of the sort expressed by Professor Hoghughi, above, but more generally unleashes the most savage atavistic instincts of revulsion, hatred and demands for retribution and revenge. Understandably so. And even more understandably if the murderer or assailant is a woman, the acknowledged giver and protector of life – especially young, unformed life. On a recent visit to Holloway I was reminded by the staff that nonces, women convicted of murdering or abusing children, are frequently segregated from other inmates for their own safety, so powerful is the sense of outrage of the other women and the ferocity with which they sometimes attack such offenders.

Society's summary condemnation of such women as evil, mad or in some way 'possessed' by malignant forces demonstrates, however, how little comprehension exists of the influence that early environmental factors or present socioeconomic deprivation – or a combination of both – may have on individual psychology and behaviour, distorting perception and diminishing reason and self-control to the point where a woman is ultimately driven to such desperate and unimaginable extremes. Today infanticide is relatively rare and justly reviled as a heinous crime, yet when it does occur it is seldom a premeditated act of genuine wickedness or the result of extreme psychopathology. This has always been true. Even the most cursory glance at the long, blood-soaked history of infanticide throughout the ages and in all parts of the world, reveals that until the beginning of this century the disposal of newborn babies deemed surplus to a community's requirements, a task usually undertaken by their mothers, with or without the help of midwives or female relatives, was the principal method of family planning, especially in countries where law or custom dictated the number of children permitted to each couple.

Although we have long held it to be a repugnantly barbaric custom, rather like cannibalism, practised by only a few primitive savage tribes subsisting in some godforsaken distant wilderness, nothing could be further from reality. Children's lives have been cheap, even valueless, since time immemorial. In Ancient Sparta, Athens and the Roman Empire, the killing of weak, sickly or deformed infants who would be incapable of breeding healthy stock was either mandatory or socially sanctioned, and although murdering healthy babies was not exactly approved of, neither was it condemned as an evil crime. Japanese farmers used to describe infanticide as a form of 'thinning out', no different to the ordered cultivation of the rice fields.

Not hate, evil or lunatic savagery, but for the most part craven despair and a ruthless determination to survive, especially when resources are scarce, have always lain behind the slaughter of infants. Among the fierce, male-dominated Yanamamo tribe of South Venezuela, rather than invoke the wrath and murderous violence of their menfolk on witnessing the birth of a daughter, many women would instead immediately kill the girls at birth, since the primary emphasis is on breeding aggressive males in order to perpetuate the tribe's prized quality of 'waiteri' – ferocity. In the South Sea Islands, notably Melanesia and Polynesia, infanticide was universally practised, while the aborigine women of Australia killed their newborn routinely to escape punishment for rearing too many children. Common over long periods in various Hindu castes and in the Swahili culture, the poorer the community, the scarcer the resources, the greater the reliance on infanticide to allow the strong and able to survive.

Nor did the teachings of Christianity or the veneer of moral probity count for much when poverty forced women to choose between life and death for her infant. How terrifying was the prospect of one's soul roasting in the fires of eternal damnation compared to being flung out into the streets with one's newborn by family or employer to await slow death by starvation, exposure and incurable disease? In Britain, as in other European countries, infanticide was far from unknown, especially among uneducated, working-class women, prompting Disraeli to write in his novel *Sybil*: 'Infanticide is practised as extensively and legally in England as it is on the banks of the Ganges.'

As recently as Victorian times, poverty, lack of effective contraception, the unavailability of safe abortion and the moral stigma of bearing a child out of wedlock, drove both married women and single girls, many of whom were servants who became pregnant after being sexually assaulted by their employers, to 'allow' their child to die shortly after birth. So high was the turnover in the business of 'special delivery' of infants that until the introduction of the Midwives Act in 1902, untrained women drifted part-time into the delivery-cum-abortion racket to augment the meagre wages they earned as chars or washerwomen. For others it became a grisly, full-time trade, and the scandal of Britain's 'lying-in houses', where babies were 'arranged' to be stillborn, was not exposed until 1868 – when it turned out that large areas of London's most salubrious districts, for example St Marylebone, were a hot-bed of infant massacre and casual baby 'disposal', with corpses often to be found in public parks and ditches. Just as ignoble, and unmistakable in its intended objective, was the practice, common in nineteenth-century Florence and throughout France, of sending babies away to wet nurses in the countryside, often never to be seen or heard of again.

Yet given the alternatives, including starvation, homelessness, disease, dismissal from employment and public opprobrium and ostracism, the common practice of strangling, stifling or drowning one's newborn, piercing the vital organs or brain with needles and other sharp objects or simply leaving it outdoors in the cold to freeze to death must have seemed a far kinder, more humane option for many an unfortunate and desperate mother, as well as her wretched, unwanted offspring. Today in some countries of the world, and not necessarily the most backward, we may be sure that the custom persists: women of the nomadic Ayoreo Indians in South America were, as recently as the late 1960s, reported by anthropologist Paul Bugos to be committing infanticide, again in a desperate bid for survival. The most likely victims are weak, premature babies, who are seen as incapable of later reproducing healthy offspring themselves, or too much at risk of developing and passing on diseases which are rife in the community. In addition, because of a taboo on having sex with unwed mothers, fear of not being able to find a husband leads many single girls to kill their child at birth. Young lives are particularly expendable at times of warfare, especially if the woman is unmarried, because it is thought a child cannot survive such dangerous times without a father, who might be absent at war for long periods or be killed in battle. In parts of Pakistan the practice also reportedly still exists. And very recently, in 1992, one of China's most prominent women, Chen Muhua, head of the All-China Women's Federation, stated publicly that millions of Chinese baby girls have systematically been killed in the past decade alone – a result both of enduring ancient custom and the 1979 one-child family policy – warning that unless the butchering ceases 'armies of bachelors' now numbering 20 million would reach 50 million by the year 2,000.

Too Close for Comfort

Although decreased poverty and disease, the advent of welfare services, moral permissiveness, and, most importantly, the availability of reliable contraception and safe abortion have, in theory, eliminated the nightmare of unwanted children, Home Office statistics on crime testify to the fact that children most at danger of becoming murder victims are aged under 12 months. In 1989 there were 71 cases of child homicide – 12 per cent of all homicides – and three-quarters were killed by their parents, including step-parents and co-habiting partners. However, as a reflection solely of cases recorded by the police, this is likely to be a conservative estimate, since the true extent of such killings, like many domestic crimes, remains unknown. Establishing whether a baby was stillborn or stifled at birth can be a notoriously difficult business, as is proving whether the sudden death of a young child is due to accident, disease, cot death (Sudden Infant Death Syndrome) or filicide. In the introduction to a recent book investigating the mysterious deaths in America over fourteen years of nine small children, allegedly due to SIDS, which were eventually found to have been caused by their mother, Marybeth Tinning, who had worked in a paediatric ward and volunteer ambulance corps, John L. Emery, Emeritus Professor of Paediatric Pathology at the University of Sheffield, remarks that: 'I have studied over 6,000 baby deaths and over 2,000 of these as unexpected deaths – among these there were many where I found no anatomical cause for death.'

Throughout history and up until the present day, it has always been women with whom babies and young children spend the overwhelming majority of their time, in close proximity and intimate contact. Given that the task of childcare falls overwhelmingly on women's shoulders perhaps we should not be so confounded that carers can turn into killers, whether by accident or design, or that an infant, by virtue of its helplessness, is likely to be the most immediate target of a woman's destructive impulses, even though it may also have been the recipient of her most tenderly loving and protective urges.

Increasingly, research shows that it is no coincidence that many of the women found guilty of child abuse and murder should be involved in the 'caring' professions, or, conversely, that accounts of 'regimes' of torture, maltreatment and killing within institutions for other vulnerable members of the community, including the disabled and elderly, are just as likely to include female as male offenders. What ultimately makes Beverley Allitt's fifty-nine day 'reign of terror' on Ward 4 of Grantham and Kesteven Hospital so deeply chilling, apart from the nature of the crimes, is not that the killer was a woman, or one who killed as part of the 'natural' female role of care-giver, but that her gender and nurse's uniform seemed to grant her *automatic* immunity from suspicion.

How many more children, old or frail people must suffer and die needlessly before we finally begin to comprehend that if society continues to persuade women that their sole access to real power lies in motherhood – and women continue to be persuaded of this – then some will certainly go on to abuse that power? How much more reassuring to brand Beverley Allitt a demon than to try to dig beneath the complex, murky psychology that makes her a pathetically inadequate and destructive human being. Or to continue baying frenziedly for her blood, than to ask ourselves why all capacity for rational and balanced thought evaporates each time a woman stands in the dock, having 'betrayed' all that is expected of her sex and the apparent virtuousness that it stands for. Society needs its demons as well as its saints, and as a figure of evil, Allitt, at least in Britain now, has no equal. As a totem of evil she rivals that arch-demon Myra Hyndley, who could never have realistically hoped for parole because she remains, as Allitt will for decades to come, a salutary reminder of corrupt femininity, the personification of the extreme end of the Madonna–whore spectrum of womanhood.

Any woman falling from Madonna-like grace is still calculated to inspire not compassion or desire for understanding but a naked and venomous wrath. Which is why the most unsettling of all truths for society to accommodate is that such occupations as paediatric nursing may come to represent a vital, at times dangerous, source of power and means of self-aggrandizement for women with a chronic, lifelong sense of inadequacy, offering a chance to gain attention, approval and praise from their patients and the patients' parents as well as from their peers. What other occupation can be so guaranteed to impart a sense of being needed and valued, a need that may become addictive if it was lacking in one's early formative years? As Joyce Egginton concludes in her study of the events leading up to Marybeth Tinning's murder conviction, ever since her first job as a nurse's aide this former neglected child was drawn to positions which entailed caring for others and thereby could be counted on to appease her need to be recognized as a skilled contributor to a worthy cause – a role she embellished by lying about overcoming dangerous situations, saving lives and coping with crises, all of which turned out to be largely fictitious or else purposely manufactured by her.

In the case of another celebrated American serial baby killer, Texan nurse Genene Jones, whose combined prison sentences totalled 159 years for the murder of up to sixteen babies in her care, similar patterns of behaviour originating in her past history are clearly discernible. A childhood traumatized by the early death both of a beloved brother and her father and constant criticism from an alcoholic mother generated her own aggressive outbursts, promiscuity and heavy drinking. As a young divorced single mother who had no scruples about beating her child, she developed an almost fanatical obsession with illness and medicine, eventually qualifying as a vocational nurse, becoming employed in the paediatric intensive care unit of a large hospital. In this role she could assuage her craving for attention and praise by adeptly stepping into the role of lifesaver in emergency situations, situations in which she experienced such a euphoric, almost sexual sense of excitement and power that she began increasingly to initiate such crises herself, fatally harming babies on her ward with lethal drug injections in order to gain glory for her heroic attempts to save them. The Jones case gained recent notoriety in Britain because of seeming parallels with the Beverley Allitt case. At one point it was even suggested that the Jones murders – outlined in a book called *The Death Shift*, published in 1990 – had served as a blueprint for the killings at the Lincolnshire paediatric unit.

Although, in this case, the extent of Nurse Jones's early personal suffering appears to pale into insignificance in comparison to her subsequent evident psychotic derangement, experts who have studied such extreme examples of the need for personal power and attention, the compulsion to lie and manipulate people and situations with complete disregard for the distinction between right and wrong, stress that such psychotic tendencies very often have their origins in early childhood neglect. Or, more precisely, that they evolve as a result of the adverse effects of such neglect on a young child's acquisition of social and learning skills as well as on the development of its cognitive processes, particularly in relation to personal accountability and the ability to link cause and effect with regard to responsible and irresponsible social behaviour. It is as a result of this inability to differentiate between the likely outcome of destructive and non-destructive acts, the blurring of the boundaries between right and wrong, that personality disorders such as extreme narcissism, with its characteristic craving for attention, are believed to develop. With hindsight it is easy to spot the early warning signs of Beverley Allitt's personality disorder. In her case the need for attention took the form of a relatively rare, bizarre behavioural disorder called Münchausen Syndrome in which sufferers seek sympathy and medical attention for imaginary or self-induced illnesses, or as in Allitt's case – in whom Münchausen Syndrome both preceded and later co-existed with Münchausen Syndrome by Proxy – injure themselves in order to obtain medical treatment or gain admission to hospital.

The drama of a hospital setting has proven particularly enticing for those women who go on to injure not themselves but their children, in a horrendously grotesque variant of the disorder called Münchausen Syndrome by Proxy. In such cases, as typified by Beverley Allitt and Genene Jones, obsessions with symptoms of ill health, frequently accompanied by either extensive self-taught medical knowledge or medical training, cause nurses or mothers to endanger their own or other children's health, sometimes fatally, with the aim of engineering a full-blown potentially deadly real-life crisis. This allows them to bask in the importance of taking centre stage to play a crucial role in that child's subsequent survival. Or, as it happens, in their death.

As described by Britain's foremost expert on the syndrome, Professor Roy Meadow of St James's Hospital in Leeds, who has documented over 300 such cases, so compelling is such women's search for attention that their capacity for cunning and dexterity in deliberately injuring their children to produce apparently inexplicable, sometimes fatal, 'mystery' illnesses apparently knows no bounds. Once they have managed to get their child admitted to hospital they invariably thrive on the attention given to them by the medical staff, rarely leaving the building, and forming close relationships with nurses, junior doctors and other patients. For such women, life only takes on true meaning within the context of drama and tragedy, in which their child's life becomes a plaything, its fate hanging by a thread. One mother, when asked why she had fabricated her child's illness, replied that: 'I liked the sympathy, I needed my daughter to be ill so that I was important. I felt I was *somebody* on the ward,' adding that she enjoyed spending time with the doctors who treated her children and derived pleasure from the success with which she managed to outwit them.

There is as much controversy over the underlying causes of Münchausen's as there is over its long-term prognosis. Severely disordered women like Beverley Allitt are believed to be beyond cure or improvement. Yet according to Professor Meadow, all personalities, even those with a serious disorder such as this, may become modified through age and positive experience, where the need for self-abuse – of which the abuse of others is seen as a variant – declines in inverse proportion to the rise in self-worth and self-esteem. While it is currently tempting – and fashionable – to attribute a disorder like Münchausen's to early experience of sexual abuse, Roy Meadow's investigation into the history of women displaying Münchausen Syndrome by Proxy (and the 5 per cent of sufferers who are men) suggest that whatever hardship and abuse they have suffered is more likely to be emotional – especially maternal coldness – than gross physical or sexual abuse.

What does seem irrefutable is the extent of 'ordinary' women's involvement in child murder, with the numbers of female offenders virtually equalling males. Over the period from 1982 to 1989, almost half of the 474 child killings attributable to parents were committed by mothers – a staggeringly high figure since no other category of violent crime reflects such a high percentage of female participation. Even a cursory look at the different responses by the courts to male and female filicide shows the degree to which mothers who kill are believed to be in need of medical treatment and rehabilitation. In a recent study of 395 parents suspected of murdering their children, 44 per cent of whom were mothers, a large number were given prison sentences for manslaughter. In contrast to the fathers, however, who were more commonly convicted of manslaughter on grounds of provocation or lack of intention to kill or cause serious harm, a vast number of the mothers had their murder charge reduced to manslaughter on the grounds of diminished responsibility, or infanticide – a crime that refers specifically to the killing of a child under 12 months by its mother. While less than 10 per cent of the mothers convicted of manslaughter were imprisoned, compared to over 50 per cent of the fathers, almost half of the mothers were given hospital orders in which psychiatric treatment was specified and/or non-custodial supervisory sentences. In almost all the infanticide cases the women were given probation orders.

That women who kill their children have tended in the past, and continue to be, leniently treated by the courts in that they are less likely than men to be convicted of murder or sent to prison cannot be denied. This ties in neatly with the 'chivalry hypothesis' frequently propounded in criminal literature, that since it is not in women's normal nature to commit crimes they are less likely to be arrested, charged, prosecuted or imprisoned. But exactly what philosophy underpins this apparent chivalry – and does it really serve women's best interests?

Good Girls, Bad Girls

The legal definition of infanticide begs numerous questions about the way society persists in viewing female crime as evidence of illness, rooted in women's reproductive biology, rather than as a salutary warning of the frequently intolerable pressures resulting from our idealization of motherhood, socioeconomic deprivation and lack of social or familial support. The fact that this is a female-only offence, murder committed during a specific 12-month post-natal period when a woman's mind, according to received wisdom, is likely to be unbalanced by hormonal disturbance due to childbirth and lactation, speaks volumes about the attitudes that have led to the construction of archetypal images of mothers who kill. These tend to fall into three different categories: the mad, the sad and the bad, killing either because they are mentally disturbed, pathetically incompetent victims of social injustice, or 'wicked' women whose apparently promiscuous lifestyle and selfish, uncaring attitudes cause them to be judged as social and moral reprobates, unfit for motherhood and untypical of their sex. Not surprisingly, it is mainly those seen as belonging to the last category, often divorced, single, unmarried mothers with a history of drug use or alcohol dependence and a sexually 'active' lifestyle, who get the stiffest sentences.

Despite the frequency of infanticide over murder convictions, the notion that mothers may become murderously deranged as a result of so-called puerperal psychosis (PP) hinges on the scantiest of medical research. The illness is estimated to affect only one or two women out of every 1,000 and there is little evidence of the disorder, still less its milder version, post-natal depression, being a frequent causal factor in child murder. According to Ania Wilczynski, author of a paper presented at a recent British Criminology conference, PP accounts for a mere 5 per cent of cases of babies murdered by their mothers. As with PMT, although the underlying causes of post-natal depression and puerperal psychosis are believed to be of hormonal origin, the medical profession remains largely divided as to the precise mechanism that contributes to puerperal psychosis and how it actually differs from other forms of psychosis.

One finding upon which the majority of researchers are agreed, however, is that there seems to be no association between lactation and mental disturbance, thus knocking out one of the central planks upholding the medical premise for infanticide. Nevertheless, as Wilczynski discovered in her research, the boundaries of the disorder are constantly being stretched to accommodate women whose behaviour fails to fit accepted notions of caring, capable, self-sacrificing and cheerful motherhood, enabling the Infanticide Act to be liberally interpreted in England, as well as Australia and Hong Kong, where legislation is similar. Recent studies now indicate that as many as half the mothers convicted of infanticide cannot be diagnosed as suffering from any mental disorder – yet the judicial system still prefers to label them as 'mad'.

Recent research into the different convictions and sentences imposed on women who kill their children offers an intriguing, if dismal, insight into the way such women are regarded either as deviant, and thus wicked, or mentally unstable and therefore unable to cope with life's demands. Ania Wilczynski, for example, cites the case of 19-year-old Karen, a working-class girl with an early history of alcohol abuse, glue sniffing and cannabis smoking, fighting with her parents and committing minor crimes. On giving birth at 17 to her former boyfriend's baby, she wanted to have the child adopted but reluctantly gave in to her parents' pressures to keep him. There were further fights, heavy drinking, severe financial problems and petty theft for which she was arrested. She lived alone on social welfare in a council flat with no contact with the child's father. In response to her complaints about anxiety, phobias and depression, her doctor merely reached for the prescription pad, prescribing anti-depressants and later referring her to a psychiatrist who, with breathtaking insight, diagnosed her as immature, chronically anxious and prone to depression. One evening, the pressure of the baby's crying became too much and she hit and punched him, causing fatal injuries. Later, she admitted to the police that she didn't mean it, but could no longer put up with the constant crying. She was later sentenced to four years' youth custody for manslaughter on the grounds of lack of intent; application for bail was turned down.

In direct comparison is the case of Janet, a 25-year-old Filipino woman from a sheltered, middle-class family, a former nurse who married an Englishman and lived with their 2-month-old baby in a dingy council flat. She undertook all the primary childcare responsibilities, was lonely, isolated and friendless, suffered constant tiredness and vaginal bleeding long after the birth and was subjected to racist abuse from her neighbours. Her baby died from a brain haemorrhage and fractured skull after she hit his head against a wardrobe to stop him crying. Earlier she had tried to strangle him and on previous occasions had hit his head against the bathroom sink and a window frame. Initially when asked whether she suffered depression she said no, but in court admitted assaulting the baby because she was depressed and he had kept crying. She was convicted of infanticide and given a three-year probation order.

It hardly takes a sociological genius to spot the contrasting stereotyping of each of these women, the latter being the archetypal 'good wife', conforming to appropriate female behaviour – a caring profession followed by marriage and planned parenthood, selflessly dedicated to the duties of home and childcare, clean-living and non-aggressive. During her interview she was tearful and frightened, denying feelings of anger towards her baby or husband, but admitting the more appropriate symptom of depression. By all accounts, therefore, someone aspiring to be a 'good mother' who, according to the court, must have been suffering the aftereffects of childbirth even though there was no evidence of mental illness. Unlike the previous case of the unmarried teenage mother, this woman was granted bail on condition that she agreed to live at the home of her parents-in-law, where her husband also resided – so that she could be 'protected' for her own good.

The teenage girl was seen as 'bad' rather than 'mad', despite the fact that she had not been driven to assault her baby before the one, fatal act and despite the appallingly adverse circumstances of her prior background and present difficulties as a single mother. Her unmarried status and earlier free and easy lifestyle, aggression, drinking habits, lack of outward warmth and motherliness and relative absence of any visible anguish or remorse after the murder all undoubtedly contributed to an image of someone unwilling to conform to society's norms, thus invoking a more punitive sentence presumably on the basis that prison would help to reform her – overcoming her maternal shortcomings while deterring further drug and alcohol abuse. The fact that drug abuse among prison inmates is today one of the biggest problems facing the prison service, or that this particular woman appears to have had no natural inclination for motherhood, nor any desire to cultivate it, appears to have been entirely overlooked.

In both these cases, as in countless other documented evidence of 'good' and 'bad' mothers, who are either imprisoned or put on probation with psychiatric treatment aimed at persuading them to 'be a good girl' as part of the package, it is obvious that women's own 'failings', whether mental, physical, emotional or moral, are considered to be self-generated. Furthermore, they are seen first and foremost as having led to their crime, rather than the blame being attributed to the often appalling social and economic deprivations that in many cases have contributed largely to some of these alleged failings or symptoms, as well as setting the scene in which such a crime would be most likely to be committed. In the case of Elizabeth Stevenson, who in 1982 killed her two young children and then tried to commit suicide in an attempt to avoid the humiliation of eviction due to reduced financial circumstances, one wonders what good her three-year prison sentence achieved. According to Lord Wheatley, the Lord Justice Clerk, imprisonment was necessary for her to get 'assistance and help'. Yet surely the sort of help Stevenson most needed would be more appropriately provided by the housing authorities than the prison service?

The taboo we are forced to consider, though many will balk at it for fear of what horrors they rightly suspect to be lurking behind the crumbling façade of ideal motherhood, is to what degree not only the myths glorifying motherhood (including the notion that every new mother automatically loves, bonds with and knows how to care for her baby), but the often extreme pressures of motherhood itself, may in themselves lead a woman to crime. Only once we unflinchingly and openly acknowledge the real suffering sustained by women who have either no 'instinct' for mothering or whose personal circumstances drain almost all the joy and satisfaction from the role of parenthood, may we at last dare to ask not how a woman can ever assault her own child – but how it is that more women don't end up doing so?

The Final Taboo

Catalogue of Horrors

When considering violent crime, especially against children, there is surely nothing as abhorrent as murder. Or is there?

In terms of political incorrectness, one could think of few things more calculated to ignite feminist wrath than the following event, which took place in London in spring 1992: the world's first national conference on female sexual abusers. For many women, even those who might grudgingly concede that under certain extreme circumstances the occasional woman might be capable of violence, even sexual violence, against a child, the fact that this subject should be publicly debated at all, let alone given media coverage, was a non-starter from the beginning. In spite of official figures from the NSPCC estimating that 5 per cent of violence against children is committed by women, often the child's natural mother, the official line adopted by many feminist organizations is that to address the subject at all is to draw attention away from the fact that child sex abuse is about the exercise of male power.

Predictably, early rumblings of dissent were audible even in advance of the event. Writing in the *Guardian*, Sarah Nelson, the author of *Incest, Fact and Myth*, wrote a piece slamming the forthcoming conference as essentially political and misogynist in its motivation – 'part of the fight-back on behalf of "gender-free" theory and practice in child abuse' – and asking why 'so much attention is currently being paid to female sexual abusers?' It is hard to understand how the first conference ever to be held on the topic could be construed as 'so much attention' and, with a sad irony, Nelson's piece most hurt those trying to heal pre-existing injuries – the victims of female abuse. Citing

280

the *Guardian* article as the sole reason, one of the key speakers, Cianne Longden, a former surviver who is now herself a therapist working with male and female adult survivers, withdrew from the platform. Sensing the mood of hostility, she issued a statement via the organizers, Kidscape, saying she was not prepared to face the hostility and further abuse of 'being led like a lamb to the slaughter.'

Hostility and mud-slinging indeed there was, with audience members demanding precise breakdowns of statistics, challenging their significance in comparison to the overwhelming preponderance of men's sex crimes and attacking Michele Elliott, Kidscape's director, for having the effrontery to criticize Sarah Nelson's article while accusing her of betraying the trust of survivors by quoting their cases – until Elliott pointed out that those individuals had expressly asked for their experiences to be made public. Yet for all the cynical dissmissal of the event by many as yet one more manifestation of a feminist 'backlash', an attempt to make light of the scale and seriousness of male sexual abuse while blaming women for inadequate mothering skills, the picture that emerged that day was gruesome indeed, as it always is whenever survivors are able to talk openly about their suffering (which isn't often given the shame and painfulness of recalling such events, or the very frequent tendency for victims to repress the memories and deny the abuse ever happened).

One of the enduring myths surrounding female sexual abuse is that because of women's essentially caring, gentle natures – as well as their physical and sexual characteristics – the word 'abuse' must be a misnomer, a contradiction in terms, and what we are really talking about are loving expressions of intimacy and caring that may border on the erotic or be mistaken by the child as sexual behaviour or abuse, such as mothers caressing and fondling their children in ways that inadvertently include genital contact with the capacity to arouse. This is one misconception of which we must rid ourselves entirely if the full horror of certain types of abuse is ever to be acknowledged and victims genuinely helped to recover from their trauma.

The real truth could not be further removed from such cosy,

soft-focus images of touchy-feely innocence. Drawing on the experiences of 127 adult survivors of female abuse who contacted Kidscape, Michele Elliott quoted cases of female sexual violence which included penetration of the vagina or anus with fingers, bottles, rose stems and sticks, which consisted often of enforced mutual masturbation, encouragement of children aged 7 or 8 to suck the mother's breasts and even full sexual intercourse. Three-quarters of the survivors were women, a quarter men, with half the women and three-quarters of the men having suffered abuse by their mothers, the remainder by grandmothers, aunts, stepmothers, babysitters, nannys and other female 'authority' figures. Abuse by a mother or female relative tended to begin at an early age, usually around four or five, often continuing through adolescence and sometimes into adulthood, especially if the victim was male.

What is staggeringly obvious is that to be the victim of female sexual abuse today is to be as isolated and helpless as were women and children twenty or even ten years ago who had been sexually assaulted by men and sought in vain for help and advice in coping with their distress. This, then, is society's last lingering taboo, a crime that remains cloaked in secrecy, myth and feminist ideology. Like rape and incest victims of the 1960s and 1970s, this group tended to be dismissed as jokers or fantasists or both. Three-quarters of the men who contacted Kidscape found no one willing to help or believe their stories. One man was told by his psychiatrist that he was obviously having incestuous fantasies about his mother – a classic Freudian Oedipal interpretation. Another man, when attempting to seek help for his 9-year-old daughter after she had disclosed abuse by her mother, was turned away by three organizations on the grounds that they 'didn't deal with this', while a fourth remained undecided about whether to help, suspecting that he must be the abuser. Yet another father was told he could not bring his daughter for counselling because men were not admitted to the centre.

Women who have been assaulted by a woman may come up against different types of denial and antipathy, finding themselves, precisely because of their sex, in an inescapable double-bind. Cianne Longden has discovered through her own bitter personal experience that for a woman to disclose being abused by another woman is likely to evoke particularly strong reactions. 'It can feel like a betrayal of your own sex to say that they are capable of such appalling acts. Because female sexual abuse arouses such strong reactions, particularly in other women, survivors fear being ostracized, receiving anger and criticism or being gossiped about.' Longdon quotes the words of one of her own clients, who recalls: 'When I first told that my aunt had sexually abused me for years, my family was blown apart. They accused me, amongst other things, of making it up, of being evil, insane and just wanting attention. What hurt most is that it was the female members of my family who were the most venomous and vindictive.'

As if their suffering and trauma were not sufficient, survivors such as these may find themselves in a bizarre Kafkaesque nightmare of inverted sexism where, in order to escape further ridicule and opprobrium, they pretend that their abuser was actually a man, in order at least to obtain some measure of help. Says Longdon: 'In every case the change of gender within these disclosures was a result not of fantasy or imagination but of the parochial attitude of society and professionals. I understand the pressures placed on survivors to conform to this need to deny that women sexually abuse. My first attempt at disclosure was met with shock and disbelief. This, combined with my counsellor's attempt to convince me that it must have been a man and not a woman who sexually abused me, left me feeling bruised, battered and wondering if I was crazy.'

Given that 96 per cent of all survivors admitted that the abuse adversely, often dramatically, affected their lives, leading to dependence on alcohol and drugs, attempted suicide, confusion and doubt over personal gender identity, inability to sustain relationships, depression as well as unresolved guilt, shame and anger, the fact that little or no help and support has been forthcoming for the majority of these survivors is nothing short of scandalous. Especially when you consider that a frequent confession made by survivors was feeling the urge to abuse children themselves, or actually doing so – confirming yet again what we know from survivors of male violence and sexual abuse, that the pattern becomes tragically repeated through generations of conditioning and learning by example, or as a consequence of the abused child angrily seeking revenge for his or her own abuse.

The Motherhood Myth

If ever an issue was screaming out to be further investigated and addressed, openly and honestly, without kid gloves and faint heart – let alone the sort of blinkered, hysterical gender-bias and sociosexual 'correctness' that bedevils some quarters of family violence research – it is this one. Since the overwhelming majority of rapists, child sex abusers and attackers are indeed men, moreover men who often display a deep-seated hatred of women, sometimes linked to a sense of sexual inadequacy, then, given that so many male survivors of *female* violence or sexual abuse also confess to feeling angry and violent towards women, is it not time we looked more closely at the types of violence endured and the identity of the perpetrators within the early history of men who commit sex crimes?

I am well aware that by proposing that we take female sex abuse seriously and suggesting that we investigate whether there may be some association, perhaps even – dare one say it – occasionally a causal connection between this and male violence, many women, certainly those who regard violence and aggression as evils committed principally by men against women and children, will want to see my head on a chopping block, or at best condemn me for betraying my sex by uttering not merely the unutterable, but the unthinkable. Yet whatever inference might be drawn, I am not proposing that women are the real monsters in the nursery, responsible for nurturing future generations of molesters and rapists. What I am urging, however, is that we *do* begin to wrap our brains around the hitherto unthinkable, painful and threatening as it might be. After all, if, as is by now generally acknowledged by psychologists, doctors and criminologists alike that very many (though by no means all) abused children grow up to become abusers and criminals, then given that so many assault victims are little girls, how can we in all conscience continue to turn a blind eye to the possible future implications of their early experiences? By denying that a woman has the potential to harm, violate, molest and injure another child very possibly because of some inner compulsion associated with her own childhood injuries, are we not, by implication, also guilty of denying or invalidating the seriousness and pain of the assaults she was forced to endure?

There is little mystery as to why the issue of female abuse makes us feel so profoundly uneasy. For in confronting and accepting its existence, we are forced to challenge and possibly demolish the three most powerfully held and all-pervasive beliefs enshrined in feminist doctrine. The first can be summed up by the maxim 'no penis, no problem', and is based on the premise that since violence and aggression are male characteristics, inextricably linked to male sexuality, *ipso facto* men must make up the overwhelming majority of sexual abusers. And so they do – but the 5 per cent or more who are not male will not go away no matter how often you go over the arithmetic. Secondly, if women, according to centuries of received wisdom, are supposedly not inherently sexually aggressive then how can we seriously suspect them of possible abuse, unless perhaps when they are threatened or coerced by a man to assist or partake in his violent acts? And yet the concept of female sexual passivity has now become so ludicrously alien that it hardly merits a passing nod. Thirdly, and most threateningly, is that to accept women may be capable of violence, including sexual abuse, against small children is to undermine our entire belief and trust in how women should 'naturally' relate to children, their own or anyone else's. To admit that women who care for children, be they mothers, grandmothers, aunts, nannies or nurses, are sometimes capable of harming them, wilfully and repeatedly, is just one small step away from destroying the sanctity of motherhood. Not to put too fine a point upon it, the alleged existence of a universal maternal 'instinct' with which all women are said to be born, and by which the majority are still expected to prove their 'true' womanhood, is beginning to look not only extremely dubious but seems to be propounding a socio-religious doctrine undermined by numerous hidden weaknesses.

In taking female sexual abuse seriously, are we guilty of the ultimate and final heresy, the destruction of the myth of motherhood? Or by toppling her from her pedestal and revealing her feet of clay, do we finally do our 'ideal' paragon of female virtue the inestimable service of admitting her limitations and failures, her frailties –and her vices? Certainly by confronting the potential evils and abuses of which some women seem capable, we stand with a finger poised uncomfortably near a detonator that could explode the very last remaining foundation stone upon which family values are constructed. Yet confront it we must – as we had, only recently, to confront the horrific reality of male sexual abuse and violence against children. Not to do so, and worse, to summarily dismiss the possibility that women may commit such acts, is to perpetuate the suffering and isolation of victims, and by denying their experiences we are all guilty of inflicting further, grave 'secondary' abuse.

Which also prompts the question, what to do about identifying and rehabilitating the offender? As increasing evidence emerges, especially from countries such as Sweden and Belgium, it seems that there is little to be gained in the way of restoring family cohesion or healing an abused child's emotional injuries by imprisoning an abusive parent. With the advent of a less harshly punitive, more humanitarian approach towards the problem of family violence as a whole, it also appears that counselling and rehabilitation for the entire family, with special emphasis on providing treatment and help for the abuser, male or female, so as to reduce the likelihood of reoffending, is crucially important to the future of both victim and perpetrator. It is therefore obvious that a further injustice which inevitably results from society's failure to confront the reality of female assaults on children is the perpetuation of ignorance as to *why* women commit such acts in the first place.

Mothers and Sons

Ironically, one of the main stumbling blocks to women's readiness to admit the possibility of female abuse seems to be that stories of victimization are increasingly being voiced by men, as well as women. Until very recently men could be assured of having doors slammed violently in their faces when attempting to seek help or gain credibility as victims, a status which women, understandably in view of the large numbers of female victims of domestic violence and sex crimes, have claimed as their exclusive preserve. One need only compare the recent proliferation of support groups and helplines available for female rape and domestic violence victims to the virtual absence of any such centres or services for male rape survivors or battered husbands to realize that when it comes to victim support, equality between the sexes is a long way off. At the same time it is largely *because* of the recent vociferousness of the women's movement on the suffering and needs of victims of violence, and the organization, at grass-roots community level, of support services to provide for those needs, that men — under that amorphous umbrella, the 'men's movement' — are now beginning to speak out about their own experiences, including abuse by other men as well as women. Whether by doing so, the 'gender-appropriate' roles of victim and offender will become less polarized is debatable; the greatest tragedy will be if the opposing factions become even more deeply entrenched.

However, the debate does seem to be gathering momentum. Ten years ago it would have been inconceivable that an event such as the London Kidscape conference could have taken place. And just a few weeks after the conference, in New York, I tuned into the *Phil Donahue Show* which was covering a topic he claimed to be 'perhaps the most under-reported crime in all of criminology': the rape of sons by their mothers. One by one, four grown men as well as numbers of phone callers told haltingly, angrily, sometimes tearfully, of suffering and degradation inflicted on them usually from early childhood. One 45-year-old's earliest memory was as a toddler, lying between his naked mother's legs and being confronted by her vagina. Haltingly he recalls being invaded by near paralysing waves of fear, wondering whether perhaps she was wounded. In due course, when she forces his head between her thighs and demands that he use his tongue, his most searing memory is of her anger and criticism of his failure to please and satisfy her. By far the most painful part of the abuse was not the act itself, as much as he dreaded it, but that he could not get close to her. The resulting punishment took the form of emotional coldness; there were days on end, he says, when she would not talk to him or touch him. Later, when he was 12 or 13, his mother would get into bed with him, manipulating his penis until it became semi-erect, then having full sexual intercourse sitting on top of him. Donahue, clearly shocked and incomprehending, asks how any male, especially a young adolescent, can manage to maintain an erection. Another guest explains that terror of punishment acts as a powerful stimulant to maintain an erection, stating baldly that the response becomes almost Pavlovian: knowing you'll get beaten if you don't maintain it for long enough ensures you keep it up as long as you can. To nods and murmurs of assent, he asserts unequivocally that this has little to do with sexuality but everything to do with the abuse of power, a bitter and repugnant truth which many of these men have only recently been able to address, let alone accept, in striving to come to terms with its effects.

Another caller rings in to say that it wasn't until he went into therapy and began remembering how as a child he was anally assaulted and emotionally brutalized by his mother that he realized why now, as an adult, he is drawn into abusive sexual relationships. A further remark, thrown in casually as an after-thought, that his mother was exceptionally gifted intellectually and academically and his family background was middle class and affluent, is a salutary reminder that such abuse cuts across social rank and upbringing. Someone points out that perhaps too much is being made of the sexual element, since in his experience there is only a very thin line between physical violence and sexual abuse. The consensus among many here is that in our prurient fascination with the sexual, we forget that parents who abuse children physically may be initially driven through sexual energy, but the boundary between the two forms of violence is so faint as to sometimes vanish altogether, a view which elicits agreement from those who remember interpreting the intensity of their mothers' anger as an attack on their masculinity. In the experience of one survivor, the eventual realization that his mother was probably abused herself has helped put his own abuse into clearer perspective, while not lessening the pain. Two participants, in frank exchange, remark on the fact that for some women, becoming mother to a child, especially a boy, opens up endless possible avenues to act out their hatred of men in general, and to extract revenge on someone who might become a future perpetrator of violence against women. As one man sees it, the sexual abuse of children amounts to no less than the enactment of a symbolic form of murder, since the only way to kill someone, in the psychic sense, yet not literally take their life, is to penetrate their body via its orifices.

Revelations such as these are for the most part doubly shocking, not only because the idea of women committing such acts of depravity may disgust and boggle the imagination – but also because these offences rarely, if ever, are brought before the courts, and female sex offenders have so far escaped the exposure and vilification experienced by men, remaining virtually invisible in the eyes of the law. The reason for this is down to simple, straightforward sexism – which in this case, at least so far, has worked to women's positive advantage. As we know, the offence of rape or sexual assault by a man of a woman is notoriously difficult to prove in court, since culpability or innocence rest on the crucial issue of consent. Reverse the roles, with the woman being charged with sexually assaulting a boy, which many would claim by definition to be logistically impossibile, and the chance of finding a woman guilty of such a crime becomes almost nil. Almost – but not entirely.

The legal age of consent, which is 16 for sexual intercourse between a man and a woman, was established in 1885 in Britain primarily to protect young girls from the advances of older men. (In the case of male homosexual acts, the law is intended to protect boys from the moral dangers of homosexual relationships, and the age of consent is 21.) Yet as Dr Susan Edwards points out in her book *Women On Trial*, nowhere is there statutory provision specifically forbidding a woman to have sex with a boy under 16. In 1948, writing in the *Journal of Criminal Science*, Sir William Norwood East observed that, 'It is still not a criminal offence *ipso facto* for a woman to seduce a boy under the age of 16'.

Had it not been for a case that took place in 1981, we might still be unaware of what actually *does* constitute indecent assault by a woman. The 15-year-old boy was staying in Patricia Faulkner's house and one evening, after he had watched a horror film on televison and confessed to being scared, she invited him to sleep in her bed, whereupon she allegedly pulled him on to her, took his penis and placed it inside her, thus initiating sexual intercourse, to which he had consented. Unfortunately for Patricia Faulkner, the fact that the boy was under 16 rendered him automatically incapable of giving consent to any sexual intimacy, which otherwise would have provided her with a defence. Secondly, as he was under 16, according to case law she had committed a criminal offence by the mere act of foreplay, which *she* did to *him*, even though it was the boy, not she, who ended up being the more active party!

On being charged with indecent assault Faulkner appealed against the conviction, stating as her reason that in touching the boy as a prelude to intercourse she could not be guilty of an assault. The judge however dismissed the appeal on the grounds that this constituted a 'passive indecent assault'. Although this particular case does seem rather ludicrous, it has set an important precedent for the future, making it possible forthwith for a charge of indecent assault to be brought against a woman.

Suspending Disbelief

Although ten or even five years ago it might have been argued, with a modicum of justification, that the statistics for female violence and abuse of children were too negligible to warrant any serious investigation (although the fact that 2 to 5 per cent of known cases should be deemed too insignificant to bother about is deeply alarming in itself), today it is impossible to seek refuge behind any such argument. On the *Donahue Show*, one counsellor who has worked with hundreds of adult survivors of both sexes told the audience that at least half were abused by their mothers. Experts working in the field of child abuse are now beginning to concede that the actual figures for female violence against children are probably significantly higher than official estimates, and certainly in excess of the conservative 2 per cent quoted by the NSPCC or the Home Office records which put female sex crimes at 3 per cent.

One therapist from a Shrewsbury-based counselling centre remembers that the first child she worked with as a counsellor in 1987 had been abused by his mother. 'About 25 per cent of the hundreds of children I have worked with since that time have said a woman sexually assaulted them. It is no longer a surprise to me when children mention a woman as the assailant, but what is a surprise is this figure of 2 per cent. If that's true, the whole 2 per cent workload for the country is somehow ending up on my casebook.'

In America, Michigan psychotherapist Kathy Evert, who recently conducted a 450-question survey of ninety-three women and nine men who were abused by their mothers, has commented that, 'no one, including me, knows the true extent of sexual abuse by females, especially mothers. About 80 per cent of the women and men reported that abuse by their mothers was the most hidden aspect of their lives.' Interestingly, Evert in part echoes the views put forward by the men on the *Donahue Show*, that suppressed anger in women surfaces in the form of abuse against their child – except that in her experience it is daughters, rather than sons, upon whom mothers project their own self-hate most intensely through brutal physical punishments.

Writing in the *British Medical Journal* in 1990, Robert Wilkins, consultant child and adolescent psychiatrist at Paxton Family and Young Persons' Unit in Reading, argues for a suspension of disbelief among specialists, challenging the accepted view that sexual abuse is perpetrated almost exclusively by men on women and girls. Citing recent research by David Finkelhor, co-director of the Family Research Laboratory at the University of New Hampshire, that estimates 13 per cent of abuse may be perpetrated by women, Wilkins seems to confirm Michele Elliott's own fears – based on growing files at Kidscape – that the much-touted 5 per cent may be an under-representation of the problem. According to Childline, the children's telephone advice organization established by Esther Rantzen in 1987, and which between then and 1992 had answered 2,130,000 calls and collected 213,000 written records of phone calls and letters from young people, in 29 per cent of all reports of physical abuse – which may or may not include a sexual element – women are named as the primary abuser. Invidious as it is to separate sexual, physical and emotional abuse, regardless of the sex of the offender, Childline counsellors admit that between 1990 and 1991, 15 per cent of all letters and transcribed phone calls clearly reveal sexual abuse, in which 91 per cent of the perpetrators were male, 9 per cent female.

Nor do such findings support the popular theory, which has informed the official feminist line on child abuse, that women who abuse are either psychotic or do so only when threatened with punishment by their male partner if they do not collude in his own violent or incestuous behaviour. Most American and British studies to date show that, like male abusers, females have a very low incidence of mental illness – one study of forty women offenders cites one in ten as psychotic – and are perceived by children and young people to be mentally stable, perfectly ordinary, often likeable individuals, giving the lie to the image of such women as crazed lunatics, cackling crones or witches who might have stepped straight out of a Grimms' fairy tale.

All of which renders this a far greater taboo and more painful to acknowledge than even the spectre of male abuse. The 'average' violent or abusive mother or aunt, nurse or baby-sitter seems for the most part so *nice*, so completely trustworthy – in much the same way that convicted psychopaths like Dennis Nilsen and Peter Sutcliffe gave the impression to neighbours and colleagues of being quiet, unassuming and caring individuals. And therein lies the supreme tragedy of female violence towards children. If this seems to us, as it must, the apogee of wickedness and inhumanity, it is because little imagination is required to comprehend that the scale of emotional devastation resulting from such violation is so intense and unendurable and its effects so lasting and pervasive precisely *because* they occur within the context of the nurturing love, dependence and trust which the victim has for the abuser. Especially when she is the child's mother or substitute mother-figure.

When the betrayal of innocence, the infliction of pain, fear, shame and terror, come from the person who is a part of you, gave you life and to whom you have no choice but to turn first, and always, for safety and love, then how can the home, let alone the outside world, ever seem an unthreatening place again? And if a child, of either sex, cannot feel sexually safe with a woman, let alone its own mother – who can it ever feel safe with? Furthermore, the sense of betrayal, of abandonment and loss of love may be similar, indeed equally devastating, whether a mother independently violated the child, or whether she stood by passively, unable or unwilling to protect the infant from another person's violence.

Unwilling – or unable? That surely is the crux of many incidents involving female abuse. For it is at this point, when we seek to apportion blame for violence done to a child, that we risk becoming trapped in the most treacherous of moral quagmires. Outrage and a sense of justice tell us *someone* must be found guilty, but with the exception of a few clear-cut cases where proof is undeniable, accurate identification of guilt is neither as simple nor likely to be as fair and demonstrable as it seems. In particular, our growing recognition of the prevalence of male violence towards women and children raises innumerable, often unanswerable questions about the degree to which women who become trapped in violent relationships fail to protect their child and therefore must be considered guilty of contributing to its abuse. How do we judge a woman who has undergone an apparent metamorphosis, from protector and guardian of young life to helpless bystander or accomplice in its destruction? Do we pity her as a victim or denounce her for being a criminal? The moral issues raised each time a case of child abuse or murder makes the headlines, whether the woman played an active role in the crime or was deemed guilty of contributary negligence, are as impossible to resolve as is the outrage and incomprehension evoked by such cases.

Recently we have seen such cases as the death of baby Chanel, whose mother, Sally Emery, was sentenced to four years' imprisonment in 1992 for failure to protect her child from its father's violence, and in the United States there was Hedda Nussbaum, who allowed herself to become so helplessly dominated by the violence and drug-dependent, depraved lifestyle of her husband, lawyer Joel Steinberg, that she failed to protect their foster child Lisa from his repeated vicious physical batterings that finally led to her death.

There are many who passionately believe that no sentient individual, let alone a mother, has the right to assume the role of passive bystander; or even that no normal woman would have so little compassion and empathy for a child's suffering as to allow it to be abused and injured, no matter how much her own safety was at risk. Yet these are dangerous assumptions, which fail to take into account women's subjective, mind-altering experience of violence, just as the commonly held suspicion that rape victims who don't put up a struggle have somehow provoked their attacker fails to do so. The more one understands how and why certain women become disabled through 'learned helplessness', the mechanism which is believed to contribute to loss of judgement, personal responsibility, freedom of choice to act independently – and in this case to act in the best interests of their child – the less just it seems to judge 'passive' offenders by the moral criteria that normally govern free choice and responsible action. A woman who initiates violence, who acts alone, must surely be judged differently (though not necessarily condemned as more destructive or wicked), than one acting in terror of her husband's threats of further or worse violence, towards herself, or the child, or both, if she doesn't comply with his demands.

Even more crucial, especially where sole offenders or initiators of abuse are concerned, is to avoid the temptation to lump together abusers of both sexes in the mistaken belief that they are motivated by identical impulses and desires. Although so far a vastly under-researched, misunderstood and myth-ridden subject, what little we know about female 'perversion' indicates significant and fundamental differences between sexually deviant behaviour by men and women, not least in its effects upon the perpetrator. According to forensic psychotherapist Dr Estela Welldon, nowhere is this more evident than in perversions of motherhood, in which women with an overwhelming sense of powerlessness and lack of self-esteem may be drawn to pregnancy and parenthood as a means of compensating for this inadequacy. In offering women instant and automatic power, authority and complete control over another human being whose dependence for its emotional and physical well-being and survival is total, motherhood may prove, for those lacking any other source of gratification, the ultimate power trip. Female sexual abuse, particularly maternal incest, represents the most tragically grotesque misuse and abuse of that power.

More than that, however, according to Estela Welldon, since a baby is a creation of the woman's own body, an extension of her own self, its abuse can be interpreted as yet another, albeit extremely distorted, reflection of women's tendency to project otherwise inexpressible hatred and fury against their own bodies, more commonly achieved through anorexia, bulimia, drug addiction and self-mutilation. It may be seen, therefore, as lying at the extreme end of a broad spectrum of female self-destructiveness, yet something which damages both abuser and victim.

And therein lies the paramount distinction between male and female abusers: a man, lacking the degree of intimate, ongoing emotional involvement with his child, is more easily able to create distance between himself and his victim, allowing the child to become depersonalized, a pure 'object' designed for personal gratification. As Welldon perceives it: 'In both sexes there is the desire and intention to dehumanize the person you abuse, to engulf, intrude and invade the victim's body for one's own gratification. But while a man chooses an outside object and uses mainly the penis to assault, women not only involve their entire body, because of the widespread distribution of erotic zones but, by abusing a child who is a part of themselves, retain an emotional link and ongoing attachment to the object of abuse which makes them suffer enormous remorse and guilt. It becomes another self-inflicted wound. By comparison, a man knows he is doing wrong but can cope with his inner conflict by keeping his perversion "encapsulated", entirely separate from his ordinary life.'

The terrible irony of that difference is that abusive women, forced to live night and day on intimate terms with their victim, suffer so greatly from self-loathing, depression, anxiety and guilt, that any sense of power, gratification or triumph which comes from abusing their child is purely fleeting. According to Welldon, since her initial powerlessness is triggered by stress and self-hatred in the first place, the very emotions which arise from abusing are those guaranteed to compel a women to repeat that behaviour over and over again. Sometimes that compulsion may be overcome by alternative forms of self-destructiveness, such as cutting, binge-eating, drug or alcohol abuse.

In her study on female perversions, *Mother, Madonna, Whore*, Welldon describes one woman, a criminal with numerous convictions, who hated her baby intensely and was only able to overcome violent urges to kick it by fixing on different parts of her body as a 'baby substitute' and attacking these instead. Yet by the time she gave birth to her second child she admitted all her spare body parts had been, as she put it, 'used up', and she ended up regularly battering the baby, after each occasion being physically sick. The clue to understanding such acts is the fact that physical punishment and sexual assaults by women of their own and sometimes other people's children may take place alongside self-injury, or a history of previous self-injury and also that *all of these* are increasingly recognized by therapists as the 'acting out' of repressed fury and vengeance against their own abusive, unloving mother or primary carer. Shame, contempt and hatred for one's own body, resulting in its systematic mistreatment and destruction, says Welldon, invariably result from parental neglect, punishment and abuse of that body and its needs and sensations from early infancy. Women's attacks on themselves and their babies suggest the degree to which the identity of their abusive or neglectful mother has become subsumed into the woman's own perception of herself as bad, dirty, unwanted and unlovable. Given that analysis, there is no mystery as to why repetitive self-generating patterns of abuse by mothers, or mother figures, must be suspected of going back at least three generations.

As revelations about female sexual abuse become more widespread, the more apparent it becomes that we would be misguided to count on it being less violent and less harmful than a man's. It has often been suggested when suspicions about female abuse have arisen that physical intimacy involved in many maternal actions may be too easily misinterpreted as abuse. Yet as professionals who work with children have repeatedly pointed out, children are for the most part extremely capable at distinguishing between physical contact that is affectionate and caring and that which is sexual and intended to provide the adult with gratification. In some cases extreme gentleness, a subtle rather than a brutal overstepping of the boundaries between parental intimacy and erotic contact, undoubtedly characterizes such assaults by women. However, as we know from incest survivors' experiences, this may also apply to the behaviour of some male abusers, and can hardly be used as an argument either to minimize the damage arising from the abuse or to vindicate the actions of the abuser. And let's not kid ourselves. Some accounts of female violence, both sexual and non-sexual, simply beggar belief as to the extent of their depravity and icy heartlessness. Whether you classify it as sexual abuse, or you take away the sexual element and call it simply punishment, the horrors now coming to light often defy all comprehension.

Sue Hutchinson, who runs a telephone counselling line for abuse victims, has commented that at least half the callers describe female abusers as being more violent and humiliating. Indeed, there have been reports from various agencies and support organizations in Britain and America of crimes so repugnant that they could by no wildest stretch of the imagination be mistaken for anything other than the exercise of power and domination. Consider for example the following:

A mother hangs bulldog clips on her daughter's nipples because she is jealous of the shape of her breasts, while regularly beating her for minor transgressions.

A girl is forced by her mother to perform oral sex and violently penetrated with objects, from early infancy until the age of 12.

An adolescent girl's mother regularly plays with her breasts and nipples and inserts objects into her vagina to 'see if I was normal'.

A female relative enters an 8-year-old girl's bedroom at dead of night and roughly inserts objects into her anus and vagina, afterwards threatening to cut out her tongue if she tells anyone.

A 13-year-old girl is regularly subjected to 'gang rapes' by her mother and her mother's women friends, which include acts of grotesque humiliation involving bottles and candles.

A 4-year-old child is repeatedly anally assaulted by a woman doctor in whom her family have had complete trust for numbers of years.

A young teenage girl phones a London helpline for victims of sexual abuse to ask how to end the increasing violence to which she is subjected, usually through her mother's boyfriend pinning her down while her mother sexually abuses her.

Until we suspend our disbelief and start accepting the truth behind these allegations, nothing can be done to help either the victims or the perpetrators of these frightening abuses.

More Sinned Against Than Sinning
Although we all like to pride – and reassure – ourselves that

we can recognize the perpetrators of evil deeds when they cross our path, trying to spot a female abuser is as pointless an exercise as trying to find a simple, clear-cut reason why anyone abuses. So recent is the recognition by doctors, therapists and counsellors of the phenomenon, so few, until now, the numbers of victims prepared to admit abuse, let alone reveal that their abuser was female, that compared to the research into patterns and profiles of male sex crimes, almost nothing is known about female perpetrators. One of the findings to emerge from a recent and rare American study into female offenders is that a woman's own early upbringing may have a marked bearing on the type of abuse she later commits. Psychologists Jane Matthews and Ruth Mathews of Transition Place, a rehabilitation centre in St Paul, Minnesota, for men, women and youngsters convicted of sexual crimes, have discovered that such women can be broadly classified into four different groups.

The first, and frequently most unnoticed by society, is the 'Teacher–Lover', an older woman who takes it upon herself to teach a young adolescent boy, either within the family or outside it, about sexuality. Jane Matthews has found that these women are drawn to young boys because they feel powerless and uncomfortable in a relationship with an adult man. Genuinely convinced that they can do no harm by seducing young boys, these women have the hardest time thinking of themselves as criminals, believing that if anyone should get the blame, it's the boy. In view of society's implicit sanction of these relationships, the glorification of such liaisons in popular culture and literature, from Colette's novel *Cheri* to films such as *The Graduate* and *Souffle au Coeur*, this is hardly surprising. Although, unlike many other types of offenders, this group tend not to have been abused as children, seducing under-age youngsters is seen by many therapists as a sign of unexpressed, intense anger which becomes 'acted out' sexually against their victim, who, compared to an adult male, seems a safe target. 'Except that the backlash can be terrible,' explains Matthews. 'The boy often ends up feeling used, that he's sold out his sexuality to an old person, and becomes angry at the woman for what she's done. The guiltier and more confused about his sexuality he feels, the more aggressive his attitude towards the woman becomes.'

By comparison, hardline cases make up the bulk of the second category of so-called 'Predisposed Offenders'. These are the repeaters and copiers, women whose own early childhood abuse, usually by multiple offenders within the immediate family, has created a blueprint for future relationships. Accustomed to being hurt, betrayed and used by those who should have taken care of them, these women's personalities are blighted by low self-esteem, poor learning skills, low peer status and the lack of any expectation of a caring, non-threatening relationship. As was the case in their own childhood, they will typically choose as victims their own children, or a child relative.

'This is the kind of woman who despite her actions is desperately needy, increasingly isolated,' says Matthews. 'One of my clients describes pacing the floor at night, desperate for human contact, not wanting to abuse her daughter, but just frantically needing some flesh to flesh human contact. So after pacing for hours, she finally goes into her daughter's bedroom, just to look at her. She starts by simply stroking her child's cheek, then her neck, and begins to feel more and more safe, warm and calm. Then she goes on, finally starts fondling the girl's vagina. This is when she panics, remembering the horror of when it was done to her. She withdraws in terrible guilt. The child then feels abandoned – doesn't know what she's done to cause the mother to pull away, go out of the room. Later on, when rows and conflicts come up between mother and daughter, the abuse is used as a threat by the parent, who warns the daughter that if she doesn't obey her, or does something naughty, then "*I'll do that to you.*" These are the women who see themselves as criminals and tend often to turn themselves in to the authorities, having nothing but guilt and remorse for what they've done.'

The third category is the 'Experimenter–Exploiter', characterized by women who experienced a rigidly puritanical and strict upbringing in which sex was never discussed and sex education prohibited. Often unaware of what they are doing, they may – usually when acting as babysitters – start to explore and experiment with small children, perhaps because of something they may have seen by accident on television or a magazine, or heard other girls talking about. More serious, by comparison, are those who may commit grave offences but do so unwillingly, at least at first, and under pressure or violent threats from a husband or lover – the fourth category, the 'Male-Coerced Offender'. Like the predisposed category, these women were also frequently abused as children, though less consistently and usually by someone outside the family. Essentially passive by nature, they tend to gravitate towards relationships with violent men who manage to dominate and control them almost entirely. 'To say that these women suffer from low self-esteem would be a gross understatement,' believes Matthews. 'They invariably hate themselves and believe that they were born evil. And although many in this group were not abused, they end up living with men who *were*. Lack of personal strength and assertiveness is what they are most aware of in themselves and would most wish to possess.' Tragically, one outcome of this absence of inner strength is that in 44 per cent of cases the women in this category, although first forced to commit abuse by their partners, go on to initiate the abuse themselves on later occasions, usually when the husband is absent.

These findings are by no means exclusive to America. Since that study began, another long-term study currently under way in Leeds, undertaken by paediatricians and consultant psychologists from St James's Hospital and Leeds General Infirmary working in tandem, has confirmed much of Matthews's research into offender profiles. Additional characteristics the Leeds team have found to be common among female child sex abusers are high levels of anxiety, sometimes coupled or alternating with extreme aggression, a tendency to regard the child they have abused as being 'more sexual' than themselves, a sense of social and emotional isolation resulting in, as well as from, the inability to form positive adult relationships with men and a strong need to re-enact the sexual abuse they had experienced as children. Consultant psychologist Helga Hanks particularly stresses that when women themselves become the 'powerful, controlling perpetrator' they perceive a sense of control and seem to gain physical release from tension. As she says: 'This becomes a powerful motivator to repeat the abusive behaviour.'

As the whole wretched tragedy of intra-familial abuse unfolds, with its now familiar, self-perpetuating patterns, what is increasingly clear is how much abusive, violent behaviour is a legacy handed down from generation to generation. And although we know that by no means all victims of violence go on to become offenders themselves, more and more it seems that the majority of abusers have themselves had some personal experience of abuse. The crucial question is whether such acts, horrendous as they often are, can justifiably be condemned as crimes when the perpetrators are likely to have been as sinned against as sinning?

The Seeds of Hate

Were Hans Christian Andersen or the Brothers Grimm alive today and asked to create new macabre tales of cruelty and sadism they would be hard pressed to imagine any scenario more grisly than the experiences of Willa Woolston and her two sisters. Their childhood, outlined indelibly in two British TV documentaries, is on a par with the most menacing Boschian impressions of hell.

Between the ages of 6 and 12, Willa and her younger sister were systematically and brutally 'tortured' – the exact word each of them uses – by their stepmother. Although the elder sister escaped victimization, her own vivid memories of the two smaller girls' suffering and terror have mentally scarred her for life. It wasn't until Willa interviewed her on camera that the full remembrance of the past flooded back in all its gruesomeness: memories of their stepmother locking the youngest girl into a dank, filthy cellar and forcing her to crawl from one corner to the other and back again while licking the filth off the floor with her tongue, of her stripping off all her 7-year-old sister's clothes, tying her to a metal chair in the back yard and leaving her outside for an entire blisteringly hot summer day, without food or drink. The elder sister recalls: 'I've never seen such blisters. I had to lie in bed and hear her cry that night and the next night. How do you think of things like that? That's got to be insanity. Sane people don't do things like that. Sane people don't hang children up in the basement by their wrists so that their feet are hardly touching the ground, and leave them like that all night. She was incredibly inventive. Incredibly.'

The memory of that cellar, the scene of those horrors, is something the younger sister has been unable to put out of her mind. 'It was so scary. That was the place where we had ropes tied around our wrists and we were hung from the pipes.' Neither Willa nor her sister remember how long they were left to hang in the cellar or how often the assaults occurred, only that they were were usually tortured separately, and on numerous occasions. The only word they can think of that describes their stepmother's motivation is *power*. They both remember the floor of the cellar being particularly filthy because water would flood the area, bringing in mud. 'That was pretty repulsive to me, that really was,' says the younger sister on recalling how she was commanded by her stepmother to lick the dried mud off the floor. 'That was just power. That's gross, that is really grotesque.' Also grotesque and inhumane was her habit of dragging one of them, naked, shrieking and sobbing, into the bathroom and forcing them under an ice-cold shower, or ordering them to eat up the remains of food that on occasions they had vomited on to their plate during a meal.

Difficult, even impossible, as it is for anyone who did not suffer abuse or torture as a child to understand, Willa does not regard her stepmother as insane – indeed, there was never any suggestion of mental illness – nor does she revile her for being evil or perverted. The films she made about her past evoked an overwhelming and unprecedented level of public response: nearly 400 calls were made to the fifteen helplines manned by trained counsellors, which had been set up in anticipation of a certain amount of feedback. The senior counsellor on the helpline, Erica Karpaiya, recalls that: 'The counsellors were particularly shocked by the numbers of women phoning to report abuse by women on women.'

After transmission of a second documentary, further examining the effects of the torture on the girls' adult lives and relationships with their partners and children, 34 per cent of callers who rang in did so to say that the abuse they had suffered was the same as that depicted in the programme.

Having set up the Child Abuse Survivor Network and talked to many survivors of female abuse and torture, Willa emphasizes the importance of recognizing the abuse and neglect suffered by her stepmother, which in turn played a crucial part in forming her future behaviour towards her stepdaughters. 'Her father left the family when she was still little, her mum became an alcoholic and went to work full time. Her role became that of the surrogate parent; the child had to become the caretaker of the mother, who might have fallen downstairs or could not take care of the family because of drinking and overwork.'

But surely, as in any similar case of gross violence, there are potentially incalculable dangers in letting offenders like Willa's stepmother off the hook simply on the grounds of their own early trauma, and the fact that she had no opportunity to vent the anger and resentment she felt towards her own parents other than through torturing helpless infants? Can we justifiably ignore the issue of personal accountability, of moral conscience? Must we assume that some suffering is so great that it creates a moral vacuum where otherwise there would have been processes effectively controlling our baser impulses and guarding our freedom to choose between harming or protecting another human being?

I think not. Were that the case then the incidence of parental violence perpetrated, say, by former child survivors of German concentration camps or Soviet gulags would now have reached epidemic proportions, yet we know that, if anything, the opposite applies. Far more persuasive is Willa's argument that her stepmother is not solely and exclusively to blame for the hell that was her and her sister's childhood because there were others, principally her father, as well as the family GP and her schoolteachers, who she believes knew full well from evident symptoms of abuse what was going on, but chose to do nothing to help. Apportioning blame and identifying irresponsibility is thus never the simple, clear-cut affair it first seems. And so it was, according to Willa, with her stepmother, who herself had sought help from others in coping with her secret childhood burden. 'I feel she was badly let down by society. She sought help twice but wasn't able to find it. This is something I know from my own personal experience, as well as from other victims. I cannot forget that my father closed his eyes to the torture we suffered. You musn't forget that my stepmother had no power over her own self and her own life, despite exerting power over us. She never had any power in her life, and the most dangerous situation is when a person who despairs because they are being abused and are powerless is ignored, offered no help. The inevitable response pattern of desperation over the years develops into an ingrained pattern of personality.' For other women, the guilt and self-loathing which overwhelms them each time they abuse may prove strong enough, if not to inhibit repeated offences, at least to drive them to sound an alarm, as in the bizarre tendency of one of Estela Welldon's patients to telephone the police to warn them each time she felt the urge to go on the prowl around the local playground looking for children to molest. It is above all this inability to excuse or justify their acts, their propensity for self-blame, that distinguishes the female from the male abuser.

To the rest of us on the outside looking in, blaming the abuser – identifying one sole villain – gets us nowhere. Evil does not occur in a vacuum and refusing to recognize the circumstances that allow violence to begin and to flourish unchecked constitutes a far graver betrayal of the needs of survivors, thus making us all in some way, through reason of silence or blindness, partly guilty for the crime. According to former psychoanalyst Alice Miller, one of the world's most outspoken authorities on the causes and effects of child abuse, there can be no doubt whatsoever that all acts of violence, sexual or non-sexual, constitute the gravest of crimes – the crime of psychic injury. She knows this as much from her own memory of the 'terrorism' exerted by her mother as from the thousands of men and women who have contacted her over the past decade, identifying with the abuses arising from the 'poisonous pedagogy' that masquerades as child rearing which she describes with shocking candour in her books. No one has revealed more vividly or with greater insight the terrifying 'repetition compulsion' that drives a parent who was once themselves abused, violently punished or neglected to project a lifetime's repressed anger, fury, hatred and resentment against their parent on to their own child in a vain attempt to avenge the earlier injustices that were done to them.

As Miller sees it, a child, especially one's own, becomes a primary transference figure, to whom a parent or parent-figure relates *as if it were their own parent* and whose behaviour and needs often unconsciously, yet automatically, awaken our own unrecognized, long-repressed animosity towards our parents. 'Actually, children are often abused because they remind us of our parents,' says Miller. 'To them it was forbidden to show our rage, but with our children we have no such inhibitions.' In Miller's view we still live in a largely child-inimical society in which the power game of child rearing takes precedence over the rights of the child. This was clearly demonstrated by the recent controversy in Britain over the rights and wrongs of spanking and slapping and the fact that 63 per cent of British mothers smack their 1-year-old babies and 97 per cent admit to regularly smacking their 4-year-olds. Smacking is commonly used as a 'container' for the parent's own unwelcome feelings. 'If you, as a mother, become enraged because your child dares to speak back, there can be a repressed experience behind your rage. Either he reminds you that you were forbidden to speak up or his criticism reminds you of a parent who constantly criticized you. To avoid this pain, our tradition of child rearing offers an easy outlet. You can slap the child, pretending you do it for his own good, that he needs to learn good manners.'

Unlike many experts on child abuse, Miller is unequivocal in the indictment of her own sex. Her refusal to single out men as the chief perpetrators of child abuse has evoked the ire of many feminists who accuse her of demonizing the role of mothers and inculcating further unnecessary guilt in women generally. In turn, Miller, although an avowed feminist, castigates feminism for perpetuating children's suffering through refusing to acknowledge that very often the *only* outlet a woman may find for her feelings is through power over her child. And until the women's movement fully confronts this thorniest of all issues, it is destined to remain imprisoned within its own ideological limits. 'The feminist movement will forfeit none of its strength if it finally admits that mothers also abuse their children. In cases of sexual abuse it is those very mothers who suffered similarly in childhood and have kept it repressed who are blind and deaf to the situation of their daughters. They cannot bear to be reminded of their history, so they fail the child.'

By following this logic through to its most extreme conclusion, Miller forces us to traverse spectacularly dangerous territory. In a recent book, *Banished Knowledge*, she describes the early childhood history of a male serial killer of women, whose mother, a prostitute, wanted a daughter rather than a son, and soon after the birth began hitting him whenever he failed to stay out of her way, nearly killing him through her violence on a number of occasions. Until the age of 7 the boy was forced to wear his hair long, like a girl, and when his schoolteacher finally gave him a haircut the mother almost beat the teacher to death. On being interviewed after his conviction and imprisonment for the multiple killings, the murderer admitted that he went out cold-bloodedly each day with the express intention of killing a woman, as if this were his normal day's work. When asked whether he thought his mother's violence might have contributed to the murders he entirely denied that she could have had any adverse influence on his behaviour.

Miller, however, sees the murders, the first of which he committed when aged 14, as a direct result of the repression of his past, representing either the unconscious desire to kill women because by not being female himself he had failed to gain his mother's love, or to gain attention, the attention he had never been given by her. Although conceding that of course the man is guilty of the murders he committed, Miller adds that: 'Once we are prepared to look at the surrounding circumstances we can no longer say that his mother is without guilt. The murderer says that his mother cannot be blamed for what happened to him, and society agrees with him. In my opinion this mother *made her son a murderer* [my emphasis] even if the son doesn't know it, even if society and the mother herself don't know it or don't want to know it. It is this very lack of awareness that is so dangerous. To prevent future crimes, the danger of this ignorance must be clearly recognized.'

Contentious and chilling as this might sound, Miller's words are beginning to take on a more widespread and insistent resonance, chiming increasingly with the warnings of others involved in the investigation and treatment of offenders, particularly females, and especially young female offenders whose victims tend to be youngsters of their own age, or else toddlers or babies. Talking at a recent public conference, the director of counselling of one of Britain's largest child counselling organizations commented on the increasing number of children reporting abuse at the hands of other children, including female children.

Two particularly disturbing recent studies into the backgrounds of young people who abuse or commit violent crimes, including murder, point to abuse as a common feature of early childhood. A committee of enquiry into the incidence of abuse by young people, set up by the National Children's Home charity, found that one third of sexual abuse is carried out by youngsters aged under 18, many of whom had themselves suffered early abuse. Typical cases included a 4-year-old girl who had been abused by both parents and was found to be already very 'sexualized' in her behaviour. Another 10-year-old was discovered to have assaulted twenty-nine other small children. Nor do the types of abuse uncovered by the report conform to the image many of us have of the sort of furtive, covert violations that go on behind closed doors. The report emphasizes that much abuse may be highly organized and planned, involving both parents, or groups of relatives and neighbours. It warned also of the dangers of allowing children to see pornographic material, including sexually explicit videos, because of the possible link between this and the child's tendency to develop sexually abusive behaviour.

Another recent investigation into the experiences and needs of Section 53 offenders – young people aged between 14 and 25 in long-term custody – came to the disturbing conclusion that 50 per cent of youngsters who had committed violent offences had themselves suffered some form of abuse. Yet in the opinion of Gwyneth Boswell of the University of East Anglia, who undertook the research, the actual figure may be as high as 90 per cent. So serious is the perceived problem that the report recommends further in-depth investigation to discover its true nature and extent. Whether or not such an investigation gets the go-ahead, of one thing we may rest assured: the overwhelming majority of perpetrators of violence and abuse will certainly turn out to be male; the burning questions that will hopefully be answered is what proportion will turn out to be female and what, if anything, distinguishes their early experiences of personal victimization from those of non-offending survivors of abuse.

It Isn't Over Till You See the Blood

Patterns of Destruction

The bathroom, as always, has been specially cleaned. The scrubbed white basin has freshly laundered towels laid alongside, and on the glass shelf she has laid out all the necessary equipment: antiseptic solution, cotton wool, bandages and – most important – a gleaming new razor blade. Now the ritual can begin. With near trance-like absorption and loving care, she takes the razor, rolls up her sleeve and begins slowly yet firmly to score a series of neat, parallel lines down the length of her forearm, from wrist to crook of elbow, first five, then another five alongside, making sure to avoid cutting into a vein or artery. Noticing on the outer edge of her arm the reddish scars of similar recent incisions she now delicately begins opening these up again, until finally the finely traced fretwork of bloodlines is complete: twenty long, fine incisions, all oozing blood. There is no pain. And as the blood begins to flow more freely, the effect begins to work: Zandra is at last released from the angry tension that for the last week has gnawed at her guts, crushing her head in an inescapable vice grip. The tightness, the unbearable tension, all are suddenly gone. Instead, a sense of peace and of being fully alive replaces the zombie-like numbness.

As she washes away the blood, disinfects and bandages her wounds, Zandra knows she can live life fully again – until the next time the inner fury and hatred, whose cause she cannot even identify, become too overwhelming to live with. 'I always know a few days, even weeks, before that it's going to have to happen. However much I try to put it off, I know it's just a matter of time until I can't stand the pressure building up inside me any longer. It takes me over to the point that I can't concentrate on anything else any longer, and the world, my own being, becomes unreal. The cutting makes me feel incredibly calm and in control. Seeing the flow of blood gives me a sense of release – it's as if it was washing away the bad feelings trapped inside me.'

The phenomenon of compulsive self-injury among apparently well-adjusted, healthy women with no history of mental illness is nothing new, but only now is the syndrome beginning to be more widely recognized outside the medical profession. The biggest burst of media coverage came as a result of Andrew Morton's biography of the Princess of Wales, in which reports that she had allegedly attempted to stab herself were interpreted by some women's therapy groups as evidence that she may be a 'cutter'. Though not uncommon among men and women confined to prisons, psychiatric institutions and remand centres, so-called 'cutting' (a term used to cover a wide range of self-injury) continues to confound the experts, especially where it occurs among the normal population. Although frequently associated with early childhood trauma such as incest, sexual or violent assault, loss of a parent, break-up of the family home, serious injury or surgery, and thus seen as symptomatic of the inability to resolve or openly express childhood rage, anger and hostility, especially towards parents, self-mutilation remains the most under-researched and ill-understood of all destructive behaviours.

Like bulimia, which often accompanies self-injury, it is a largely secret, thus undetectable activity, and may often be interpreted as attempted suicide, for the most part an entirely erroneous diagnosis, yet an all too understandable one in view of the ferociousness with which many self-injurers attack themselves and the types of wounds inflicted. Yet strange as it may seem, although sporadic suicide attempts may sometimes be a feature of chronic self-injury, the vast majority of self-mutilators do not cut themselves in order to end their lives, nor do they commonly even fantasize about dying. Quite the opposite. As one leading researcher, Paul Rosen, observes, while individuals with a suicidal predisposition typically feel depressed and resentful at having failed to kill themselves, the self-mutilator feels positively cheerful and glad to be alive having once set about the bloody task of carving themselves up with a razor, knife or some other sure-fire tool of destruction.

Which immediately begs the question, how can such people really be regarded by doctors and therapists as otherwise 'healthy' individuals? Isn't your average cutter actually an out-and-out masochist who secretly enjoys the pain, or a repressed neurotic perpetrating against herself acts of torture and humiliation which she would in fact dearly like to carry out against others, but for which she lacks the bottle?

Far from it. Bizarre and grotesque as it seems, the problem of self-abuse cannot be neatly summed up, and continues so far to elude easy classification. What is beginning to emerge is that cutters are no more 'mad' or deviant than the thousands of closet or self-confessed anorexics, bulimics or compulsive over-eaters that carry on normal working and domestic lives with a greater or lesser degree of success. True, they have problems, but in contrast to many bulimics and anorexics they frequently appear to have those problems well under control – which, when you begin to probe the lives of chronic cutters, appears to be in itself a very large part of the problem. For, contrary to expectation, the average cutter's life is the very model of efficiency, good scheduling and self-awareness. To use current pop-psycho jargon, their behaviour offers a vivid example of what it means to be a 'control freak'. Razors, knives, broken glass, sharp sticks or stones are the instruments of choice for ensuring that it is they who control the stress and pain of being alive, rather than the other way round.

This then is the real tragedy – the pattern is so deeply engrained that it becomes an integral, ingrained part of the whole lifestyle and, more importantly, a necessary life*skill*. What is also staggering is the great numbers of cutters, both male and female, that seem to exist. Hospital studies reveal that over 100,000 people in the UK are treated in hospital each year as a result of deliberately self-inflicted injuries which, apart from cutting, may include burning, beating, punching, banging, slashing, biting, gouging out of parts of the body, face and head, using any variety of weaponry which may be picked up randomly if to hand, or carefully selected as the preferred, even necessary, instrument of destruction.

Although by no means unique to women (young men make up a very large percentage of self-mutilators, outnumbering women in hospital wards and specialist clinics such as the Barnes Unit at Oxford's John Radcliffe Hospital), females are four times more likely to self-injure than men, although their aim generally is never to injure themselves seriously enough to warrant medical attention. This fits in with the extraordinary paradox that the last thing most self-mutilators want is to kill themselves or to persuade others that they have tried to do so. What it also suggests is that the real figure for self-mutilation undoubtedly far exceeds the official estimate.

There is a certain consistency to the patterns of behaviour shared by many self-injurers. These are as mystifying as they are tragic. In one US study involving fifty-two self-mutilating adolescents aged between 14 and 20 from four different treatment centres, out of a total of 293 reported incidents 97 per cent were non lethal, although 60 per cent repeatedly attacked themselves, half of them resorting to varying techniques such as cutting and punching themselves or burning and hitting their head or face against walls and other hard objects. None of the subjects felt any pain while inflicting these injuries and in the majority of cases the reason given for the assaults was the overwhelming need to seek relief of tension and expression of anger, or perhaps also sometimes depression, coupled with the conviction, rarely misplaced, that this release would occur. Such continual reinforcement of the effectiveness of self-injury undoubtedly provides a powerful incentive for repetition. In short, cutters carry on cutting because it works.

Which explains why, to the outside world, a woman who carves up her limbs or beats herself up usually comes across as confident, sociable and in control of her life, rather than as a pathetic victim of some inner neurosis. Like Zandra, a 35-year-old TV researcher, such women tend to be young, ranging in age from pre-pubescence to early middle age, intelligent and talented, according to a report by the *British Journal of Medical Psychology*. Their most devastating handicap, often all-pervasive yet hidden from the outside world, is low self-esteem, the single most disabling trait in women when it comes to healthy expressions of anger and aggression. To listen to the inner torment that plagues many self-mutilators is to witness the fulfilment of that most prophetic of psychoanalytic clichés: women's inability to express anger outwardly and instead to turn it inwards against themselves.

What is truly shocking, however, is the degree of violence with which many women use their bodies as a vehicle for their anger against others, violence that apparently knows no bounds. Anne, a bulimic, became so disgusted with her continuous pattern of binging and vomiting and her inability to break the habit that finally one day she grabbed a kitchen knife and plunged it into her stomach. 'It was the only way I could gain control,' she remembers.

Diane, who developed bulimia following a traumatic divorce, got to the stage of cutting herself three times a week, finally slashing her throat twice, seriously, with a razor. Confined to a closed psychiatric ward for a period afterwards, the majority of the nursing staff accused her of being manipulative and attention-seeking, demonstrating a callous lack of insight or understanding, a sadly common attitude among medical staff dealing with attempted suicide and self-injury cases, which reflects the absence of serious research into the problem. The prevalence of such attitudes also indicates why so many self-mutilators go out of their way to inflict their injuries slowly and with care, in order to avoid contact with doctors and hospitals. Briony, an ex-cutter, never had any illusions that anyone would be able or willing to understand her compulsion. 'I'd fix on one part of the body and cut it to the bone. I did it because I was screaming inside. I felt I had the whole world's problems on my shoulders and no one would listen. The blood did my crying for me and I didn't have to bother anyone with how I felt.'

The Silent Scream

For some, cutting may prove to be, literally, a double-edged sword, assuaging one set of problems and replacing them with others. It was Freud who originally suggested that when a person commits or attempts suicide, it is not themselves they really wish to kill, but someone else close to them. Cutting certainly seems to reflect much of the truth of that assertion. 'For me it's all rage – rage at other people and the inability to express it. And cutting is bloody satisfying,' is how one woman puts it, admitting, however, that the relief brought about by cutting is often tainted with regret and shame, as well as sadness at witnessing the disfigurement of her own body, a body she confesses she values and basically loves.

However, according to psychologists trying to prise some nugget of meaning from such behaviour, the real issue is more complex than simply the venting of anger and fury against one's body because of an inability to let it out elsewhere. One of the principal keys to understanding the underlying mechanism of self-abuse is the frequent absence of pain during laceration itself. There is a theory that this is caused by a chemical imbalance whereby the body produces excess levels of endorphins – natural morphine-like substances secreted by the brain under extreme stress to raise the pain threshold following injury and shock caused by warfare, natural disasters or accidents. But this is all together too facile an explanation. Certainly absence of pain gives self-injurers the scope to brutalize their bodies extensively and repeatedly, with a viciousness that would be intolerable to the rest of us, but the crucial question is what causes this predisposition to numbness in the first place? After all, many cutters do feel pain and discomfort *after* the act, so it isn't just a matter of abnormal biochemistry or faulty brain circuitry. We know, for example, that endorphin levels rise in *response* to stress, shock or injury, so the absence of pain may denote an effect rather than a cause of the inner turmoil that leads to the 'silent scream' of self-injury. Particularly persuasive, when you listen to cutters' own experiences as well as therapists' observations, is the concept of 'body alienation', a kind of existential nightmare which seems to afflict the great majority of self-abusers.

The origins of such experiences are believed to go back invariably to an early history of unresolved anger and anxiety caused usually by parental abandonment, neglect or mistreatment and often traceable to the very earliest pre-verbal stages of infant development. Certain women (and men) who have been unable to resolve those early conflicts during childhood and adolescence may find themselves incapable of openly expressing anger, rage, hostility, guilt or anxiety. And, more to the point, when such emotions arise, whatever the immediate cause – whether a dispute with a colleague, a row with a partner, being insulted or ignored by an official – they automatically begin to feel overwhelmed and threatened, in a sense 'ambushed' by an advancing, unstoppable tide of feeling. The inability to cope effectively with their emotions compels them to seek relief elsewhere, either through externalizing or 'acting out' by deliberately attacking other people or objects or 'introjecting', which is the secret back route that leads to self-injury. In rare cases, some women may alternate unpredictably between both extremes of behaviour. It is as a result of this inner stress and conflict that mind and body switch automatically to an emergency defence against the perceived imminent eruption of uncontrollable rage and fury, a psychosomatic state psychologists call 'depersonalization'.

Self-injurers describe this typically as a physical numbness or aura of unreality which, in extreme cases, makes it difficult or impossible to distinguish oneself from other objects around one, creating an unsureness of the very existence of one's own body as a separate entity from the surrounding environment. Coupled with such somatic sensations – or, more precisely, lack of sensations – there is also an all-pervasive sense of inner emptiness and deadness. The condition bears a remarkable resemblance to the post-traumatic stress disorder (PTSD) symptoms of combat or disaster survivors or the desensitization described by hostages or political prisoners following interrogation, whereby they would wake up feeling as if their own face or limbs did not belong to them.

For self-injurers, cutting seems to offer a fast, effective means of restoring physical feeling and a sense of reality, brought about through redefinition, via blood and eventual pain, of personal bodily boundaries. What it really amounts to is a bizarre self-rescue mission which for the most part succeeds remarkably well. In their book *Self-Mutilation*, Robert Ross and Hugh McKay, who have worked extensively with self-abusers, suggest that cutting may in some ways be interpreted as an existential 'statement', providing confirmation, albeit violent and bloody, of one's existence and personal identity – I bleed therefore I am.

According to Hazel Redsull, a British teacher and art therapist and author of a comprehensive study of adolescent self-injury, the only way to understand – and overcome – cutting is to recognize it as a coping strategy rather than a wanton, senseless act of self-destruction. From her observations of cutters, there is much of the copycat element in self-abuse, especially in schools and young offender institutions, where the behaviour is learned from others who openly display their wounds and describe the positive benefits derived from inflicting them. 'It is like a virus that goes around an institution and becomes more and more catching,' she explains. 'It seems to be related to the attention gained by the cutting from the staff in the care of the wound – and from peers. Yet once those individuals have been helped to overcome the tendency to depersonalize and can learn to communicate in other ways, the behaviour usually ceases. What they also learn is that cutting doesn't communicate the anger and hurt they want to convey, usually to their parents, because once you've cut yourself the anger is dissipated so it is no longer communicable.'

When women choose to leave visible signs of their injuries, the motive is often to punish the object of their anger, as in the case of the girl who cut her arms and bled into the washbasin, leaving her mother to confront the horror of her daughter's actions. Another girl left bloodstained sheets and bedspread for her girlfriend to see 'because I wanted to punish her as well as myself'.

The addictive quality of obtaining relief through injury and the numbing effects of depersonalization can be difficult to overcome, especially in older women who have been cutting themselves for many years, sometimes since childhood. For one thing, lack of pain makes it possible for ever more savage injuries to be inflicted, often unwittingly. Diane, who ended up cutting her throat twice, admits, 'It was like a release, but it used to scare me that it was so painless, and I sometimes felt I wouldn't know when to stop.'

Some women develop an awareness of a 'second self', a separate part of themselves which stands back objectively observing the damage being done yet remains powerless to stop it. Nandi, a successful, high-flying stockbroker, recalls lying on her bed punching herself and clawing her flesh until it bled, while another part of her looked on cynically from above and mocked. 'There was this cool, rational, detached me, standing aside, saying, "Oh yes, that's very clever, isn't it? So you really think doing this to yourself is going to help your problems and unhappiness, do you?" And knowing full well that this sensible other part of me was right, while still being compelled to scratch and scratch away more feverishly until the blood finally came, and in the end I *did* feel pain – I wanted desperately to feel the pain. I also knew full well that what I was doing would give me the release I needed, like having a good cry or a sexual orgasm, but that in the long run it would achieve nothing positive in terms of being more capable of expressing anger, which I have never been able to do.'

Some mutilators, having reached an advanced stage of depersonalization, become increasingly calculating in the strategies they use in carrying out these acts, coolly premeditating how, when and where is best to do it, and then going about the task with all the stately formality of a Japanese Seppuku ritual. A woman like Zandra knows well ahead of time when she is likely to attack herself and will usually pre-plan with elaborate precision the location and timing, laying in 'stocks' of bandages, TCP and cotton wool, to treat her wounds. Others, perhaps because their anger has been sparked unexpectedly by a specific incident or because their emotional threshold is lower, may turn on themselves with a sudden and extreme ferocity, indiscriminately using whatever weapon comes most immediately to hand, including knives, scissors, broken bits of glass, china or light bulbs, caustic or flammable materials, boiling water or lit cigarettes, sometimes punching or beating themselves or banging their head and face against a wall, inserting abrasive or sharp-edged objects into their vagina, swallowing glass, ripping out their hair or gnawing away at their limbs, lips or inner mouth.

Because so much deliberate self-injury is repetitive and follows ritualistic, predictable patterns, many psychiatrists regard it as a part of the whole repertoire of obsessive-compulsive disorders such as continual hand washing, repeated hygiene procedures or home-safety checks, yet in contrast to these, many cutters will go out of their way to ensure complete secrecy of their habit, injuring only those parts of the body they know no one will see and deliberately choosing clothes guaranteed to cover up scars and wounds. It is certainly no coincidence that so many self-mutilators are unmarried, separated or live alone. Nandi emphasizes that every time she beats and scratches herself she makes a conscious effort to bruise and lacerate only those parts of her body always covered by clothing. Hence, no matter how strong the underlying emotional impulse or horrific the degree of mutilation, this remains an intensely lonely and private act, which may begin early on in childhood or, most commonly, at puberty, around the age of 12 or 13, and often continue throughout adolescence and into adulthood.

A typical long-term self-abuser is Lorraine, 43, abandoned by her mother in infancy and sexually abused by her father and brother. She had a baby at 15, which died two days after being born. Lorraine began jabbing her arms with sticks and pebbles when she was 6 and by her teens she was regularly cutting her wrists with pieces of glass which she kept hidden in a bedroom drawer.

Although it is not unknown for very small infants, even babies, to injure themselves deliberately and repeatedly (Robert Ross describes babies of a few weeks old typically seeking a mother's attention by slapping themselves or head-banging, behaviour also exhibited by many distressed animals), if there is a prime time for deliberate self-mutilation, that time is adolescence, beginning commonly around the onset of menstruation, often extending for indefinite periods into adulthood, when early experiences of parental rejection may resurface, painfully and vividly, after years of effective suppression and denial. Now, at this vulnerable stage, the physical changes and emotional ferment of puberty, stressful at the best of times, may cause repressed emotions to boil up and overflow as anger, hatred and resentment, as well as pain and depression, are forced to seek an outlet – with often devastating consequences.

Acting Out

It is during this major transitional phase of puberty that many girls and young women, like teenage males, are likely to act out their hostile and aggressive tendencies, turning adolescence into a violently cataclysmic rite of passage – often one seemingly without end – marked by bullying, fighting, vandalism and assaults against others as well as the self. Most confusing of all, especially to those who live and work with them, are those angry female adolescents who veer uncontrollably and frighteningly from one aggressive mode to another, displacing their anger inwardly as much as outwardly, with each attack symbolizing a powerful expression of unfocused rage which feminist psychotherapist Susie Orbach defines as a basic defence against other more painful and intolerable emotions associated with early childhood development. Without full understanding of the origins of that early pain – against which the anger has come now to serve as a defence – any attempt to control or resolve violent behaviour, whether directed outwardly or inwardly, is doomed to fail.

Through her work as a therapist with aggressive, self-harming youngsters, Hazel Redsull has had ample experience of women's propensity for lashing both outwards and inwards. Virtually every girl with whom she has come into contact has had an early history of childhood trauma and admitted that the underlying motive for their violence was to express anger at a parent or parent figure, sometimes compounding the destructiveness of their actions by drug taking, glue sniffing, alcohol dependence and promiscuity. One girl, who remembers being made to feel unimportant and worthless by her family throughout her early years, at the age of 12 was informed suddenly, in front of her entire family, that the woman she thought was her mother was in fact her grandmother and that her real mother was her elder sister. From then on she periodically overdosed on drugs, scratched and cut herself continuously, smashed semi-precious household objects and burned or otherwise damaged her younger sister's clothes; all this she admitted doing in order to deliberately hurt her mother and family, yet also in the hope of attracting her mother's attention.

Such cases tragically illustrate a classic ploy used by angry individuals who cannot directly articulate their feelings but will instead resort to making others angry. What in reality they crave – especially if their anger is due to parental neglect – is attention and approval. When this turns out to be unforthcoming and apparently unattainable, anger at least guarantees attention of another sort from the parent, and as such must serve as second best to love and affection.

American psychotherapist Louise Kaplan has observed that virtually every young woman who consults a doctor or therapist with a history of self-cutting has endured a childhood made miserable by their mother's unresponsiveness, self-preoccupation, emotional coldness and lack of empathy. She describes the self-mutilator as treating her skin on a conscious level with supreme detachment, as if it were dead, but unconsciously, through acts of cutting and blood-letting, attempting to bring it to life. Such repeated attacks can therefore be seen as a desperate attempt to assuage the unsatisfied needs of infancy – in particular the absence of skin contact and tactile stimulation. To Kaplan, it is hardly a coincidence that a woman deprived as a child of maternal caresses, kisses, cuddles and strokes, should so often choose the surface of the skin as a target for her destructiveness. Deprived of early experiences that should have instilled a sense of self-worth and self-protectiveness, the self-mutilator ultimately cannot meet her body's needs in any way other than destructively.

Another girl who until the age of 9 had a close, loving relationship with her mother, only to lose that intimacy as result of the arrival on the scene of a stepfather and, soon after, a newborn baby, reacted to this virtual 'abandonment' by extensively and severely cutting herself, becoming a heavy drinker and regularly fighting at school. 'I used to get very frustrated, go around slamming doors, stamp my feet and started going out a lot, fighting at school. I was always a tomboy, I wanted to be a boy so I could look after myself. I always wore jeans or trousers. I didn't trust anyone since my mum let me down. I've been like that ever since.'

As Redsull has discovered through her work, when self-injury and delinquency are combined, the full force of fury driving that behaviour becomes awesome and palpable. 'I have worked as an art therapist with a girl who was inflicting damage on herself. She was, however, putting out plenty of anger also. The day before we began our sessions, she and another girl who was exhibiting very similar behaviour had broken into the school and had completely vandalized the place. There was plenty of anger there. The sight just made you gasp; the sheer energy of the anger. Furniture tipped over, books strewn about, plants, paint, earth, glue, anything to hand about and up the walls. I was wondering quite how I would ever contain this girl's feelings in the sessions.' Redsull found that the girl alternated regularly between violent self-injury, accompanied by fears about the effects of this, and equally violent damage to property.

To attempt to make sense of such extremes of chaotic behaviour is to be confounded by perplexing contradictions and paradoxes at almost every turn, mainly because both forms of violence so often turn out to be different sides of the same coin, generated by similar feelings of furious impotence, frustration and personal inadequacy – a problem as common among many violent aggressive males as it is among delinquent and self-abusing females. If there is any significant difference between the modes of aggression displayed by adolescent boys and girls, it concerns the environment in which anger is expressed.

Nadia, a social worker and therapist who worked in a young person's home in South London, an assessment unit which in effect served as a last-ditch rescue centre for teenagers whose backgrounds included deprivation, abuse and neglect of every variety and degree, recalls aggression being as rife among the girls as the boys, although location and patterns of destructiveness distinguished between the two. Whereas boys would typically express their violent impulses outside the home, engaging in petty theft, drunken brawls, vandalizing public property, the girls habitually brought violence *into* the home. 'Once the boys arrived back at the home having gone on the rampage in the streets, they were easy enough to control. But the reverse was true of the girls. Their anger and violence emerged mainly within the centre, their aggression being expressed against themselves through self-injury, drug abuse, drunkenness, fighting the staff or one another and being generally unruly. It's as if females only feel able to let out their aggression within the "safe" confines of a domestic or residential setting, or after looking for trouble outside, getting high on drugs or alcohol, being promiscuous or, worse, getting gang-banged by groups of youths, taking all the fury and aggravation associated with those bad experiences back into the home where they would let it out against other girls or against the staff.'

Seen from the perspective of social deprivation, extreme youth and growing accessibility of drugs, female destructiveness could be construed as partial confirmation of what in our rising moral panic we perceive as the total fragmentation of the social fabric; violence in women has always been deplored because it represents the final unravelling of the seams holding the last tatters of that weave together. Yet what cannot be denied is that such behaviour invariably represents the symptom or by-product rather than the cause of that disintegration.

Although there is no clear cut overall causal relationship between crimes of violence and alcohol consumption (in the rest of Europe, especially the south, where alcohol consumption even among youngsters is higher, hooliganism and other violence is far lower than in the UK), there is cause for alarm over the ill-effects of alcohol – and drugs – on very young women, especially those whose family and social background is unstable or violent. Judging by the experiences of youth workers, the volatile fusion of teenage emotional instability, intensified by environmental stress and powerful, addictive chemical substances, can turn a woman, as it may a man, into a potentially lethal weapon of destruction.

Under-age drinking appears to be reaching epidemic proportions: a 1993 British study revealed that one in twenty 14-year-olds drinks more than the weekly intake recommended for adults, which makes 90,000 children in the UK heavy drinkers. The study, involving 18,000 secondary school children, shows that one in twenty 14- and 15-year-old girls drinks on average more than fourteen units of alcohol per week, the equivalent of the two glasses of wine per day suggested as the safe level for adult women. A survey by Whitbread indicates that in 1991, 20 per cent of violence in their 1,600 British pubs involved fights between women customers. Now add to this the growing menace of drugs ranging from cannabis and Ecstasy to heroin, cocaine, crack and 'ice', an amphetamine-based version of crack whose addictive quality and tendency to induce aggression is far higher than generally recognized, and the picture of rising destructiveness among young women takes on blood-curdling dimensions.

In large cities, especially such notorious high-crime areas as Manchester's Moss Side, addiction among girls and young women leading to heightened aggression is a growing phenomenon, according to drug-counsellors and youth workers. Nor need a girl become a fully fledged drug addict in order to run the risk of self-destructive or dangerous behaviour. According to Sheila Henderson who has studied women's participation in the current 'rave culture', involving mainly the use of 'semi-soft' recreational drugs like Ecstasy and all-night dancing at clubs where the blaring, pulsating sound of 'acid rock' provides another potent drug, young women, aged 14 to 24, today expect to achieve more intense and long-lasting thrills, physical and mental, through the combination of music and chemicals. Unlike the disco scene of the 1960s and 1970s, since the late 1980s, says Henderson, women have become less inhibited about going out alone or in groups to dance, drink, take drugs and enjoy themselves, usually with no intention of looking for boyfriends or casual sex. If they do want sex they have little hesitation in approaching and propositioning a man they fancy. As she discovered, the drugs used are largely 'uppers' as opposed to the popular 'downers', like cannabis, which were favoured in previous decades, and the girls define themselves primarily through their independent single status, their high level of 'street-cred' and their self-confessed 'right' to seek out pleasure and experiment with activities that are dangerous and forbidden.

Of the two types of destructive behaviour, the inwardly and the outwardly projected, for women self-injury actually seems in many instances more likely to deliver the necessary fast release from tension, even yielding some degree of emotional satisfaction – especially among those who openly exhibit their self-inflicted injuries, thus validating their actions through other people's reactions. By comparison, fighting or delinquent behaviour among many young women frequently backfires, leaving them feeling as inadequate as before, if not more so, because of the realization of how much fear and dislike their actions cause among their peers, family and friends, which can be seen as a reflection and reinforcement of the disapprobation of society generally.

However, to what degree other people's responses to female aggression and destructiveness are to blame for this backfiring, and how much women's own instinctive subjective responses are a contributory factor, is difficult to tell. Almost certainly the answer is a mixture of both. The guilt and anxiety that often arise in the wake of a violent outburst do tend to support many psychologists' belief that women grow up to respond to aggressive situations and anger in other people, as well as their own feelings of anger, with anxiety and fear – hence their frequent avoidance of the sort of hostile confrontations that men as a whole will face with equanimity or even purposely seek out as a means of asserting their image and 'proving' their masculine identity.

Pornography of the Mute – A Means of Self-Realization?
While working at Grandview School in Ontario, an institution for adolescent delinquent girls, Robert Ross and Hugh Bryan,

both psychologists as well as professors of criminology, have discovered an extraordinary capacity of many of the 'carvers' for finding ever more ingenious means to show off their wounds, projecting and enhancing their status by openly exhibiting their scars as if they were a signature of their personal identity: 'Some of our girls with carving scars on their arms would deliberately adopt a style of dress which would accentuate the shock value of their cuts, such as short-sleeved or tank-top shirts. Some would even choose the colour of their clothes in order to provide a bold contrast with their scars.'

In defining their public identity through scarring and lacerating their bodies, these girls were in fact acting no differently from the hundreds and thousands of male inmates incarcerated in prisons and other correctional institutions for whom this is a notoriously popular means either of asserting individuality or else publicizing membership of an 'in group'. Research into prison life shows that self-mutilation, like becoming tattooed, is often the only way for an inmate to obtain status in an anti-establishment culture – a socially approved way of opposing the *status quo*. And with the advent of the nihilistic punk culture with its fashion for the insertion of studs, rings and safety pins into lips, noses, ears and other parts of the body, such body markings – sometimes referred to, without trace of irony, as epidermal 'art' – have come to assume a far deeper anti-social significance, a symbolic two fingers up to the outside world.

Among the girls at Grandview, as at other approved schools, the same ethos seems to prevail, with cutting and other self-inflicted injuries signifying group membership and scars serving as a kind of identity badge, similar to tattoos. Thus most of the girls at Grandview were specifically coerced into carving themselves in order to avoid ostracism or to prove their allegiance to the group or for a girl to demonstrate the depth of her affection if another threatened to reject her. Yet what intrigued Ross and Bryan most of all was how frequently the actual act of cutting, far from being a private act of anguish, became an elaborate ritual, an occasion of importance – and self-importance – marked by dramatic ceremony and esoteric symbolic accompaniments such as chanting, gestures and swearing of oaths, analogous to the initiation rites practised by primitive tribal cultures. The researchers admit that they and the staff never ceased to be amazed at the 'skilled choreography of it all'. Interestingly, the importance and ceremony accorded such public acts of mutilation seemed to be associated with rule-breaking as a form of attention seeking, while cutting was frowned upon. Once staff permitted it and ceased focusing on it as a misdeed, the girls no longer got a buzz out of flaunting the rules and the rate of cutting dropped.

The more they worked with the girls, the more Ross and Bryan were struck by the extent to which the female self-mutilators appeared in general to be far more preoccupied with their bodies than is usual among other individuals, often seeming to view their skin as a primary, sometimes exclusive, source of self-satisfaction. Like other psychologists who have studied cutting, they noted that mutilators responded to their bodies very much as if it were a love-object (although hate-object would seem more appropriate, given the degree to which they punished and disfigured it), becoming preoccupied and obsessed with their bodily sensations and processes in a manner common to very young children. Also, like infants, many of the girls were completely self-centred and narcissistically in need of attention, displaying very violent and sudden outbursts of rage if their needs and desires were not immediately met.

It is this tendency for cutters to turn their bodies into fetishistic objects, coupled with the complex, hidden meaning of those acts, which has led psychotherapist Louise Kaplan to call self-mutilation the 'pornography of the mute'. Unlike conventional forms of pornography whose appeal is upfront, unsubtle and all too evidently constructed around a pleasure principle, here, according to Kaplan, the terrors and forbidden desires of infancy are made visible, yet in a language that eludes comprehension.

In identifying this phenomenon, researchers appear to have found if not the whole answer, then certainly a major explanation to the question of why so many women experience an anger 'problem', and frequently end up turning it against themselves. It is impossible to gain a broader picture of women's subjective experiences of anger as a negative force without going back to the earliest days, weeks and months of infancy, when the newborn, as was originally observed by the controversial child analyst Melanie Klein, experiences its earliest conflicts between love and hate, contentment and the wish to destroy, anxiety and anger at the mother's breast. From her work with very small children, often as young as two, Klein noted that the newborn brings with it into the world two violently conflicting drives, one life-enhancing and loving, the other imbued with hate, greed, envy and resentment, and one or other of these predominates at different times depending on the baby's sense either of frustration or fulfilment at the breast.

Thus emerged the notorious and much challenged concept of the 'wicked infant', furiously driven to attack and try to destroy the mother during its earliest development. From birth on, at first unable to experience itself as an individual living entity, separate from the breast and from the mother, the 'inner world' of the infant, as described by Klein, is almost entirely shaped and coloured by the primal experiences of, first, being merged with the mother as one inseparable, interfunctioning unit and, later, by the amount of conflict, anger, fear and frustration that may accompany the growing infant's realization of itself as a separate individual – a process known as 'separation-individuation' which takes place during the first years of infancy.

Klein postulated that it is during the earliest symbiotic stage of the mother–child relationship, when the newborn still perceives itself as indistinguishable from the breast, and later, from the mother herself, who is both idealized as wholly 'good' and vilified as wholly 'bad', that any 'bad' experiences associated with inadequate care, neglect or abandonment and abuse are interpreted by the child as caused not only by the omnipotent 'bad' mother but, *ipso facto*, by its own 'badness'.

Much influenced by Klein's explanation of this early merging of mother–child identity, as perceived by the child, and the child's 'splitting' of its own terrifying or pleasurable experiences into separate good or bad objects – as personified first and foremost by the mother – feminist psychoanalysis has made much of the fact that little girls, compared to boys, are often destined to remain partially merged with the mother's identity, or at least fail to fully establish their own distinct and separate boundaries of existence.

This has also led to the notion of women's perception of their skin and bodies as 'containers', both literal and symbolic, for all their frightening, painful, demeaning and shameful experiences. It is because those experiences commonly embrace bodily functions such as menstruation, the development of secondary sexual characteristics and erotic arousal which herald the transition from childhood to sexual maturity, that early puberty and adolescence are the most likely periods at which girls may be driven to self-injury.

Dr Margaret Mahler, a pioneer in ego psychology and child development, coined the term 'separation-individuation' to describe the period between 18 months and 3 years of age when the growth of the child increasingly leads it to separate from its mother and become its 'own' person, a process which may be fraught with trauma and setbacks and never be successfully completed if the mother is too clinging, over-possessive or controlling. This may lead not only to the girl child's continuing over-dependence, insecurity and anxiety (if one senses oneself to be an extension of the primary care-giver rather than an individual in one's own right, then to sever that connection may seem terrifying beyond belief and tantamount to being deprived of love and protection), but to a conviction that the mother's faults and failings are, in actual fact, one's own.

Hence a child who senses danger in expressing anger against the mother may feel safer letting the fury out against itself – the attack becoming in effect directed against the mother-in-the-self – or simply repressing the anger altogether. This symbiosis, which becomes particularly acute if the mother rejects, punishes or abandons the child who dares to express anger, thereby reinforcing her image as the 'bad' mother, is far more common among mothers and daughters than among mothers and sons, mainly because – being of the same sex – girls separate later than boys and they will more naturally continue to mirror themselves in their mother's image. Sometimes they will never separate fully, a problem that is intensified if they are taught by their mother's example, chastised by both parents and indoctrinated by their culture into believing that anger in females is unwelcome and wicked.

This confusion of mother–child identities casts some light on the dual meaning of self-injury. For example, the relief felt by cutters at seeing the blood flow from their injuries has been attributed as much to a purging of impurities – the elimination of the unwanted, internal 'bad' mother – as to a soothing, therapeutic act designed to bring comfort, relief from tension and a sense of 'wholeness'.

According to feminist psychoanalytic theory, which has been greatly informed by the work of pioneering child psychologists such as Margaret Mahler, Donald Winnicott and Ronald Fairbairn, women's 'anger problems' are nearly always the product of an incomplete or traumatic process of separation/individuation, in which anger is a taboo, inseparable from anxiety, unable to be freely or safely expressed by the child for fear of rejection, loss of love or the threat of abandonment. It is for this reason that anger is believed so often to become automatically transmuted into fear, guilt or panic in many women's experiences. In view of the fact that the majority of self-injurers have an early history of abuse, neglect or desertion by the parent or parent-figure (i.e. adoptive or foster mother), there can be little mystery as to how and why they should have become incapable, from infancy, of differentiating between anger and anxiety.

In regressing to a state of numbness and detachment between mind and body prior to cutting themselves, women like Nandi and Zandra seem to be exhibiting classic signs of what Fairbairn called a 'schizoid split', whereby a part of the ego withdraws from the outer world when its needs are unrecognized or denied. The anger and hostility which a child feels for its parent is, according to Fairbairn, invariably a response to frustrated needs, yet the greater the threat of danger due to withdrawal of parental protection the more likely the child, and later the adult – especially where their identity remains merged with that of their mother – is to experience conflict and fear over expressing anger and, by denying it, pushing it into the deepest, most hidden subconscious recesses.

Equally pertinent, both in the case of women who 'act out' their anger and those who suppress it, is Donald Winnicott's notion of the 'false self', created by the insecure neglected infant to ensure parental love and care. With the 'true self', i.e. the child's spontaneous uniquely individual identity, increasingly pushed under, its existence denied and ignored during the course of infant development, the capacity for a woman with a well-erected, impermeable false self to fully confront and identify her true inner needs, especially those involving anger, may be diminished to the point of total extinction. Describing the difference between a child's normal, healthy capacity for 'hot displeasure', occasional bouts of resentment and fury towards parents who are fundamentally loving and supportive, and the tendency towards the 'cold malice' of hatred, child psychotherapist John Bowlby also pinpointed abandonment and separation, actual or threatened, as crucial to our understanding of the nature of dysfunctional anger as displayed by children or grown women whose hatred and rage towards a parent may verge on the murderous, whether they express it or not.

As Bowlby observed, frustrations of a less obvious nature, such as when a parent demands that the child act as caretaker, in effect becoming a pseudo-parent to them, as is more common in mother–daughter than mother–son relationships, can evoke just as much anger, usually densely interwoven with guilt and anxiety, as do more obvious forms of neglect or rejection. So, while boys are just as likely as girls to experience conflicts and frustration over early expression of anger towards a parent, for them the whole process of separating and differentiating from the mother is facilitated by being self-evidently of the opposite sex, while their conditioning also encourages them to express or sublimate their anger externally through physically rigorous games and sports, acts of prowess, fighting – whether for real or for 'play' – and other modes of overt, socially acceptable forms of aggression, often unavailable to girls.

* * *

One way to understand cutting, therefore, is to see it as a desperate, short-lived attempt by the imprisoned 'real self' to express its needs and communicate its anguish. Before the real self can feel free to express anger and fury, it must comprehend that it is *safe* to articulate those feelings and that love, care and acceptance by a loved one, whether a parent, partner, child or close friend, will not be withdrawn as a result. Yet the difficulty of coming to this realization – that showing anger does not automatically eradicate another person's love – keeps many cutters straitjacketed by the boundaries of their false self, their actions dictated by the counterfeit persona that has known only dysfunctional modes of anger. In addition, the knowledge that cutting can be relied upon to provide satisfaction and release of anger, however perverse it might seem, can come to be perceived as vastly reassuring and comforting to many women – which is not necessarily true for their counterparts, those who become so vehemently possessed by fury that they can only discharge it through unpremeditated, wantonly ferocious attacks on other people and property.

The Anger Problem

Hard as it is to understand how a woman who mutilates her own body can actually end up believing – and convincing others – that she has more of a grip on her emotions and functions more efficiently in daily life than one who expresses her anger spontaneously and directly, what defies comprehension even more is that many of the women who are openly aggressive are also the least confident or assertive of these two groups – an apparent paradox as common among violent men as their female counterparts. That both forms of behaviour induce either a sense of self-control or a release which are largely illusory and short-lived and can amount to a severe disability is undeniable. So, too, is the fact that beneath the self-deception most women are well aware of their anger 'problem' and would dearly love to overcome it, but find themselves stymied by their own shaky self-image. And while anger may well be the impulse that kickstarts the engine which sets off attacks on the self or on others, the oil that greases the whole destructive mechanism of displaced aggression is invariably made up of equal components of guilt and anxiety. Thus, even where a woman appears able to 'let out' her anger, this can turn into a form of indirect self-injury, resulting in a 'boomerang effect' in which her violence merely succeeds in reinforcing the negative self-image she is battling to overcome.

Talking to a group of women from CAST, a London-based organization that provides support for former prisoners as well as offering creative outlets for their internal conflicts, including anger, which may either have led to or resulted from their involvement in crime and the penal system, the boomerang effect of displaced anger becomes painfully evident. As Kim, a strikingly attractive, articulate woman in her late twenties sees it, no matter how much status and clout a girl derives from her reputation as a fighter, when you cannot identify and resolve the real cause of your anger or direct it at the appropriate target, no amount of aggressive action will dissipate the inner tension or neutralize the fear which triggers the aggression in the first place. If anything, like a chronic inflammation or pain whose origins remain undiagnosed yet whose symptoms the sufferer constantly suppresses or temporarily alleviates with powerful drugs until the next upsurge of discomfort, anger that is linked to long-standing psychological injury is guaranteed to return ever more forcibly once the 'high' of fighting wears off.

Kim, who comes from a violent home where she both witnessed and bore the brunt of physical and verbal aggression, fought often and well at school and throughout her teens, taking on boys as well as girls and usually winning.

'It was the only way of expressing my anger – I didn't know any other way. I wouldn't purposely walk away from potentially explosive situations as I would now. As a youngster I enjoyed and needed that adrenalin rush, the heart beating faster, the mixture of fear and excitement – actually it's excitement caused by fear, and I'd get into fights, all my friends egging me on and praising me when I'd won. I got a sense of personal affirmation through fighting. I felt I was somebody. There was that element of a power trip in it too. But what was really happening, I now realize, is that my anger was always aroused by fear – fear of situations, fear of people.'

This psychological intertwining of fear and anger – just as prevalent among violent men as women – in Kim's case goes back to memories of a father who only ever communicated his displeasure with his wife and children through violent outbursts, and brothers who acted similarly. In the dysfunctional family, where certain emotions such as humiliation, loneliness, shame and anxiety become too painful to bear, the growing child often learns that the quickest exit from pain is via anger, guaranteeing an instant short-circuit of all other troublesome emotions. To this end Kim set about perfecting a tough-girl image to protect her vulnerability, yet remaining all the while partially aware that it was not a role to which she was fully suited. 'In my family, if you were ever hurt by something you'd immediately express it through anger, physical or verbal. I was very wrapped up in being hard, rebellious, naughty – but I did have a conscience about it. And once I'd been expelled from my first senior school for fighting I did begin to see that although I might impress some people by my violence, in the end you lose your friends and end up with more enemies threatening to wreak vengeance. I found that being violent was the best way of creating constant fear and drama in my life. I'd be walking through the streets worrying about who I'd bump into who'd got it in for me! My way of toning down the violence later on at school was to become a joker, to impress people.'

Today Kim's adolescent fury is far from fully resolved. Aware of her aggressive tendencies and the devastation they can wreak, she remains caught between a rock and a hard place, damned if she fights, damned if she doesn't. 'You tell me – what's a healthy expression of anger for a woman? What do you do with all that energy? Men are allowed to be violent, but not us. I don't fight any more and I avoid violent situations whenever possible, but all that's happened is that I moved on to having violent relationships with men, this time with me being on the receiving end, even though I'd give back as good as I got. It goes back to the old childhood thing of anger and violence being the only way you know how to communicate.

'Nowadays, as I get older, the fear element is stronger in me and it stops the anger coming out. But I find that walking away from things is quite humiliating because of the way I used to be once, remembering how at 15 I'd have done something extreme to get back at someone and prove myself. And I haven't yet found a way of feeling that I can be somebody without having to do it by beating people up. I'm aware that my anger with myself may come out against those I care for and I realize that although I thought I'd managed to deal with my anger it's really still there inside. I've just pushed it down again, yet I know I need to sort it out because by festering and boiling away inside me it makes your head explode – I get lots of very bad headaches from just feeling angry for months on end, not knowing why, or what to do about it. Once I would have gone out and punched somebody and felt better. But now I know it wouldn't have done any lasting good at all. I can feel rage, indignation and resentment towards people and things all the time, like if somebody just brushes against me on the escalator I think, how bloody *dare* they, I want to yell and whack them, and it does my head in. But most people won't accept your anger, not if you're a woman. If you express it freely you get caught up in a power struggle.'

On a first encounter, the female 'toughs' who get together at CAST, like most of the women who have spent long periods in jail and/or in institutionalized care, appear formidably hard-edged, iron ladies all, their vulnerability and reluctance to trust anyone belied by an apparent brittle self-confidence projected in diverse forms – from quiet, glaring, don't-mess-with-me defensiveness to a raucous piss-taking jocularity, St Trinian's crossed with men's locker-room braggadocio. But scratch the surface and you discover how much is sham and showy bravado. Comfortable though they claim to be with their violent behaviour, whether in the past or the present, and their image as aggressive women, most acknowledge that it has failed to confer true assertiveness or impart a sense of control over their lives, let alone resolve the pain of inner emotional conflict.

In contrast to those women for whom an aggressive attitude appears to have led to a real sense of empowerment and enhanced self-esteem, most notably among those who achieve success in quintessentially male-dominated sports or professions, or even those who end up treading a criminal route, such as Brooklyn's female crack dealers or Chicago's Vice Queen gang members, perceiving themselves for the first time ever as being in charge of their lives, no longer victims to be used and abused by others, *these* women clearly have a problem with their anger and aggression. They feel ill at ease within themselves and are anxious or ambivalent about the effects of their behaviour. Being angry bothers or upsets them, inducing guilt, depression or anxiety. In this respect they are remarkably similar to those women who habitually turn their anger inwards, through attempted suicide or self-injury. The release of anger is temporary, often incomplete, the residual side effects often counter-productive, and the underlying pain – against which they use anger as a shield – as constant and enduring as ever.

Which of the two modes of aggressive behaviour is the most self-destructive or difficult to resolve is hard to determine – especially in a culture which still persists in labelling female aggression as unacceptable, irrational and usually a case for medical intervention or punishment. How much of women's 'anger problem' lies within themselves and how much is due to society's harshly negative responses to and treatment of women who express themselves in what is still regarded as anomalous, unfeminine behaviour? Does the fault – if fault it be – lie within the woman, or within her environment? The kind of negative feedback that even self-assertive, authoritative, let alone aggressive, women can count on from society is hardly conducive to the healthy outward expression of any so-called hostile or 'dark' emotion and certainly not to the spontaneous venting of anger or fury. So, even if she ends up feeling guilty or ashamed about her behaviour, the woman who acts out her anger, albeit unreasonably and against an unjustifiable target, at least knows that this feeling exists and 'lives' in a specific location, unlike those who develop a void to be filled with more 'acceptable' emotions such as guilt, compulsion to please or over-achieve, depression or low self-worth. Thus, the 'acter-out' is free of one major handicap, the lack of awareness of the existence of her anger, thus avoiding the emotional myopia that puts this one emotion at the top of the list of psychological 'blocks' for so many women. For restraint in expressing anger invariably boils down to a fear of one's internal aggressive drive. When a woman cannot openly act out her anger and instead conceals it under the guise of self-mutilation, or even in the form of eating disorders and other obsessive-compulsive behaviours, the most common cause is her own terror at what devastation her anger might wreak – whether it be rejection by others or the possibility of causing death and destruction through the unleashing of her hitherto suppressed power.

The more appalling the prospect of the harm her anger might cause, the deeper the self-injurer drives her fury, hatred and desire for revenge underground into the deepest recesses of the psyche. For Catriona, a 60-year-old translator who grew up in America's Midwest in an atmosphere of continuous, spontaneous violence vented principally by her father against her mother, and her brothers against each other and against her, shame and self-blame were the only emotions which she could readily identify. As a child, and later on as an adult who eventually became an alcoholic, anger was an emotion as foreign to her as the most obscure Aboriginal dialect – even after five years of psychotherapy, three times a week. 'I had discovered in therapy that there were incestuous goings-on between my brothers and me – not exactly outright sexual abuse but still things that obviously felt wrong and shameful. My reaction had been to take responsibility for this wrongdoing and develop a deep sense of shame that entirely engulfed any feelings of anger. I didn't even know what anger felt like – though I'd witnessed it enough times, God knows.'

Eventually, after years of therapy failed to locate even the faintest grain of hostility or anger, Catriona's therapist persuaded her to undergo a new form of 'total anger immersion' which involved being blindfolded, listening through earphones to powerful music based on themes of anger – in this case Holst's 'Mars' movement from *The Planets* – and taking the drug Ecstasy to reduce emotional inhibition. 'I don't remember much about the session at all,' says Catriona, 'except that after it was over I was overcome by the most profound and deeply agonizing shame that I had ever experienced in my entire life. My one intention and my one need as I left my therapist that day was to commit suicide, as fast as possible. This was shame of a sort I felt entirely incapable of living with. I was lucky in that a friend had come by the apartment who prevented me taking the pills with which I intended to kill myself. Now, looking back, it is incredible to me that my anger was bound up with shame so all-pervasively, that this was all I could come up with when exposed to such an immense onslaught of anger-provoking influences.'

Three years on, having moved on to group therapy and joined Alcoholics Anonymous, Catriona can now increasingly begin to recognize the stirrings of anger within her but alongside those feelings, or immediately afterwards, is the familiar, residual shame and guilt for allowing herself to consciously experience those feelings.

Just as terrifying to many women who cannot feel or communicate their own anger is the threat of danger posed by other people's anger. As a self-mutilator, Nandi recognizes the mechanism that causes her to release the mounting tension of stored fury through the letting of blood. Two years of therapy, sessions with a psychiatrist and now group therapy encounters have made it patently obvious to her why she cannot show anger openly, but that insight has so far failed to yield a better outlet for her feelings.

'I was 11 when my father had a nervous breakdown and never went to work again. My mother became the breadwinner and there were six of us in the family, all high achievers, all intending to go to university and become successful professionally. The strain placed on my mother came out in horrific, grotesque displays of verbal abuse, directed mainly at my father. The tension at home was constant and terrible, made worse by having to put on a respectable front, a façade of normality, to neighbours and friends in our very conventional, Orthodox Jewish community. I saw my role in all this as being my mother's protector and having to rescue her from my father whom I perceived as harmful, the cause of all her grotesque outbursts of anger, and the stress-related ill health she developed after his breakdown. It was a sudden growing up. After 11 I was no longer a child.

'I was 20 when Dad killed himself. By that time I'd already discovered that my younger sister was bulimic and cutting herself. I used to think she must be clinically mad and quite abnormal. Yet somehow that perception of her self-injury doesn't impinge on what I do to myself now, which feels totally normal and necessary. It is still quite impossible for me to get angry openly, even when I've tried punching cushions and attempted to scream and shout as part of an anger-venting exercise – I am physically incapable of screaming, shouting or being in any way violent, except when scratching and beating myself up. I'm too terrified of the memory of my mum's outbursts when I was little. My instinct is that if I show anger, there will be a catastrophe, someone will die – well, my dad did die, didn't he? So you can understand the unconscious connection.

'When I'm angry inside, shivering and boiling up, I think about how it would be to just hurl all the china and glass against the walls and express it that way, then I start attacking myself. Somehow that seems safer – my body is worth less to me than my dinner service.'

Nandi was also reminded in group therapy to what degree she could be incapacitated by other people's anger, as well as her own. 'There was a girl one evening in the group who went all out in one of those anger-ventilation exercises, kicking and hammering a cushion as an outlet for the stored-up hatred of her father. Shortly after she began, all my control and calm just fell apart. It was a shock sensation, like being a roller blind that's jerked and releases very fast and suddenly upwards. There's no more control, your fear just engulfs you. I fled the room in tears and howled for hours afterwards, remembering the havoc caused by my mum's anger.'

Although self-mutilators like Nandi have contained their anger to the point where they know exactly when and where it is safe to let it out – namely in complete privacy and against their own bodies – there are those whose past experience of early abuse and the resulting build-up of hatred and resentment is such that it has crystallized, rather than clouded, their recognition of their own capacity for violent action, to the point where they purposely withdraw into themselves for fear of losing control and severely harming others. The principal way many have learned to cope with their experiences is not to feel; to feel is to be angry and to be angry is to unleash a force so potentially deadly in its consequences as to be unthinkable.

Listening to the horrific, blood-curdling experiences of a group of prisoners from Bedford Hills, New York's top security women's prison, one is struck how understandable, even justifiable, some women's violent and criminal actions become when judged within the overall context of their past history of abuse – abuses often so inhumane and vicious that many were unable to describe their suffering to me without breaking down in tears, or leaving the room.

Of the twenty prisoners I talked to at Bedford Hills, most had long-term or life convictions for committing or acting as accessories to crimes of violence, including murder. Compared to other women prisoners who regularly mutilate themselves, attempt to commit suicide – and succeed – or else regularly and viciously attack their fellow prisoners or prison warders, this group could be described, without irony, as the fortunate ones. Unlike the majority of prisoners of either sex anywhere in the world, most were involved in an almost unique group therapy programme, an ongoing rehabilitative project involving weekly or fortnightly sessions led by the initiator of the programme, psychologist and prison worker Sharon Smrlish. They are fortunate in happening to be locked up in what is currently acknowledged to be America's most progressive women's prison, in terms of psychological rehabilitative facilities, and have therefore been given an opportunity to re-examine, work out and, if possible, resolve the most deep-rooted and damaging effects of early childhood abuse and deprivation. Many still remain for the most part chronically psychologically numb, their personalities often fragmented or split into two or more separate parts. Some are only beginning to awake and acknowledge their own identity after years of fantasizing that someone else, not they themselves, was living through their previous experiences, while others still struggle to escape a state of psychic half-death, where trust cannot be placed in others for fear of betrayal, rendering human relationships based on reciprocal care and affection a virtual anathema.

Every one of those women, most of them under 40, had been subjected to often appalling degrees of sexual abuse and violent beatings by one or more members of their family — including sometimes their mothers or sisters. Also, as happened frequently, when they were either placed in care or adopted by foster parents they continued to be abused by these secondary 'care-takers'. Some left home before reaching their teens, usually living rough on the streets, sleeping around, turning to prostitution and petty crime in order to survive. Most recall being raped at least once by strangers, sodomized, beaten senseless and left for dead.

The phrase that came up repeatedly in our talks was 'looking for love, looking for someone who would be kind and take care of me'. Predictably, every one of these women became involved with a 'dream man' in her teens, someone she initially perceived as a 'saviour' or a 'knight in shining armour, who gave me everything, made me feel special and loved'. But this respite tended to be cruelly brief. The men with whom these women became involved were invariably drug addicts or drug dealers, gangster hit men, con men, pimps, liars — and they liked to beat up women. Thus the cycle of abuse became re-established, the women ending up as battered wives or girlfriends, becoming pregnant, often bearing numbers of children by different men, becoming addicted to hard drugs and alcohol and committing crimes of violence usually less through cold, premeditated volition than randomly and in a chaotic, desperate bid to get money or to fit in with their husband's or boyfriend's plans.

Here, then, we have a random selection of some of America's most 'dangerous' and 'violent' female criminals. Yet the one emotion that was *never* expressed during the time I spent with them, although discussed in the abstract or to describe past events, was anger. For all their personal past acts of violence —

the burglaries, muggings, killings, beatings up of frail and elderly victims, car thefts, slashings, shootings and stabbings – the lasting impression is of victims, who have been too long on the receiving end of other people's anger to be able to express their own hatred and need for revenge freely or openly. So emotionally and spiritually crippled by the violence of their early past are women like these – who, as research tells us, make up the majority of the violent female prison population – that they know full well the potential power of the fury they carry around inside them. As I was told over and over again, theirs is a fury that could, and would, kill were it to be released.

Kate, who grew up in Harlem, tells me she was 5 when she first started formulating her 'hit list'. First listed were members of her family, to be followed by boyfriend, husband and in-laws, whom she vowed one day to kill. On the list are all those who ever beat her, sexually abused her, raped her or threatened her with death, along with anyone who acted this way towards her grandmother, the single good, caring person she ever had in her life. Kate's hit list numbers about a dozen or more men and women – many of whom she managed to physically attack and injure during her early nightmare years spent alternately with her relatives, her foster parents and her boyfriend and his family.

Today the anger inside her lies subdued but very much alive, an omnipresent knot of tension which she cannot allow to unravel for fear of the havoc that would ensue. 'Anger is a very dangerous area for me now. Not only do I avoid getting into aggressive confrontations because I know that if I were to get angry suddenly I'd snap and certainly kill somebody, but I avoid getting close enough to anyone to feel any kind of emotion, including affection. Don't anyone come too near me or try to touch me physically or I'll go crazy-mad.'

Another prisoner in the group, Melanie, explains that for her, as for many of the others, the 'anger problem' isn't so much an inability or inhibition about expressing the emotion but more a cross between a phobia of aggressive circumstances and a constant conscious effort to avoid the sorts of situations and conflicts which may trigger anger. 'Anger is loss of control, and in losing control I fear – no, I *know* that I'll kill – so I avoid any situation that might make me lose control. The memory of the hate and desire to kill I had when I saw my grandfather kill my mother and then set the house on fire to cover up his crime, with all us children in it, has stayed with me for life. Later I wanted to kill the man I lived with who used to stomp my face into the pavement when he got angry, chain me to a radiator and kick me in the stomach when I was pregnant. Until two years ago I just wanted to kill everybody. I didn't allow myself to get close to anybody. That was the only way to avoid feeling anger and the urge to kill.'

It seems almost inexplicable that women who once proved their capacity for ruthless violence and wantonly destructive acts – and certainly seemed uninhibited about openly expressing anger – should now regress to the point where anger becomes such a dangerous no-go area. Yet it is precisely *because* their anger has a life-long history of underlying pain, *because* anger as an emotion has become so charged with memories of potential or actual extreme violence, that even the faintest visceral gnawing of irritation, discontent or hostility is sufficient to trigger an instant action replay of past horrors, a rerun of events associated with being harmed and with harming others. Why, once you know the full implications of igniting an incendiary device or clambering around the rim of a smouldering volcano, would you knowingly and willingly repeat that nightmare again? It is precisely because they have had the message drummed into them so unforgettably and incessantly that anger equals violence, which in turn leads to injury, pain and dehumanization, of themselves as of others, that women like Kate and Melanie and hundreds and thousands of other women both inside and outside prisons and institutions around the world have consciously or unconsciously allowed their anger to become numb or to turn it inwards towards themselves, rather than unleash it on the outside world.

Warrior Women

Nothing to Fear But Fear Itself

It is night-time and a stale, oppressive humidity hangs in the air. The streets are ill lit and empty. This is the South Bronx, one of New York's most derelict and notoriously crime-ridden areas inhabited largely by unemployed and poor Hispanic and black families, their lives and homes under twenty-four-hour threat from the gangs of marauding teenagers and children, some as young as 9 or 10, many high on crack or heroin, desperate enough to shoot or stab anyone for the price of a fix. Murder and shootouts with the police, like arson, are so commonplace they no longer make the papers, while rape, mugging, burglary and looting are too much a part of daily life for anyone to bother reporting them to the police.

A stocky black woman in jeans and leather jacket, carrying two bags of shopping, walks briskly out of a supermarket, making her way purposefully past the rows of dilapidated, half burned-out tenements, the debris-strewn parking lots and piles of uncollected refuse. Suddenly, a small, wiry figure, male, aged no more than 17, darts out from behind the shell of a wrecked transit van. He looks frightened, with manic eyes and a mean tightness about his mouth. Pulling a gun from his anorak pocket, he points it at the woman. 'Gimme yoh leather jacket, bitch,' he snarls. 'Jes yoh fuckin' take it off right now and hand it over, cunt.'

She stands rigid, facing the gun, and slowly places her shopping bags on the ground beside her. Then, without warning, like an instantaneous barrage of machine-gun fire, she lets rip, spitting her words clearly with a voice of bloodcurdling power and piercing shrillness, building to a screaming crescendo, descending to a low, gravelly snarl at base level. It is the sound of red hot, raw and lethal fury. 'Ya fuckin' asshole. Ya wanna have this jacket, ya asshole motherfucker? Well, let me tell ya this, asshole, ya gonna have to take it offa me yourself if ya want it so bad. Ain't no way I'm gonna undo the zip, take it off, and hand it to ya. No way ya fuckin' cocksucker [voice rising to a banshee scream] 'cos I fuckin' worked for this coat, I fuckin' worked my ass off for it, and ain't no one helped me get it. So, ya know what I'm gonna do? I'm gonna pick up my shit here and I'm gonna go right on and visit my friends up the road there. Now *you* can do what the fuck you wanna because I'm gettin' outta here right now.'

The diatribe over, she gathers her shopping and begins to step past him. The boy, ashen faced, mouth agape, runs off as from a rabid beast, up an alleyway into the night.

It was the kind of extreme high-danger situation that the best self-defence teachers only set up at the end of a very advanced course when students are ready for the final test of the speed and aggression of their reactions. Only this was no mock-up, it was the real thing. And it was the mugger's tough luck to have chosen as his prospective victim one of New York's strongest and most fearless women. Unhappily for him, her speciality just happens to be the security and crime prevention business. Even by black belt Linda Ramezy's standards, this was a hair-raising touch-and-go confrontation. Yet the relish with which she recounts the episode to me indicates clearly the pride she feels in her capacity for self-defence, her unwavering conviction that women have much to lose by passivity yet everything to gain by exploring the extremes of their aggressive potential.

She and others like her have proven this repeatedly. The outcome of her set-to with the Bronx mugger yet again proves the point this 48-year-old jujitsu expert has so far made to over 3,000 students throughout the USA, namely that an attacker does not generally expect his intended female victim to react aggressively or violently. Women just don't behave that way, do they? Men, in particular, do not expect a strange woman whom they confront to shout or use obscene and threatening language. So, never underestimate the deterrent power of surprise. It may be all that's needed to avoid becoming a crime statistic. And that's even before you lam into your attacker with kicks and punches. Contrary to received wisdom on how women can best avoid violent assault, experiences like Linda Ramezy's are not the exception to the rule but, according to some researchers, offer confirmation of how successfully rage and fury can be channelled in defence of one's life and well-being. Unless, that is, a woman is too disabled by a lifetime's practice of being polite, helpful and dignified. Is disabled too strong a word? Almost certainly not, since it is these qualities of docility and quintessential female niceness which mothers, with society's implicit approbation, so assiduously cultivate in their daughters that criminals count on when choosing their prey. When asked why he targeted women, a sex attacker who was recently convicted of numbers of such assaults replied that it was 'because they are soft and cannot struggle'. What more salutary reminder can there be of the powerful image of female helplessness?

The truth is that many women can be hard when they need to be, and physically capable of a lot more than just struggling. Granted, Linda Ramezy may be in the front rank of America's strongest, most alert and confident women, outside the armed forces, and her job is to teach self-defence not only to women but to men, including trainee security guards – all of which makes her atypical – but it is crucial not to miss her point about physical aggression being only one weapon in a woman's armoury of self-defence.

'Attitude and the right verbal attack may be all that's needed to scare a would-be assailant. For the most part I've protected myself verbally. It scares them right off, shows them you're in control. They don't know what you'll do next so they usually don't wait to find out,' says Linda, a former sexual assault survivor. Things she has done to protect herself in the past include punching a man to the ground, grabbing a razor that was being used to threaten her and slashing her assailant with it, and disabling a man attempting to choke her with his hands. 'I will do anything I have to to protect myself. I'd rather be judged by twelve than carried by six! When it's either my life or his there can be no room for negotiation – like pleading or being nice on the chance he'll respond. Incapacitate him so you can get away. There are a hundred different ways to do that, I teach them all, and you don't have to be young, agile, strong or fit, anyone can learn if properly taught. The toughest thing for women to overcome is years of being taught to be accommodating and pleasing. In certain situations this attitude has to be completely reversed. You have a perfect right, if your space is invaded and you feel threatened, especially by a stranger, to strike first, ask questions later.'

However, until attitudes towards what is 'appropriate' female behaviour radically change, it may be unrealistic, as well as asking too much of the majority of women, to cultivate both the mental toughness and the physical wherewithal of someone like Linda Ramezy. As research is beginning to indicate, there *are* very significant differences in mentality and self-perception between women who possess the capacity to fight, attack and aggress, physically as well as verbally, and those who cannot or would not dare to react in this way. Not surprisingly, these differences can be traced right back to women's childhood upbringing.

In their earliest studies of women who have resisted and successfully avoided rape, American researchers Pauline Bart and Patricia O'Brien discovered that what distinguishes 'avoiders' from actual victims is their initial reaction of all-consuming rage and indignation at the attacker for even daring to intrude on their space. More importantly, despite often extreme fear, they find themselves able to think clearly and act fast, reacting promptly and assertively, putting up a longer, more vigorous protest and using more varied and imaginative strategies than those who were raped. Even more telling, however, is the background shared by many of the 'avoiders'. Although most were physically active and had studied self-defence, their success in avoiding rape was not solely determined by physique, age or the ability to fight. Interestingly, they were more likely as children to have played a contact sport, like football. As the researchers point out, football teaches women something that every boy knows, but few girls ever learn, that physical contact, including being knocked to the ground, is not necessarily a life-threatening occurrence and need not incapacitate one's physical responses.

Most crucial of all seems to have been these women's early socialization with regards their own anger and aggression. Contrary to the majority of women's experiences, rape avoiders were invariably brought up by parents who encouraged them to take care of themselves at an early age, to stand up to bullies and not give in or seek protection if caught in a fight with other children. Not surprisingly, they grew up to be independent, adept at practical tasks and coping with emergencies, and were able to express anger without any of the guilt or hesitation that inhibits women who were socialized to adhere to traditional behavioural norms. As adolescents, rape avoiders had fewer dreams of marriage, motherhood and domesticity as a sole future ideal, tending instead to look ahead to the challenge of a career, and chose female role models who personified strength and independence.

All of which raises a number of deeply disturbing questions related to the way girls are brought up by their parents and the advice they are later given, as adults, about how best to protect themselves against violence. Such evidence suggests that in pursuing their official line to women about the inherent dangers of acting aggressively, especially when confronted by a potential assailant, the police and other crime prevention advisers may well be rendering women a gross disservice. More than that, by advocating niceness, caution and passivity as opposed to nastiness and aggression, the experts are either displaying extreme ignorance or deliberately flying in the face of some pretty conclusive new evidence to the contrary. For instance, a recent US study conducted by the FBI involving over 2 million female victims of sexual attack showed that those who resisted assault using verbal or physical aggression actually doubled their chances of avoiding rape while not increasing their chances of serious injury. Another recent FBI study consisted of showing convicted muggers and sex attackers a film of mothers collecting their children from school and asking them which women they would be likely to select as easy targets for assault: invariably the men singled out those whose behaviour and appearance indicated the least amount of confidence.

It must be high time, in the light of such findings, that society in general realizes that all those allegedly socially advantageous aspects of feminine behaviour like gentleness, politeness, consideration and the urge to help and conciliate, may, in certain circumstances, prove dangerously counterproductive by signalling that female targets are easy targets. Apart from almost certainly increasing rather than diminishing a woman's chances of victimization, ought we not to face the unpalatable fact that such qualities, by advertising women's helplessness, may also actively encourage rather than deter men's readiness to commit sexual and other violent crimes? Taking a fairly innocuous example, a common feature of obscene phone calls now virtually at epidemic level in Britain is the high incidence of multiple calls made by the offender to the same woman. British Telecom advise women to hang up promptly and without any response, but the police believe that the reason why one man will continue to pester the same victim is the inability of most women to deliver a swift and adequately aggressive rejoinder during the initial encounter.

The most worrying aspect of today's current and highly contagious 'fear wave' that continues to spread, particularly among women living in urban communities, is that it not only strengthens the sense of belonging to a victim culture but, by limiting women's freedom of movement, helps create an impression of even greater powerlessness. By the promotion of such harebrained enterprises as female-only taxi services, female-only trains and buses, or by advising women not to sit near or look at men in railway carriages or in the street, we effectively reinforce, *ad nauseam*, the image of female vulnerability. And if, as seems evident, compliance, fear and passivity are not the predominant qualities women are born with, then it is surely crucial that we make every possible effort, as parents of female infants or as adult women, to trust in – even cultivate – those aggressive instincts that are integral to all human survival. Apparently, however, this is not the direction in which certain authorities wish to see women headed. In striking directly at the heart of our most cherished precepts of what is deemed safe, acceptable female behaviour – safe and acceptable for whom, one might ask – research such as the recent FBI studies seem to have created a furore over how women should best protect themselves.

No prizes for guessing from which sector of the community the noisiest dissent may be heard. A prime example of reactionary bluster comes from Chief Inspector Brian Hewett of the Home Office Crime Prevention Centre, recently shown on TV lecturing police officers on the advice to be given to women for their own safety. Still pursuing the time-honoured tradition of placing the responsibility for reducing the opportunities a man has to commit an assault firmly on the woman, by urging her to act unprovocatively and cautiously, thus restricting her freedom of movement (and elevating her fear level), Hewitt is shown presenting a slide cartoon of a woman in boxing gloves, one foot firmly placed on the chest of a prostrate man. Without a glimmer of humour he asks his audience: 'I don't want female dominance at all. Do you, lads?' When asked about the value of self-defence training, he states guardedly that women should regard it as no more than a pastime 'like pottery or needlework'.

Actually, Inspector Hewitt does have a point, albeit one arrived at unintentionally. So badly taught is the majority of self-defence training, so woefully inadequate in its range of skills, techniques and readiness to run the whole gamut by simulating as realistically as possible the variety of violent situations a woman may find herself in, that their value in fending off or escaping an attacker may be negligible. Where classes are taught exclusively by women this is particularly true.

Hearing Linda Ramezy run through the hypothetical scenarios of assault and self-defence tactics, it is clear how far we women have allowed ourselves to be divorced, not just physically, but also mentally, from our basic survival instincts. Every self-defence teacher will tell you that by far the most difficult tactic to teach women, one from which almost all instinctively and often permanently recoil, is stabbing one's fingers in an assailant's eyes. Teacher Paddy O'Brien says that it is only by posing deeply traumatic hypothetical situations to her students, such as asking them if they would attack an assailant in this manner were he threatening the lives of their children, that they finally admit they would. How many women, especially those already somewhat nervous and tentative about learning self-defence, would feel instantly comfortable about having to confront this catalogue of possible horrors, let alone the no-holds-barred approach Ramezy teaches her students and the uncompromising phraseology with which she does it?

'Women have mostly to learn ground techniques – on the ground is most likely where they're going to end up if attacked. So, I ask what if he pushes you down and he drags you? What do you do? What if he grabs one leg while you're kicking – then what? Or he's trying to smash your head into the ground? That's something a lot of men can't even get out of. I teach what it's like being choked from every conceivable angle, being dragged from all sides in every manner, having your hair pulled in all ways. What can you do to get away if he pins your arms with his knees? Or if he unzips his pants and wants to force *it* in your mouth? If he tries to rape you from behind, how to get out of an anal assault, or incapacitate him even once he's about to penetrate you. There are ways to temporarily disable some-one for long enough to get yourself out of all manner of situ-ations, ways that have nothing to do with being physically strong, fit or sporty. But you have to be taught them properly. Most women are *not* taught properly. Take the blow or grab to a man's groin – something all women learn in defence classes. But they rarely learn it well. You must know exactly *where* to strike. Most think it's about striking the penis. It isn't. It's about getting the balls! When I teach them, I teach how they've got to strike it, kick it, squeeze it, pull it, bite it, yank it, twist it, drag it – put the whole damn thing in the blender! Don't leave nothing. There's no room for hesitation or doubt. When you're through my course, you will be so empowered, your fears and self-image will never be the same again.' And as if to ensure no possibility or room for doubt, she shows me letters and testi-monies from individual women, heads of universities, colleges and educational authorities, for whom Ramezy's courses have proved to be an important first step in trusting their capacity to defend themselves against all forms of harassment and assault, subtle or overt, physical or verbal.

Equal Among Men

Linda Ramezy is one of a rapidly growing number of awesomely 'superstrong' women, some very young, some less so, whose self-confidence seems unassailable and whose assertiveness and sense of self-esteem is inextricably linked to their physical strength and stamina and their ability to match, if not surpass, that of most men of a similar physique and height. By entering professions and sports hitherto firmly off-bounds to women, as for example boxing, arm wrestling, bullfighting, weightlifting, martial arts, the armed services and police units involved in riot control, this evolving breed of what might almost be classified as post-feminist 'warrior women' are proving to be as much an inspiration to young girls representing a uniquely different type of role model as a source of unease and alarm among men. The speed and success with which brawny, 'ballsy' women are making their mark and challenging the *status quo* thankfully show no sign of abating. In 1991 the first women were allowed into the French CSR, armed police units famed and feared for their tendency to resort to extremes of physical restraint against urban demonstrators, and although in 1987 the British Police Federation wanted to withdraw women PCs from front-line duty in riots, violent picketing, football games and pub brawls, today women at the London Metropolitan police training centre in Hendon undertake arduous physical training alongside their male colleagues and can expect no let-up or preferential treatment because of their sex.

And yet the truth remains that the image of a woman trained to use her body as a deadly weapon to fight, attack, even to kill, whether in sport, war or self-defence, is still seen in most realms of society as a sexual anomaly and nothing short of a deadly threat to the established order, a kick in the teeth for society's most cherished images of civilized – and civilizing – womanhood. In spite of the fact that kick boxing, for instance, has become the fastest growing martial art for women in Britain, many of whom graduate from self-defence training to competing in tournaments, and although there are some thirty or forty women boxers currently fighting on the British circuit, undeterred by the Amateur Boxing Association's refusal to recognize women's boxing as a legitimate sport, any mention of a woman pulling a punch is still usually met either with derision or outraged disbelief, from either sex.

Take Bernard Levin's impassioned tirade against a pretty, petite and entirely unaggressive woman called Sue Atkins, whose only crime happens to be a talent for boxing, 'as disgusting a notion' he claims as ever to have heard.

Why do some men, including me, always open a door for a lady, give her our seat on a bus, pick up something she has dropped, refrain from swearing in her presence? ... the battering of the breasts signals something far more deeply shocking than the inevitably seedy surroundings and conditions in which female fighting takes place ... why, then, should they not beat each other to pulp in the boxing ring? Because creation, or evolution, built their bodies, and the purpose of their bodies, differently from those of men. Let Sue Atkins and her kind wait until men give suck and only then put on the gloves.

In her book *On Boxing*, author Joyce Carol Oates is no less vitriolic on the subject of women who undertake the sport, probably reflecting the majority of women's views on this most overtly macho of all activities: 'the female boxer ... cannot be taken seriously – she is parody, she is cartoon, she is monstrous. Had she an ideology, she is likely to be a feminist.'

Although there are many who subscribe to that last theory, the irony is that the majority of women boxers, weightlifters and exceptionally strong sportswomen are certainly not noted for overt feminist sympathies or radical views, tending, in spite of their unconventional activities, to espouse many traditional views on men, marriage and motherhood.

Mercifully, despite the entrenched chauvinism demonstrated

by men like Bernard Levin and Inspector Hewitt (which would be risible were it not taken so seriously by so many) and despite the crippling fear of crime that dominates so many women's lives, out of all proportion to the actual risks, greater numbers of women than ever before are beginning to take the initiative in changing their behaviour and attitudes while toughening up their bodies. And not before time. The received wisdom, that by turning women into fighters and making them more aggressive you destroy their civilizing influence in society and endanger what hopes for peace and harmony remain, possibly raising fatalities and injuries along with the crime rate by provoking further male aggression, is not only so much errant piffle, but is unlikely ever to be substantiated. After all, does a man's capacity to slug a criminal who is threatening his life or the safety of someone close to him make him any less likely to be a loving husband and caring father? Ironically, strong women, because they are aware of their competence and skill in defending themselves and enjoy their positive self-image, seem to be far less likely to behave violently, commit crimes or display unprovoked and misplaced anger and aggression – or, indeed, to condone such behaviour in other women.

Although perfectly capable of delivering a hefty left hook that would knock the average woman or man out cold, British women's lightweight boxing champion (now retired) Sue Atkins, the object of Bernard Levin's ire, confesses disgust at seeing women involved in street or pub brawls. 'It's a sickening spectacle in either sex. I'd never lose control and fight someone out of rage, in public. That's why I believe boxing should not be banned but rather encouraged in boys' schools, as well as girls', because it provides an outlet for energy and aggression and teaches you what skilful sparring and avoiding being hit and injured are all about.'

British kick boxing title holders Ann Holmes and Anne Quinlan, who both began studying martial arts as children, deplore the public image of female boxers as either lesbians or rough, foul-mouthed harridans, fists permanently clenched in readiness for a brawl. That image is one which entirely belies the true skill and artistry of kick boxing, a sport still dismissed simply as a crude variation of street fighting, devoid of rules and technique. Compared to women's boxing, which Britain's Amateur Boxing Association refuses to recognize as a legitimate sport — a shortsighted policy which permits unlicensed matches to take place in which contestants fight without proper rules, hence increasing the risk of injury — Thai boxing and kick boxing, although in many ways more violent and potentially lethal, are governed by strict and precise rules about which parts of the body may be used to kick and punch and where the permissible targets are on an opponent's body, all of which makes for rigorous and disciplined training of both men and women, attracting students who are more likely to be motivated by hard work and perfectionism than aggression.

Anne Quinlan, who began martial arts training at 11 when her application to join a local boys' boxing club was turned down, believes women often reach a far higher standard than the men because they have to work harder in order to be accepted as serious athletes by the men with whom they train. 'We become equal to men when training. There's no preferential treatment, so you feel you are good enough to do anything the boys do. You soon learn this is not for softies! It was what I'd always dreamed of: to be treated and allowed to train as a student, not as a woman. As far as my own determination is concerned, I think I'd gained a tremendous amount of initial confidence, prior to my boxing career, from having knocked down a man in the street who tried to attack me.'

Ann Holmes sees women's presence in boxing, as in most predominantly male sports, as entirely beneficial, since they can invariably be counted on to raise the quality and standard of work all round because of their out and out commitment to hard training and setting themselves ever higher challenges. It is clear that the cachet of breaking chauvinist barriers and being accepted by their male peers is the earliest and toughest challenge a woman in a man's sport has to face — and since acceptance is only accorded to those who demonstrate ability and toughness, it also offers the greatest measure of success.

According to Sue Atkins, becoming accepted proves not only your dedication but the ultimate irrelevance of gender. 'You become just another boxer to them once they see you're serious.' American kick boxing champion Elba 'Cookie' Melendez, 5 foot 4 inches and weighing eight stone, who has fought both women and men, admits her ultimate turn-on is to work out in one of New York's 'hardcore' sleazy all-male gyms on 42nd Street, frequented largely by tough guys from rough neighbourhoods who would be out on the streets mugging and doing drugs were they not hooked on bodybuilding and boxing, and see their attitude change from hostility or contempt to unadulterated admiration and respect. 'Usually, after a few minutes, they can't believe what I'm doing. It blows their minds. They come up and tell me I'm hitting the bag better than a lot of the guys. I've ended up getting nothing but respect and help. You cease being a woman to them and become simply another athlete.'

Kick boxer Lisa Howarth, who began judo training at 12, has no illusions about women as the nobler, less aggressive sex, believing that those women who become proficient at boxing or martial arts often do better than expected in sparring and competitions both because of the indomitable grit needed to overcome men's condescension and hostility as well as an extra mental edge that triggers the will to win. 'They tend to be more aggressive and bitchy towards each other than men when their pride is involved. A man doesn't mind sometimes giving in to another man, he doesn't really believe his basic physical ability will be questioned. But it's different for a woman who is out to prove herself – for her there is usually far more at stake.'

Despite some female boxers' perceptions of themselves as inherently more aggressive than other women, this may be merely wishful thinking, since so far there is no scientific evidence to support such a theory. Dutch psychologist Stephanie Van Goozen recently carried out a number of intriguing experiments designed to measure levels of anger arousal in different groups of women, including those fanatically involved in aggressive sports such as wrestling, kick boxing and rugby and others who practised non-aggressive ones like swimming. Van Goozen and her colleagues at the Institute for Emotion and

Motivation at Amsterdam University's Faculty of Psychology, created a laboratory setting specifically intended to induce anger, irritation and frustration; without being forewarned about the conditions they would experience or informed about the real objective of the study, subjects were confined to an uncomfortably hot and humid room, directed to perform a number of stressful and difficult tasks and subjected to unfriendly treatment. As many as 85 to 90 per cent of the women reported becoming angry, even though unaware that this was the aim of the study.

Yet when broken down into subgroups, the women involved in aggressive sports felt no more anger than their supposedly 'less aggressive' counterparts. Further studies intended to measure the psychological and physiological effects of anger through such indicators as blood pressure and heart rate, facial expressions, vocal intensity and aggressive behaviour also failed to single out the female boxers, rugby players and wrestlers as being in any way more volatile or erratic when experiencing feelings of anger. What intrigued Van Goozen even more, after the experiments had been completed and the data analysed, was the disappointment of her 'high-aggression' sportswomen, who regarded themselves as definitely more aggressive than the average woman in the street. 'They were really extremely disappointed when they heard the experiment had been about measuring levels of aggression, and that they had not proved to be especially aggressive. It ran contrary to everything they believed about themselves.'

As I see it, both Van Goozen's studies, as well as the attitudes and beliefs expressed by some of her subjects whose self-image could be interpreted as 'aggressive', inadvertently reveal two key elements that are central to our understanding of the distinction between aggression and assertiveness in women, yet which researchers in all disciplines from psychology and sociology to biology and chemistry tend habitually to gloss over. One is the degree to which society's continued labelling of certain emotions and behaviour as either wholly and consistently 'good' or 'bad' colours our individual subjective attitudes towards those emotions and behaviour in ourselves. The other is our tendency to confuse what are traditionally regarded as male traits – assertiveness, competitiveness and emotional detachment – with aggression, simply because *all* these seem to contravene accepted female behaviour. To anyone who believes women to be by nature passive or submissive, any behaviour to the contrary will presumably appear idiosyncratic, a deviation from the norm, rather than part of a spectrum of normal behaviour that ranges from passivity at the one end to extreme violence at the other. Aggression, notoriously difficult to define, especially in women, is in the eye of the beholder – which rather echoes the view of that controversial opponent of psychiatry Tomas Szasz, that there is no such thing as madness, only behaviour which is deemed socially unacceptable by the world at large.

Thus it seems that Van Goozen's kick boxers and wrestlers may well have convinced themselves that they were aggressive by the standards of more conventional female behaviour, when actually all they really are is more confident, authoritative, outspoken and physically strong than many of their contemporaries. Falling into the trap of confusing aggression with assertiveness – and erroneously regarding anger as the inevitable wellspring of aggression, an emotion thus likely only ever to produce unwelcome, destructive effects – is something of which even the most self-confident women are capable. Such is society's ambivalence about female dominance and power that studies continue to indicate to what extent very assertive women are criticized by both sexes – but overwhelmingly by other women – for being pushy, unattractive (by conventional standards), threatening and aggressive. Could it be that reluctance to invite any such 'negative' labelling continues to hold back many women from developing their fullest potential for constructive or positive aggression?

If this is indeed the case, then it is depressing to speculate how much those women who allow themselves to be trapped by convention or handicapped by fear and doubt may be missing in terms of personal power and control over their lives. Despite the evident mixture of relish and pride Linda Ramezy takes in telling you how she herself has fought or wisemouthed her way out of situations of seemingly inescapable danger, the overall impression she gives is of deep inner balance and calm, almost charismatic self-possession. 'I am immensely powerful, unbelievably invincible, and because of that, more relaxed than at any other time in my life. [She began studying ju-jitsu in her late thirties.] Everything I teach is what I myself learned through trial and error. Working with men: I hit them a certain way, and they drop, so I know it works. In fact I am now *more afraid* of fighting than I am of being fought, because I know what I have in my power to do to someone.'

This apparent paradox underlines two of the most crucial factors distinguishing very strong women who have consciously trained their bodies and minds to exceptional levels of efficiency from those who are merely aggressive and angry, spoiling for a fight or an opportunity for some displaced violent outburst arising from an anger whose basic cause is habitually ill-identified. One such factor is control. It is as if by developing a sense of being in control of what might, to other women, be regarded as stressful, fear-inducing, menacing situations, that the very assertive and physically capable woman also manages to control to a large degree any potentially disabling, counter-productive feelings that threaten to overwhelm her. The other is insight. Dangerous or aggressive as they may appear to the outside world, women who box, wrestle, lift heavy weights or practise martial arts to an advanced standard are forced to recognize and identify their anger essentially through locating its precise source, as well as to find the least destructive yet also sufficiently self-satisfying way in which to express or dissipate it, if they are to avoid wreaking untold damage against themselves and their opponents. With the capacity for attacking, injuring, even for killing, comes the realization of responsibility for those powers – a reckoning that is particularly acute for women since, unlike men, few grow up accepting that brute strength and the capacity for fighting and injuring are a natural, even an optional, part of their existence.

Also, it is precisely because of the confidence and self-worth that comes with immense physical strength and capability that the need to act aggressively or to prove her toughness is so much less for a woman. Unlike men who often experience their sporting or athletic prowess as an extension of the aggression-orientated macho culture they inhabit in the world outside, adding to their status among the lads in the pub or changing room, women, once a fight or competition is over, usually feel little urge or compulsion to flaunt their strength outside the realms of their sport.

It appears that the process of becoming physically powerful and being able to demonstrate, quantify and repeatedly test and prove one's strength, in itself provides many women with the building blocks for the creation and reinforcement of self-esteem and self-confidence. Physical endeavour in the end may provide the catalyst that finally leads to the resolution of inner conflicts and the banishment of life-long feelings of powerlessness and frailty. In some ways what this amounts to is a reverse form of psychotherapy, working on the psyche from the outside in.

Looking back on her sickly adolescence, marked by memories of rejection, lack of confidence and a long period of anorexia during which she nearly died and was finally hospitalized at five and a half stone, there is nothing in Katherine Monbiot's background that suggests why or how, at 27, she should be voted the world's sixth strongest woman at an international event in Japan or become Britain's champion arm wrestler, often working against men to improve her strength. 'For me, the experience of having been weak and helpless through anorexia meant I had to prove something by going entirely the other way. The confidence I gained having proved my strength in arm wrestling and weight training eventually made it safer for me to express my femininity. It's OK to be softer once you've shown publicly that you can be hard.'

By her own admission the residual anger, much of it against her parents for first sending her away to boarding school at a young age and later on for sending her to hospital to be forcibly fed, has in part been dissipated through physical exertion and what remains has usefully fuelled her physical endeavours. 'At first I was really very shocked, just before my first big international competition, at this huge surge of anger that welled up. I thought, God, where's *that* coming from? It's a peculiar feeling but it's a good feeling too. It's very much part of the adrenalin kick, which always makes one feel great. Maybe it's stuff that's there in all of us but most of us can't express it in our everyday lives. This sort of activity is a way to deal with anger and frustration in an acceptable way.'

Just as for male athletes, there are some unexpected dangers and temptations. Women who compete in very rigorous, high-aggression sports, or those who play contact sports, soon come to learn that while some anger may enhance performance, all too often if triggered at the wrong time or in excess, apart from causing injuries, it may destroy the capacity to perform well. Predictably, the 'killers' in sports, be they male or female, are those who have been tempted to boost their muscle bulk and power by taking steroid drugs. For former British champion bodybuilder Zoe Warwicke, taking body-building drugs may have made the title easier to win but, as she later confessed in a *Guardian* interview, it was at the devastating cost of becoming consumed and depleted by constant, round-the-clock steroid induced animal fury – what athletes refer to as 'roid' rage. 'My sexual organs grew six times bigger. I lost my boobs. Got a square chin, a deep voice and an Adam's apple. I went to sleep with anger, woke with anger – like a drug-induced white rage. It's all right being a tomboy through your own choice – but this was alienating me from my own sex.'

Certainly, as growing numbers of women enter top-level athletics, the spectre of steroid-linked aggression is something which needs to be addressed very seriously by athletes, trainers and doctors alike. Although the secrecy shrouding drug abuse is such that few studies of the effects of anabolic steroids in men, let alone in women, have so far been conducted, one 1985 study involving ten weight-trained women athletes revealed that apart from developing such side effects as facial hair and a deeper voice, eight women noted increased aggressiveness, which in part proved beneficial because it enhanced their drive to practise and compete, but which also caused an unacceptable number of problems in their relationships with colleagues and family.

With growing recognition and concern about the link between anabolic steroid use and aggressive, violent behaviour, one can only hope that the myths surrounding the purported 'masculinizing' effects of sport on women will be placed in their limited and proper context – which means the context of drug use only.

Zoe Warwicke won the championship in 1985, and came clean about her steroid abuse in 1988. Looking back on an interview I did with her in 1983 when she was 23, had been training for ten years and was obviously gearing up for the big time, it is fascinating, with hindsight, to pinpoint the comments and views she held then, reflecting an attitude some sports psychologists might identify as an early warning of a woman becoming too dangerously 'high' on her strong-woman image for her own good, too addicted to winning, at any cost.

'You've got to be prepared to go to hell and back again,' Warwicke impressed upon me, detailing with zealous fervour the punishing training regime and endless permutations of weight training necessary to obtain the desired cut, bulk, rip and tuck of the various muscle groups. 'It's not a pussyfooting job, it's deadly serious. It becomes like a natural drug, your self-esteem becomes huge. You're the ultimate woman walking around. It's not about looking like a man, that's not what women weightlifters are about. It's about trying to attain our ideal body image.'

It wasn't until the end of our talk that she mentioned something which I now see as a vital clue as to how a talented, hardworking girl, obviously passionately committed to a sport she loved, became too obsessive and too determined to win at any costs, with the disastrous results she later described. 'In the beginning I took up training because of how I was treated. At school I was small and skinny and got picked on by a big-busted bully! I started weight training and was never a victim again.' What these remarks seem to reflect is the tragedy that can result when a woman, consciously or unconsciously, uses her body's strength (as does a compulsive slimming fanatic) as a defence armour or carapace against inner feelings of inadequacy, guilt or anger. When self-image, as in Warwicke's case, becomes inextricably linked to and dependent on performance and winning, with greater energies invested in the outcome rather than the actual playing or practice of sport, then what invariably results is the swapping of one set of emotional problems for other psychological frailties, such as the inability to concede defeat or recognize personal limitations. Such enslavement to unrealistic and unattainable goals is *not* part of the recipe for equality or happiness.

Despite such pitfalls, women are now excelling in virtually every area of previously male-dominated endeavour. Even in a traditionally repressive, religious country like Spain, where women's sexual and social liberation is a very recent phenomenon, the braggadocio displayed by today's young women determined to enjoy the same freedoms, recognition and power as the most macho of men – as for example in the bullring – shows just how speedily centuries of conditioning can be overcome when the opportunities exist. To a leading 'torera' like Christina Sánchez de Pablos, Spain's glamorous 20-year-old prima donna of the corrida, there is no shame, doubt or squeamishness about being a killer, one who kills frequently in her case, totalling an average of fifty or more bulls per year, and who gets well paid and fêted for it. 'When I kill well – which means the bull dies immediately – I feel immensely good. I have shown that I have the strength, the courage, everything a man has to have, to excel as a bullfighter.' The Paris-based Brigitte Bardot Foundation for animal welfare has publicly condemned women bullfighters as a disgrace to their gender, claiming that 'if a woman's qualities of softness, love and tenderness become those of violence, brutality and force, we have much to fear for the future.'

But then bullfighters, male or female, do not regard this as a violent or brutal activity. Women, like men, are quick to adopt the erotic poetry of seduction and power peculiar to Latin machismo, bordering on the sado-masochistic, used to celebrate bullfighting as a genre of art. Another 20-year-old torera, Laura Valencia, speaks in quasi-mystical, macho-erotic terms of killing as the artist's signature on a masterpiece: 'It's the final confirmation of one's creation. I feel very proud. For most people, the greatest thing for a woman to do is to give birth to a child. For me the most important thing is to walk in a circle around the ring, holding my trophy, the ears cut from the bull I have just killed.'

With increasing numbers of women describing their new-found freedoms and strengths in such uncompromisingly aggressive, yet at the same time, joyous terms, one wonders for how much longer competition can continue to be classified by some women as a feminist taboo and aggression or the desire for power condemned as an essentially male and therefore ignoble and reprehensible demerit?

So what of the much vaunted physical dangers facing women who become involved in such rough sports? As sports writer Adrianne Blue has pointed out, men's greater weight, speed and power, as well as their anatomy, make them just as, if not more, likely to sustain serious injuries in all contact sports. Compared to women's reproductive organs, protected by a hard bony casing, strong ligaments and musculature, the male genitalia are a 'sitting duck' inviting pain and injury. Women who box generally wear reinforced protective breast shields, and there have been no reports of serious injuries other than fractured wrists and elbows, broken or bloodied noses, cut lips and eyelids – which may well make the average male blanch, but are insignificant compared to the horrific injuries that are only possible when men with the power and build of Frank Bruno or Gary Mason set about smashing and beating one another to pulp over twelve rounds, compared to women's modest three.

As 'Cookie' Melendez sees it, there is an inherent contradiction in the argument that women shouldn't fight or box because of the risk of disfigurement or injury. 'What people don't see, or don't want to see, is that the chances of a woman who can't defend herself getting beaten up, disfigured, maybe killed out in the streets by an attacker are greater – so where's the logic?' It's a good point.

The Double Standard

To succeed, as have women like Melendez, Monbiot and Atkins, takes brawn – but what else? What are the requisite qualities for breaking permanently free of constraints, unlearning once and for all centuries of conditioning, to overcome the opprobrium and censure invited by striving to become more 'like a man'? Are such women born naturally possessing qualities such as competitiveness and the need for regular 'highs' derived through physical risk and stimulus, qualities waiting to be developed within a challenging environment? Or, on the contrary, is it through the act of striving against adversity to gain access to territories created, proprietorially guarded and monopolized by men, that those women experienced a catharsis which led to true empowerment?

The answer is almost certainly a mixture of both. That our culture and, more specifically, the hitherto 'closed' male world of sport does not welcome or approve of women muscling in on this terrain is obvious to anyone who has talked to or observed the experiences of women who *do* excel in that world. There remains a persistent belief that 'real' women are neither physically nor psychologically equipped to succeed at certain sports to the same degree as men and that the risks of extreme injury are prohibitively high. From her earliest school days, throughout adolescence and into adulthood, the average girl in most developed countries can still expect to meet opposition, discrimination or incomprehension if she wishes to play rough and tumble contact sports such as football, especially if she wants to play with boys, or race against them in track events for stiffer competition, or tries to join a boxing club, or hopes to compete in such events as the triple jump, pole vault or hammer, all of which remain exclusively male events at the World Olympics. This discrimination endures not only because the activities themselves are perceived as masculine, too physically taxing and dangerous for women's inferior strength, but also because some of the dominant mental and behavioural qualities needed to pursue them are simply not congruent with stereotypical views of womanhood – ideal womanhood, to be precise. Therein almost certainly lies the crux of the problem, the criteria by which women are judged when they enter 'hard' sports being both unjust and false.

For a woman to develop a passionate dedication to such activities as say, boxing, mountaineering, bullfighting or martial arts, she must be in some way 'addicted' or, to be more precise, increasingly compelled to seek out the thrills, satisfaction, challenge, sense of pride and triumph afforded by successful participation in her chosen sport. These are the women who conform to the so-called 'Type-T' personality identified by University of Wisconsin psychologist Frank Farley, who defines such individuals by their unusually strong need for excitement, thrills and risk-taking, which in men tends to manifest itself through the pursuit of physical adventure, in women through mental challenge. However, with increased female participation in 'male' sports and pursuits, Farley foresees the likelihood of ever more 'physical' Type-T self-expression in women. What such women demonstrate is a tendency to express and define their personalities through initiating action and 'doing' – deemed masculine traits – rather than through reacting and 'being' – seen as quintessentially female qualities.

Yet, despite Frank Farley's utterly plausible assertion, to many an outside observer the amount of ruthlessness, isolation, self-will, bossiness, stoicism, aggression, even arrogance, let alone the calculated risk-taking needed to stay the course in high-danger, physically punitive sports, still appears irreconcilable with the accepted womanly qualities of caring, unselfishness, social responsibility and emotional stability. The notion of a woman who either lives as a loner, solely for her sport, or puts her family and personal life second to the fulfilment she craves from scaling the Himalayas, fording rapids, lifting weights, fighting and killing bulls or sparring with fellow humans is still likely to be seen as irresponsibly driven to risk life and limb to satisfy her own selfish desires. If she has no personal life, is childless and lives alone, she will often be dismissed as a pathetic oddity. As a wife and mother, the 'career-adventuress' automatically becomes a moral reprobate, incurring odium for neglecting her family's welfare while threatening her children with the possibility of having to grow up as orphans – an accusation constantly levelled at mothers who work in the armed services and volunteer for high-risk positions in the front line at times of war.

Fair comment, one might say, and perhaps valid enough in the case of mothers with young children. But no prizes for spotting the double standard. Such arguments carry – or should carry – just as much weight and legitimacy in the case of married men and fathers who undertake hazardous hobbies and professions, including the armed forces. The real truth, as always emerges when moralists argue against the right of women, especially wives and mothers, to engage in active combat in the armed forces, is that the idea of a woman being free to explore, develop and define her identity and attain fulfilment outside or alongside the sphere of domestic relationships remains deeply unsettling, even threatening, to society as a whole. We talk of a woman being 'possessed' or 'driven' to such extremes as if manipulated by forces outside her control, which from the experiences of female soldiers, pilots, etc., we know is patently untrue. And the uncomfortable truth remains that as long as we persist in defining such women as radically different, nonconformist 'heroines' who attract special attention and awe precisely *because* of their sex, then we continue to reinforce, whether explicitly or implicitly, traditional notions of womanhood as the invaluable emollient and everlasting super glue that binds our social fabric.

Whether mothers should be allowed, let alone encouraged, to go off to war has, especially since the Gulf War, become one of the most emotive, hotly disputed issues involving the equality of women. Journalist Sally Quinn of the *Washington Post* has described it as an example of 'feminism gone awry' to which Democratic congresswoman Pat Schroeder, an ardent advocate of women's right to equal opportunities within the services, retorted that if the *Post* had sent Quinn to cover the war 'she would have tried to get a Pulitzer Prize and would have had a fit if someone said, "You should stay home, you have small children"'. As Schroeder has also pointed out, no one pats men on the head and asks whether they feel bad that they aren't at home with the family – which undeniably many do.

Ironically, despite the furore over women as combatants, in America public opinion is remarkably in favour of full female participation in war. In a nationwide poll conducted just before the Gulf War began, 52 per cent of respondents agreed that women in Saudi Arabia should be involved in the fighting, although this declined to 47 per cent once the war had started. A survey conducted by the women's magazine *McCalls*, less noted for its militant feminist sympathies than for its endorsement of Middle American values, found that four out of five (84 per cent) of women questioned agreed that women should fight in the war – a 5 per cent higher approval rate compared to the previous year's poll. Broken down, the figures are even more telling: 66 per cent of mothers with daughters said they would not oppose their daughters going into combat and a significant 44 per cent said they themselves would be prepared to fight, while nearly all those questioned felt strongly that a woman in the armed forces, regardless of whether she is a mother or not, should have the same rights and responsibilities as her male counterparts.

What the involvement of 34,000 American women troops (out of 540,000) in Operation Desert Storm helped establish with demonstrable finality is how razor-thin and artificial is the putative dividing line between support and combat roles, safe areas and danger zones, making a mockery out of the ethic of chivalry that bars women from combat for their own protection. The truth is that once deployed in any part of a war zone, whether as a nurse, police officer, radio operator in predominantly civilian areas or as a support worker for combat units, piloting helicopters, driving tanks or trucks to deliver and unload ammunition, ferrying supplies or individuals from allegedly 'safe' to 'unsafe' territory, women are just as likely as men to be hit, injured or killed by enemy fire. As we saw from news coverage of events, the frequent targeting by enemy forces of command headquarters and supply functions away from the front line makes an absurd charade of the policy of concentrating women in those positions for reasons of safety. As Pat Schroeder remarked: 'The Persian Gulf helped collapse the whole chivalrous notion that women could keep out of danger in the war. We saw that the theatre of operations had no strict combat zone, that Scud missiles were not gender-specific – they could hit both sexes, and unfortunately they did.'

The spectre of seeing women's bodies blown to bloody smith-ereens on our TV screens, of wives, daughters, girlfriends, sisters and mothers being shipped home in body bags, was always the bottom line of most people's opposition to full female partici-pation in war. Yet the fact that society's outrage does not extend equally to the massacre of young men or, more to the point, civilian casualties including women, children, babies, the elderly and infirm, indicates the speciousness and hypocrisy of that particular argument. Equally hypocritical is the uproar over sending women off to a possible 'fate worse than death' – some-thing which, again, seems to worry men far more than women.

What is striking but perhaps not altogether surprising is how rarely women's experiences of serving in the Gulf in the most dangerous of circumstances – including injury, capture, torture and rape – in any way fits in with men's expectations of how incapacitated a female would become as a result of such traumas. What we have is another more extreme version of the argument concerning those other familiar bogeys, PMT and menstruation, which men continually refer to as major obstacles to women's efficiency despite the fact that professional women whose jobs depend on physical stamina, fast reflexes and acuity of mind rarely if ever experience themselves as being at the mercy of their monthly rhythms and cycles. Indeed, that women's judgement, their physical and mental reactions are on average unaffected by hormonal flux is a proven medical fact. Clearly, it is the men who have the biggest problem in accom-modating to the idea of women in battle – not the women themselves.

The revelation, made over a year after the Gulf War ended, that one of the women soldiers captured by the Iraqis had been subjected to a brutal sexual assault, despite being severely injured after her helicopter crashed in enemy territory, made spectacular headline news. Giving evidence in June 1992 at a US Presidential Commission on the role of women in the mili-tary, Major Rhonda Cornum, mother of a 15-year-old daughter, decorated with three bravery medals, sent shockwaves around the world with her statement that, 'Being raped by the enemy should be considered an occupational hazard of going to war.' Which, roughly translated, means: 'Fuck you, chauvinist Pentagon pigs – what right do you think you have to dictate to women what control they have over their bodies?'

Undoubtedly, incidents such as rape of female soldiers are more likely to become part of the already unthinkable obscenity of war. Another American PoW, Melissa Rathbun-Nealy, who was injured and captured by Iraqi troops when her truck came under fire near the Saudi–Kuwaiti border, admitted after her release to having been viciously kicked and beaten while in captivity. Yet there is little sign that women such as these ever went into the services expecting an easy ride. If men ever had illusions about captured women soldiers being treated more leniently or chivalrously, now is the time for them to be shattered. And if, as has been suggested, women should be discouraged from active service on the grounds that if captured alongside male colleagues the sound of their distress while suffering possible assault or torture in captivity would be unbearably traumatic and demoralizing for the men in neighbouring cells, one's only reaction can surely be that this is a problem the men must learn to sort out for themselves.

The claim that by allowing women to fight on equal terms with men you risk undermining military traditions of discipline, male solidarity and cohesion, not to mention the danger of romantic and sexual involvement that might endanger the efficient smooth functioning of a troop or regiment, is seen by the pro-women's lobby as simply an excuse to divert attention away from the real issue: men's reluctance to allow women access to senior, prestigious, well-paid positions in the military. Let's not forget that this remains, after all, the last bastion of old-brass male supremacy.

In an interview just a few days before she was killed when her helicopter flew into power lines, Major Marie Rossi observed that: 'Sometimes you have to dissociate how you feel personally about the prospect of going into war. But personally as an aviator and a soldier, this is the moment that everybody trains for

– that I've trained for – so I feel ready to meet a challenge.' Rossi was an experienced pilot who flew dozens of supply missions to advancing divisions in Iraq and was one of the first American officers to cross into enemy territory when the ground assault began; her humility and courage typically represent the attitude of many of her female colleagues. 'What I am doing is no greater or less than the man who is flying next to me. I think if you talk to the women who are professionals in the military, we see ourselves as soldiers.'

And if some women in the military give the impression of arrogance, emotional coldness, even hardness, should we really be unduly upset or mystified? Who ever criticized a man for controlling his emotions or retreating into himself in order to focus his attention and energies entirely on the rigorous task at hand, or for being bossy and dominating in the line of duty? Sergeant Theresa Lynn Treloar, whose job as head of a twenty-three-man one-woman team in the US army brought her closer than any woman to the front lines in the Gulf, was notoriously nicknamed the Ice Lady for her confidence and efficiency. Yet she rightly dismisses such labels as unavoidable for a competent woman in her position. 'A female in an all-male unit is creating a pattern. I was given the opportunity to turn this job down. I chose this and I knew what I was getting into.' Her superior, Captain Michael Mendell, paid her the ultimate compliment by stating: 'She is the only woman I know who carries an M-16 rifle, a light anti-tank weapon, an AT-4 and grenade. I would trust her to cover my back in any situation.' Yet Sergeant Treloar is aware that her career has been hindered by her sex. Some male soldiers are quick to judge her because she is a woman, and her professionalism is often mistaken for coldness. Conversely, when a woman displays legitimate signs of anger, as when another person fails to carry out a task efficiently or promptly, this may be interpreted as female emotionalism.

What many men have yet to accept is the degree of professionalism and pride that women can bring to dangerous and responsible jobs in the military. Talking about the night when Iraqi Scud missiles were headed for the base where she had been posted as head of a Patriot missile platoon, Lieutenant

Phoebe Jeter remembers the initial shock at realizing that she was responsible for firing US missiles in defence. Taking that responsibility head-on, she triumphed, ordering thirteen Patriots to be fired and destroying at least two Scuds, thus becoming the first and only woman to shoot down a Scud and winning an Army Commendation Medal. Having initially joined the army for 'some adventure' she then made an infinitely more valuable discovery about herself: 'I learned I could do *anything* that I want to.'

The Final Frontiers

In the same way that vast numbers of women now expect to define themselves through their work, so they must be able to claim as their inalienable right the freedom to test and hazard their bodies not only for pure sensory fulfilment but as a means of expressing personal identity, in the same way that men have striven to since time immemorial. Far from being out of control and at the mercy of random external or neurotic forces, the single factor that most distinguishes the superstrong or 'warrior' woman is her determination and ability to develop control over her fears, doubts and her physical responses as well as over environmental factors.

Indeed, it is the very process of developing this control that seems to be one of the chief liberating experiences for such women. In the view of Debbie Koehn, American mountaineer, sailor, skier and adventurer, married with one young child, who is the first woman to first climb, then ski down a number of South American peaks, the ultimate liberation comes from working through potentially disabling fears and doubts. 'I've come through the other side of fear to success. That feeling transfers to everything in my life. It's an important aspect of developing my being.' That isn't to deny the ever-present existence of sometimes life-threatening danger in her activities. 'But at least I'm in control,' she says. 'My life is not in the hands of someone else – a pilot, a driver, some government, or another external force. If something goes wrong it's me. I feel very whole about that.'

For a woman who, like the majority of her sex, until very recently was conditioned by parental influence as well as by society's dictates to accept her powerlessness and lack of control over her actions and destiny as normal and irreversible, the sense of liberation and autonomy experienced by going so far beyond the bounds of permissible female endeavour may prove the ultimate in self-empowerment.

Take the background of one such 'heroine', the 32-year-old French mountaineer Catherine Destivelle, who in 1991 was the first climber ever to open up a route on the unconquered south-west face of the Dru. Introduced as a young child by her father to the challenge of rock climbing, by 16 she had already achieved considerable success at tackling the Alps. Interestingly, the need for danger, for testing her limits, diverted her temporarily – as it does many young men – into a rough, clandestine world of gambling, smoking, heavy drinking, late nights, poker playing and general debauchery, which she admits led eventually to physical and mental burnout. 'I gambled all night long in Paris . . . I smoked a lot and destroyed my body and only slept for three hours at night,' she recalls. A few years later, however, 'La Grande Catherine', as she is dubbed by her compatriots, had regained control of her impulses and health, going on to become the world's most successful female freestyle climber. Although renowned when very young for her delight in overtaking men on difficult ascents, the key to her strength and success, as is the case with so many mentally tough and physically competent women, is her reluctance to join groups, teams or partnerships, preferring instead the rigours of the lone life. Perhaps it is that mental incisiveness, cold, accurate and deadly as an ice-pick, that seems more chilling in a woman than in a man. 'There are boys who dream of doing what I do but mentally they don't have what it takes,' comments Destivelle. 'I armour myself to think only about how to go forward. I tell myself I am a climbing machine.'

Such iron will and disciplined control does not come without a strong underlying streak of ruthless self-interest. But whether this is greater than the steely singleness of purpose and the manipulative powers a career-orientated woman, or man, might

show in climbing to power within politics or a corporate institution is debatable. The only difference is that the rewards
adventuring women describe are harder for most of us to identify with since they are not based on financial or hierarchical
values but concerned with an altogether more visceral – almost
primal – feedback, a constant challenge to and affirmation of
being alive. Why should we be surprised to hear that another
legend in mountaineering, the late Wanda Rutkiewicz, who
died while driving herself to the edge of human endurance
during the final push to the summit of Kanchenjunga, the
world's third highest peak, used to alienate fellow climbers with
her domineering, arrogant attitude and determination not to
allow the death of colleagues on an expedition to deter her from
climbing on, regardless? Without such single-mindedness and
absence of sentimentality – a quality too often mistaken for
human feeling – could she have become a legend among climbers, still fearless and fiercely heroic until her death at 49, the
first woman to conquer K2, the third to climb Everest, or make
twenty-two expeditions in seventeen years, ascending eight of
the world's fourteen highest peaks, an achievement she shared
with just thirteen men? I believe almost certainly not.

American pilot Grace McGuire talks of having worked seven
days a week, often foregoing food and sleep, to prepare for a
round-the-world flight intended to recreate the route pioneered
by Amelia Earhart, and she admits the project has 'destroyed
everything'. When she says, 'I have no social life, I eat, sleep
and breathe this project,' should we regard her as any more
ruthlessly obsessive about her work than Margaret Thatcher –
or, come to that, Mother Teresa? Should we not envy and cheer
a woman who can claim, 'I'm not happy if I'm not fighting for
my life. It sounds mad, but it's true. I'm not happy unless I'm
roughing it and in control'? It must be worth questioning
whether it is the woman with her eye on a seat on the board
or the woman plotting her next ascent up some as yet unscaled
Himalayan peak who is destined ultimately to reap the more
treasured and enduring reward – and who will be forced to give
up or compromise least of her spirit and integrity in doing so.

*   *   *

Women are nearly at the point of acceptance. Nearly — but not quite. Nor will they fully succeed until society's attitudes change and the media's depiction of strong, angry, aggressive, powerful women as in some way freakish alters in their favour. As with so many undigested half-truths and erroneous beliefs concerning matters related to health, body chemistry and psychology of the sexes, the dual-edged concept that athletics and 'male' pursuits masculinize women and, the corollary, that only unfeminine women take them up seriously in the first place, still seems cast in stone.

Why else are women in sport still generally criticized, even derided, for appearing 'butch' or behaving in an unacceptably aggressive manner when similar behaviour by a male athlete would evoke no response at all, let alone attract the sort of tongue-clicking indignation the public appears to revel in? Consider the shockwaves caused among sports commentators by tennis star Monica Seles's habit of grunting on the court, accompanied during Wimbledon fortnight by unflattering press photos of Seles's snarling expression and lengthy discourses on the acceptability of such off-puttingly provocative behaviour. One can only wonder whether a grunting Boris Becker or Stefan Edberg would have elicited so much agitated comment or conjecture. Almost certainly not. Yet the rather depressing message implicit in media images and comments on female athletes is that it's fine to excel and win, but only if done in a ladylike manner. No sweat, no signs of aggression, no butch grimacing, no messy or mannish haircuts and, above all, no rippling muscles, please. What clearer illustration exists than in the world of tennis where, although women have a high profile and a relatively long history of success, suspicion and ridicule are still aroused by those failing to conform to conventional stereotypes? Any suggestion of 'brute' strength or lesbianism is above all calculated to provoke attacks of the most hurtful and personal nature, such as Auberon Waugh's vitriolic outburst in the *Spectator* some years ago:

Perhaps she would have grasped at least part of the reason [why the crowds allegedly don't love her] if she had been able to watch herself play against the deliciously pretty Miss Gabriela Sabatini, from Argentina, at Wimbledon on Thursday's television. The sad and beastly truth, for all to see, is that Ms Navratilova, through no fault of her own, is extremely ugly . . . ugly women have to be really exceptionally pleasant to be loved . . . ugly women (like very small men) are often bitter, aggressive and chippy . . . a significant number of these bitter malevolent women have adopted lesbianism as their cause . . . I wonder if Ms Navratilova's failure to be loved by the crowds has anything to do with her self-proclaimed lesbianism?

Quite apart from its needless savagery, it is difficult to determine which aspect of this offensive diatribe is the more startling: the personalized hatchet-job and, by implication, the deprecation of all women who fail to conform to narrow, set standards of attractiveness or the fallacious claim that Navratilova lacks crowd-appeal. Anyone with any grain of knowledge about tennis can testify to the howling falsity of that statement.

In a nutshell we there have a neat summing up, albeit in extreme form, of what many men find most disturbing about women in sport: their usually powerful physique, their sweatiness, dishevelled hair (or short, boyish styles chosen for practicality), their fighting spirit − grunts and all − and, most of all, their developed muscles. No other quality is more calculated to upset sensibilities and arouse controversy than female musculature. Muscle development, or its lack, is without doubt the single major and most emotive criterion by which society's perception of 'real' femininity is finally judged. Understand this and you begin to understand the basis of the near-primitive reactions, ranging from horror and repulsion to patronizing amusement, that fulminate in the breasts of so many non-athletic men and women when confronted with images of powerful female athletes in whom the wondrous machinery that powers their victories is clearly on display. There can be little question that the world views the physiques of women like Fatima Whitbread, Florence Griffith-Joyner and Tessa Sanderson, not to mention champion bodybuilders and weightlifters, with awe, certainly, but awe usually tinged with revulsion or pity or both. Rare is the man, or woman, who would honestly and wholeheartedly endorse journalist Simon Barnes's eulogy in *The Times* to female Olympic athleticism:

> But there was one more hope and inspiration to the Games: perhaps the hero I have been looking for throughout the enthralling fortnight in Barcelona – Hassiba Boulmerka . . . It was a performance that radiated strength. It was, somehow, a performance of particular physicality. Some athletes glide across the track and seem scarcely to touch the ground: Boulmerka muscled her way through the air, shouldering the stuff aside and hammering her way around the stadium. She radiated physical and mental strength. Eyes blazing, biceps pumping, she ran as if she were squashing myths and archetypes with every stride . . . I would like to add my own cheers: for Africa, and for women.

It is impossible to escape the delightful irony of not a poet, not a feminist, but a Fleet Street journalist, normally the most archetypal specimen of chauvinism, being so overwhelmingly enthralled by the awesome magnificence of an evidently powerful woman. The more glorification and idealization there is by the media of women like Boulmerka and the more women there are with the guts and grit to emulate this alternative vision of womanhood, the sooner we will be able to claim, finally and with confidence, to have become our own women. Free for the first time ever from the tyranny of biology. For ever – and irrevocably.

377

Afterword

We cannot claim yet to have reached the stage where female aggression has ceased to make banner headlines and no longer provokes outraged incomprehension and divisive, ill-informed debate. Yet if not now, that day must come in the not too distant future. Given that this can only occur once destructive, criminal or anti-social behaviour by women is accepted as relatively commonplace – not to be condoned or excused but understood as a reflection of one aspect of women's normal range of experience and self-expression – this might sound like a perverse, even irresponsible vision of the future. Until such a time, however, there is no mistaking the freakshow element that attaches to each publicized episode of female violence, with 'masculine' traits such as anger, rage, hostility, dominance and destructiveness summarily condemned as unnatural, and especially chilling when they occur in women. During the writing of this book there has been a marked increase in the number of incidents involving women's violence as reported by the press, including a growing tendency among journalists, male and female, to disclose in shocked disbelief their own experiences of being mugged, threatened, robbed or physically assaulted and their property vandalized by delinquent, sometimes crack-addicted females operating singly or in gangs. Meanwhile, claims that violent crime by women has escalated to unprecedented levels in a relatively short time – the latest figures given are a 250 per cent rise since 1973 – and 12 per cent in 1993 alone – continue to be conspicuous not just for their implied dark prophecy of a world devoid of the female qualities of compassion and care, but for their notable absence of any attempt to explain this development by placing it within a balanced socio-economic perspective.

The most depressing aspect of the rising moral panic over

female violence is that it is non-violent, unassertive, law-abiding women who often have the most to lose when those who are aggressive or transgress the accepted female role are caught in the firing line of vituperative hysteria. This much has become painfully evident to me while researching this book. We are, after all, still only talking about a small, if steadily increasing, number of women who exhibit recognizably violent behaviour. Men still remain the chief perpetrators of violence, especially in its grossest forms, and it is women who are frequently at the receiving end – often because they remain too timid, too passive, too frightened by their own habitually suppressed aggressive impulses to imagine any alternative to being a victim, largely through social conditioning and early upbringing. It is women like these, who remain most susceptible to society's prejudices and primitive beliefs, who continue to experience the most irreducible stress and major conflict when it comes to acknowledging, understanding and expressing any impulse arising from the unmentionable dark nether zone of their psyche. In that the apparent increase in crimes of violence by women is now becoming one of the most important and explosive areas of social debate – frequently sparked through the outcry over juvenile crime, in which girls increasingly participate – one must fervently hope that interest in the topic may eventually cease to hold mere novelty value. Only then will we progress beyond the tired old question of whether post-feminist women are 'turning' more aggressive, and why, and turn our minds instead to the most significant question of all: how this complex, inherently normal, human mechanism has managed until now to remain so well controlled, suppressed, sublimated or denied by the great majority of women, often at quite appalling and devastating cost to their personal lives and psychological equilibrium.

Since, as I have tried to establish, female aggression as a force of nature is neither new nor aberrant – to interpret women's increased violence, lawlessness and aggression as evidence of dysfunctional biology is to confuse opportunity with pathology and mistake adaptation for aberration – it must become increasingly obvious that for the first time in history, as women stride out into the hitherto exclusively male-dominated world, participating as equals in all spheres of life, so the need and opportunity for them to marshal their existing potential for what was until recently deemed unfeminine and hence unnatural behaviour must increase. The problem with criticizing Margaret Thatcher, as many do, for her iron-clad megalomaniacal style on the grounds that she was too much like a man is that it ignores the more crucial issue of whether such behaviour is desirable or necessary even in a man. The existing lunatic premise that all aggression is unacceptable because men are guilty of indulging in its worst, most sickening excesses, offers no sound basis for understanding how similar forces are experienced and manifested by women. And by failing to understand this, how can we hope to offer protection and help to the still largely unrecognized victims of female violence?

Acceptable or no, there can now be no turning back – female aggression is a phenomenon with which we will only become more, not less, familiar with in the next millennium. In my view this does not portend the threatening, apocalyptic vision shared by many. Quite the contrary. It signals the approach of a less inequitable, unjust world in which the subordination of women was taken for granted, where women at last are becoming equipped to overcome male domination and oppression. We might do worse than accept the aggressive female as the most powerful symbol of women's liberation.

Bibliography

Chapter 1 – The Rise of Machisma
Pietro Calderoni, 'Chi Ha Paura Di Rosetta?' *Epoca*, 17 February 1993

'Camorra Color Rosa', Laura Maragnani/Silvia d'Alessandro. *Panorama*, 30 May 1993

A. Juno & V. Vale (eds), 'Angry Women', Re/Search Publications, San Francisco, USA, 1991

F. Adler, *Sisters In Crime*, McGraw Hill, New York, 1975

A. Campbell, *Self-Report of Fighting by Females*, B. J. of Criminology, Vol. 26, No. 1, January 1986

A. Campbell, *Female Gang Members' Social Representation of Aggression.* Paper presented at the 44th Annual Meeting of the American Society of Criminology, New Orleans, 4–7 November 1992

M. Chesney-Lind, *Girls, Gangs and Violence: Anatomy of a Backlash*, ibid.

Federal Bureau of Investigation, *Crime in the United States – 1977*, Washington DC, US Department of Justice, 1978

Federal Bureau of Investigation, *Crime in the United States*, Washington DC, US Department of Justice, 1992.

Criminal Statistics, England and Wales, 1990, HMSO, 1992

Prison Statistics, England and Wales, 1990, HMSO, 1992

Report on Women Offenders And Probation Service Provision: Report of a Thematic Inspection. HM Inspectorate of Probation/Home Office, London, 1991

Criminal Justice Act, Section 95, 'Gender and the Criminal Justice System', HMSO, London, 1992

The British Crime Survey, Home Office Research Study 111, HMSO, London, 1989

F. Heidensohn, *Women and Crime*, Macmillan, London, 1985

D. Klein & J. Kress, *Any Woman's Blues*, in Crime and Social Justice, No. 5, Spring/Summer 1976, pp. 34–49

O. Pollack, *The Criminality of Women*, University of Pennsylvania Press, Philadelphia, 1950

J. Ussher, *Women's Madness: Misogny or Mental Illness?*, Harvester Wheatsheaf, London, 1991

F. Adler, *The Criminology of Deviant Women*, Houghton Mifflin, Boston, 1979

D. Klein, *The Etiology of Female Crime: A Review of the Literature*, Issues in Criminology, 8, Fall 1973, pp. 3–30

C. Lombroso, *The Female Offender*, T. Fisher Unwin, London, 1895

H. Mannheim, *Comparative Criminology*, Routledge & Kegan Paul, London, 1965

C. Vedder & D. Somerville, *The Delinquent Girl*, Charles C. Thomas, Springfield, Ill., 1970

W. I. Thomas, *The Unadjusted Girl*, Little, Brown, Boston, 1923

C. Smart, *Women, Crime and Criminology*, Routledge & Kegan Paul, London, 1977

C. Smart, *The New Female Criminal: Reality or Myth?* B. J. of Criminology, Vol. 19, No. 1, 1979

W. A. Bonger, *Criminality and Economic Conditions*, Little, Brown, Boston, 1916

S. Freud, *The Complete Psychological Works*, J. Strachey (ed.), The Standard Edition, Hogarth Press, London, 1953

S. Freud, *Three Essays on the Theory of Sexuality*, Hogarth Press, London, 1953

J. Wheelwright, *Amazons and Military Maids*, Pandora, London, 1989

R. Miles, *Women's History of the World*, Michael Joseph, London, 1988

S. Macdonald, P. Holden & S. Ardener (eds), *Images of Women in Peace and War*, Macmillan, London, 1987

P. Reeves-Sanday, *Female Power and Male Dominance*, Cambridge University Press, Cambridge, 1981

V. Broido, *Apostles Into Terrorists*, Smith (Maurice Temple) Ltd, 1978

R. v. Krafft-Ebing, *Psychopathia Sexualis*, Staples Press, London, 1965

J. Abray, *Feminism in the French Revolution*, American Historical Review, 80

D. G. Levy, H. Branson, A. White & M. D. Johnson (eds), *Women in Revolutionary Paris 1789–1795*, University of Illinois Press, Urbana, 1979

C. R. Berkin & C. M. Lovett (eds), *Women, War and Revolution*, Holmes and Meier, New York, 1980

S. Rowbotham, *Women's Resistance and Revolution*, Penguin, London, 1972

N. L. Goldman (ed.), *Female Soldiers – Combatants or Non-Combatants?* Historical and Contemporary Perspectives, Greenwood Press, Westport, Conn., 1982

H. Fisher, *The Sex Contract*, Granada, London, 1983

A. Oakley, *Sex, Gender and Society*, Smith (Maurice Temple) Ltd, London, 1972

E. Badinter, *Man/Woman: The One is the Other*, Collins Harvill, London, 1989

M. H. Klaus & J. K. Kennell, *Maternal-Infant Bonding*, Mosby, St Louis, 1976

B. S. Anderson & J. P. Zinsser, *A History of Their Own: Women in Europe from Prehistory to the Present*, Vols 1 & 2, Penguin, London, 1988

Women In Special Hospitals, a one-day conference, London, 30 October 1990

A. Mandaraka-Sheppard, *The Dynamics of Aggression in Women's Prisons in England*, Gower, Aldershot, 1986

P. Carlen (ed.), *Criminal Women*, Polity Press, London, 1985

S. Casale, *Women Inside*, Virago, London, 1989

U. Padel, *Insiders*, Virago, London, 1988

T. Parker, *Life After Life*, Pan, London, 1991

K. Muir, *Arms and the Woman*, Sinclair-Stevenson, London, 1993

B. Barnsley, *Flowers in Hell*, Pandora, London, 1987

S. Read, *Only a Fortnight*, Bloomsbury, London, 1989

K. Daly, *Women's Pathways to Felony Court: Feminist Theories of Lawbreaking and Problems of Representation*, S. California Review of Law and Women's Studies, 1993

K. Daly, *Gender, Crime, and Punishment*, Yale University Press, 1994

Related reports in: *Guardian*; *Evening Standard*; *New York Magazine*; *Sunday Express* magazine; *Time*; *New York Times*; *Sunday Times*; *The Times*; *Sacramento Bee*

Chapter 2 – Caution: Being Feminine Could Damage Your Health

S. Milgram, *Obedience to Authority: An Experimental View*, Harper and Row, New York, 1974

P. G. Zimbardo, *The Cognitive Control of Life*, Scott, Foresman, Glenview, Ill., 1969

P. G. Zimbardo & F. L. Ruch, *Psychology and Life*, Scott, Foresman, Glenview, Ill., 1975

P. G. Zimbardo, *The Human Choice: Individuation, Reason and Order Versus Deindividuation, Impulse and Chaos*, 1970, in W. J. Arnold & D. Levine (eds), Nebraska Symposium on Motivation, 1969, University of Nebraska Press, Lincoln

P. Brain, *Mindless Violence? The Nature and Biology of Aggression*, Inaugural lecture delivered at University College of Swansea, February 1990

R. Baron, *Human Aggression*, Plenum Press, New York, 1977

E. I. Megargee, *Undercontrolled and Overcontrolled Personality Types in Extreme Antisocial Aggression*, Psychological Monographs, 1960

R. H. Bailey, *Violence and Aggression*, Time-Life Books (Nederland) B.V., 1977

G. Siann, *Accounting for Aggression*, Allen and Unwin, London, 1985

P. Marsh & A. Campbell, *Aggression and Violence*, Basil Blackwell, Oxford, 1982

A. Frodi, J. Macaulay & P. R. Thome, *Are Women Always Less Aggressive Than Men? A Review of the Experimental Literature*, Psychol. Bulletin, Vol. 84, No. 4, pp. 634–60

A. Blue, *Grace Under Pressure*, Sidgwick and Jackson, London, 1987

M. R. Lefkowitz, *Women In Greek Myth*, Duckworth, London, 1986

F. Dahlberg (ed.), *Woman the Gatherer*, Yale University Press, New Haven, Conn., 1981

J. B. Lancaster, *Primate Behaviour and the Emergence of Human Culture*, Holt, Rinehart and Winston, New York, 1975

E. E. Maccoby & C. N. Jacklin, *The Psychology of Sex Differences*, Stanford University Press, Stanford CA., 1974

V. Franks & E. Rothblum, *The Stereotyping of Women*, Springer, New York, 1983

Plutarch's Lives (*Caius Marius*), The Dryden Translation, revised by H. Clough, Dent, Everyman's Library, 1962

N. Tanner & A. Zilhman, *Woman in Evolution: Innovation and Selection in Human Origins*, Signs, J. of Women in Culture and Society, 1 (3), 1976

N. Tanner, *On Becoming Human*, Cambridge University Press, 1981

A. L. Zilhman, *Women and Evolution: Subsistence and Social Organisation Among Early Hominids*, Signs, J. of Women and Society, 4, 1974

S. Goldberg, *The Inevitability of Patriarchy*, William Morrow, New York, 1973

M. Hang, D. Benton, P. F. Brain, B. Oliver & J. Mos, *The Aggressive Female*, CIP-Gegevens Koninklijke Bibliotheek, Den Haag, 1991

R. Leakey & R. Lewin, *Origins*, Macdonald and Jane's, London, 1977

E. Morgan, *The Descent of Woman*, Souvenir Press, London, 1989

R. B. Lee & I. DeVore, (eds), *Man The Hunter*, Aldine-Atherton, Chicago, 1968

R. Bleier, *Science and Gender*, Pergamon Press, New York, 1984

J. Archer & B. Lloyd, *Sex and Gender*, Cambridge University Press, Cambridge, Mass., 1985

M. Dobrizhoffer, *An Account of the Abipones, an Equestrian People of Paraguay*, John Murray, London, 1822

Bibliography

R. Flannery, *The Position of Women among the Mescalero Apache*, Primitive Man, 5, 1932, pp. 26–32

J. Lombard, *The Kingdom of Dahomey*, in D. Forde & P. M. Kaberry (eds), *West African Kingdoms in the 19th Century*, Oxford University Press, 1967

M. J. Hersovits, *Dahomey: An Ancient West African Kingdom*, 2 vols, J. J. Augustin, New York, 1938

N. Chagnon & P. Bugos, *Kin Selection and Conflict, an Analysis of a Yanomamo Axfight*, in N. Chagnon, W. Irons (eds), *Evolutionary Biology and Human Social Behaviour*, Duxbery, Nth Scituate, Mass., 1979

A. L. Zihlman & N. Tanner, *Gathering and the Hominid Adaptation*, in L. Tiger, H. M. Fowler (eds), *Female Hierarchies*, Beresford Book Service, Chicago, 1979

J. Nicholson, *Men and Women*, Oxford University Press, 1984

L. Berkowitz (ed.), *Roots of Aggression: A Re-examination of the Frustration–Aggression Hypothesis*, Atherton Press, New York, 1969

A. H. Buss, *Aggression Pays*, in J. L. Singer (ed.), *The Control of Aggression and Violence: Cognitive and Physiological Factors*, Academic Press, New York, 1971

A. H. Buss & A. Durkee, *An Inventory for Assessing Different Kinds of Hostility*, J. of Consulting Psychology. Vol. 21, No. 4, 1957

K. Lorenz, *On Aggression*, Methuen, London, 1966

J. Money, *Sexual Signatures*, Harrap, London, 1976

J. Money & A. A. Ehrhardt, *Man and Woman, Boy and Girl*, Johns Hopkins University Press, Baltimore, 1972

R. Stoller, *On the Development of Masculinity and Femininity*, 1968, in W. C. Young (ed.), *Sex and Gender*, William Wilkins Co., 1972

A. Walker, *Women Physiologically Considered*, J. & H. G. Langley, New York, 1850

A. Fausto-Sterling, *Myths of Gender*, Basic Books, New York, 1985

D. Maxwell-Hudson, *The Delicate Sex*, in A. L. Hammond & P. G. Zimbardo (eds), *Readings on Human Behaviour*, Scott Foresman & Co., London/Boston, 1988

A. Montagu (ed.), *Man and Aggression*, Oxford University Press, 1968

S. B. Hrdy, *The Langurs of Abu: Female and Male Strategies of Reproduction*, Harvard University Press, Cambridge, Mass., 1977

S. B. Hrdy, *The Woman That Never Evolved*, Harvard University Press, Cambridge, Mass., 1981

S. B. Hrdy & G. Hausfater (eds), *Infanticide: A Comparative and Evolutionary Perspective*, Aldine, New York

P. Draper, *Kung Women: Contrasts in Sexual Egalitarianism in Foraging and Sedentary Contexts*, in R. Reiter (ed.), *Towards an Anthropology of Women*, Monthly Review Press, New York

J. R. Lion MD, *Pitfalls in the Assessment and Measurement of Violence, A Clinical View*, J. of Neuropsychiatry, 3, No. 2, 1991

D. Bear MD, *Neurological Perspectives on Aggressive Behaviour*, ibid.

E. F. Coccaro MD, *Development of Neuropharmacologically Based Behavioural Assessments of Impulsive Aggressive Behaviour*, ibid.

L. T. Yeudall, et. al. *A Neuropsychosocial Theory of Persistent Criminality*, in *Advances in Forensic Psychology and Psychiatry*, Vol. 2, 1987

W. H. Reid (ed.), *The Psychopath: A Comprehensive Study of Antisocial Disorders and Behaviour*, Brunner/Mazel, New York, 1978

C. S. Wisdom, *'Does Violence Beget Violence?' A Critical Examination of the Literature*, Psychol. Bulletin, V. 106, 1989

C. S. Wisdom, *The Cycle of Violence, Science*, 244, 1989

C. S. Wisdom, *A Tail on an Untold Tale: Response to Biological and Genetic Contributors to Violence: Wisdom's Untold Tale*, Psychol. Bulletin, V. 109, 1991

L. F. DiLalla & I. I. Gottesman, *Biological and Genetic Contributors to Violence: Wisdom's Untold Tale*, Psychol. Bulletin, V. 109, 1991

G. Wilson, *The Great Sex Divide*, Peter Owen, London, 1989

J. M. Dabbs et al., *Saliva, Testosterone and Criminal Violence among Women*, in *Personality and Individual Differences*, 9, 1988

H. F. L. Meyer-Bahlburg, *Sex, Hormones and Female Homosexuality, a Critical Examination*, Arch. of Sexual Behaviour, 8, 1979

F. Purifoy & L. Koopmans, *Androstenodione, Testosterone and Free Testosterone Concentration in Women of Various Occupations*, Social Biology, 26, 1980

H. F. Harlow & M. K. Harlow, *The Effect of Rearing Conditions on Behaviour*, in J. Money (ed.), *Sex Research: New Developments*, Holt, Rinehart and Winston, New York, 1965

F. Heidensohn, *The Deviance of Women*, B. J. of Sociology, V. 19, 1968

A. Oakley, *The Myth of Motherhood, New Society*, 25 February 1970

S. Van Goozen et al., *Androgens, Negative Mood and Anger in Women*, paper presented at Xth World Meeting of the International Society for Research on Aggression, 'From Conflict to Cooperation: Multidisciplinary Studies on Aggression in Animals and Humans', Siena, Italy, 6–11 September 1992

S. Van Goozen et al., *Hormonal Research Over the Menstrual Cycle*, ibid.

J. B. Hutchinson, *Sex Hormone Action on Brain Mechanisms of Aggression* (plenary lecture), ibid.

Symposium: *Sex Differences in Perception and Response to Threat*, ibid.

Bibliography

Symposium: *Female Aggression, ibid.*

Symposium: *Hormonal and Neurochemical Correlates of Aggression, ibid.*

Symposium: *Defensive Mechanisms in Animals and Humans, ibid.*

K. Björkqvist *et al.*, *Styles of Aggression and Sex Differences: A Developmental Theory, ibid.*

J. Condry & S. Condry, *Sex Differences: A Study in the Eye of the Beholder*, Child Development, 47, 1976, p. 817

A. Storr, *Human Destructiveness*, Routledge, London, 1991

A. Storr, *Human Aggression*, Pelican, London, 1970

C. J. Jung, *Modern Man in Search of a Soul*, Kegan Paul, Trench, Trubner, London, 1945

A. Arendt, *Eichmann in Jerusalem*, Penguin, London, 1963

E. Fromm, *The Anatomy of Human Destructiveness*, Penguin, London, 1977

M. Caplan & D. Hay, *Fighting Among Babies: The Origins of Human Conflict?* Paper presented at the British Psychological Society Developmental Psychology Conference, 14 September 1991, University of Cambridge

M. M. Lefkowitz, L. D. Eron, L. O. Walder & L. R. Huesmann (eds), *Growing Up to Be Violent*, Pergamon, New York, 1977

S. L. Bem, *The Measurement of Psychological Androgyny*, J. of Consulting and Clinical Pyschology, 42, pp. 155–62

S. L. Bem, *Sex Role Adaptability: One Consequence of Psychological Androgyny*, J. of Personality and Social Psychology, 31, 1975, pp. 634–43

K. Deaux, *The Behaviour of Men and Women*, Brooks/Cole, Monterey, CA, 1976

O. Hartnett, G. Boden & M. Fuller (eds), *Sex Role Stereotyping*, Collected Papers, Tavistock Publication, 1979

M. D. Gall, *The Relationship Between Masculinity–Femininity and Manifest Anxiety*, J. of Clinical Psychology, 25, 1969, pp. 294–5

I. K. Broverman *et al.*, *Sex Role Stereotypes and Clinical Judgements of Mental Health*, J. of Consulting and Clinical Psychology, 34, 1970, pp. 1–7

S. L. Abramowitz *et al.*, *The Politics of Clinical Judgements. What Non-liberal Examiners Infer About Women Who Do not Stifle Themselves*, J. of Consulting and Clinical Psychology, 41, 1973, pp. 385–91

D. H. Baucom *et al.*, *Relation Between Testosterone Concentration, Sex Role Identity and Personality Among Females*, J. of Personality and Social Psychology, 48, No. 5, 1985, pp. 1218–26

V. O. Long, *Relationship of Masculinity to Self-esteem and Self-acceptance to Female Professionals, College Students, Clients and Victims of Domestic*

Violence, J. of Consulting and Clinical Psychology, Vol. 54, No. 3, pp. 323–7

G. L. Schindler, *Testosterone Concentration, Personality Patterns and Occupational Choice in Women*, Unpublished doctoral dissertation, University of Houston, 1979

S. Faludi, *Backlash*, Chatto & Windus, London, 1992

Chapter 3 – The New Female Criminal

L. Maher & R. Curtis, *In Search of the Female Urban Gangsta: Change, Culture and Crack Cocaine*, chapter prepared for B. Raffel-Price and N. Sokoloff (eds), *The Criminal Justice System and Women* (2nd Edition), 1992

L. Maher & R. Curtis, *Women on the edge of crime: Crack cocaine and the changing contexts of street-level sex work in New York City*, Crime, Law and Social Change 18, 1992, pp. 221–58

D. Baskin, I. Sommers, R. Tessler & H. J. Steadman, *Role Incongruence and Gender Variation in the Provision of Prison Mental Health Services*, J. of Health and Social Behaviour, Vol. 30, 1989, pp. 305–13

I. Sommers & D. Baskin, *Sex, Race, Age and Violent Offending*, Unpublished paper

I. Sommers & D. Baskin, *The Situational Context of Violent Female Offending*, paper presented at the 43rd Annual Meeting of the American Society of Criminology, San Francisco, November 1991

I. Sommers & D. Baskin, *Female Initiation into Violent Street Crime*, paper presented at the 44th Annual Meeting of the American Society of Criminology, New Orleans, November 1992

J. Laub & M. J. McDermott, *An Analysis of Serious Crime by Young Black Women*, Criminology, 23, 1985, pp. 81–98

S. Simpson, *Caste, Class and Violent Crime: Explaining Difference in Female Offending*, Criminology, 29, 1991, pp. 115–36

N. Weiner & M. E. Wolfgang (eds), *Violent Crime, Violent Criminals*, Sage, Newbury Park, CA, 1989

W. J. Wilson, *Studying Inner-City Social Dislocation*, American Sociological Review, 56, 1991, pp. 1–14

E. Dunlap & B. D. Johnson, *The Setting for the Crack Era: Macro Forces, Micro Consequences (1960–92)*, paper for publication in the J. of Psychoactive Drugs, 27 May 1992

L. M. Pickens & D. A. Kinney, *Reconceptualizing the Role of Gang Membership for Young Women: A Case Study of an Urban Public High School*, paper presented at ASC 44th Annual Meeting, November 1992, New Orleans

Bibliography

E. Dunlap & B. D. Johnson, *Who They Are and What They Do: Female Dealers in New York City*, ibid.

J. Moore, *Chicanas and East Los Angeles Gangs*, ibid.

L. Fishman, *Then and Today: Black Female Gangs of the Sixties*, ibid.

M. Chesney-Lind, *Girls, Gangs and Violence: Reinventing the Liberated Female Crook*, ibid.

A. Campbell, *Female Gang Members' Social Representation of Aggression*, ibid.

R. A. Robinson, *Theories of Power and the Study of Female Delinquents*, ibid.

K. Faith, *Historical Perspectives on Female Crime: From Witches to PMS*, ibid.

P. Carlen, *Women, Crime and Poverty*, Open University Press, Milton Keynes, 1988

P. Carlen, *Women's Imprisonment*, Routledge and Kegan Paul, London, 1983

A. Block, 'Aw! Your Mother's in the Mafia': *Women Criminals in Progressive New York*, Contemporary Crises, 1, 1977, pp. 5–22

In the Psychiatrist's Chair (Toyah Wilcox) BBC Radio 4, 28 December, 1992

'Girl Gangs in Los Angeles', *Woman's Hour*, BBC Radio 4, 28 July 1992

C. Tchaikovsky & M. Benn, *Dangers of Being a Woman*, Abolitionist, No. 23, 1987

G. Robertson, *Correlates of Crime among Women Offenders*, Med. Sci. Law. Vol. 30, No. 2, 1990, pp. 165–74

A. Campbell, *The Girls in the Gang*, Basil Blackwell, 1984

E. Miller, *Street Woman*, Temple University Press, Philadelphia, 1986

R. Huff (ed.), *Gangs in America*, Sage, Beverly Hills, CA, 1990

W. Brown, *Black Female Gang Members in Philadelphia*, Int. J. of Offender Therapy and Comparative Criminology, 21, 1977, pp. 221–8

S. E. Merry, *Urban Danger*, Temple University Press, Philadelphia, 1981

L. T. Fishman, *The Vice Queens: An Ethnographic Study of Black Female Gang Behaviour*, paper presented at the 44th Annual Meeting of the ASC, New Orleans, November 1992

J. W. Coid, *Sadistic and Compulsive Homicidal Urges in Female Psychopaths*, paper presented at the Second International Conference: Psychodynamics and the Adolescent and Female Offender, International Association for Forensic Psychotherapy, London, 26–28 March 1993

J. W. Coid, *An Affective Syndrome in Psychopaths with Borderline Personality Disorder?* B. J. of Psychiatry, 162, 1993, pp. 641–50

J. W. Coid, DSM-111 *Diagnosis in Criminal Psychopaths: A Way Forward*, Criminal Behaviour and Mental Health, 2, 1992, pp. 78–94

J. W. Coid, *et al.*, *Self–Mutilation in Female Remand Prisoners 11: A Cluster Analytic Approach Towards Identification of a Behavioural Syndrome*, Criminal Behaviour and Mental Health, 2, 1992, pp. 1–14

Related reports in: *New York Times; Daily Mail; Today; Sunday Times*

Chapter 4 – In Cold Blood

J. Flanner, *Paris was Yesterday (1925–39)*, Angus & Robertson, London, 1973

L. Gribble, *Such Lethal Ladies*, Chivers Press, Bath, 1985

E. J. Swasey, *The Importance of Women to the Future of Gun Ownership*, paper presented at the ASC Conference, New Orleans, 4–7 November 1992

J. R. Davis, *Possession of Guns Among Probationers*, *ibid.*

V. Bugliosi, *The Manson Murders*, Penguin, 1974

J. Levin & J. A. Fox, *Mass Murder: America's Growing Menace*, Plenum Press, New York, 1985

J. Levin & J. A. Fox, *Female Serial Killers*, in C. C. Culliver (ed.), *Female Criminality: The State of the Art*, Garland Publishing, New York, 1993

K. Segrave, *Women Serial and Mass Murders: A Worldwide Reference, 1580–1990*, McFarland & Co. Inc., Jefferson, NC, 1992

B. Malinowski, *The Sexual Life of Savages*, Beacon Press, Boston, 1987

When Women Rape Men, Psychology Today, Vol. 17, September 1983, pp. 74–5

Bryant Gumbel's interview with Aileen Wuornos on NBC *Today Show*, New York, 5 May 1992

'Making of a Serial Killer', Nick Broomfield's documentary about Aileen Wuornos, Channel 4, 31 March 1993

S. Epstein, *The First Female: The Case of Aileen Wuornos*, paper presented at the 44th Annual Meeting of the American Society of Criminology, New Orleans, November 1992

S. Russell, *Damsel of Death*, Virgin Publishing, London, 1992

A. Kirsta, *Victims: Surviving the Aftermath of Violent Crime*, Century, London, 1988

E. MacDonald, *Shoot The Women First*, Fourth Estate, London, 1991

Bibliography

A. Burton, *Urban Terrorism*, Leo Cooper, London, 1975

R. Morgan, *The Demon Lover*, Methuen, London, 1989

D. E. Georges-Abeyie, *Women as Terrorists*, Terrorism: An International Journal, Vol. 1, No. 1, 1977

E. Ganter, *Conversation with Leila Khaled*, Courage Aktuelle Frauenzeitung, West Berlin, No. 8, August 1981

S. MacDonald, P. Holden & S. Ardener (eds), *Images of Women in Peace and War*, Macmillan, 1987

J. Bryant, *This Soldier Still at War*, Harcourt Brace Jovanovich, New York, 1975

D. Ward, J. Jackson & R. E. Ward, *Crimes of Violence by Women*, in D. Mulvihill *et al.* (eds), *Crimes of Violence*, US Government Printing Office, Washington DC, 1969

Task (Protection & Training Services) Ltd, *Aggression: The Female of the Species*, p. 12

J. E. Hodge (Rampton Hospital), *Addiction to Crime*, paper presented at the first DCLP annual conference, University of Kent at Canterbury, 3–5 January 1991

D. M. Gresswell (Rampton Hospital), *Psychological Models of Addiction and the Origins of Maintenance of Multiple Murder*, ibid.

S. L. Bradshaw, C. D. Ohlde & J. B. Horne, *The Love of War: Vietnam and the Traumatized Veteran*, Bulletin of the Menninger Clinic, 55, pp. 96–103

E. Staub, *The Psychology and Culture of Torture and Torturers*, in P. Suedfeld (ed.), *Psychology and Torture*, Hemisphere Publishing Corp., New York, 1990

J. R. Nash, *Look For The Woman*, Harrap, London, 1984

M. Haritos-Fatouros, *The Official Torturer: A Learning Model for Obedience to the Authority of Violence*, J. of Applied Social Psychology, 18, 1988, pp. 1107–1120

H. V. Dicks, *Licensed Mass Murder: A Sociopsychological Study of Some SS Killers*, Basic Books, New York, 1972

M. Midgley, *Wickedness*, Ark, London, 1986

R. J. Lifton, *The Nazi Doctors*, Basic Books, New York, 1986

R. J. Lifton, *The Genocidal Mentality*, Macmillan, London, 1991

J. Dimsdale (ed.), *Survivors, Victims and Perpetrators: Essays on the Nazi Holocaust*, Hemisphere Publishing Co., New York, 1980

E. Staub, *Altruism and Aggression: Social and Biological Origins*, Cambridge University Press, 1986

E. Staub, *The Roots of Evil*, Cambridge University Press, 1989

E. Staub, *Psychological and Cultural Origins of Extreme Destructiveness and Extreme Altruism*, proof of chapter to appear in W. Kurtiner &

J. Gewirtz (eds), *The Handbook of Moral Behaviour and Development*, Lawrence Erlbaum Associates, New York

E. Staub, *The Origins of Caring, Helping and Non-Aggression*, in S. and P. Oliner (eds), *Embracing the Other*, New York University Press, New York

E. Staub, *Values, Helping and Well-Being*, an unpublished study

Related reports in: *Daily Mail*; *Guardian*; *France-Soir*; *Sunday Times*; *Daily Express*; *Evening Standard*; *Today*; *Time*; *Sacramento Bee*; *Newsweek*; *The Times*; *Observer*; *USA Today*; *Palm Beach Post*; *New York Times*; *Independent*

Chapter 5 – Deadly Intimacies

C. A. Bullock & G. P. Waldo, *Homicides in Florida: Female Murderers*, paper presented at a seminar on Female Homicide Offenders, part of the proceedings of the 44th Annual Meeting of the American Society of Criminology, New Orleans, November 1992

A. J. Shields & P. J. Hanke, *Sentencing Variations of Women Convicted of Homicide in Alabama*, ibid.

E. Gilbert, *Women and Homicide: The Role of Age and Race*, ibid.

T. Danner *et al.*, *The Female Chronic Offenders: Exploring Bio-Historical and Offense Pattern Dimensions for Incarcerated Female Felons*, ibid.

C. K. Gillespie, *Justifiable Homicide*, Ohio State University Press, Columbus, 1989

A. Browne, *When Battered Women Kill*, The Free Press, New York, 1987

M. Symonds, *The 'Second Injury' to Victims of Violent Crimes*, Evaluation and Change (special issue), 1980, p. 38

Betty Broderick interview on *Oprah Winfrey Show*, 19 January 1993, Channel 4

S. Edwards, *Female Sexuality and the Law*, Martin Robertson & Co., 1981

S. Edwards, *Policing Domestic Violence*, Sage, New York, 1987

S. Edwards, *Battered Women Who Kill*, New Law Journal, 5 October 1990

S. Edwards, *Women On Trial*, Manchester University Press, 1984

S. Lees, *Naggers, Whores and Women's Libbers: Provoking Men to Murder*, paper presented at the British Sociological Association Conference, Southampton University, 1989

J. Radford, *Retrospective on a Trial*, in *Sweeping Statements*, Women's Press, 1984

'I Shot My Husband and No One Asked Why', a Scarlet TV Production for Channel 4, 20 June 1988

Bibliography

'Women on Death Row', *Inside Story*, documentary, BBC 2, May 1992

J. Radford, *Sentenced to Life Imprisonment for Resisting Male Violence: Man-Made Law Denies Justice for Women*, Rights of Women Bulletin, Autumn 1991

J. Radford, *Policing & Male Violence, Policing Women*, in J. Hanmer, J. Radford & E. A. Stanko (eds), *Women, Violence and Social Control*, Hutchinson, London, 1989

Kiranjit Ahluwahlia on *Dispatches*, Channel 4, 25 February 1991

Criminal Statistics, England and Wales, 1990, HMSO, 1992

J. Radford, *Self Preservation: Proposal for a New Defence to the Charge of Murder*, paper submitted by Right of Women to the Royal Commission on Criminal Justice, 1992

Southall Black Sisters, *Domestic Violence and the Law on Provocation*, unpublished article, 1991

Domestic Homicide Statistics, 1982–1989, the Home Office, presented to the House of Commons by Mr John Patten, 17 October 1991

W. Buck & S. Walklate, *Male Versus Female Homicide*, paper presented at the British Psychological Society's Division of Criminological and Legal Psychology Conference, University of Salford, 22 February 1993

W. Chan, *The Battered Woman Syndrome: Its Role in the Law of Self-Defence*, paper presented at the Third European Conference of Law and Psychology at Oxford University, 18 September 1992

H. Kennedy, *Eve Was Framed*, Vintage, London, 1993

C. P. Ewing, *Battered Women Who Kill*, Lexington Books, New York, 1989

H. Kohut, *The Restoration of the Self*, 1977

E. M. Schneider & S. B. Jordan, *Representation of Women Who Defend Themselves in Response to Physical or Sexual Assault*, in E. Bochnak (ed.), *Women's Self Defence Cases: Theory and Practice*, the Michie Company Law Publishers, Charlottesville, VA, 1981

L. E. Walker, *The Battered Woman Syndrome*, Springer, New York, 1984

M. E. P. Seligman, *Helplessness: On Depression, Development and Death*, W. H. Freeman, San Francisco, 1975

R. J. Gelles, *An Exchange/Social Control Theory of Intrafamily Violence*, in D. Finkelhor, R. Gelles, G. Hotaling & M. Straus (eds), *The Dark Side of Families*, Sage, Beverly Hills, CA, 1983

I. K. Broverman *et al.*, *Sex Role Stereotypes and Clinical Judgements of Mental Health*, J. of Consulting Psychology, 34, 1970, pp. 1–7

E. M. Lewis, *An Experimental Analogue of the Spouse Abuse Cycle*, paper presented at the National Conference for Family Violence Researchers, University of New Hampshire, Durham, July 1981

K. O'Donovan, *Battered Women Who Kill: Legal Aspects*, paper presented at 'Perspectives on Female Violence', national conference at St George's Hospital Medical School, London, 7–8 March 1991

S. Yeo, *Battered Woman Syndrome in Australia*, New Law Journal, 8 January 1993

B. Mitchell, *Distinguishing Between Murder and Manslaughter*, New Law Journal, 5 and 12 July 1991

N. Kaser-Boyd & S. R. Balash, *Battered Woman Syndrome in the Courtroom*, C.A.C.J. Forum, Vol. 19, No. 4, 1992

N. Kaser-Boyd, *Post-Traumatic Stress Disorders in Children and Adults: The Legal Relevance*, in Western State University Law Reporter, 1993

N. Kaser-Boyd, *Rorschachs of Women Who Commit Homicide*, J. of Personality Assessment, Vol. 60, 3, 1993, pp. 458–70

H. Maguigan, *Battered Women and Self-Defense: Myths and Misconceptions in Current Reform Proposals*, University of Pennsylvania Law Review, Vol. 140, No. 2, 1991

Related reports in: *The Times; Sunday Times; Sunday Telegraph; Guardian; New York Times; Evening Standard; Los Angeles Times; Orange County Reporter*

Chapter 6 – Battered Husbands: The Invisible Men

K. Brown, unpublished study of violence between domestic partners

S. Smith, D. Buchan, D. Barker & G. Bodiwala, *Adult Domestic Violence*, Health Trends, 24, 1992, pp. 97–9

W. G. Godberg & M. C. Tomlanovitch, *Domestic Violence Victims in the Emergency Department: New Findings*, J. of the American Medical Association, 251, 1984, pp. 239–64

M. J. George, *A Preliminary Investigation Of Instrumental Abuse of Men*, a report for Submission to the Home Affairs Select Committee, 1992

M. D. Pagelow, *The Battered Husband Syndrome: Social Problem or Much Ado About Little*, in N. Johnson (ed.), *Marital Violence*, Sociology Review Monograph 31, Routledge and Kegan Paul, London, 1985

Family Law, Domestic Violence and Occupation of the Family Home, The Law Commission, No. 207, HMSO, 1992, London

E. Shorter, *The Making of the Modern Family*, Basic Books, New York, 1975

S. K. Steinmetz, *The Battered Husband Syndrome*, Victimology, 2, Nos 3–4, 1978

S. K. Steinmetz, *The Cycle of Violence*, Praeger, New York, 1977

Bibliography

S. K. Steinmetz, *Wife-beating, Husband-beating: A Comparison of the Use of Physical Violence Between Spouses to Resolve Marital Fights*, in M. Roy (ed.), *Battered Women*, Van Nostrand Reinhold, 1977

S. K. Steinmetz, *Cross-Cultural Marital Abuse*, J. of Sociology and Social Welfare, 8, 1981, pp. 404–414

S. Steinmetz & J. S. Lucca, *Husband Battering*, in V. B. Van Hasselt et al. (eds), *The Handbook of Family Violence*, Plenum, New York, 1988

E. Pleck, *et al.*, *The Battered Data Syndrome: A Comment on Steinmetz's Article*, Victimology, Vol. 2, Nos 3–4, 1977–8, p. 682

L. H. Bowker (ed.), *Women and Crime in America*, Macmillan, New York, 1981

D. R. Miller & G. Swanson, *The Changing American Parent*, Wiley, New York, 1958

A. Shupe, W. A. Stacey & L. R. Hazelwood, *Violent Men, Violent Couples*, Lexington Books, New York, 1987

E. Pizzey & J. Shapiro, *Prone To Violence*, Hamlyn, London, 1982

E. Pizzey, *Choosing a Violent Relationship*, New Society, 23 April 1981

E. Pizzey, *Scream Quietly or the Neighbours Will Hear*, Pelican, London, 1979

R. Breen, unpublished master's thesis on violence between couples, University of Texas at Arlington, May 1985

R. J. Gelles & M. A. Straus, *Intimate Violence*, Simon and Schuster, New York, 1988

R. J. Gelles, *The Violent Home: A Study of Physical Aggression Between Husbands and Wives*, Sage, Beverly Hills, CA, 1974

R. E. Dobash & R. P. Dobash, *Women, Violence and Social Change*, Routledge, London, 1992

M. McLeod, *Women Against Men: An Examination of Domestic Violence Based on an Analysis of Official Data and National Victimisation Data*, Justice Quarterly, Vol. 1, 1984, pp. 171–93

R. L. McNeely & G. Robinson-Simpson, *The Truth about Domestic Violence: A Falsely Framed Issue*, Social Work, Nov–Dec 1987, pp. 485–90

G. Margolin, *The Multiple Forms of Aggressiveness Between Marital Partners: How Do We Identify Them?*, J. of Marital and Family Therapy, Vol. 13, 1987, pp. 1977–84

C. Levinger, *Sources of Marital Dissatisfaction Among Applicants for Divorce*, American J. of Orthopsychiatry, 36 (5), pp. 803–807

I. Oswald, *Domestic Violence by Women*, The Lancet, December 1980, p. 1253

J. Turner, *Behind Closed Doors*, Thorsons, London, 1988

M. A. Straus & G. T. Hotaling (eds), *The Social Causes of Husband–Wife*

Violence, University of Minnesota Press, Minneapolis, 1980

M. A. Straus, R. J. Gelles & S. K. Steinmetz, *Behind Closed Doors: Violence in the American Family*, Sage, London, 1988

M. E. Wolfgang, *Victim-precipitated Criminal Homicide*, J. of Criminal Law, Criminology and Police Science, 48, 1957, pp. 1–11

R. Stark & J. McEvoy, *Middle Class Violence*, Psychology Today, 4, November 1970, pp. 52–65

C. Tavris, *Anger: The Misunderstood Emotion*, Touchstone, New York, 1989

A. Campbell, *Out of Control: Men, Women and Aggression*, Pandora, 1993

Weekend Live, 'Battered Men', Central Television, 22 March 1991

Phil Donahue Show: Battered Husbands (transcript 05137), Multimedia Entertainment Inc.

K. Dalton, *Once A Month*, Fontana, London, 1987

K. Dalton, *Menstruation and Crime*, British Medical J., 2, 1961, p. 1752

K. Dalton, *Premenstrual Syndrome Goes to Court*, Peter Andrew Publishing Co., Droitwich, 1990

K. Dalton & L. Taylor, *Premenstrual Syndrome: A New Criminal Defence*, California Western Law Review, 1982

Related reports in: *Time; Newsweek; Guardian; Vanity Fair; Spectator*

Chapter 7 – Killer Carers

Video shown at the Second International Conference of the International Association for Forensic Psychotherapy, *Psychodynamics and the Adolescent and Female Offender*, London, 26–28 March 1993

M. Gardiner, *Deadly Innocents: Portraits of Children Who Kill*, Hogarth Press, London, 1977

D. Selbourne, *The Spirit of the Age*, Sinclair-Stevenson, London, 1993

L. Manshel, *Nap Time: The True Story of Sexual Abuse at a Suburban Day-care Centre*, William Morrow, New York, 1990

D. G. Kilpatrick, *et al.*, *The Psychological Impact of Crime: A Study of Randomly Surveyed Crime Victims*, submitted to the National Institute of Justice, Washington DC, 1987

D. G. Kilpatrick & L. J. Veronen, *Stress Management for Rape Victims*, in D. Meichenbaum & M. E. Jaremko (eds), *Stress Reduction and Prevention*, Plenum, New York, 1983

D. G. Kilpatrick, L. J. Veronen & C. L. Best, *Factors Predicting Psychological Distress among Victims*, in C. R. Figley (ed.), *Trauma and its Wake*, Brunner Mazel, New York, 1984

Bibliography

M. Tooley, *Abortion and Infanticide*, Clarendon Press, Oxford, 1983, in M. Kohl (ed.), *Infanticide and the Value of Life*, 1978

L. Rose, *Massacre of the Innocents*, Routledge & Kegan Paul, London, 1986

K. A. Johnson, *Women in the People's Republic of China*, in S. Chipp & J. Green (eds), *Asian Women in Transition*, Pennsylvania State University Press, University Park, 1980

S. Delamont & L. Duffin, *The Ninteenth-century Woman: Her Cultural and Physical World*, Croom Helm, London, 1978

M. Haug, D. Benton, P. F. Brain, B. Oliver & J. Mos (eds), *The Aggressive Female*, cip-Gegevens Koninklijke Bibliotheek, Den Haag, 1992

J. Eggington, *From Cradle To Grave*, W. H. Allen, London, 1989

P. Elkind, *The Death Shift*, Corgi Books, London, 1990

R. Persaud, *When Carers Become Killers*, General Practitioner, 4 June 1993

S. R. Meadow, *Munchausen Syndrome by Proxy: The Hinterland of Child Abuse*, the Lancet, 13 August 1977

R. Asher, *Munchausen Syndrome*, the Lancet, 10 February 1951

A. R. Nichol & M. Eccles, *Psychotherapy for Munchausen Syndrome by Proxy*, Archives of Diseases in Childhood, No. 60, 1985

H. Allen, *Justice Unbalanced*, Open University Press, Oxford, 1987

P. T. D'Orban, *Women Who Kill Their Children*, British J. of Psychiatry, 134, 1979

A. Oakley, *From Here to Maternity: Becoming a Mother*, Penguin, London, 1986

Criminal Statistics England and Wales, 1989, HMSO, 1990

E. S. Meltzer & R. Kumar, *Puerperal Mental Illness, Clinical Features and Classification: A study of 142 Mother and Baby Admissions*, British J. of Psychiatry, 147, 1985

K. Robson & R. Kuman, *Delayed Onset of Maternal Affection After Childbirth*, B. J. of Psychiatry, 136, 1980, pp. 347–53

H. Kennedy, *The Courtroom Process*, paper presented at the Perspectives on Female Violence Conference, St George's Hospital Medical School, London, 8 March 1991

D. Mawson, *Psychiatric Perspectives on Female Violence*, ibid.

A. Wilczynski, *Images of Parents Who Kill Their Children*, paper presented at the British Criminology Conference, University of York, 24–27 July 1991

A. Wilczynski & A. Morris, *Rocking the Cradle: Mothers Who Kill their Children*, in H. Birch (ed.), *Moving Targets*, Virago, London, 1993

Related reports in: *The Times*; *Evening Standard*; *Sunday Times*

Chapter 8 – The Final Taboo

Comments recorded at Kidscape First National Conference on Female Sexual Abusers, 31 March 1992

M. Elliott, *What Survivors Tell Us – An Overview*, in M. Elliott (ed.), *Female Sexual Abuse of Children: The Ultimate Taboo*, Longman Group UK, 1993

The Phil Donahue Show: Sons Raped by their Mothers (transcript 3459), Multimedia Entertainment Inc.

S. Edwards, *Women on Trial: A Study of the Female Suspect, Defendant and Offender in the Criminal Law and Criminal Justice System*, Manchester University Press, 1984

NSPCC Fact Sheet: *Children and Families in 1992*

H. Vanderbilt, *Incest: A Chilling Report*, Lear's, February 1992

R. Wilkins, *Women Who Sexually Abuse their Children*, British Medical Journal, Vol. 300, 5 May 1990

D. Finkelhor & D. Russell, *Women as Perpetrators*, in D. Finkelhor (ed.), *Child Sexual Abuse: New Theory and Research*, Free Press, New York, 1984

K. C. Faller, *Women Who Sexually Abuse Children*, Violence and Victims, Vol. 2, 1987, pp. 263–76

E. Welldon, *The Psychodynamics of the Female Abuser*, paper presented at the Second International Conference of the International Association for Forensic Psychotherapy: 'Psychodynamics and the Adolescent and Female Offender', 26–28 March, London, 1993

A. Bentovim, M. Tranter, E. Dooley, N. Eastman & H. Kenedy (*chair*), *The Criminal Justice System and the Female Abuser*, seminar, *ibid.*

E. Welldon, *Mother, Madonna, Whore: The Idealisation and Denigration of Motherhood*, The Guildford Press, New York, 1992

C. Sheldrick, *Female Perpetrators of Sexual Abuse*, paper presented at 'Perspectives on Female Violence', St George's Hospital Medical School, London, 7–9 March 1991

R. Mathews, J. K. Matthews & K. Speltz, *Female Sexual Offenders*, The Safer Society Press, Orwell, USA, 1989

J. K. Matthews, *Working With Female Sexual Offenders*, in M. Elliott (ed.), *Female Sexual Abuse of Children*, Longman Group UK Ltd, 1993

H. G. I. Hanks & J. Saradjian, *Women Who Abuse Children Sexually: Characteristics of Sexual Abuse of Children by Women*, The Journal of Systemic Consultation & Management, Vol. 2, 1991, pp. 247–62

L. Kelly, *Unspeakable Acts*, Trouble and Strife, 21, Summer 1991

E. Bell, *With Our Own Hands*, Trouble and Strife, 16, Summer 1989

K. Lobel (ed.), *Naming the Violence: Speaking out about Lesbian Battering*, Seal Press, 1986

'My Demons', *Video Diaries*, BBC 2, 12 May 1990

'My Demons: The Legacy', *Video Diaries*, BBC 2, 5 September 1992

A. Miller, *The Drama of the Gifted Child*, Basic Books, New York, 1981

A. Miller, *For Your Own Good*, Virago, London, 1983

A. Miller, *Thou Shalt Not Be Aware*, Pluto Press, London, 1985

A. Miller, *Banished Knowledge*, Virago, London, 1990

A. Miller, *Breaking Down the Wall of Silence*, Virago, London, 1991

J. Newson & E. Newson, *The Extent of Parental Physical Punishment in the UK*, Approach (Association for the Protection of All Children Ltd), London, 1989

National Children's Home: *Children Sexually Abusing Other Children – the Last Taboo? A Report of the Committee of Enquiry into Children and Young People Who Sexually Abuse other Children*, 1992

G. Boswell, *Section 53 Offenders: An Exploration of Experiences and Needs*, The Prince's Trust, June 1991

Related reports in: *Guardian; Spectator; Independent*

Chapter 9 – It Isn't Over Till You See the Blood

C. T. Gualtieri, *The Measurement of Self-Injurious Behaviour*, J. of Neuropsychiatry, vol. 3, No. 2, Spring 1991

F. A. Elliott, *Neurological Aspects of Antisocial Behaviour*, in W. H. Reid (ed.), *The Psychopath: A Comprehensive Study of Antisocial Disorders and Behaviours*, Brunner/Mazel, New York, 1978

K. Hawton & J. Catalan, *Attempted Suicide*, Oxford University Press, 1987

M. A. Simpson, *The Phenomenology of Self-mutilation in a General Hospital Setting*, Canadian Psychiatric Association Journal, 20, 1975, pp. 429–33

M. A. Simpson, *Self-mutilation*, British J. of Hospital Medicine, 16, 1976

R. J. Rosenthal, C. Rinzler, R. Wallsh & E. Klausner, *Wrist-cutting Syndrome: The Meaning of the Gesture*, American J. of Psychiatry, 128, 1972, pp. 1363–8

Bristol Crisis Service for Women, *Women and Self-Injury*, 1991

H. Redsull, *Deliberate Self-injury in Adolescents: A Special Study*, Art Psychotherapy Diploma, 1989

L. J. Kaplan, *Female Perversions*, Penguin Books, London, 1993

Stress and Addiction Amongst Women: A Report of a Working Group of the Women's National Commission, Cabinet Office, London, 1988

P. Marsh & K. Bibby, *Drinking and Public Disorder*, The Portman Group, 1992

G. T. Wilson *et al.*, *Alcohol and Anxiety Reduction in Female Social Drinkers*, J. of Studies on Alcohol, 50, 1989, pp. 226–35

W. Windle & G. M. Barnes, *Similarities and Differences in Correlates of Alcohol Consumption and Problem Behaviours among Male and Female Adolescents*, The International J. of Addictions, 23, 1988, pp. 707–28

B. Saunders, *Psychological Aspects of Women and Alcohol*, in *Camberwell Council on Alcoholism*, 1980

B. Hutter & G. Williams (eds), *Controlling Women*, Croom Helm, 1981

S. Henderson, *Women, Sexuality and Ecstasy Use*, paper given to a Symposium on Ecstasy organised by Leeds Addiction Unit and Northwest Regional Drug Training Unit, Leeds, 6 November 1992

S. Henderson, *Luvdup and Deelited*, a paper presented at the 6th Conference on the Social Aspects of AIDS, Southbank Polytechnic, 9 May 1992

H. Deutsch, *The Psychology of Women*, Vol. 1, Grune and Stratton, 1944

C. P. Oberndorf, *The Role of Anxiety in Depersonalisation*, International J. of Psychoanalysis, Vol. 31, 1950, pp. 1–3

P. Schilder, *Image and Appearance of the Human Body*, International Universities Press, New York, 1950

K. Menninger, *A Psychoanalytic Study of the Significance of Self-Mutilations*, Psychoanalytic Quarterly, 4, 1935, pp. 408–66

J. Mitchell (ed.), *The Selected Melanie Klein*, Penguin Books, London, 1986

M. Klein & J. Riviere, *Love, Hate and Reparation*, Hogarth Press, London, 1937

M. Klein, *The Psychoanalysis of Children*, Hogarth Press, London, 1959

M. Klein, *Criminal Tendencies in Normal Children*, British J. of Medical Psychology, Vol. 7, pp. 177–92

J. Bowlby, *Attachment and Loss, Vol. 2, Separation – Anxiety and Anger*, Basic Books, New York, 1973

P. Gallwey, *Unconscious Mental Defences Against Violence in Women*, paper presented at Perspectives on Female Violence, National Conference, St George's Hospital Medical School, London, 7–8 March 1991

C. Pritchard, *Self-Violence in Women in the UK and European Community*, *ibid.*

L. Eichenbaum & S. Orbach, *Understanding Women*, Penguin Books, London, 1985

D. W. Winnicott, *The Child, the Family and the Outside World*, Penguin, London, 1965

D. W. Winnicott, *The Maturation Processes and the Facilitating Environment*, International Universities Press, New York, 1965

R. Stoller, *Sex and Gender, the Development of Masculinity and Femininity*, Vol. 1, Maresfield Library, H. Karnac, London, 1984

M. Mahler, *On Human Symbiosis and the Vicissitudes of Individuation*, International Universities Press, New York, 1968

H. Kohut, *The Restoration of the Self*, International Universities Press, New York, 1977

J. F. Masterson, *The Search for the Real Self*, The Free Press, New York, 1988

D. Pines, *A Woman's Unconscious Use of Her Body*, Virago, London, 1993

C. Thompson, *On Women*, M. R. Green (ed.), New American Library, New York, 1986

Related reports in: *Bella; Sunday Times*

Chapter 10 – Warrior Women

V. Bozzi, *Assertiveness Breeds Contempt*, Psychology Today, Vol. 21, September 1987, p. 15

V. Bozzi, *Women In Sports: What's Changed?* Psychology Today, Vol. 23, October 1989, p. 70

M. D. Lamkin, *Power* (address, 24 October 1986), Vital Speeches of the Day, Vol. 53, December 1986, pp. 151–4

C. Potera, *Women's Mental Edge*, Women's Sports and Fitness, July 1986, p. 55

S. Faludi, *Backlash*, Chatto & Windus, London, 1992

P. A. Marchbanks, L. Kung-Jong & J. A. Mercy, *Risk of Injury from Resisting Rape*, American J. of Epidemiology, Vol. 132, No. 3, 1990

S. E. Ullman & R. A. Knight, *Fighting Back: Women's Resistance to Rape*, J. of Interpersonal Violence, Vol. 7, No. 1, March 1992

P. B. Bart & P. H. O'Brien, *Stopping Rape: Successful Survival Strategies*, Pergamon, London, 1985

D. Caignon & G. Groves, *Her Wits About Her*, The Women's Press, London, 1985

R. Wyre, *Women, Men and Rape*, Perry Publications, Oxford, 1986

'Eve Strikes Back', TV documentary, BBC 2, 29 March 1993

J. C. Oates, *On Boxing*, Bloomsbury, London, 1987

S. Van Goozen, N. Frijda & N. Van de Poll, *Anger Manifestations in an Experimental Paradigm: Studies in Women*, paper presented at the Xth World Meeting of the International Society for Research on Aggression, Siena, Italy, 6–11 September 1992

V. Minor & H. E. Longino (eds), *Competition: A Feminist Taboo?* The Feminist Press, New York, 1987

C. A. Oglesby (ed.), *Women and Sport: From Myth to Reality*, Lea and Febiger, Philadelphia, 1978

A. Blue, *Grace Under Pressure*, Sidgwick and Jackson, London, 1987

K. F. Dyer, *Catching Up The Men*, Junction Books, 1982

R. H. Strauss *et al.*, *Anabolic Steroid Use and Perceived Effects in Ten Weight-Trained Women Athletes*, JAMA, Vol. 253, No. 19, 1985

J. E. Wright, *Anabolic Steroids and Athletics*, Exerc. Sport. Sci. Rev., Vol. 8, 1980, pp. 149–202

J. Mills, *Living on the Edge*, Women's Sports and Fitness, March 1986, pp. 24–9

K. Muir, *Arms and the Woman*, Sinclair-Stevenson, London, 1993

J. Wheelwright, *It Was Exactly Like the Movies! The Media's Use of the Feminine During the Gulf War*, paper presented at the Women at War: Images of Women Soldiers Conference, Florence, Italy, 15–16 November 1991

C. H. Enloe, *The Militarization of First-Class Citizenship: Some Lessons from the Gulf War*, ibid.

L. Sebesta, *Women and the Legitimation of Force: The Case of Female Military Service*, ibid.

P. Hanna, *Women in the US Military: How They Fare Psychologically*, ibid.

J. Hicks Stiehm, *Arms and the Enlisted Woman*, Temple University Press, Philadelphia, 1989

Maj. Gen. J. Holm, *Women In the Military*, Presidio Press, Novato, CA, 1982

Related reports in: *Vogue; Health; The Times; Guardian; Newsweek; New York Times; Observer; Women's Sport and Fitness; Sunday Times; Ebony; Financial Times*

Index

Index

My Mother/My Self

Nancy Friday

Why are women the way they are? Why, despite, everything, do we find so much of ourselves mysterious? Where do the dependence, the longing for intimacy, the passivity come from?

Drawing on her own and other women's lives, Nancy Friday shows compellingly that the key lies in a woman's relationship with her mother – that first binding relationship which becomes the model for so much of our adult relationships with men, and whose fetters constrain our sexuality, our independence, our very selfhood.

'Brilliant. Courageous. Moving. One of the most important books I have ever read about my mother, myself and my life.'
Washington Post

'A book most women will want to read and every man ought to.'
Michael Korda

HarperCollins Paperbacks – Non-Fiction

HarperCollins is a leading publisher of paperback non-fiction. Below are some more titles on women's issues that are available or will become available from spring 1994.

- ☐ WHAT DO WOMEN WANT?
  Luise Eichenbaum and Susie Orbach £5.99
- ☐ PLEASURE Margaret Leroy £5.99
- ☐ MY MOTHER/MY SELF Nancy Friday £6.99
- ☐ JEALOUSY Nancy Friday £6.99
- ☐ THE CINDERELLA COMPLEX Colette Dowling £6.99
- ☐ THE WOMEN'S HISTORY OF THE WORLD Ros Miles £5.99
- ☐ THE RITES OF MAN: LOVE, SEX AND DEATH IN THE MAKING
  OF THE MALE Ros Miles £5.99
- ☐ DEADLIER THAN THE MALE Alix Kirsta £5.99
- ☐ SEXING THE MILLENIUM Linda Grant £6.99
- ☐ THE SILENT PASSAGE: MENOPAUSE Gail Sheehy £5.99

You can buy HarperCollins Paperbacks at your local bookshops or newsagents. Or you can order them from HarperCollins Paperbacks, Cash Sales Department, Box 29, Douglas, Isle of Man. Please send a cheque, postal or money order (not currency) worth the price plus 24p per book for postage (maximum postage required is £3.00 for orders within the UK).

NAME (Block letters)_____

ADDRESS_____

_____

While every effort is made to keep prices low, it is sometimes necessary to increase them at short notice. HarperCollins Paperbacks reserve the right to show new retail prices on covers which may differ from those previously advertised in the text or elsewhere.